Hiking

Oregon's Southern Cascades and Siskiyous

Help Us Keep This Guide Up to Date

Every effort has been made by the author and editors to make this guide as accurate and useful as possible. However, many things can change after a guide is published—trails are rerouted, regulations change, techniques evolve, facilities come under new managment, etc.

We would love to hear from you concerning your experiences with this guide and how you feel it could be improved and kept up to date. While we may not be able to respond to all comments and suggestions, we'll take them to heart and we'll also make certain to share them with the author. Please send your comments and suggestions to the following address:

The Globe Pequot Press
Reader Response/Editorial Department
P.O. Box 480
Guilford, CT 06437

Or you may e-mail us at:

editorial@globe-pequot.com

Thanks for your input, and happy travels!

A **FALCON** GUIDE ®

Hiking

Oregon's Southern Cascades and Siskiyous

Art Bernstein

FALCON®

GUILFORD, CONNECTICUT
An imprint of The Globe Pequot Press

A FALCON GUIDE®

All photos by author unless otherwise noted.
Cover photo by Tom and Dee Ann McCarthy

Library of Congress Cataloging-in-Publication Data is available.
ISBN 1-56044-898-9

♻ Text pages printed on recycled paper.

Manufactured in the United States of America
First Edition/First Printing

Contents

Part II The Siskiyous

Acknowledgments

My thanks to the employees of the federal agencies that administer the lands and trails described in this book. As always, they proved uniformly gracious (if you'll pardon the pun) and bent over backwards to be helpful and provide information. Liz Stevenson-Shaw of the Umpqua National Forest stands out in this stellar group. Other helpful Forest Service employees include Frank Erickson, Chris Dent, Jim Good, Jeanne Sheehan, Gary Bartlett, Janice Schultz and Dwight Johnson. At Crater Lake National Park, John Broward, Kent Taylor, and Mary Rasmussen were extremely accommodating, as was an unidentified switchboard operator. The author spent an illuminating couple of hours talking to Roger Fishman, director of the Spirit of the Rogue Visitor Center at Lost Creek Lake. The woman at the front desk at the BLM Medford District office also provided a wealth of readily shared information. And the author was awed by the USGS topo map collection at the Medford (Jackson County) Public Library. And finally, Monty Elliott, head of the Geology Department at Southern Oregon University, came through with some fascinating information the day before the manuscript was mailed to the publisher.

In addition, the author would like to thank Molly Jay, David Lee, Jay Nichols, Mike and Kathy Uhtoff (if you're ever in Ashland, stop by the Northwest Nature Shop), Gail Manchur, Ross Tocher, Kimmie and Steve Polinger, Robin Rose, Aryeh Hirschfield, Randy Kieling, Tim O'Connor, Patricia Bernstein, Jennifer Bremer, Sara Bernstein, and Anna Bernstein. Thanks also to Jacqueline O'Leary, Brandon Bremer, and George Bremer.

Legend

Interstate	(5)
U.S. Highway	(97) (199)
State Highway	(230) (46)
Forest Road	4201
Interstate Highway	⟹
Paved Road	⟹
Unpaved Road	⟹
Trailhead	○
Featured Trail	▬ ▬ ▬ ▬ ▬
Secondary Trail	– – – – –
Featured Way Trail	••••••••••••
Way Trail	··················
Pass or Saddle	‿
Mine Site	⚒
River	∿
Creek	～
Lake	▨
Waterfall	∿∥
Spring	⌐○
Marsh	☤

Town	○ **Roseburg**
Picnic Area	⊼
Campground	⛺
Parking Area	Ⓟ
Bridge	⏝
Cliff	⏦⏦⏦⏦
Building	■
Peak	⛰ 9,782 ft.
Overlook/Point of Interest	▣
Ditch	⌒⌒
Power Transmission Line	•—•—•—•
National Forest/ Wilderness Boundary	— – — – — ·
County Boundary	▦▦▦▦
State Boundary	OREGON CALIF.
Map Orientation	N ↑
Scale	0 0.5 1 Miles

Locator Map

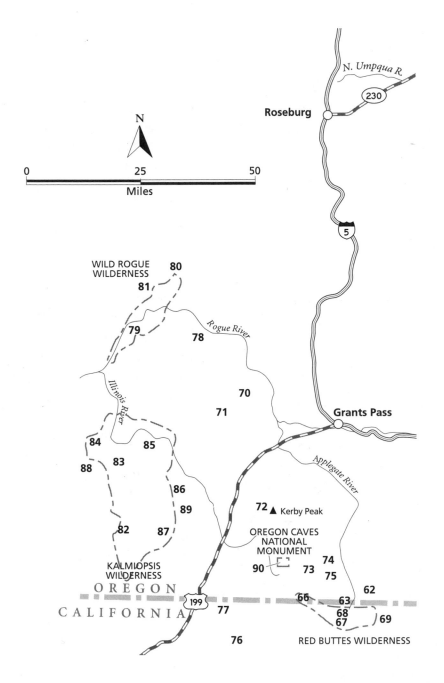

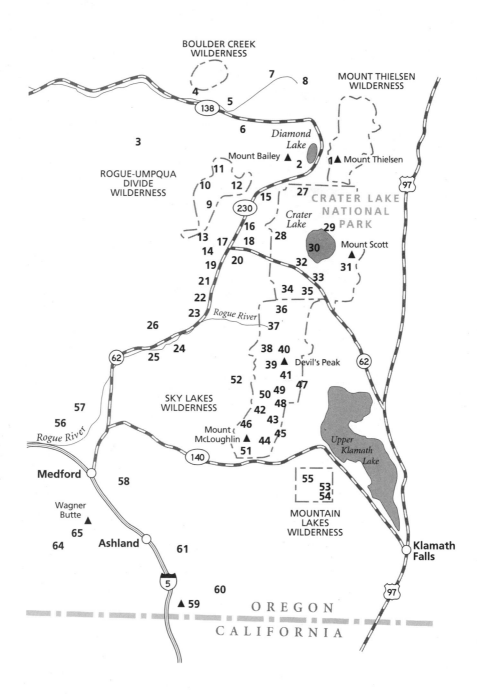

Introduction

HIKING IN OREGON'S SOUTHERN CASCADES AND SISKIYOUS

Southern Oregon ranks near the top among natural regions in the United States, not only in scenic magnificence but in the number of hiking trails from which to admire that magnificence. Within a two-hour drive of Medford (Southern Oregon's largest city), it is probably possible to go hiking every weekend for a lifetime and never run out of trails. Nineteen federal wilderness areas, 11 national forests, two national parks, two national monuments and six national wildlife refuges await trail enthusiasts.

High on the list of Oregon scenic wonders are the ancient and rugged Siskiyou Mountains, with their knife-edge ridges, botanical oddities, and spectacular river canyons. Visitors come from all over the world to raft and hike the lower Rogue and Illinois Canyons.

And then there are the Cascades. This majestic range, with its broad volcanoes, dominates not only Southern Oregon but the entire Pacific Northwest, from Northern California to British Columbia. The string of towering volcanic peaks form the main barrier between the Northwest's verdant western valleys and its eastern deserts. In Southern Oregon, Cascades highlights such as Crater Lake, Mount McLoughlin, and the canyon of the upper Rogue River cast a magical spell on visitors.

Trail jurisdictions. Of the 91 primary hikes described in this book (not counting more than 100 optional hikes), 30 lie mainly on land administered by Rogue River National Forest, headquartered in Medford, Oregon. Eleven hikes lie mostly within Winema National Forest, headquartered in Klamath Falls. Twelve hikes fall under the jurisdiction of Umpqua National Forest, headquartered in Roseburg, and 18 hikes are under the aegis of Siskiyou National Forest, headquartered in Grants Pass. That's 71 national forest hikes. In addition, 9 hikes are mostly located within Crater Lake National Park, 6 are on land Administered by the U.S. Bureau of Land Management, one sits on property owned by the Nature Conservancy, two occupy land managed by the U.S. Army Corps of Engineers, and one, believe it or not, is in a Medford City Park. A final hike lies within Oregon Caves National Monument, which is administered by the National Park Service.

Much labor has gone into designing and maintaining these trails and the agencies responsible are to be commended and thanked. The best way to repay their efforts is to treat the land with respect.

Fees. As this book is being prepared, the Pacific Northwest Region of the USDA Forest Service is in the third year of a three-year pilot program of trailhead parking fees. On the Rogue River and in the Siskiyou National

Forests, there is currently a $3 daily parking fee at most improved trail-heads, which must be paid at a Forest Service office during business hours (some are open Saturdays). A $25 annual permit is also available. Fees are in effect from May through September. Umpqua and Winema National Forests, which do not charge fees, have elected not to participate but may be required to as the program expands. There is talk of raising the fee to $5, with a $50 fine for violations. As of the year 2000, no fines were assessed.

As the pilot program progresses, fees may be further modified and there may be other changes as well, so you might want to call first or check the Internet to see about cost. Appendix A provides phone numbers and web-sites for agencies that administer the trails in this book. Eventually, the new program will be linked to other federal and state fee systems, including the Forest Service's Golden Eagle program and the Golden Age program for seniors.

On-site, self-service fee stations are being phased in very slowly. These should prove helpful to tourists passing though or spur-of-the-moment hikers who cannot access Forest Service offices during business hours.

The Pacific Crest Trail (PCT). The Pacific Crest Trail (2000) follows the crest of the Sierra Nevada and Cascade ranges for 1,800 miles from the Mexican border to the Canadian border. It is considered America's most challenging trail and hiking its entire length is a noble and worthy accomplishment.

About 90 miles of the PCT traverse the Southern Cascades and Siskiyous. This book gives the best hikes of those 90 miles. Readers who would like more information on the PCT will find many publications containing mile-by-mile narratives.

In this book, you'll find the PCT enthusiastically described as it crosses Devil's Peak, the Sky Lakes Basin, Mount Thielsen, the south end of Crater Lake National Park, and the Red Buttes. Less scenic sections, like the 30-mile stretch across the Dead Indian Plateau, which mostly follows old logging roads have been mercifully omitted.

For those lacking the time or patience to hike the entire route, concentrating on the path's highlights is probably the ideal way to experience this national treasure. PCT hikers (and readers) should bear in mind that: (1) one person's highlight is another person's low-light and vice-versa and (2) you can never predict when an unheralded highlight will appear out of nowhere. A good example is the junction of the Pumice Flat and Pacific Crest Trails in Crater Lake National Park. The lead-in routes leave much to be desired. But the actual junction, in a tiny grass-and-wildflower basin surrounded by white-rock ledges, is exquisite.

Winter activities. There are downhill-ski areas in the Southern Cascades at Pelican Butte, near Klamath Falls, and at Mount Bailey, near Diamond Lake. Both are accessible via commercial snowcat and have no lifts. The nearest ski areas with lifts are at Mount Ashland, near Ashland (in the Siskiyou Mountains), Mount Shasta (just over the state line in California), and Mount Bachelor (near Bend). Diamond Lake has a rope-tow hill for inner tubes and snowboards.

Established cross-country ski trails (plus a few snowmobile trails) may be found in Crater Lake National Park and in the surrounding national forests, but only five main roads are kept open in winter in the Southern Oregon Cascades (Oregon Highways 140, 62, 66, 138, and 230). Side roads in the snow zone can get buried under as much as 20 feet of snow. To park in a snow zone in Oregon, including at ski resorts, an annual Sno-Park Permit is required, available at any Forest Service or Department of Motor Vehicle Office, or at the ski areas.

No roads through the snow zone of the Siskiyou Mountains are maintained in winter. The Happy Camp Road, out of Cave Junction, is kept cleared only to the Page Mountain Winter Sports Area, a cross-country ski site.

ADJACENT AREAS

Central Oregon Cascades. The many trails, alpine lakes, and volcanic summits of the central Oregon Cascades, including Mount Jefferson and South Sister, Oregon's second- and third-highest peaks, are wonderfully described in this book's companion FalconGuide, *Hiking Oregon's Central Cascades.*

Northern California Cascades. The Cascade Range continues into Northern California for 125 miles. While there are far fewer lakes and trails in the California segment than in the Southern Oregon segment, Northern California boasts two of the Cascades' mightiest peaks. At 14,161 feet, Mount Shasta is second in the Cascades only to Washington's Mount Rainier. Many consider Shasta, 50 miles south of the Oregon border and a solitary, heavily glaciated volcano, to be America's most beautiful mountain. Some people worship Mount Shasta.

Fifty miles south of Mount Shasta, Mount Lassen is the only peak in the contiguous 48 states besides Mount St. Helens to erupt in the twentieth century, having done so between 1914 and 1917. Lassen also erupted in the nineteenth century, as did the Medicine Lake Highland, just east of Mount Shasta. The Medicine Lake Highland, in terms of basal area, is the largest volcano in the Cascades (and in the United States), although it's only 8,000 feet high. Lava Beds National Monument and Burnt Lava Flow, also just east of Shasta, last erupted in the eighteenth century.

Oregon Coast. The Southern Oregon Coast is a geological province in its own right and unrelated to the Siskiyous, although there are chunks of the Siskiyous in the Coast Range and vice-versa. The Oregon Coast is an extremely popular recreation destination, with many scenic drives, spectacular turnouts, secluded and not-so-secluded beaches, windswept headlands, and more than its share of hiking trails.

The best-known Oregon Coast pathway is the Coastal Trail, extending some 300 miles from Clatsop Spit, at the mouth of the Columbia River, to the California line. Redwood National Park, just over the state line in California, also boasts many outstanding trails.

There are two small native redwood groves in Oregon, both on the Chetco River out of Brookings. Other than that, the species' range pretty much comes to a screeching halt at the state line.

HOW TO USE THIS GUIDE

Selection of hikes. The hikes chosen for this guide lead to significant natural features, such as a lake, a mountaintop, a free-flowing creek or river, or a waterfall. There were selected over dozens of perfectly good trails in the southern Cascades that simply lead from one random point to another. We also omitted were trails that too closely parallel roads, trails that lead to places where you can drive, and trails following the shores of reservoirs or large, highly developed lakes with road access.

To use this book effectively, please note the following items:

Highlights

This short description of each hike includes those special natural features for which it was chosen as well as any other aspects that make the trail outstanding.

Type of hike

Hikes fall into the following categories:

Day hike. Best for a short excursion only, usually less than 6 miles one way. These short trails may lack water or suitable camping sites.

Backpack. Best for backpacking with at least one night in the backcountry. Many overnight hikes can be done as day hikes if you have the time and stamina.

Loop. Starts and finishes at the same trailhead with no (or very little) retracing of your steps. Sometimes the definition of a "loop" is stretched to include creative shapes (like a figure eight or lollipop). Sometimes a loop requires a short walk on a dirt road to get you back to the trailhead.

Out and back. Traveling the same route coming and going.

Shuttle. A point-to-point trip that requires two vehicles (one left at each end of the trail) or a pre-arranged pickup at a designated time and place. One effective way to manage the logistical difficulties of shuttles is to arrange for a second party to start at the other end of the trail. The two parties then rendezvous at a pre-determined time and place along the trail and trade keys.

Total distance

This figure gives the total distance hiked. In an out-and-back hike, the number is twice the length of the trail. Measuring trail distances is an inexact science at best. In this guidebook most distances have been taken from map measurements and from in-the-field estimates. Most wilderness trail signs do not include distances, and when they do you can bet they are just somebody else's best guess. Forest Service signs round the posted trail length to the nearest 0.5 mile. In a few instances, the text gives mileages that differ from the Forest Service's trail signs, based on the author's best calculations.

Keep in mind that distance is often less important than difficulty and that distances given only indicate map distances. Since maps reflect only the horizontal, a trail shown on the map as 1 mile but which climb a steep slope, is actually longer than a mile. Most hikers average about 2 miles per hour, although a steep 2-mile climb on rocky tread can take longer than a 4-mile stroll through a gentle river valley.

Mileages in the seven chapters that are continuations of other hikes (Hikes 30, 40, 41, 43, 49, 50, 55, and 77), are calculated from the beginning of the described hike, not from the trailhead where you parked your car.

Difficulty. Difficulty ratings are inherently flawed: what's easy for you might be difficult for me. Still, such ratings serve as a general guide and give a useful approximation of a hike's challenge. Remember to factor in your own fitness level when interpreting the rating and planning your trip.

In general, a gradient of less than 300 feet per mile is considered "easy" and a gradient over 600 feet per mile is considered "strenuous." Everything in-between is "moderate." A rating may be modified by the presence of steep sections on an otherwise easy trail and by the trail's overall length. It's hard to call any trail less than 1 mile "strenuous" unless it climbs more than 1,000 feet. On the Fish Lake Trail (Hike 11), the average rise is only 250 feet per mile over 4 miles but the climb is concentrated into 1.5 strenuous miles while the rest is virtually level. It is rated "moderate." On Union Peak (Hike 34), the path is rated "easy for 5 miles, strenuous for 0.5 mile."

Elevation gain or loss. This figure shows the highest and lowest elevation only. Elevations that are taken from topo maps are rounded to the nearest 100 feet. If the elevation change is less than 200 feet, the figure is listed as "minimal."

The accompanying elevation profiles are not meant to be a detailed foot-by-foot account of the route, but serve as a quick glimpse of the overall elevation change.

Best months. Winter snow lines in southern Oregon average between 3,000 and 4,000 feet while trailhead elevations in this book range from 400 feet (Rogue River Trail at Agness) to 7,700 feet (Mount Scott). Trailheads above 4,500 feet are usually accessible by mid-May. The highest trail segments (over 9,000 feet), may not become passable until July or later. Snowfall varies greatly from year to year and storms can temporarily bury even the lowest elevations. In spring, even when the snow at lower elevations has melted and the trail is clear, swollen creeks and rivers may block your way.

Summers are fairly mild in the mountains, so heat and humidity usually aren't problems. When it's 100 degrees in Medford, it's 20 degrees cooler at 5,000 feet. The only places where summer heat can be a problem are the Table Rocks (Hikes 56 and 57), Viewpoint Mike (Hike 25), Roxy Ann Peak (Hike 58), and the lower Rogue and Illinois Canyons (Hikes 77, 78, and 84). All have low-elevation trailheads and are best avoided when the temperature in Medford or Grants Pass is over 90.

Summer highs in Medford average between 85 and 105 degrees. Rain is rare in the valley areas in summer but terrifying localized thunderstorms, with lots of lightning, may occur in the mountains. These happen three or four times a year and usually touch off dozens of forest fires, which can make it difficult to see or breathe. Winter highs in Medford average in the 40s and 50s. The first snowfall usually shows up some time in November, with a snowpack developing by mid-December.

Maps. This section lists the applicable USGS 7.5-minute topo map or maps for each hike. Other maps are also helpful. The Rogue River and Siskiyou National Forest recreation maps show nearly every trail in this book, even those outside the Rogue River National Forest (except for the six North Umpqua area trails in Umpqua National Forest). More detailed Forest Service topographic maps are available for the Sky Lakes Wilderness, the Mount Theilsen Wilderness, the Rogue-Umpqua Divide Wilderness, the Boulder Creek Wilderness, the Mountain Lakes Wilderness, the Red Buttes Wilderness, the Kalmiopsis Wilderness, and the Siskiyou Wilderness (but not the Wild Rogue Wilderness). By far the most detailed maps are the USGS 7.5-minute topographic quad maps, which are given in the Maps section of each hike. The drawback is that they don't cover much area. While USGS maps are fascinating to peruse, Forest Service wilderness maps are much more practical.

Forest service maps are available at outdoors stores and at any Forest Service supervisor's office or ranger district. Maps may also be ordered on-line. Each National Forest has its own website (see Appendix C).

Special considerations. Sometimes you should be aware of special circumstances before deciding on a hike or getting ready for one. You may want to know, for example, if you'll run into horse traffic, or mosquitoes, or if you should bring extra water. This section tells you what to expect.

Finding the trailhead. Directions in the Cascades are given from Medford, southern Oregon's largest city, except for the North Umpqua Area, where directions are given from Roseburg, located 100 miles north of Medford on Interstate 5. In the Siskiyous, directions are from Grants Pass, Brookings, Gold Beach, or Powers. If coming from somewhere else, modify the directions accordingly using a state road map and the Rogue River, Siskiyou, Winema, or Umpqua National Forest maps. Note: The primary purpose of the "Finding the trailhead" section is to assist the reader in locating the route on a map prior to the trip. It is not advisable to use this section as your sole source of directions. The heading also describes points where markings on the ground may be ambiguous.

Parking and trailhead facilities. This section tells you where to park and how much room you're likely to find for your vehicle.

Key points. This heading includes all trail junctions, whether the hike turns there or not. It also gives major landmarks. Mileages are given within 0.1 mile but often reflect only a best estimate. The designations "go right," "go left," or "go straight," indicate either a change of trails or the direction to go if the route is unclear.

Options. These are either alternate routes leading to the same destination as the main hike or short side trips not noteworthy enough to warrant their own section. Trails usually end up listed as options because they contain only secondary highlights or are somehow less desirable than the featured hike. In general, the main hike describes the shortest route, except when there's a compelling argument for a longer route (as in Hike 11: The Fish Lake Trail is much more scenic than the shorter Beaver Swamp Trail).

BACKCOUNTRY REGULATIONS

- Wilderness permits are not required in Oregon.
- Trailhead parking fees are required in Oregon. (See the previous section, "Fees.")
- Camp only in appropriate places. (See "Zero impact," below.)
- Stay on trails (where possible) and don't create shortcuts.
- Dispose of human waste in a cat hole at least 200 feet from all water sources and campsites.
- Dispose of bathing water and dishwater well away from water sources.
- Use campstoves rather than cooking fires whenever possible or eat cold meals.
- Carry out all trash. If you can pack it in, you can pack it out.
- Limit group size to ten or less.
- Suspend food out of reach of animals.
- Do not feed or in any way disturb the wildlife. Do not leave behind food scraps.
- Do not operate any mechanized vehicle in the wilderness.
- Do not destroy, deface, disturb, or remove from its natural setting any plant, rock, animal, or archaeological resource.

ZERO IMPACT

Nowadays most wilderness users want to walk softly, but some aren't aware that they have poor manners. Often their actions are dictated by the outdated habits of a past generation of campers who cut green boughs for evening shelters, built campfires with fire rings, and dug trenches around tents. In the 1950s, these practices may have been acceptable. But they leave long-lasting scars, and today such behavior is absolutely unacceptable.

Because wild places are becoming rare and the number of back country visitors is mushrooming, a new code of ethics is growing. Today, we all must leave no clues that we were there. Enjoy the wild, but leave no trace of your visit.

THREE FALCON PRINCIPLES OF ZERO IMPACT

- Leave with everything you brought in.
- Leave no sign of your visit.
- Leave the landscape as you found it.

Most of us know better than to litter—in or out of the backcountry. Be sure you leave nothing along the trail or at your campsite. Pack out all items, no matter how small, including orange peels, flip tops, cigarette butts, and gum wrappers, and do your best to pick up any trash others leave behind.

Follow the main trail. Avoid cutting switchbacks and walking on vegetation beside the trail. Don't pick up souvenirs, such as rocks, antlers, or wildflowers. The next person wants to see them too, and collecting them violates many regulations.

Avoid making loud noises on the trail (unless you are in bear country) or in camp. Be courteous—remember, sound travels easily in the backcountry, especially across water.

Carry a lightweight trowel to bury human waste 6 to 8 inches deep at least 200 feet from any water source. Pack out used toilet paper.

Go without a campfire. Carry a stove for cooking and flashlight, candle lantern, or headlamp for light. For emergencies, learn how to build a no-trace fire.

Camp in obviously used sites when they are available. Otherwise, camp and cook on durable surfaces such as bedrock, sand, gravel bars, or bare ground.

Leave no trace—and put your ear to the ground and listen carefully. Thousands of people coming behind you are thanking you for your courtesy and good sense.

Details on these guidelines and recommendations of Zero Impact principles for specific outdoor activities can be found in the guidebook *Leave No Trace*. Visit your local bookstore, or call (800) 243-0495 for a copy.

BEING PREPARED: BACKCOUNTRY SAFETY AND HAZARDS

The Boy Scouts of America have been guided for decades by what is perhaps the single best piece of safety advice—Be prepared! For starters, this means carrying survival and first-aid materials, proper clothing, compass, and topographic map—and knowing how to use them.

Perhaps the second-best piece of safety advice is to tell somebody where you're going and when you plan to return. Pilots must file flight plans before every trip, and anybody venturing into a blank spot on the map should do the same. File your "flight plan" with a friend or relative before taking off.

Close behind your flight plan and being prepared with proper equipment is physical conditioning. Being fit not only makes wilderness travel more fun, it makes it safer. Here are a few more tips:

- Check the weather forecast. Be careful not to get caught at high altitude by a bad storm or along a stream in a flash flood. Watch cloud formations closely so you don't get stranded on a ridgeline during a lightning storm. Avoid traveling during prolonged periods of cold weather.

- Avoid traveling alone in the wilderness and keep your party together.

- Don't exhaust yourself or other members of your party by traveling too far or too fast. Let the slowest person set the pace.

- Study basic survival and first aid before leaving home.

- Before you leave for the trailhead, find out as much as you can about the route, especially the potential hazards.

- On day hikes, know what time it gets dark and turn back with plenty of time to spare.

- Don't wait until you're confused to look at your maps. Follow them as you go along, so you have a continual fix on your location.

- If you get lost, don't panic. Sit down and relax for a few minutes while you carefully check your topo map and take a compass reading. Confidently plan your next move. It's often smart to retrace your steps until you find familiar ground, even if you think it might lengthen your trip. Lots of people get temporarily lost in the wilderness and survive— usually by calmly and rationally dealing with the situation.

- Stay clear of all wild animals.

- Make sure your first-aid kit includes a sewing needle, snake-bite kit, aspirin, antibacterial ointment, antiseptic swabs, butterfly bandages, adhesive tape, adhesive strips, gauze pads, two triangular bandages, codeine tablets, two inflatable splints, Moleskin or Second Skin for blisters, 3-inch gauze, CPR shield, rubber gloves, and lightweight first-aid instructions.

- Make sure your survival kit includes a compass, whistle, matches in a waterproof container, cigarette lighter, candle, signal mirror, flashlight, fire starter, aluminum foil, water purification tablets, space blanket, and flare.

Lastly, don't forget knowledge is the best defense against unexpected hazards. Read up on the latest in wilderness safety information in Falcon's *Wild Country Companion.*

Lightning—you might never know what hit you. Mountains are prone to sudden thunderstorms. If you get caught in a lightning storm, take special precautions. Remember:

- Lightning can travel ahead of a storm, so take cover before the storm hits.

- Don't try to make it back to your vehicle. It isn't worth the risk. Instead, seek shelter even if it's only a short way back to the trailhead. Lightning storms usually don't last long, and from a safe vantage point, you might enjoy the sights and sounds.

- Be especially careful not to get caught on a mountaintop or exposed ridge; under large, solitary trees; in the open; or near standing water.

- Seek shelter in a low-lying area, ideally in a stand of small, uniformly sized trees.

- Avoid anything that attracts lightning, like metal tent poles, graphite fishing rods, or pack frames.

- Crouch with both feet firmly on the ground.

- If you have a pack (without a metal frame) or a sleeping pad with you, put your feet on it for extra insulation against shock.

- Don't walk or huddle together. Instead, stay 50 feet apart, so if somebody gets hit by lightning, others in your party can give first aid.

- If you're in a tent, stay in your sleeping bag with your feet on your sleeping pad.

Hypothermia—the silent killer. Be aware of hypothermia—a condition in which the body's internal temperature drops below normal. It can lead to mental and physical collapse and death. Hypothermia is caused by exposure to cold and is aggravated by wetness, wind, and exhaustion. The moment you begin to lose heat faster than your body produces it, you're suffering from exposure. Your body starts involuntary exercise, such as shivering, to stay warm and makes involuntary adjustments to preserve normal temperature in vital organs, restricting bloodflow in the extremities. Both responses drain your energy reserves. The only way to stop the drain is to reduce the degree of exposure.

With full-blown hypothermia, as energy reserves are exhausted, cold blood reaches the brain, depriving you of good judgment and reasoning power. You won't be aware that this is happening. You lose control of your hands. Your internal temperature slides downward. Without treatment, this slide leads to stupor, collapse, and death.

To defend against hypothermia, stay dry. When clothes get wet, they lose about 90 percent of their insulating value. Wool loses relatively less heat; cotton, down, and some synthetics lose more. Choose rain clothes that cover the head, neck, body, and legs and provide good protection against wind-driven rain. Most hypothermia cases develop in air temperatures between 30 and 50 degrees, but hypothermia can develop in warmer temperatures.

If your party is exposed to wind, cold, and wet, watch yourself and others for uncontrollable fits of shivering; vague, slow, slurred speech; memory lapses; incoherence; immobile, fumbling hands; frequent stumbling or a lurching gait; drowsiness; apparent exhaustion; and inability to get up after a rest. When a member of your party has hypothermia, he or she may deny any problem. Believe the symptoms, not the victim. Even mild symptoms demand the following treatment:

- Get victims out of the wind and rain.

- Strip off all wet clothes.

- If the victims are only mildly impaired, give them warm drinks. Then put them in warm clothes and a warm sleeping bag. Warm victims further with well-wrapped water bottles filled with heated water.

- If the victims are badly impaired, attempt to keep them awake. Put each victim in a sleeping bag with another person—both naked. If you have double bags, put two warm people in with each victim.

Fording rivers. Early summer hiking in the Southern Cascades and Siskiyous may involve crossing streams swollen with run-off. When done correctly and carefully, crossing a big river is safe, but you must know your limits. None of the hikes in this book has major fords.

Know those cases where you simply should turn back. Even if only one member of your party (such as a child) might not be able to follow larger, stronger members, you might not want to try a risky ford. Never be embarrassed by being too cautious.

Be cougar alert. Cougar encounters are extremely rare and many veteran hikers never even see a cougar in the wild. However, the big cats, also called mountain lions or pumas, are potentially dangerous. It is wise to educate yourself before heading into cougar habitat.

To stay as safe as possible when hiking in cougar country, follow this advice:

1. Don't let small children wander away by themselves.

2. Don't let pets run unleashed.

3. Know how to behave if you encounter a cougar.

See Falcon's *Mountain Lion Alert* for more details and tips for safe outdoor recreation in cougar country.

Be bear aware. The first step of any hike in bear country is an attitude adjustment. Being prepared for bears doesn't only mean having the right equipment, it also means having the right information. Black bears (there are no grizzlies in Oregon) do not as a rule attack humans, but they may pose a danger if you handle your food improperly. At the very least, letting a bear get human food may contribute directly to the eventual destruction of that bear. Think of proper bear etiquette as protecting the bears as much as yourself.

Camping in bear country. Staying overnight in bear country is not dangerous, but the presence of food, cooking, and garbage adds an additional risk to your trip. Plus, you are in bear country at night when bears are usually most active. A few basic practices greatly minimize the chance of encounter.

To be as safe as possible, store everything that has any food smell. Ziplocked bags are perfect for reducing food smell and help keep food from spilling on your pack, clothing, or other gear. If you spilled something on your clothes, change into other clothes for sleeping and hang clothes with food smells with the food and garbage. If you take them into the tent, you aren't separating your sleeping area from food smells. Try to keep food odors off your pack, but if you fail, put the food bag inside and hang the pack.

Be sure to finalize your food storage plans before it gets dark. It's not only difficult to store food after darkness falls, but it's easier to forget some juicy morsel on the ground. Store food in airtight, sturdy, waterproof bags to prevent food odors from circulating throughout the forest. You can purchase dry bags at most outdoor specialty stores, but you can get by with a trash compactor bag. Don't use regular garbage bags as they can break too easily.

See the diagrams below for different ways to hang a bear bag. If you have two bags to hang, divide your food into two equal sacks. Use a stone

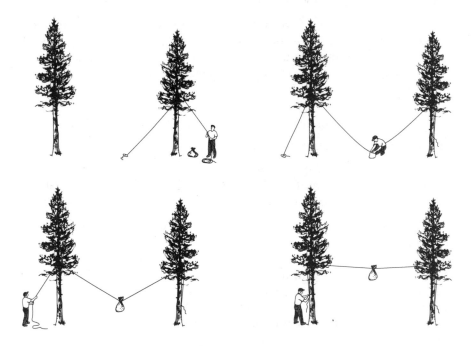

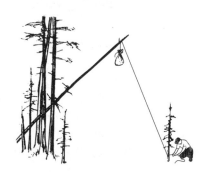

to toss the end of a piece of nylon cord (parachute cord is fine; under most circumstances there is no need for the heavier stuff) over the limb well out from the trunk, then tie half your food to the end. Pull the food up to the limb, then tie your remaining food sack onto the cord as high as you can reach. Stuff the excess cord into the food sack, then use a stick to push the second sack several feet higher than your head. The first sack will act as a counterweight and descend a few feet, but it should remain at least as high as the second sack. In the morning, use a stick to pull down one of the sacks.

Don't get paranoid about the types of food you bring—all food has some smell. By consciously reducing the number of dishes (pack out all food scraps) and amount of packaging, consuming everything on your plate, and paying careful attention to storage, you not only make your back-packing culinary experience more enjoyable and hassle free, but also more bear-proof.

Read Falcon's *Bear Aware* by Bill Schneider for complete information on camping in bear country.

Remember rattlesnakes. Rattlesnakes strike humans only out of self-defense, when they're startled or otherwise afraid. The solution, of course, is to avoid scaring them. Look where you place your feet and hands when hiking in rattlesnake country (which means most of the trails in the South Cascades and Siskiyous, but especially lower, warmer elevations). Fortunately, they almost always warn you of their presence with their tell-tale rattle.

If you encounter a rattlesnake, slowly back away and give it a chance to retreat. Almost invariably, it will seize the opportunity and slither away. If it doesn't, simply give the snake a wide berth and leave well enough alone. Do not throw rocks or sticks at it.

If bitten by a rattlesnake, don't panic. Rattlesnake bites can make you sick but are rarely fatal to healthy adults. Use a snake-bite kit immediately to extract as much of the venom as possible. (It may actually be a "dry bite" in which no venom is delivered—intended only to frighten you.) Do not run or otherwise speed up your circulation, as that increases the spread of the venom in your blood stream. Keep the bite site lower than your heart to decrease the spread of venom. Get medical attention as soon as possible, preferably within an hour.

NATURAL HISTORY

The Cascades. The story of the Oregon Cascades is the story of volcanoes—lots and lots of volcanoes—dating back 50 million years and more, strung out along the Pacific "Ring of Fire," and fueled by the westward advancement of the North American continent. Even the much older mountain systems in the region, such as the Siskiyous, which are not considered volcanic, have an ultimate volcanic origin. Oregon is also dotted with ancient isolated volcanoes, such as Saddle Mountain near Astoria, which are not associated with the Cascades or Siskiyous.

The Cascades are America's most extensive volcanic chain by far. They stretch from Mount Lassen in California to Mount Garibaldi in British Columbia. The highest summits are California's Mount Shasta (14,161 feet) and Washington's Mount Rainier (14,445 feet). The range, of course, is not limited to the high peaks and crest areas. In southern Oregon, the system essentially extends (east to west) from the Klamath Basin to Interstate 5. The freeway follows the geological boundary almost exactly.

The Cascades can be divided into the Western Cascades and the High Cascades. The Western Cascades, around 40 million years old, lie west of the High Cascades and are highly eroded and much older than the High Cascades. Of the areas in this book, the Soda Mountain area and the Rogue-Umpqua Divide belong to the Western Cascades. The string of immense, young, still-active volcanoes rising immediately east of the Western Cascades is called the High Cascades. The High Cascades date back only 10 million years.

The major peaks of the Cascade Range all belong to the High Cascades, which reach their maximum height in Southern Oregon and Northern California. In Washington, scattered High Cascades peaks such as Mount Rainier and Mount Saint Helens poke up through the more prevalent Western Cascades. In Southern Oregon, only isolated remnants of the Western Cascades have escaped the High Cascades' relentless advance.

Ten million years from now, the towering composite volcanoes of the High Cascades (a composite volcano is made up of both ash and lava), such as Mount Shasta and Mount McLoughlin, will have eroded away to their innermost skeletons (lava is pretty soft) and will resemble Pilot Rock or Rabbit Ears. Meanwhile, a few dozen miles east, another volcanic chain will have risen up. This hypothetical new system will no doubt be called the "Really High Cascades," if there are people around.

You might ask why, if the Cascades are so volcanically active, there were only two significant eruptive episodes during the twentieth century. Look at it this way: Two eruptions per century equals 20,000 eruptions in a million years and 200,000 eruptions in 10 million years. That's a lot of eruptions. There were six eruptions in the nineteenth century.

The major volcanic event influencing southern Oregon occurred at Mount Mazama, a heavily glaciated, 11,000-foot mountain between Mount Shasta and central Oregon's South Sister. About 7,000 years ago, Mazama erupted with a fury that sent an ash plume around the world and inundated the Rogue River Valley with lava as far away as (what is now) Shady Cove. Having thus spilled its guts, the peak's empty innards caved in, forming a giant, steep-sided crater called a "caldera." The pit eventually filled up with rainwater and snowmelt to become Crater Lake. The Mountain Lakes basin (Hikes 53, 54, and 55), the Medicine Lake Highland near Mount Shasta, and Newberry Crater, near Bend, have histories similar to Crater Lake, although their calderas are less recent and less dramatic.

The Klamath Mountains. The Klamath Mountains geological province extends from Redding, California, to Roseburg, Oregon, and from Medford almost to the coast. Within the province, a number of distinct ranges can be identified, including the Trinity Alps, the Salmon Mountains, the Trinity Divide, the Marble Mountains, and the Siskiyou Mountains.

The Klamath system appears related both to California's Sierra Nevada and the Blue Mountains of northwest Oregon. All date back around 200 million years. Several theories attempt to explain this relationship. The "Island Theory" suggests that the Klamaths broke off from the main chain and drifted out to sea, forming an offshore island until more recent uplift moved the beach to its present location. The "Crescent Theory" in contrast, hypothesizes an underground connection between the three ranges buried beneath the Cascades. Of course the ranges may also be entirely unrelated.

The Siskiyou Mountains. As with other ranges of the Klamath Mountains, the Siskiyous are inconsistently defined. Forest Service maps confine them to the ridge immediately north and west of the Klamath River in Oregon and California (including Mount Ashland, the Red Buttes, and the Siskiyou Wilderness). In addition to the above, most geologists include as part of the Siskiyous the entire Klamath system in southern Oregon, including everything south of Roseburg, west of the Cascades and east of the Coastal Ranges.

The name *Siskiyou* is a Cree word meaning "bob-tailed horse." The Cree still live in western Canada. An early explorer (possibly Peter Skene Ogden), so the story goes, purchased a bob-tailed race horse named Siskiyou on a visit to the Cree. In the 1820s, at what is now Siskiyou Summit on Interstate 5, the horse died in a snowstorm. So distraught was the owner that he named the pass after his dearly departed equine. The title was later applied to the entire mountain range, a national forest, and a California county.

Serpentinite. It is theorized that the North American continent is slowly moving westward and overriding the oceanic crust. Near the surface, the crust is composed mostly of basaltic lava flows. Deeper down, it is made of a coarse granite called "peridotite." Both basalt and peridotite have relatively little sodium, potassium, and silica. They contain potentially minable amounts of nickel, copper, chrome, platinum, and magnesium.

As the oceanic crust disappears under the advancing continental mass, layers of crust are believed to shear off and adhere to the continent. Where this has occurred, peridotite, being very soft, oozes upward between the rock formations like mud oozes between one's toes. Once near the surface, peridotite metamorphoses into serpentinite.

There is more peridotite and serpentinite in the Klamath Mountains than anywhere else on the continent. The largest single mass is about 15 miles wide and 30 miles long. Vulcan Lake (Hike 82), is located on this formation.

Sepentinite and peridotite are both greenish black, shiny and slightly greasy to the touch. They weather to a distinctive, rough-textured, reddish tan rock or to a bright orange soil. The quickest tipoff to the presence of serpentinite or peridotite is that they support entirely different vegetation than other rock types. Most of the vegetation is stunted and strange looking, and includes many rare and endangered plant species.

In addition to Serpentinite, the Siskiyous Mountains contain a variety of rock types representing several periods of uplift and erosion. A basic ingredient, more extensive in California than Oregon, is a lovely white granitic rock (granitic rock is a large-crystalled lava which hardened deep underground and never made it to the surface) called "quartz-diorite," formed in the Age of Dinosaurs at the core of a long-vanished range. Other intrusions of granitic and lava rock followed, especially during a period of volcanic activity 150 million years ago.

The most common rock in the lower Rogue Canyon and many other areas of the Siskiyous, is an ancient, partially metamorphosed (chemically altered in place over a long period of time) basaltic lava called "greenstone." Greenstone's numerous cracks and fissures are often filled with white quartz. Quartz veins may be accompanied by flakes of gold and silver, which gave rise to the region's colorful mining history. Other rock types in the Klamaths also contain gold-bearing quartz.

Patches of sedimentary rock, particularly limestone and sandstone, also dot the Klamaths. Much of this ancient material has metamorphosed into schist and marble.

Marble lenses, more common in the Klamaths than one might imagine, dissolve along fracture lines to form caves, usually with spectacular flowstone and stalactite formations. The region's best known marble deposits adorn Oregon Caves National Monument and the Marble Valley. The latter lies just south of the California line, in the Marble Mountains.

There are no marble or limestone caves in the Cascades. And there is no gold or silver there, either.

Glaciers. A major geological factor shaping the Southern Oregon mountains is glaciation. The most recent North American Ice Age, between 1 million and 10,000 years ago, was confined in Western North America to the mountains. While evidence of past glaciation can be found throughout the region, it occurred most extensively in the Sky Lakes region. The region's largest single ice mass once covered the Sky Lakes Basin while Oregon's longest and most spectacular glacier once moved down the Middle Fork of the upper Rogue. The south fork of the Illinois, in the Siskiyous, was also heavily glaciated.

Glaciers are adept at quarrying and bulldozing rock. Signs of past glaciation include valleys with a U-shaped profile, elongated rubble heaps called "moraines" and amphitheater-shaped basins called "cirques," marked by a steep horseshoe-shaped cliff on one side and a lake at the cliff's base.

Nearby Mount Shasta remains glaciated, as does the South Sister, near Bend. Mount McLoughlin was once heavily glaciated on the northeast flank but those glaciers have gone the way of the rest of the Ice Age glaciers. The glaciers on Mount Mazama were blasted to smithereens during the eruption 7,000 years ago.

Plant associations. The southern Oregon Cascades and Siskiyous lie at the crossroads between the California Forest Region, the Pacific Northwest Forest Region, and the Pacific Coast Forest region. Incense cedar, sugar pine, white fir, and Shasta red fir are California species while western red cedar, western hemlock, Pacific silver fir, and noble fir are Northwest denizens. Coastal species include red alder and Port Orford cedar. Douglas-fir shows up everywhere in the West, from South Dakota to New Mexico to Alaska to Baja California.

A major botanical demarcation seems to be the Rogue-Umpqua Divide. North of the divide, Pacific silver fir, Alaska cedar and Western redcedar, three dominant Northwest tree species, are found in abundance. South of the divide, those species are almost completely absent.

In addition to its sky blue lake, Crater Lake National Park is also famous among botanists for its trees, being the only place where every West Coast true fir species (genus *Abies*) can be found. An observant hiker can find white fir, grand fir, noble fir, Pacific silver fir, subalpine fir, and Shasta red fir (a variety of California red fir). Douglas-fir is not a fir, hence the hyphen. It, too, is found within the park.

As you hike the Southern Oregon region, be aware of forest associations (species that are often found together). Associations may be the result of elevation (whitebark pine and mountain hemlock inhabit the highest elevations, with oak, ponderosa pine, and grass dominating the lowest elevations), north slope-south slope differences (north slopes are much shadier and cooler), fire history (lodgepole pine, manzanita, and whitethorn ceanothus require frequent fires to reproduce), riverbank areas (Oregon ash, red alder, willow), and so forth.

The resident plants also vary depending on whether you're on the Cascades' western or eastern slope. The west side is warmer and rainier while the east side is a drier and colder rain shadow, where storms moving in from the pacific are deterred by the mountain range. Quaking aspen and western juniper barely show their faces west of the divide but are abundant to the east. Ponderosa pine grows at higher elevations on the east side than on the west and is far more abundant there. The east side of the Cascades is often referred to as "pine country," although many other tree species also grow there.

There are so many wildflowers species in Southern Oregon that the hike descriptions only name a few of the most prominent or interesting. There are hundreds of species to be found; some low-elevation, some high-elevation, some riverbank, some shade-loving, some sun-loving, some endangered (especially on serpentinite areas of the Siskiyous), some everywhere you look. The chapters drop a few names but offer no descriptions.

If the subject interests you, look up the ones mentioned before you leave home or pack a wildflower guide (always a good idea).

Plants to avoid. Poison oak is common on lower elevation dry sites but may also turn up in woods below 4,000 feet. Look for straight, light-tan stems, tiny greenish-white berries, and the telltale three leaflets per leaf stem, with the two outside leaflets lobed on the outer edge only and the middle leaflet lobed on two edges. Poison oak is similar to poison ivy (which is not native to Oregon) and is a member of the sumac family. Like poison ivy, poison oak can grow up the side of a tree as a clinging vine. It usually is a small, clonal shrub with stems growing in colonies. People who claim to be immune to poison oak are advised not to press their luck because they could become allergic at any time.

The only place mentioned in this book where the author has observed stinging nettles is along the Upper Rogue River Trail. It can also be found at Lava Beds National Monument, in the desert east of Mount Shasta, just over the state line in California. These are two very different sites. If you touch a nettle, it feels like a mild bee sting for an hour or so, then goes away. Look for a tall herbaceous plant with large, heart shaped leaves and a spiked head covered with little greenish-white beads. The little beads cause the stinging reaction.

Wildlife. The most impressive large mammals you're not likely to run across in the Southern Oregon Cascades and Siskiyous are black bear, Roosevelt elk, red fox, and cougar.

Black bears are pretty timid and tend to run away, unless you have food on you or inadvertently threaten their cubs. Cougar attacks are also extremely rare. See the previous sections on these animals under "Being prepared: backcountry safety and hazards."

Elk hunters, who know where to look, are much better at finding elk than a common hiker. Roads in the Tom and Jerry and Red Blanket Creek areas are closed in winter because they're elk wintering ranges. You'll find lots of droppings when the roads first open up in April. The Sphagnum Bog Trailhead (Hike 28) area boasts several resident elk.

Hikers are likely to see Columbian blacktail deer (they have black tails and are very small), quail, ground squirrels (including chipmunks), gray squirrels, coyotes, any of a hundred songbird species, and few redtail hawks. The nearby Lower Klamath National Wildlife Refuge, south of Klamath Falls, is home to dozens of species of waterfowl, from snow geese to ruddy ducks to sandhill cranes. The refuge is the second-largest bald eagle area in the United States (after Alaska) and winter is best for viewing. If you're extremely observant, you might also spot a mule deer at the refuge.

Critters to avoid. Rattlesnakes are unlikely to bother you, but they do turn up from time to time. See the "Remember rattlesnake" section under "Being prepared: backcountry safty and hazards."

Yellowjackets turn up in abundance, mostly near lakes following dry winters. They can be aggressive and you can get stung from time to time but it's usually not severe unless you're hypersensitive. A lot of places in the region are named after yellowjackets (see Hikes 3 and 13).

Ticks are tiny flat arachnids with armor-plated bodies. Their bite can not only get infected, but can cause Lyme disease, which you don't want to catch. To avoid tick bites, check yourself for ticks any time foliage, especially broadleaf shrubs, brushes against your head, neck, or upper body. The author has had success dislodging ticks, if they're not too deeply embedded, by twisting them counterclockwise, despite assertions that this is an old wives' tale. If the tick's head is embedded, a hot match head is supposed to be very persuasive.

Mosquitoes are abundant in the wet, forested, middle-elevation areas of the southern Oregon Cascades—notoriously so in the lake basins of the Sky Lakes Wilderness. One side effect of the snowiest year ever (1999), was that is was also the most mosquito infested year ever. In some places in the Sky Lakes, thousands of aggressive, swarming mosquitoes filled every square foot of vacant space, making life miserable for visitors. Natural mosquito repellants were ineffective against such numbers. Industrial strength DEET barely held them in check.

It should be noted that on most Sky Lakes excursions, mosquitoes are not an issue. They largely disappear within a week or two after the snow melts so August, September, and October are relatively comfortable. The Siskiyous are much less mosquitoey than the Cascades because there isn't as much marsh.

HUMAN HISTORY

Native tribes and early settlement. The first human residents of the Rogue River region the Takelma and Tututni, were called the "Rogue" Indians (*Coquin* in French); because White explorers, at the turn of the nineteenth century, made certain judgments regarding their behavior. Though intended as an insult, the name stuck and was later applied to a river, any number of businesses, and a community college in Grants Pass.

Evidence suggests that Native American populations between the mouth of the Rogue and Crater Lake never exceeded a few hundred souls. Mostly hunters and gatherers, they lived a quiet life with minimal impact on the land (except for a habit of occasionally setting forest fires to improve deer habitat).

Having heard stores about White efforts to subdue and eliminate native tribes farther east, the Takelma and Tututni did everything they could to make the first White visitors and settlers feel unwelcome. Two early recipients of their hostility in the 1820s, were Peter Skene Ogden and Joe McLeod. Ogden, Utah, is named for Peter Skene while McCloud, California, is named for Joe McLeod. (They weren't much at spelling in those days.)

According to an early account, McLeod found the local Indians "obnoxious" and described their behavior as "impudent" and "troublesome." They "went so far as to take the peoples' kettle from the fire and help themselves to the contents."

Relations between the native tribes and the European settlers were never good. In the early 1850s, a one-two punch was delivered to the local natives. The first was the Oregon Land Donation Act of 1850, which opened nearly all land in the territory to white settlement without providing any compensation to the existing inhabitants. The act gave 320 acres of land to any white person 18 years of age or older.

Then, in 1852, gold was discovered near the Lower Rogue River. This led to a number of skirmishes between the miners, settlers, and U.S. Army on one hand, and the native tribes on the other. Within a very short time, the area became one of the most populated in Oregon, with Jacksonville as the principal city.

The Takelma were briefly assigned all the land on the top of the Table Rocks as their reservation but continued harassing settlers and vice-versa. This led to the Rogue Indian Wars of 1855–1856. The series of one-sided confrontations culminated in the Lupton Massacre, in which 2 soldiers and 27 native women and children perished.

The Takelma and Tututni are mostly gone now.

Other nearby tribes. The history of the tribes immediately east of the southern Cascades, just outside the area discribed in this book, is no less tumultuous than that of the more westerly Takelma and Tututni. The Modoc and Klamath tribes were forced onto the Klamath reservation in the mid-1800s. Because the two groups were traditional enemies, the Modoc soon chose to leave. Attempts to return them to the reservation culminated in the Modoc War of 1872, in which 27 Modocs, led by Captain Jack, holed up in a hastily constructed fortress amid the jumbled lava rocks at the edge of Tule Lake, in what is now Lava Beds National Monument. The tiny group held off several hundred U.S. Army regulars for six months.

Lava Beds, Captain Jack's Stronghold, Tule Lake, and Lower Klamath Lake are well worth a visit, for the scenery, the history, and the wildlife. Also of interest there are Petroglyph Point at Lava Beds and Glass Mountain and Medicine Lake, immediately south. The site of a World War II Japanese internment camp may be seen at Newell, just south of the town of Tulelake.

Mining. Southern Oregon was a focal point of the Western gold rush in the 1850s through the 1870s. The regions first two county seats, Jacksonville (Jackson County) and Waldo (Josephine County) began as mining settlements. Gold mining in Southern Oregon is entirely confined to the Siskiyous. There were flurries of gold mining activity in the 1940s, when elaborate dredges were brought in, and the 1970s. It remains a popular pastime.

During World War II, an attempt was made to develop Josephine County's serpentinite areas for nickel and chrome mining. Both produced low-quality ores and, the effort, for the most part was quickly abandoned. However, the only nickel mine in the United States, near Riddle, north of Grants Pass, operated until the mid-1980s.

Timber and ranching. After the gold miners left in the 1870s, ranchers and timber people moved in. Hundreds of towns were established around tiny steam-powered sawmills, with the finished product shipped by rail to San Francisco and Portland. The primary ranching crops were (and are) pears and hay in the Rogue Valley and cattle and potatoes in the Klamath Basin. Timber products remained basic to the region's economy through the 1970s.

The State of Jefferson. Southern Oregonians and residents of the California far north have much in common besides shared mountain ranges. Both areas are inhabited by highly independent pioneer types who find themselves frequently disturbed that their region's small population gives them little influence in their far-off state capitals. Over the years, efforts have been made to combine the two areas into a State of Jefferson. Some of the efforts (those of 1941 especially) have been serious and resulted in violence. Although the state of Jefferson is mostly a state of mind, real or mythical, the area is a magnificent place, stretching from the redwood coast to Mount Shasta to the North Umpqua to the Klamath Basin.

Crater Lake National Park. Although Crater Lake was long revered by the Klamath tribe as a dwelling place of the gods, it wasn't visited by people of European ancestry until 1853, when three itinerant gold miners happened across it. John Wesley Hillman is credited with the actual discovery. Since there is no gold or any other precious metal anywhere in the southern Cascades (the only minable commodities are pumice, obsidian, and gravel), it's nice to know their time wasn't wasted.

William G. Steel is credited as the motivating force behind the lake's designation as the nation's fifth national park in 1902 (after Yellowstone, Yosemite, Mount Rainier, and the Grand Canyon). The park predates the National Park Service by 14 years.

LAKE SUMMARY

While most of the major lakes mentioned in this book contain fish, that is only because they are regularly stocked by the Oregon Department of Fish and Wildlife. In most of the stocked lakes, fish do not reproduce and are unable to survive the winter. A few major lakes, principally Blue Lake and Crater Lake, are not stocked. North and South Lakes, two of the seven lakes in the in the Seven Lakes Basin, are not stocked. Of the 200 lakes, ponds, and puddles in the Sky Lakes Wilderness, only 31 are both stocked and mentioned in this book. A half-dozen others are stocked but not located near any established trail.

Fish Lake, in the Rogue-Umpqua Divide Wilderness, is the largest (and deepest) wilderness area lake mentioned in this book (90 acres). Lake Harriette, in the Mountain Lakes Wilderness, comes in second at 70 acres. Both are much larger than any of the Sky Lakes. Island Lake (40 acres) is the largest of the Sky Lakes, followed by Long Lake (37 acres), Alta Lake (32 acres), Middle Lake (30 acres), Red Lake (29 acres), and Squaw Lake (26 acres). By contrast, Upper Klamath Lake covers 72,000 acres while Crater Lake encompasses 17,600 acres. The Siskiyous contain only a few very small lakes.

The following list includes only stocked lakes mentioned in the text. The stocking program is dependent on available funds and could be cut back or discontinued at any time.

Rogue-Umpqua Divide Wilderness

Lake	Elevation	Acreage	Depth	Fish
Buckeye	4,200	8	45	Brook trout
Cliff	4,300	5	15	Brook
Fish	3,350	90	140	Brook, rainbow

Sky Lakes Wilderness

Lake	Elevation	Acreage	Depth	Fish
Alta	6,600	32	13	Brook
Badger	5,920	9	11	Brook
Beal	5,570	5	9	Brook
Cliff	6,270	10	14	Brook
Dee	5,910	14	16	Brook
Deep	5,950	4	17	Brook
Deer	6,075	5	15	Brook
Donna	5,960	2	9	Brook
Elizabeth	6,020	3	8	Brook
Grass	6,000	25	8	Brook
Heavenly Twin, Big	5,975	25	13	Brook, rainbow, cutthroat
Heavenly Twin, Little	5,975	7	17	Brook
Horseshoe	5,720	20	12	Brook, rainbow
Isherwood	5,980	16	17	Brook, cutthroat
Island	5,906	40	17	Brook
Ivern	5,700	3	10	Brook

Long	6,080	37	9	Brook
Margurette	6,020	15	29	Brook, rainbow
Meadow	5,620	14	4	Brook, rainbow
Middle	6,100	30	12	Brook
Notasha	6,035	6	27	Brook, rainbow
Pear	5,760	25	33	Brook, rainbow
Puck N.	6,450	7	18	Brook
Puck S.	6,450	24	10	Brook
Red	6,080	29	6	Brook
Round Lake	3,860	2	12	Brook
Snow	6,080	3	8	Brook
Sonya	5,875	8	38	Brook, rainbow
Squaw	5,745	26	11	Brook, rainbow
Trapper	5,938	17	11	Brook
Wizzard	5,910	5	17	Brook
Woodpecker	5,910	3	11	Brook

Mountain Lakes Wilderness

Lake	Elevation	Acreage	Depth	Fish
Clover	6,700	1.5	8	Brook
Como	6,750	7	32	Brook, rainbow
Harriette	6,750	70	63	Brook, rainbow
Mystic	7,240	2.5	14	Brook
Paragon	6,980	3.5	8	Brook
South Pass	6,525	8.5	8	Brook, rainbow

Surrounding lakes (natural only)

Lake	Elevation	Acreage	Depth	Fish
Crater	6,178	17,600	1,996	Brook trout
Diamond	5,182	3,000	50	Brook, rainbow
Fish	4,642	350	25	Brook, rainbow
Fourmile	5,744	740	170	Brook, kokanee
Lake of the Woods	4,961	1,113	52	Brook, rainbow, kokanee
Upper Klamath	4,139	72,000	45	Rainbow

Siskiyou

Lake	Elevation	Acreage	Depth	Fish
Azalea	5,500	2	8	Brook, rainbow
Babyfoot	4,500	3	18	Brook trout
Bolen	5,370	12	33	Brook, rainbow
Miller	5,020	5	21	Brook, rainbow
Tannen	5,300	8	28	Brook trout
East Tannen	5,400	5	7	Brook
Valen	4,500	0.5	12	Cutthroat trout
Vulcan	4,600	7	30	Cutthroat trout

(courtesy of the Oregon Department of Fish and Wildlife)

Part I

The Southern Cascades

Mount Thielsen Wilderness

It's against the law, in Oregon, to utter the words "Mount Thielsen," without quickly adding the phrase, "The Lightning Rod of the Cascades." It probably has something to do with the peak's narrow, spire-shaped tip. Mount Thielsen is the raison d'être of the 55,000-acre Mount Theilsen Wilderness, immediately north of Crater Lake and east of Diamond Lake. Elevations in the wilderness range from 5,000 feet to 9,182 feet on top of Mount Thielsen. The companion FalconGuide, *Hiking the Central Oregon Cascades,* covers only the northern half of the Mount Thielsen Wilderness.

1 Mount Thielsen

Highlights:	A challenging climb to the 9,182-foot, frighteningly narrow spire tip of the "Lightning Rod of the Cascades."
Type of hike:	Day hike, out and back.
Total distance:	About 8 miles.
Difficulty:	Strenuous.
Elevation gain:	3,782 feet.
Best months:	July–October.
Map:	USGS Mount Thielsen quad.

Special considerations: Above the Pacific Crest Trail (2000) junction, this hike is strenuous and dangerous with loose scree slopes and rock scrambling near the top. It can be done without climbing gear, however. There is no water. Horse travel is not allowed above the PCT junction.

Finding the trailhead: Take Oregon Highway 62 north from Medford to Union Creek. Past Union Creek, where OR 62 swings right toward Crater Lake (at milepost 57), continue straight on Oregon Highway 230 towards Diamond Lake. Twenty-four and a half miles later, at the junction with Oregon Highway 138, where OR 230 ends, turn left and proceed 1.5 miles to the well-marked trailhead parking area on the right.

Parking and trailhead facilities: The trailhead accommodates 30 cars. There is excellent camping at South Diamond Lake, less than 2 miles from the trailhead.

Key points:
 0.0 Thielsen Trailhead.
 1.0 Spruce Ridge Trail junction.
 3.3 Pacific Crest Trail junction.
 4.0 Summit of Mount Thielsen.

Mount Thielsen

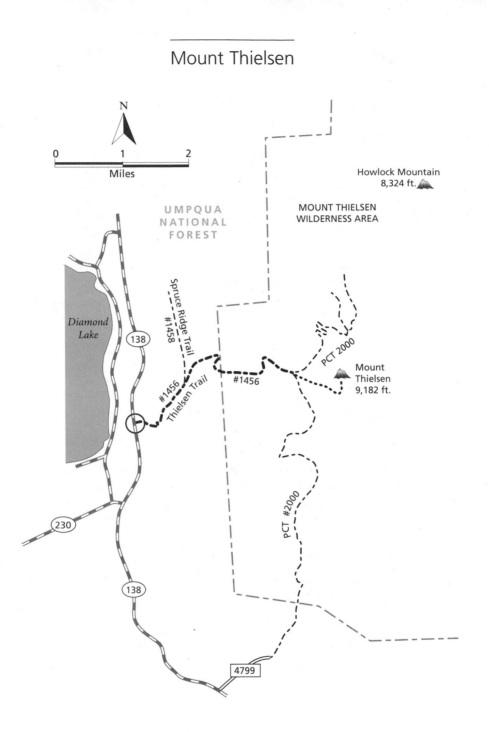

N

0   1   2

Miles

Howlock Mountain
8,324 ft.

UMPQUA
NATIONAL
FOREST

MOUNT THIELSEN
WILDERNESS AREA

Spruce Ridge Trail
#1458

Diamond
Lake

138

PCT 2000

Mount
Thielsen
9,182 ft.

#1456

Thielsen Trail

#1456

230

PCT #2000

138

4799

The hike: The ascent of towering Mount Thielsen, whose tilted spire has earned it the nickname, "the Lightning Rod of the Cascades," is probably the most difficult in this book. With its rarefied elevations and precipitous gravel slopes, the Mount Thielsen Trail soars 1,900 feet in its final mile and is like scaling the side of a bell, with every step steeper than the last.

From the trailhead, the Thielsen Trail (1456) climbs steadily but gently into a forest of Shasta fir, mountain hemlock, and western white pine. After 1.5 miles, it passes the Spruce Ridge Trail (1458). The Thielsen Trail comes around a point 0.5 mile beyond and the looming avalanche basin comprising the peak's west face emerges in all its glory.

The summit remains in view for most of the route beyond this first vista point as the forest thins, the terrain grows rockier, the trail steepens slightly, and high elevation species such as subalpine fir and whitebark pine begin to turn up. Diamond Lake is visible to the Spruce Ridge Trail junction at mile 1. It then disappears for a couple of miles, only to reemerge as the centerpiece of a mind-boggling panorama.

The Pacific Crest Trail meets the Theilsen trail at mile 3.3. The remainder of the summit route, though fairly obvious, is much more difficult. You may wish to either turn around here or content yourself with exploring a couple of miles of the PCT. Northward, the PCT winds through the avalanche basin, while to the south it makes its way among emerald meadows and multihued rock formations.

Above the PCT crossing, the Thielsen Trail (now a faint way-trail) inches up the ridge at the edge of the avalanche basin. The contorted whitebark pines gradually yield to loose gravel slopes with few solid footholds.

Eventually, the ridge peters out and you hit a sheer rock wall towering above the rim. A little scrambling just south of the rock wall takes you past the rocks and up an even steeper trail segment that traverses a precipitous scree slope to the landing at Chicken Point, which is on the east-west ridge between Diamond Lake and the Klamath Basin.

Technical gear isn't necessary to ascend the final 200-foot spire to the summit but don't feel bad if Chicken Point lives up to its name. Not everyone feels comfortable clinging to narrow ledges above 2,000-foot drop-offs. Never attempt the spire alone and watch out for people below you.

The actual summit, 4 grueling miles from the trailhead, covers about 10 feet square or less. The views are breathtaking.

Options: *Pacific Crest Trail from the south.* It's 7 miles from the Pacific Crest Trail crossing of Oregon Highway 138 northbound to the junction with the Thielsen Trail. The final 3 miles, amid craggy spires and long vistas, are extremely scenic. To reach the trailhead, take Forest Road 4579 left (north) from OR 138, 1.5 miles east of the north entrance to Crater Lake National Park. It's 0.5 mile to the parking area.

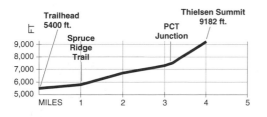

Pacific Crest Trail from the north. Pick up the Spruce Ridge Trail (1448) on OR 138 opposite the Diamond Lake turnoff for a longer but no less scenic route to the base of Thielsen. It's a 2.5-mile hike through the woods to the junction with Trail 1449. Another 2.5 miles on Trail 1449 lands you at a magnificent rocky basin and spring on Thielsen's north side, where the path meets the PCT. Heading south (right) at the PCT junction, it's not quite 2 miles (7 miles from the trailhead on OR 138), over a narrow rocky ridge and across another lovely basin, to the junction with the PCT and the Thielsen Trail.

Diamond Lake Area

Among southern Oregonians, 3,000-acre Diamond Lake may be *the* favorite High Cascades destination in both summer and winter. In addition to great scenery, 8,000- to 9,000-foot volcanoes on either side, and the Crater Lake North Entrance 3 miles away, the area boasts a restaurant, marina, bar, motel, cabins, gas station, store, and many activities. In winter, a snowcat takes skiers up Mount Bailey while near the resort there's a snowmobile rental and a rope tow for snowboarders and inner-tubers. The area boasts a couple of the most beautiful campgrounds you'll ever find. The lake is stocked with rainbow trout.

---

2   Mount Bailey

Highlights:	A spectacular hike to the top of an 8,368-foot volcanic dome rising directly above Diamond Lake.
Type of hike:	Day hike, out and back.
Total distance:	About 10 miles.
Difficulty:	Moderate to strenuous.
Elevation gain:	3,068 feet.
Best months:	Late June–October.
Map:	USGS Diamond Lake quad.

Special considerations: There is no water on this trail.

Finding the trailhead: Take Oregon Highway 62 north from Medford to Union Creek. Past milepost 57, where OR 62 swings right towards Crater Lake, continue straight on Oregon Highway 230 towards Diamond Lake for 24.3 miles. Just before the stop sign at Oregon Highway 138, look for Forest Road 6592 along the Diamond Lake south shore. Turn left, proceed for 1 mile, then turn left again on Forest Road 4795. Follow FR 4795 for 2 miles. Just past Silent Creek, turn up Spur 300. The trailhead is 0.5 mile up, at Fox Spring.

Parking and trailhead facilities: Parking at Fox Spring is ample (at least 10 cars) and there are several well-developed campgrounds nearby at Diamond Lake.

Key points:
   0.0 Fox Spring Trailhead.
   2.0 Spur 380.
   4.5 False summit.
   5.0 Summit.

Mount Bailey

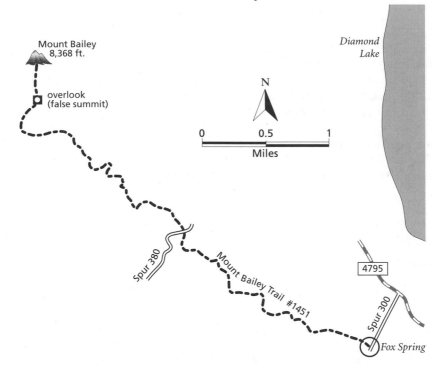

The hike: While not quite as overwhelming as neighboring Mount Thielsen, 8,368-foot Mount Bailey is a favorite among Southern Oregonians. The two giant volcanoes, Thielsen and Bailey, rise up on opposite sides of Diamond

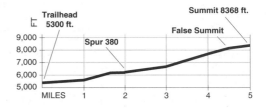

Lake, just north of Crater Lake. Mount Bailey is the one you see from the Diamond Lake Resort. Bailey is a major, if underrated Cascade Peak, 800 feet lower then Thielsen, with a beautiful and challenging summit trail. In winter, her steep, uniform cinder slopes offer one of the more unusual ski experiences, with mechanized snowcats instead of lifts ferrying skiers.

Originally named Mount Baldy because of it's domed profile, the peak became Bailey as a result of a cartographer misreading a surveyor's handwriting.

From Fox Spring, the Mount Bailey Trail (1451) begins in a lodgepole pine stand typical of Cascade volcanic regions and works its way into Shasta fir, mountain hemlock, and western white pine. Two and a half miles from the trailhead, over the forested summit of Hemlock Butte (mile 1.5, 6,309 feet), down a slight dip and beyond the wooded flat at Spur 380 (mile 2), the route steepens and breaks out into the open, passing treeline clusters of subalpine fir and whitebark pine. Most of the stretch between miles 2.5 and 4 snakes up a south-facing facet, with views of the Crater Lake rim to the south. Occasionally, the path bumps a sharp rim, revealing panoramas to the northeast of Diamond Lake and Bailey's dizzying avalanche bowl.

A half mile before the false-summit overlook, which is 4.5 miles from Fox Spring, things become quite steep. Be sure to bring water. A thousand feet before the false summit, look for a small crater 100 feet across and 50 feet deep containing a snowfield that has not completely melted in recent times.

Technically, the trail ends at the false summit. The true summit lies 0.5 mile north at the end of a precarious way-trail (a path that was never formally constructed but just grew through use). The route there drops briefly, then follows the base of a vertical rock wall, with loose gravel shooting downhill a couple of thousand feet. Eventually, the wall ends and the route starts back up, then peters out. From there, you have to scramble back to the ridgetop. It's a relatively easy walk along the ridge, around a couple more small outcrops, to the lookout base capping the flat peak.

Option: *Alternate trailhead.* You can sometimes cut 2 miles from the hike, if the gate is open, by taking the dirt Forest Road 3703 to the north (left, coming from Medford), near the summit of Oregon Highway 230, past milepost 21, 3 miles before the Oregon Highway 138 intersection. Follow the gravel road 1.8 miles to the far end of Spur 300 and turn right. Immediately after, take a left onto Spur 380. The Mount Bailey Trail crosses this narrow dirt road after 1.3 miles, where the road starts downhill. There is no trailhead sign here. Park along the shoulder. Spur 380 is usually gated.

North Umpqua Area

Douglas County's North Umpqua River area ranks prominently among Oregon's most scenic regions and contains many outstanding trails. All six trails in this section, as well as Mount Thielsen (Hike 1) and Mount Bailey (Hike 2) are located partly in the North Umpqua River drainage. The west side of Bailey, along with the entire north side of the Rogue-Umpqua Divide Wilderness, drains into the South Umpqua River, also in Douglas County.

Only one major trail in the 19,500-acre Boulder Creek Wilderness, bordering the North Umpqua near milepost 50 of the North Umpqua Highway (Oregon Highway 138), is included in this book, but it is a doozy. The hike, a steep and beautiful path from the North Umpqua to Pine Bench, includes several options.

The new 79-mile North Umpqua Trail, stretching from Rock Creek, 20 miles west of Roseburg off OR 138, to Miller Lake in the Mount Thielsen Wilderness, was constructed between 1989 and 1996 and officially dedicated in 1997. Even though the first 50 miles parallel OR 138 a little too closely, it's an impressive engineering feat. The North Umpqua may be a little prettier than the Upper Rogue. From this trail we present two highly scenic segments totaling 16 miles.

The north Umpqua area is, among other things, waterfall country and this section includes three of the state's very best outside of the Columbia Gorge and Silver Creek. Watson Falls ties for the second highest in the state, while Toketee Falls may be the most beautiful waterfall anywhere. Lemolo Falls is also spectacular.

---

3 Yellowjacket Loop

Highlight:	A beautiful loop, beginning at a lake and winding through forest, mountaintop, and multiple meadows. This is the hike most recommended by Umpqua National Forest employees.
Type of hike:	Day hike, loop.
Total distance:	5.5 miles.
Difficulty:	Moderate (easy after mile 1).
Elevation gain:	800 feet.
Best months:	June–October.
Map:	USGS Quartz Mountain quad.

Special considerations: No potable water despite crossing many wet seeps.

Yellowjacket Loop

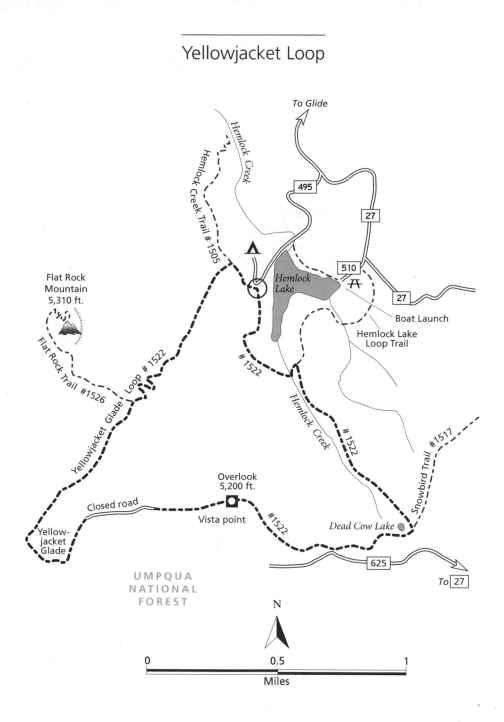

To Glide

Hemlock Creek

Hemlock Creek Trail # 1505

495

27

510

27

Flat Rock Mountain 5,310 ft.

Hemlock Lake

Boat Launch

Hemlock Lake Loop Trail

Flat Rock Trail #1526

Yellowjacket Glade Loop #1522

#1522

Hemlock Creek

1522

Snowbird Trail #1517

Overlook 5,200 ft.

Closed road

Vista point

#1522

Dead Cow Lake

Yellow-jacket Glade

625

To 27

UMPQUA NATIONAL FOREST

N

0   0.5   1

Miles

Finding the trailhead:

From Roseburg, take Oregon Highway 138 to Glide (milepost 15) and follow the Little River Road (County Road 17, becoming Forest Road 27) for 31 miles to Hemlock Lake. CR 17

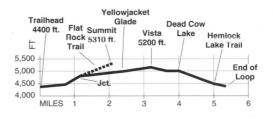

becomes Forest Road 27 at milepost 27, which is 16 miles from the Glide turnoff. The pavement turns to gravel 3 miles up FR 27. From the beginning of FR 27, it's 10 miles to Lake in the Woods Campground and 15 miles to Hemlock Lake. At the Hemlock Lake junction, turn right, towards the campground. Park at the parking area near the bulletin board and campground registration. The Yellowjacket Loop Trail begins at the bulletin board but is unmarked (trailhead signs are located 50 feet up the path). An alternate trailhead, at the Hemlock Meadows Picnic Area on the lake's east end, lengthens the route by 0.7 miles.

Parking and trailhead facilities: There is parking for eight cars at the trailhead. A campground with pit toilets is located nearby, and you can fish in the lake.

Key points:
0.0 Campground trailhead.
1.2 Junction, Flat Rock Trail (1 mile to summit).
2.2 Yellowjacket Glade.
3.2 Vista point.
3.7 Road.
4.0 Dead Cow Lake, junction with Snowbird Trail.
5.0 Junction with Hemlock Lake Loop (go left).
5.5 End of loop.

The hike: Before heading out on the trail, drive around to the boat launch on the lake's east end (the campground trailhead is on the west end). From there, you can see Flat Rock Mountain (the one with the rock outcrops), and the vista point on Yellowjacket Loop (the forested hump to the left of Flat Rock). Hemlock Lake is a 20-acre reservoir surrounded by forest and meadow.

From the campground trailhead at the bulletin board, the Yellowjacket Loop Trail 1522 heads down from the lake, to a large floral meadow crossed by a boardwalk. The meadow, like six other meadows in the next 2 miles, is home to coneflower, spirea, Queen Anne's lace, butterweed, Indian paintbrush, columbine, and above all, corn lily. At other meadows, one can spot penstemon, bleeding heart, tiger lily and other wildflower and shrub species too numerous to list here. Bear grass grows in the woods near the summit, with lots of trillium in the forest understory.

Being north of the Rogue-Umpqua Divide, forest trees consist mostly of western hemlock and Douglas-fir at the lower elevations, evolving to mountain hemlock and noble fir at the higher elevations, with Pacific silver fir at all elevations.

At the first meadow, just before the boardwalk, the Hemlock Creek Trail (1505) takes off to the right while Yellowjacket Loop begins to the left (go left). After wandering through three successive corn-lily meadows, with forest in-between, Yellowjacket Loop hits its only steep stretch, a series of forest switchbacks leading to the junction with the Flat Rock Mountain Trail (1526), near yet another large meadow.

There are two signs at the Flat Rock Trail junction, 100 feet apart. One says "Flat Rock Mountain—1 mile." The other says "Flat Rock Mountain—1.5 miles." The actual distance appears to be slightly less than 1 mile. Flat Rock Mountain offers a compelling view of Hemlock Lake with the High Cascades rising up behind. See "Options."

For 1 mile beyond the Flat Rock junction, the path continues as before except not as steeply. Wet meadows alternate with forest patches on the slope away from Hemlock Lake, just below the ridge line. Following the trail gets difficult in a couple of places due to the dense meadow foliage; if you hike in the morning, you're likely to end up with dew-soaked legs and shoes.

The trail's highlight comes 2.2 miles from the trailhead, where the path breaks out of the woods into an immense dry meadow, looks south into the South Umpqua drainage for the first time, then quickly ascends a ridgetop with a fine view of Flat Rock Mountain to the north (the peak that looks like it was chopped in half). The grassy opening where the trail emerges is Yellowjacket Glade. And yes, there are yellowjackets in Yellowjacket Glade.

Yellowjacket Glade, Mount Bailey, and Quartz Mountain from Yellowjacket Loop.

The highlight here is not Mount Bailey, on the horizon to the east, or Mount McLoughlin, on the horizon to the south, but Quartz Mountain (5,500 feet). Quartz Mountain is marked by steep bluffs, little vegetation, and what looks like volcanic ash deposits from a recent eruption on its flat summit. The "ash" is actually tailings from a quartz mine, one of the few mines in the Cascades that doesn't remove pumice or gravel. Until a few years ago, the quartz was used in the smelting process in the Riddle Mountain (Hannah) nickel mine, in the Siskiyous southwest of Roseburg, the only operating nickel mine in the U.S. When the Riddle Mountain mine closed down, they began selling the quartz to a glass manufacturer. To drive to the top of Quartz Mountain, stay on FR 27 for 3.5 miles past Hemlock Lake, then turn left on Spur 660.

Past Yellowjacket Glade, the path follows the ridgetop for 2 miles. The map shows the route following a road for 0.3 of those miles but it's a closed road grown over with grass. This is a nice area to observe forest regeneration after logging, with lots of conifer reproduction.

At mile 3.2 from the trailhead, the path reenters the woods and climbs a small, forested hillock, the vista point advertised on one of the trail signs. It's not much of a vista, but it offers the trail's only view of Hemlock Lake. A sign at the vista point informs hikers that the view north is North Umpqua drainage while the view south is South Umpqua Drainage. This is the loop's highest point. At 5,250 feet, it is less than 100 feet lower than Flat Rock Mountain.

Soon after the vista point, the path hits a real road briefly, at mile 3.7. The sign there has been knocked down and the continuing trail isn't too clear. Head uphill, just to the left of the road. The road, a gravel logging spur, runs into FR 27 after 1.5 miles (heading east, towards Mount Bailey), 2.5 miles beyond Hemlock Lake.

The path turns away from the ridgetop at mile 4 and starts downhill through an area of magnificent old growth. The route soon passes the beginning of the Snowbird Trail (1517, on the right) which ends at Snowbird Shelter, 3 miles away. The Snowbird Trail is not a good route. It hits no major highlights, keeps crossing roads and actually follows a road for 1 mile. Mile 4 on Yellowjacket Loop is marked by Dead Cow Lake. The name "Dead Cow" actually makes this 1/4-acre cesspool sound nicer than it is. The pond sort of reminds you of a tallow vat where they boil dead animals (including cows), to make candle wax. The water is stagnant and a horrible gray.

The path back to Hemlock Lake is straight, short, and in the woods until you hit bottom at mile 5, at the junction with the Hemlock Lake Loop Trail (not numbered). You then spend 0.5 mile making your way around the huge meadow that drops down into the lake. The loop ends exactly where it started.

Options: *Flat Rock Trail.* If you have time, this 1-mile side path is lots of fun. After crossing a meadowy saddle, the path ascends through the woods from 4,800 feet to a 5,310-foot summit. A cliff-top aerie offers a dramatic overview of Hemlock Lake and beyond.

Hemlock Lake Loop Trail. The Hemlock Lake Loop Trail offers an easy 2-mile trip around Hemlock Lake. It begins at the east boat ramp, which you can reach via car by going straight at the Hemlock Lake junction on FR 27. Heading south (left), the path runs through the meadows south and west of the lake for 0.7 mile before joining the end of the Yellowjacket Loop. Turn right onto trail 1522 which returns to the campground after 0.5 mile (1.2 miles from the trailhead). The path then follows the campground road (right again) for 0.3 mile to the west boat ramp. From there, the route hugs the lake's wooded north shore for 0.5 mile, returning to the starting point at the east boat ramp.

4 Pine Bench

Highlights:	A steep wilderness hike up an immense river bluff to an enchanted flat, with connections to the interior of the Boulder Creek Wilderness.
Type of hike:	Day hike, out and back.
Total distance:	4.8 miles.
Difficulty:	Strenuous.
Elevation gain:	950 feet.
Best months:	Any.
Maps:	USGS Toketee Falls and Illahe Rock quads.

Special considerations: Trails up from the river are longer than shown on the map and very steep, although the route is mostly shaded. While there is plenty of water, purifying it is a good idea. The spring at Pine Bench is delicious.

Finding the trailhead: Take the paved Medicine Creek–Soda Springs turnoff from Oregon Highway 138 (the North Umpqua Highway), at milepost 55. The turnoff is on the left if you're coming from Roseburg and is called Forest Road 4775. Almost immediately on FR 4775, a gravel road takes off left, leading to Soda Springs Dam, the Soda Springs Trailhead, a power plant, and the Boulder Creek Trailhead. Proceed 1.3 miles past the dam and over the bridge to the Soda Springs Trailhead just before the power plant.

Parking and trailhead facilities: The trailhead area, provided by Pacific Power,

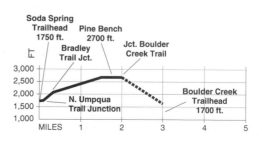

Pine Bench

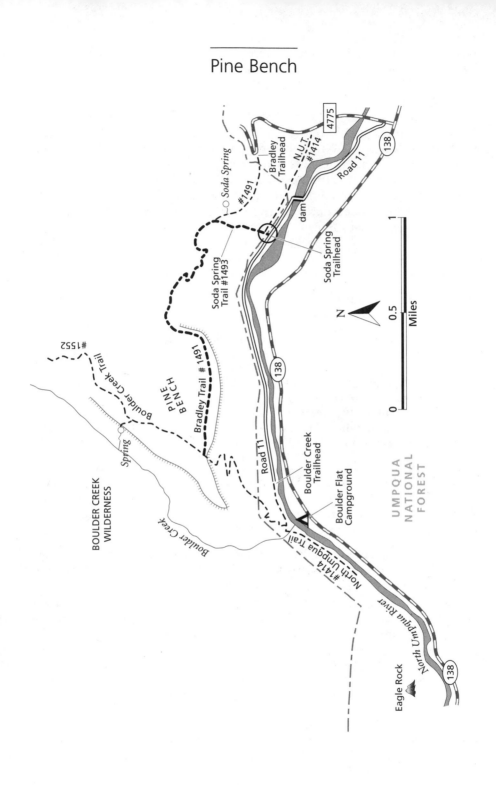

has a picnic table and room for 15 cars.

Key points:
0.0 Soda Springs Trailhead.
0.1 North Umpqua Trail junction (go straight).
0.4 Bradley Trail junction (go left).
1.5 Pine Bench.
2.0 Boulder Creek Trail junction.
2.4 Pine Bench Spring.

The hike: This short but deceptively difficult path provides no views of the river (except near the trailhead). For unusual scenic and botanical interest, however, it is a charmer. Despite the low elevation, the heavily trodden route is well shaded and comfortable year-round, with plenty of water.

You see evidence of the 1996 forest fires along much of the route. In most areas, the burn raced through the understory, slightly singing the bases of the conifer trees, which ultimately survived. At the trail's lower end, look for holes in the ground where the root wads of large trees burned away and left an impression. At Pine Bench, many acres of trees died from heat rather than actual fire. You can tell by the persistence of fine branches. If a conifer's cambium layer, between the bark and the wood, hits 150 degrees all the way around the trunk below the foliage, the tree is a goner whether it catches fire or not. The dead trees will gradually deteriorate but will provide noncompetitive shade for Douglas-fir and sugar pine seedlings (not to mention a veritable smorgasbord for insect-eating birds).

A history of repeated fires may be the reason for the abundance of pines at Pine Bench. Ponderosa pine shows up in the rainy North Umpqua valley only on extremely dry, sunny, low-elevation sites that have been burned over or clearcut. Pine Bench contains about 48 percent ponderosa pine, which is slowly yielding to Douglas-fir (also 48 percent), along with scattered sugar pine and incense-cedar. Ponderosa pine cannot reproduce in its own shade.

The Soda Springs Trailhead is the prettiest and most unusual portal into the Boulder Creek Wilderness. Located on the river, the short Soda Springs Trail (1493) begins by passing under a 10-foot-diameter pipe that carries water from the Soda Springs Dam to the power plant. You have to duck slightly to get under it.

The Soda Springs Trail meets the North Umpqua Trail (1414) after 200 feet. Technically, the NUT turns left at the Soda Springs junction, goes out the Soda Springs Trailhead, and follows the road west, past the power plant to the Boulder Creek Trailhead, bypassing the Boulder Creek Wilderness. The described hike through the wilderness across Pine Bench mostly follows the Bradley Trail (1491).

From the NUT junction, the Soda Springs Trail climbs gradually through the woods, passing a tiny stream and possibly a spring on the left. This is not the Soda Spring for which the trailhead, dam, and power plant are named. The real Soda Spring, as shown on the map, lies to the right of the trail.

The path joins the Bradley Trail (1491), also coming in from the east, 0.4 mile from the Soda Springs Trailhead. See "Options" for a description of the Bradley Trail, which can save you from climbing a couple of hundred feet and is about the same distance as the path from the Soda Spring Trailhead.

Turning left at the Bradley Trail junction, the path enters the wilderness and begins a serious ascent. The higher you get, the steeper the hillside becomes. Eventually, 1 mile from the trailhead, the path makes a couple of short switchbacks, crosses a tiny saddle and inscribes another switchback. From the tiny saddle, it's a fairly level 0.3 mile to Pine Bench and 0.8 mile to the junction with the Boulder Creek Trail. The 0.3-mile segment leading to the bench traverses a very steep, bowl-shaped slope. The river, far below, is nowhere to be seen through the dense forest.

After crossing a small rocky creek in the steep bowl, the path makes its way to the rim of Pine Bench, then out onto the flat. There are panoramas of the North Umpqua Canyon and far mountains when you first hit the rim, but no views of the river. The junction with the Bounder Creek Trail (1552) shows up 2 miles from the Soda Springs Trailhead. To explore more of the bench, including an old homestead site, and to find the nearest water (0.4 mile), turn right onto the Boulder Creek Trail.

The short trek to the spring, is flat, grassy, and magnificent. The burned trees are a tragedy but the forest will recover, although there is little observable conifer reproduction in the heavily burned or open areas. Forests tend to regenerate from the edges of live stands and that's where you find most of the newly sprouted trees. Notice that the baby Douglas-firs have been heavily munched on by deer while the baby pines have not. Look for delphinium, wild iris, houndstongue, and lots of poison oak.

For the spring, turn left at an unsigned fork in the trail, 0.4 mile from the Bradley/Boulder Creek junction. It's a couple of hundred feet on the side trail to a campsite with a stunning panorama of the Boulder Creek Canyon from atop some cliffs. The spring is slightly downhill to the left.

For a steep, quick, and beautiful descent to the river and creek mouth, and an alternate route back to the Soda Spring Trailhead, take the Boulder Creek Trail left (south) at the Boulder Creek/Bradley junction. See "Options."

Options: *Bradley Trailhead.* The hike to Pine Bench from the Bradley Trailhead is about equidistant to the hike from the Soda Spring Trailhead and saves 200 feet of climbing. The Bradley Trailhead isn't as interesting as the Soda Springs Trailhead because there are no views of the river or picnic tables. To reach the Bradley Trailhead, drive 1 mile up FR 4775 to the well-marked turnout and parking area on the left. There's room for 6 cars.

Boulder Creek Trail north from Pine Bench. From the junction atop Pine Bench, the Boulder Creek Trail takes off north (right), to the heart of the wilderness, and south (left), back down to the river. If you follow the

Boulder Creek Trail north for 0.4 mile, you arrive at a beautiful little spring whose water quickly plummets into the Boulder Creek gorge.

The Boulder Creek Trail continues for 8 miles from the Bradley Trail junction at Pine Bench to the north end of the wilderness. The initial 2 miles follow the rim above a steep canyon. Then, rounding a side creek, the path shoots abruptly down to the canyon floor, crosses Boulder Creek, and heads up the other side for 0.4 mile before meeting Boulder Creek again at mile 3. The romance with Boulder Creek here lasts only 2 miles, after which the path begins a grueling uphill climb, gaining 1,500 feet in 1 mile, before following a ridgetop the final 2 miles.

Boulder Creek Trail south from Pine Bench. An excellent loop is possible using both the Soda Springs and Boulder Creek Trailheads. Turning left (south) onto the Boulder Creek Trail from the Bradley Trail on Pine Bench, the path drops abruptly over the canyon rim, plummeting 900 feet in 1 mile, with several switchbacks, to the North Umpqua River. The descent is extremely steep but fairly wooded and not as rocky as you might expect. Look for excellent views of the river and Eagle Rock.

The Boulder Creek Trail ends at the junction with the North Umpqua Trail near the mouth of Boulder Creek. A very steep side trip right (west) on the NUT takes you to the mouth of Boulder Creek after 0.1 mile. There are lots of boulders there, and a charming footbridge.

If you head left (east) on the NUT from the end of the Boulder Creek Trail, you arrive at the Boulder Creek Trailhead after 0.2 mile. From the Boulder Creek Trailhead, it's a 1.7-mile hike along the road, which parallels the North Umpqua, back to the Soda Springs Trailhead. The total loop distance is 4.6 miles.

Should you elect to begin your hike at the Boulder Creek Trailhead instead of the Soda Springs Trailhead, as many people do, you find a shorter (1.2 miles versus 2 miles) but slightly less scenic route to Pine Bench than the Bradley Trail. As noted, the path gains 900 feet in 1 mile but it levels off somewhat after the initial few switchbacks.

To drive to the Boulder Creek Trailhead, continue on the access road past the Soda Springs Trailhead and the power plant. The road beyond the power plant is fairly rocky and full of ruts and mud puddles.

The descent from Pine Bench to the mouth of Boulder Creek offers an outstanding view of the Umpqua Rocks Geological Area, immediately west of the mouth of Boulder Creek and rising up from the north side of the North Umpqua. The area features impressive rock spires and towering formations of eroded Western Cascades basaltic lava. The most obvious formation is Eagle Rock, best viewed from OR 138, 1.5 miles west of the Boulder Creek Campground, but Rattlesnake Rock and Old Man Rock may also command your attention. There are trails into the area.

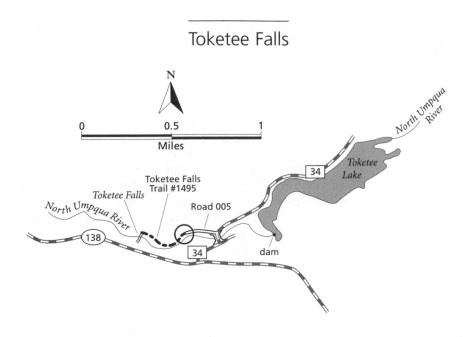

5 Toketee Falls

Highlights:	A short, easy walk to an unusual and stunningly beautiful waterfall.
Type of hike:	Day hike, out and back.
Total distance:	About 1 mile.
Difficulty:	Easy.
Elevation gain:	Minimal.
Best months:	Any.
Map:	USGS Toketee Falls quad.

Finding the trailhead: Take the Toketee Falls turnoff left (north) onto Forest Road 34 from Oregon Highway 138, the North Umpqua Highway, at milepost 59. Follow the paved FR 34 for 0.3 mile to the Toketee Falls Viewpoint parking area.

Parking and trailhead facilities: The trailhead has room for 30 cars.

Key points:
0.0 Toketee Falls Trailhead.
0.5 Toketee Falls.

The hike: This is an easy path through a dense riparian forest of Douglas-fir, western hemlock, and western redcedar to one of the world's more impressive waterfalls. You hear the falls long before you see them.

44

Toketee Falls.

From the trailhead, the Toketee Falls Trail (1495) winds through the woods briefly, then comes out atop a rock gorge just upstream from the falls. A series of stairsteps on the trail, some stone and some wooden, lead over a low crest then down to a viewing platform. There are ample guard rails.

Toketee Falls is a 120-foot plunge on the North Umpqua River. The first 40 feet drop into a collecting pool inside a strange and beautiful bowl of columnar basalt. Spilling out of the bowl, the water then falls another 80 feet before resuming its journey westward to Roseburg, Reedsport, and the ocean.

The viewing platform was rebuilt a few years ago. The old platform perched dangerously and never quite gave an adequate view. You came away feeling that the best angle for viewing Toketee Falls was from a helicopter in the middle of the river. The new platform offers a better view, accommodates more people, and is more structurally sound.

The North Umpqua Trail misses Toketee Falls because it turns away from the river immediately west (it had been running 0.2 mile inland anyhow), to make its way around Toketee Lake. Toketee Lake and Falls are the last connection either the North Umpqua Trail or the North Umpqua River have with OR 138.

---

6   Watson Falls

Highlight:	Oregon's second highest waterfall.
Type of hike:	Day hike, out and back.
Total distance:	1.2 miles.
Difficulty:	Moderate.
Elevation gain:	300 feet.
Best months:	April–November.
Map:	USGS Fish Creek Desert quad.

Finding the trailhead: Take Oregon Highway 138, the North Umpqua Highway, east from Roseburg to milepost 61, then turn right (south) onto Forest Road 37. The trailhead parking lot and picnic area are at the junction.

Parking and trailhead facilities. There are restrooms, picnic tables beside the creek, and a paved parking lot with room for 50 cars.

Key points:

0.0 Watson Falls Trailhead.

0.4 Footbridge, loop turnaround.

0.6 Base of Watson Falls.

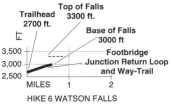

HIKE 6 WATSON FALLS

Watson Falls

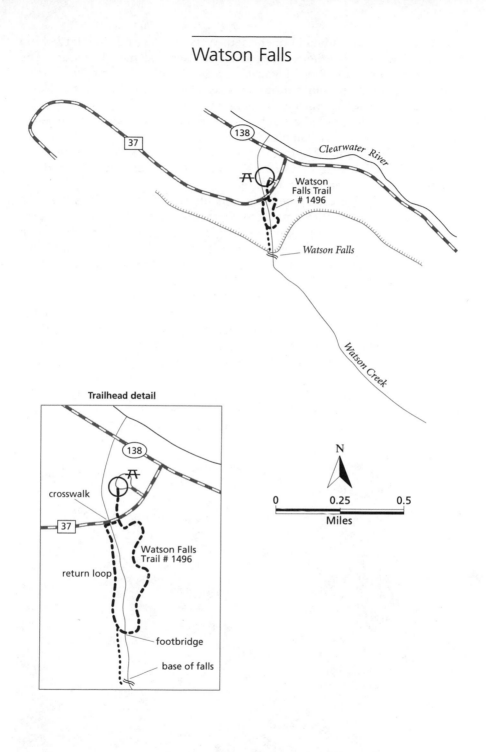

The hike: Magnificent and unheralded, Watson Falls ranks not far behind Crater Lake as a southern Oregon "must see" scenic attraction. The enchanted little trail, even if you take your time and savor every step, requires less than an hour out of your life. The falls are just off the North Umpqua Highway, 18 miles from Diamond Lake.

Watson Falls is reputedly Oregon's second-highest waterfall, although Salt Creek Falls, near Willamette Pass out of Eugene, claims the same distinction. Both plummet 272 feet. Watson and Salt Creek Falls are the highest waterfalls between Multnomah Falls (600 feet) and California's Yosemite Valley (several over 1000 feet).

The 300-foot-high escarpment responsible for Watson Falls is the nose of a giant lava flow that emanated from the Mount Bailey area some 750,000 years ago. You pass more of the giant cliffs, rising just to the south of OR 138, as you approach the Watson Falls turnoff from Diamond Lake.

The Watson Falls Trail (1496) begins in the highly developed parking area and gets considerable use. After 100 feet, it crosses FR 37, then takes up a position alongside Watson Creek. The path is fairly steep and winding and seems longer than the 0.4 mile quoted at the trailhead. It snakes its way around and over giant, moss-covered boulders and countless mini-waterfalls before emerging at a little wooden footbridge with a beautiful view of the plummeting falls. Whoever designed the bridge was a very creative individual.

Above the footbridge, the trees disappear and the main loop doubles back to the right. If you head left here, towards the falls on a side trail, you come to a switchback after 0.1 mile, with a sign that says, "To Upper Vista

Anna Bernstein and Phaedra Moyer at Watson Falls.

Point." This is not a trail to the top of the cliff, as the name suggests. The fairly steep route ends up atop the moss-covered rubble pile next to the falls after 0.2 mile. By all means, check out this short trail.

At the "Upper Vista Point" sign, you also have the option of following a rugged little way-trail that charges straight ahead to the base of the falls and one of the most enchanting, spiritually uplifting rock grottoes you'll ever see. Just below the falls, a moss-covered boulder field litters the terrain, with the white creek braiding in and out through a dozen channels. Use this route if you want to actually experience the base of the falls. None of these trails is very long and all are highly recommended.

Options: *Loop Trail.* Most people who hike to Watson Falls return the way they came instead of completing the loop. If you do stay on the loop, the return leg takes you back to the trailhead a little more quickly than the way you came in, but it lacks the dramatic views of the cascading creek and giant boulders. There is no crosswalk where the far end of the loop trail meets FR 37, so you have to walk along the road for a short distance.

Top of Falls. For the insanely adventurous, it's possible to visit the top of Watson Falls. There is no trail, however and the route is very brushy and extremely dangerous. The last few feet to the rim drop-off consists of steep, loose duff with no guard rails. The spot where the creek plummets over the cliff is fairly easy to reach although brush tends to obscure the view.

---

7 Dread and Terror

Highlight:	A beautiful 5-mile hike along the North Umpqua River, featuring old-growth forests, dozens of waterfalls, hundreds of cold springs, and a couple of hot springs.
Type of hike:	Day hike, shuttle.
Total distance:	About 5 miles.
Difficulty:	Easy.
Elevation gain:	350 feet.
Best months:	April–November.
Map:	USGS Potter Mountain quad.

Special considerations: Because the North Umpqua Trail only opened in 1996, it does not appear on the USGS topo map. On the current Umpqua National Forest map (1995), the route is only roughed in and is labeled "under construction." The map given here was provided courtesy of the Umpqua National Forest.

This section of the North Umpqua River is permanently closed to trout fishing to protect cutthroat trout, an endangered species.

Dread and Terror

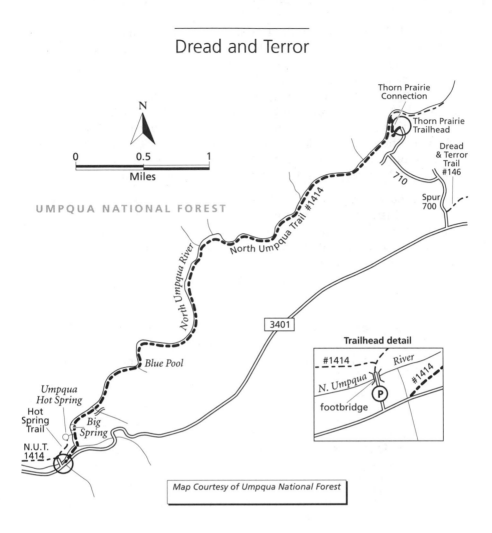

Map Courtesy of Umpqua National Forest

Finding the trailhead: Take Oregon Highway 138, the North Umpqua Highway, east from Roseburg to the Toketee Lake turnoff (Forest Road 34), at milepost 59. Proceed 2 miles up the paved Forest Road 34, then turn left onto to the gravel FR 3401. *West trailhead:* 2 miles up FR 3401, you come to the Umpqua Hot Springs parking area. The trailhead for the eastbound North Umpqua Trail's Dread and Terror section is up the road a couple of hundred feet on the left. *East trailhead:* Continue on FR 3401 for 4 miles past Umpqua Hot Springs to a side road on the left with a sign that says "North Umpqua Trail." The road is Spur 700 but there are no signs indicating that. It's 1 mile on Spur 700 to the trailhead (there are two turns so follow the signs). The trailhead accesses a short link trail called the Thorn Prairie Connection.

Parking and trailhead facilities: The Umpqua Hot Springs parking area accommodates 20 cars. Possibly three more cars could park on the road shoulder at the actual trailhead. There's a pit toilet at the parking area and a couple of campsites just across the river (over an elaborate, recently constructed footbridge). It's a 0.3-mile hike on a steep side trail to the hot springs.

Key points:
0.0 Dread and Terror Trailhead.
0.2 Campsite and Big Spring.
0.5 Footbridge, creek crossing, waterfall.
1.0 Waterfall, Blue Pool.
4.7 Junction, Thorn Prairie Connection (go right).
5.0 Thorn Prairie Trailhead.

The hike: The name "Dread and Terror" comes from Dread and Terror Ridge, a nondescript hill just south of the Umpqua River's Dread and Terror Section. The trail along the top of Dread and Terror Ridge (see "Options"), evokes neither dread nor terror and isn't even particularly interesting. The name does not come from pioneer encounters with murder, mayhem, sightings of ghosts or monsters, or menacing by crazed or mythical animals. It refers to the whitethorn ceanothus bushes for which Thorn Prairie, the flat between Dread and Terror Ridge and the North Umpqua canyon, is named. Apparently, forest workers found the thorns dreadful and terrifying to work in.

The first mile on the North Umpqua Trail (1414), from the Umpqua Hot Springs parking area to the blue pool, may be the most beautiful mile on the entire North Umpqua Trail. Heading east from the Dread and Terror Trailhead near Umpqua Hot Spring trailhead, you hit pay dirt almost immediately. While approaching a large, magnificent campsite on the river's edge downhill to the left, the trail passes over the top of a huge, gushing spring.

After dropping down to the campsite, the path passes another fascinating landmark, a large outcrop of columnar basalt (made up of hexagonal columns) covered with moss, which some hikers have dubbed the "Weeping Rock." A gentle trickle of water oozes over the 50-foot rock face, weaving in and out of the columns and sending out a pleasant spray.

The next mile, and in fact the next 13 miles from Umpqua Hot Springs to the Lemolo Lake Trailhead, passes hundreds of small springs, trickles, seeps, and wet spots. It's difficult to keep your shoes dry. The reason for all this emerging water is that the water table is very close to the surface and when the trail builders dug into the steep hillside, they tapped into frequent underground flows.

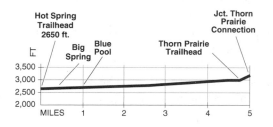

51

Dread and Terror section, North Umpqua Trail.

One of the more interesting springs is a fairly large gush of water that pours out just above the trail at one point, behind a cluster of tree roots. After 3 feet of freedom, the water disappears back into the hillside.

At mile 0.5, the path drops into and out of an enchanted grotto with a small footbridge and a fairly large waterfall. No matter how hot and muggy the weather, when you pass this falls, the temperature momentarily drops 30 degrees, with a steady wind blowing from the crashing water to your face. It feels like an air conditioner.

At mile 1, the path comes to another footbridge, over a beautiful, cascading creek that forms a pool just above the trail. It looks as though the creek emanates from a hot spring because there is steam rising off it. But the water does not feel warm (the USGS map shows other hot springs in the vicinity besides Umpqua Hot Springs). The water crashes into the pool, which seems to glow with an eerie iceberg blue in the midst of the churning and bubbling.

Beyond the blue pool, the scenery settles down somewhat. Most of the larger side creeks are across the river. Still, this is a gorgeous walk that occasionally drops down to the river's edge, then climbs 50 to 100 feet up the canyon, only to drop down again soon after.

As you approach mile 4.7, the path enters a short, marshy side channel (with skunk cabbage), which the river uses only when the water is very high. Approaching a large bend, the Thorn Prairie Connection Trail (unnumbered) shows up, with a hard turn to the right. The Thorn Prairie Connection inscribes a steep, 0.3-mile switchback that gains 250 feet of elevation as it climbs out of the densely forested canyon to the Thorn Prairie Trailhead.

Thorn Prairie, where the trailhead is located, is filled with whitethorn ceanothus bushes. Whitethorn ceanothus likes harsh, dry upland sites with frequent forest fires. A beautiful forest of young Douglas-fir (probably planted), is crowding out the whitethorn. If they can keep fires out, this will be a nice place in 20 years and they'll have to change all the names in the vicinity.

Options: *Umpqua Hot Springs.* From the Umpqua Hot Springs parking area, cross the footbridge over the river and follow the signs to the hot spring. The trail is only 0.3-mile long (or less), but very steep. The springs sit atop a large limestone formation above the river, created by deposits from the calcite-laden water that flows from the spring. A wooden open-air lean-to covers the largest of the three hot water pools (that seat six or eight). The smaller pools (seating about three each), are completely exposed. The hot springs are quite popular and while the Forest Service has no record of any problems with the large number of visitors, they are unattended and bathers use them at their own risk.

West on the North Umpqua Trail. To head west on the North Umpqua Trail, cross the footbridge and follow the Hot Springs Trail for 200 feet, past a small campsite, to the base of a dry limestone formation (there used to be a hot spring here and, in fact, it's similar to the formation at the actual hot springs). An obvious though unsigned trail takes off on the left. The North Umpqua Trail leads to Toketee Lake in 4 miles.

Thorn Prairie Connection to Lemolo Falls. If you continue east on the North Umpqua Trail from the junction with the Thorn Prairie Connection Trail, it's 6.5 miles to the top of Lemolo Falls and 8 miles to the Lemolo Lake Trailhead. The best part of this segment is the last 2 miles, from the rock gorge below Lemolo Falls to the Lemolo Lake Trailhead. The route is describe in Hike 9, under "Options."

Dread and Terror Trail. This 4-mile trail runs along the top of Dread and Terror Ridge from Spur 700 (the road to the Thorn Prairie Trailhead), to another spur road. The path is steep in spots, especially near the west end (Mile 2 climbs 800 feet. Other than that, the path is fairly level). The west trailhead is at 3,400 feet, the east railhead is at 4,400 feet, and the high point is at 4,600 feet. The route runs mostly through the woods, with no views of the river. The highlight is a logging clearcut full of planted conifer seedlings and a spectacular rhododendron display near the east trailhead.

Finding the two trailheads for the Dread and Terror Trail can be daunting. For the west trailhead, follow directions to the Thorn Prairie Trailhead, above. After driving 0.2 mile down Spur 700, you come to a shaded spot with a wooden post on either side of the road (where they sometimes gate the road). The trailhead is on the right, hidden in the bushes, 50 feet before the wooden posts. You see a sign if you look carefully. For the east trailhead, continue east on FR 3401, past Spur 700, for 1 mile, then bear left on Spur 800, a wide gravel road. Four miles later, you'll come to a fairly wide, unmarked road to the left. The trailhead is 0.5 mile down the spur road, on the left, at a turnaround next to a clearcut. There is no trailhead sign.

8   Lemolo Falls

Highlight: A short, remote, and very steep trail to a huge, thundering waterfall on the North Umpqua River.
Type of hike: Day hike, out and back.
Total distance: 3.4 miles.
Difficulty: Moderate to strenuous.
Elevation gain: 600 feet (on return trip).
Best months: April–November.
Map: USGS Lemolo Lake quad.

Finding the trailhead: Take Oregon Highway 138, the North Umpqua Highway, east from Roseburg, past milepost 73 to the Lemolo Lake turnoff at Forest Road 2610. Turn left (north) and proceed 4 miles to the gravel Forest Road 3401, on the left, just before the turnoff to the Lemolo Lake resort. Go 0.5 mile west on FR 3401 to Spur 800 and turn left, following signs to the Lemolo Falls Trail. It's another 2 miles to the turnoff to Spur 840, on the right, and 0.2 mile up Spur 840 (a narrow dirt road) to the trailhead.

Parking and trailhead facilities: The trailhead is a logging landing with room for ten cars. Follow the closed-off road, which eventually becomes a trail.

Key points:
0.0 Lemolo Falls Trailhead.
1.7 Base of Lemolo Falls.

The hike: From the trailhead, the Lemolo Falls Trail (1468) descends gently along an old road through a partial logging cut (mostly white fir, western white pine, and mountain hemlock). After 0.5 mile, the route makes a couple of sharp turns (one marked, one not marked), becomes a genuine trail, and enters the steep canyon of the North Umpqua. As you enter the canyon, a sign says "Lemolo Falls—¼ mile." The sign is a bit optimistic. Somebody has scratched in "1¼ miles," which isn't accurate, either. Judging from the map, the actual distance appears to be halfway between the two figures, or about 0.7 mile.

There are lots of rhododendrons in the canyon, which are spectacular in spring and early summer.

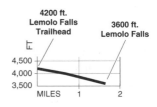

54

Lemolo Falls

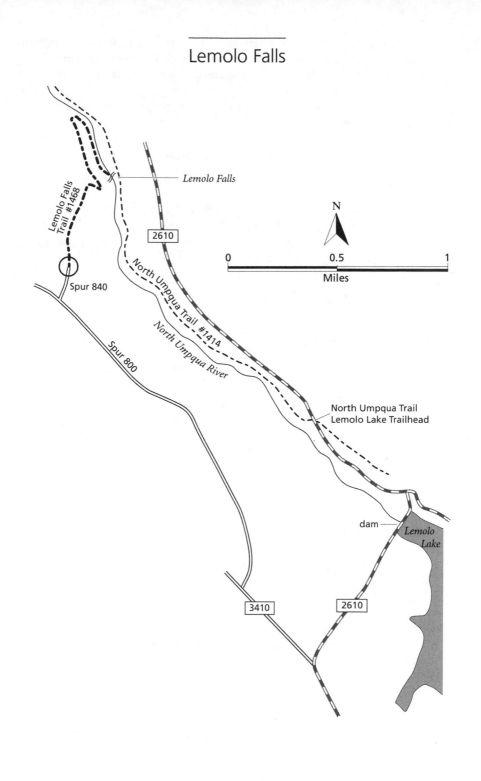

Lemolo Falls

Lemolo Falls Trail #1468

Spur 840

2610

North Umpqua Trail #1414

North Umpqua River

Spur 800

North Umpqua Trail Lemolo Lake Trailhead

dam

Lemolo Lake

3410

2610

N

0   0.5   1
Miles

After a long switchback, the path hits the river and the falls come into view. They're not quite a plunge (free-falling water), since the white liquid hugs the rock surface most of the way down. But they are immense—108 feet high with tremendous water volume much of the year. The path goes to the base of the falls, with its emerald collecting pool, constant cold breeze, and soaring mist. The walk back to your car is much more difficult than the walk in.

This route does not tie into the North Umpqua Trail (1414), which passes the top of Lemolo Falls on the other side of the river. Both routes are very nice.

Options: *North Umpqua Trail to top of falls.* It's 1.5 miles from the Lemolo Lake Trailhead of the North Umpqua Trail, located just past the Lemolo Lake Dam, to the top of Lemolo Falls. The route is a continuation of the North Umpqua Trail's Dread and Terror Section (see Hike 7). This is a beautiful walk, although it has a nasty habit of descending to the river, then climbing far up the canyon only to descend again. It does this two or three times in 1.5 miles. The NUT passes several low but very impressive waterfalls before skirting the top of Lemolo Falls.

To reach the trailhead, follow the directions to the Lemolo Falls Trailhead but continue on the paved FR 2610 for 0.8 mile past Lemolo Lake Dam, which is 1 mile past the FR 3401 turnoff. The trailhead is across a wooden auto bridge on the left.

Warm Springs Falls. As long as you're visiting waterfalls around Lemolo Lake, don't miss Warms Springs Falls. They plunge 70 feet over an immense vertical rock face of columnar basalt, much like Toketee Falls but without the rock bowl and upper falls.

To reach Warm Springs Falls, continue on FR 2610 for 2 miles past the Lemolo Lake Trailhead, to a paved (briefly) spur road to the left (Spur 680), where FR 2610 swings sharply right. It's exactly 1.7 miles on Spur 680 to the Warm Springs Falls Trailhead, which can be very difficult to find. In the middle of a large, level, conifer plantation, look for a very small turnout on the right, with the trailhead directly opposite on the left. Spur 680 crosses Warms Springs Creek 0.5 mile later.

The 0.3-mile (or less), perfectly level Warms Springs Falls Trail (1499) ends on top of the falls, which has a huge amount of water for a side creek. Look for a side trail to the right just after crossing a little dip in the trail in and out of a gully. The side trail is very steep and slippery and leads to an abrupt ledge directly above the falls. There is no guardrail so be careful. Back on the main trail, it's another 100 yards to the trail end and a much safer vista of the falls and its lovely grotto.

Rogue-Umpqua Divide Wilderness

The best place to grab a quick peek at the rugged, Rogue-Umpqua Divide range is on Oregon Highway 230, heading west from Diamond Lake. A row of peaks suddenly rises up that appears older, steeper, and more rugged than the surrounding mountains (except maybe for Thielsen, which is about as rugged as you can get). The 33,000-acre Rogue-Umpqua Divide Wilderness is a hidden gem. Ranging in elevation from 3,200 feet to 6,800 feet, the mountains not only separate the Rogue and Umpqua River drainages, they separate the California and the Pacific Northwest forest regions.

Fish Lake, in the Rogue-Umpqua Divide Wilderness, is by far the largest wilderness lake in this book (90 acres). It is the book's deepest lake except for Crater Lake.

The Rogue-Umpqua Divide Wilderness may contain more trails per square mile than any wilderness in the country. For every destination, there are multiple options, side trips, alternate routes, and trail combinations. This book attempts to list the most worthwhile hikes and best options.

9 Toad Lake

Highlights:	An easy, wildflower-laden path at the end of a magnificent scenic back road. Many items of botanical interest.
Type of hike:	Day hike, out and back.
Total distance:	4.6 miles.
Difficulty:	Easy.
Elevation gain:	679 feet (on return trip).
Best months:	June–October.
Map:	USGS Fish Mountain quad.

Finding the trailhead: Take Oregon Highway 62 north from Medford to Union Creek. Where OR 62 swings right toward Crater Lake, past milepost 57, continue straight (on Oregon Highway 230) toward Diamond Lake. One mile later, turn left, across the Rogue, onto the gravel Forest Road 6510 (becoming Forest Road 6515, which in turn becomes Spur 530 at Horse Camp). Follow signs to Hershberger Lookout, 19 miles away. The well-marked trailhead is located at mile 18, at the final switchback before the lookout.

Toad Lake

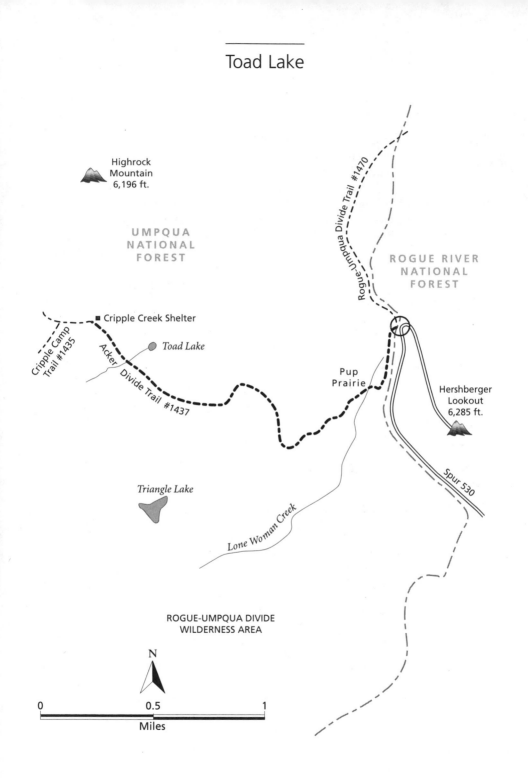

Highrock
Mountain
6,196 ft.

UMPQUA
NATIONAL
FOREST

Rogue-Umpqua Divide Trail #1470

ROGUE RIVER
NATIONAL
FOREST

■ Cripple Creek Shelter

Cripple Camp
Trail #1435

Acker
Divide Trail #1437

Toad Lake

Pup
Prairie

Hershberger
Lookout
6,285 ft.

Spur 530

Triangle Lake

Lone Woman Creek

ROGUE-UMPQUA DIVIDE
WILDERNESS AREA

N

0	0.5	1

Miles

Parking and trailhead facilities: The trailhead accommodates six cars. The nearest primitive camping is at Horse Camp, in the meadow 1 mile before the trailhead.

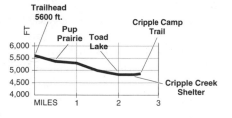

Key points:

0.0 Hershberger Trailhead.
0.5 Pup Prairie.
2.0 Toad Lake.
2.2 Cripple Creek Shelter.
2.3 Junction with Cripple Camp Trail.

The hike: If you've never been to Hershberger Lookout, you've missed one of southern Oregon's great vistas. Straddling the Rogue-Umpqua Divide, the lookout offers not only outstanding views but a magical juxtaposition of rocky outcrops, dense forest, and gentle meadow. The only place that comes to mind with a greater wildflower concentration is Mount Rainier's Paradise Park in Washington.

After crossing the Rogue River, Hershberger Road winds through woods and logging shows for 18 miles, emerging at a beautiful meadow at Horse Camp. A turnoff right, at Horse Camp, leads to Rabbit Ears, a prominant landmark, after 1.5 miles. Back on the main road, the trail to Toad Lake turns up 1 mile beyond Horse Camp, at a sharp switchback. The short (0.1 mile) trail to Hershberger Lookout begins at the road end, 1 mile past the trailhead, and should not be missed.

From the trailhead, the Acker Divide Trail (1437) to Toad Lake, on the left, shoots steeply downhill into the woods from the trailhead. Look for Pacific silver fir here. Largely absent from the Rogue Valley, the species abounds from the Rogue-Umpqua Divide northward. Look also for subalpine fir, noble fir, and mountain hemlock.

After less than 0.5 mile, you cross beautiful Pup Prairie, then the Pup Prairie Trail junction. A charming stand of Alaska yellow cedar graces the beautiful little creek crossing at Pup Prairie. Like Pacific silver fir, Alaska yellow cedar abounds at higher elevations north of the Rogue-Umpqua Divide but is rare in southern Oregon.

Beyond Pup Prairie, the Acker Divide Trail continues to weave between open floral meadow and subalpine forest before arriving at Toad Lake at mile 2. Look for Indian paintbrush, lupine, delphinium, bleeding heart, and many other species. Toad Lake sits in a beautiful meadow, although the lake itself is dry or marshy most of the year. Beaver activity is readily observed.

Cripple Creek Shelter lies 0.2 mile past Toad Lake (2.2 miles from the trailhead) while the Cripple Camp Trail is 0.3 mile past Toad Lake. The Acker Divide Trail continues on to Grasshopper Mountain, Fish Lake, and the trailheads of the Umpqua side of the Wilderness.

Options: *Grasshopper Trail.* One and a half miles beyond the Cripple Creek Shelter, the Acker Divide Trail meets the Grasshopper Trail (1574). To climb Grasshopper Mountain, turn right on the Grasshopper Trail and hike steeply uphill for 0.7 mile, until you arrive at the 0.5-mile Grasshopper Mountain Trail (1580). Turn left for the summit. If you keep going on the Grasshopper Trail, beyond the summit turnoff, you'll end up in Hike 10.

Rogue-Umpqua Divide Trail. Immediately right of the Acker Divide Trail at the Hershberger Trailhead, the Rogue-Umpqua Divide Trail (1470), takes off to the north. It's 0.7 mile on the RUD to the upper end of the Fish Lake Trail (Hike 11), amid floral meadows and a view of High Rock Mountain. At mile 1, you come to a pretty little saddle. At mile 2, you arrive at Hole-in-the-Ground, a former glacial-cirque lake thats silted in to become a meadow on the upper flank of Fish Mountain. From there, it's another 2 miles to Castle Rock and Fish Creek Valley (Hike 12).

10   Cliff Lake

Highlights:	An easy hike off the South Umpqua River to a beautiful pair of lakes, then to the top of a mountain; interesting geology.
Type of hike:	Day hike, out and back.
Total distance:	7.2 miles.
Difficulty:	Easy to Cliff Lake, then strenuous.
Elevation gain:	1,923 feet.
Best months:	May–November.
Map:	USGS Buckeye Lake quad.

Finding the trailhead: Take Oregon Highway 62 north from Medford towards Crater Lake. Turn left at the town of Trail (past milepost 24), onto Oregon Highway 227 and continue 20 miles to the town of Tiller. At Tiller, turn right up the paved

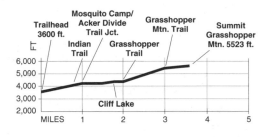

South Umpqua Road (Forest Road 28). Twenty-five miles later, turn right, up the gravel Forest Road 2823. Continue 1.5 miles to Forest Road 2830 and follow it 8.5 miles to Spur 600. The 10 miles from FR 28 to the Skimmerhorn Trailhead are well marked.

Parking and trailhead facilities: The Skimmerhorn Trailhead accommodates about 20 cars.

Cliff Lake

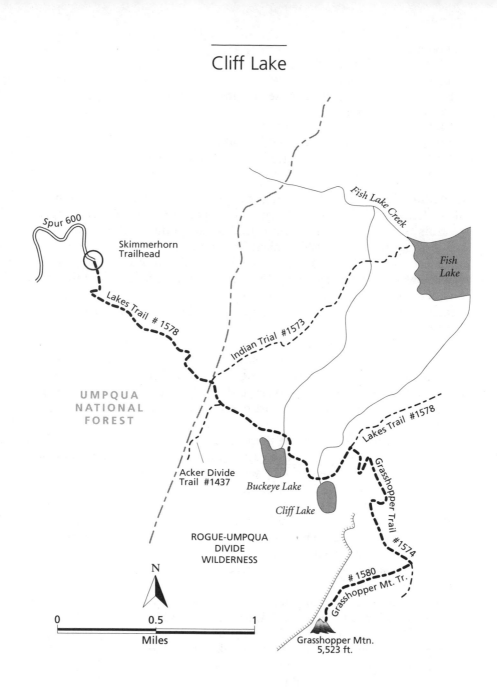

Spur 600

Skimmerhorn
Trailhead

Fish Lake Creek

Fish
Lake

Lakes Trail # 1578

Indian Trial #1573

UMPQUA
NATIONAL
FOREST

Lakes Trail #1578

Acker Divide
Trail #1437

Buckeye Lake

Cliff Lake

Grasshopper Trail

#1574

ROGUE-UMPQUA
DIVIDE
WILDERNESS

N

1580

Grasshopper Mt. Tr.

Grasshopper Mtn.
5,523 ft.

0   0.5   1

Miles

Key points:

0.0 Skimmerhorn Trailhead.

0.8 Indian Trail junction.

1.0 Mosquito Camp Trail (Acker Divide) junction.

1.5 Buckeye Lake.

1.8 Cliff Lake.

2.0 Grasshopper Trail junction (go right).

3.0 Grasshopper Mountain Trail junction (go right).

3.6 Summit of Grasshopper Mountain.

The hike: Even without knowing the geology, this is a beautiful area of lakes, dense forests, vertical ridges, and jagged summits. To fully appreciate this short, easy hike from the most popular trailhead in the Rogue-Umpqua Divide Wilderness, one must be aware of a geological event occurring 6,000 years ago. Imagine a 5,500-foot mountain, formed by ancient lava flows, suddenly breaking in half and sending millions of tons of rubble into the valley, 2,500 feet below. Such an event created the escarpment above Cliff Lake and impounded the waters of Buckeye, Cliff, and Fish Lakes.

Driving to the Skimmerhorn Trailhead along the South Umpqua is pretty interesting in itself. Be sure to stop at South Umpqua Falls. Note the abundance of western redcedar along the South Umpqua, along with the usual middle-elevation Douglas-fir and western hemlock. Western redcedar, one of the Northwest's most common trees, is largely absent from the Rogue Valley.

It's a 1.5-mile hike from the Skimmerhorn Trailhead to Buckeye Lake along the Lakes Trail (1578). The path is fairly gentle with slight upgrades in the middle. It's also remarkably wide as summer use is heavy. The lakes are at a fairly low elevation for alpine lakes, and you can often get there as late as mid-December.

Both lakes are nestled amid dense forests at the foot of the cliff described earlier. Both have excellent, level campsites nearby. Buckeye Lake is larger and reveals more of the escarpment than Cliff Lake. Cliff Lake, as the name implies, hugs the base of the cliff. Both lakes are stocked with brook and rainbow tout.

Two miles from the trailhead, 0.2 mile past Cliff Lake, the Grasshopper Trail (1574) takes off steeply uphill to the right while the Lakes Trail continues to Fish Lake (2.5 miles). One mile up the Grasshopper Trail, the Grasshopper Mountain Trail (1580) breaks off to the right. From here it's 0.6 mile to the lookout site atop Grasshopper Mountain, (elevation 5,523 feet), 3.6 miles from the trailhead.

Since the peak is pretty much a flat mesa, the first part of the climb, where the Grasshopper Trail leaves the Lakes Trail, is steepest. After ascending the cliff, the trail winds through open areas with broad vistas. The extremely jagged peak immediately west is Highrock Mountain (6,196 feet).

Option: *Fish Lake.* Fish Lake, at 90 acres, is the largest glacial lake in this book. It sits 1,000 feet lower than Cliff and Buckeye Lakes in a densely wooded valley. A steep, 5-mile loop leads to Fish Lake and back from Cliff Lake. Start the loop on the Indian Trail (1573), which joins the Lakes Trail on the left 1.2 miles from the Skimmerhorn Trailhead. Follow it 1.5 miles to the Fish Lake Trail (1570), turn right past Fish Lake, and continue for 1.3 miles to the junction with the far end of the Lakes Trail from Cliff Lake. A much easier way to get to Fish Lake is via the Fish Lake Trailhead or the Beaver Swamp Trailhead (see Hike 11).

11 Fish Lake

Highlight:	A large, gorgeous, geologically unusual mountain lake in the Rogue-Umpqua Divide Wilderness.
Type of hike:	Day hike, out and back.
Total distance:	About 8 miles.
Difficulty:	Moderate.
Elevation gain:	1,070 feet.
Best months:	April–December.
Map:	USGS Buckeye Lake quad.

Finding the trailhead: From Oregon Highway 62, east out of Medford, continue past the town of Shady Cove for 3 miles to the junction at the town of Trail. Turn left at the sign that says, "Tiller." Technically, the Trail-Tiller Road is Oregon Highway 227, but that's not obviously posted anywhere. It's 26 miles to Tiller, where you cross the South Umpqua Bridge and immediately turn right onto Forest Road 28 (the South Umpqua Road). After 24 miles on FR 28, turn right onto Forest Road 2823, then left onto Forest Road 2830 after 1.5 miles, then left onto Forest Road 2840 after 2.5 miles. It's 0.5 mile on FR 2840 to the Fish Lake Trailhead.

Parking and trailhead facilities: There are picnic tables, pit toilets, a horse loading ramp, and parking for 30 cars with trailers at the Fish Lake Trailhead.

Key points:
  0.0 Fish Lake Trailhead.
  3.0 Beaver Swamp.
  3.5 Beaver Swamp Trail junction.
  4.0 Fish Lake.

The hike: At an elevation of only 3,370 feet, Fish Lake lies well below any other glacial lake in southern Oregon. The explanation is that Fish Lake was caused not by glaciers (although it occupies an ancient glacial valley), but by damming from a tremendous landslide off nearby Grasshopper Mountain, 6,000 years ago—the same landslide that created Cliff and

Fish Lake

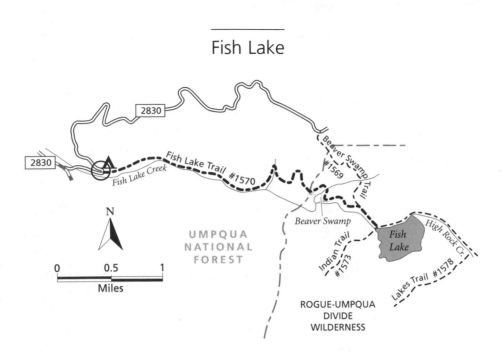

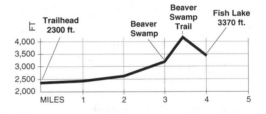

Buckeye Lakes (Hike 10). Fish Lake is accessible during any season but the absolute dead of winter. It is the largest and deepest wilderness lake described in this book.

There are two primary trails to Fish Lake, the Fish Lake Trail (1570) and the Beaver Swamp Trail (1569). Both are easy to get to (the Beaver Swamp Trailhead is 4 miles past the Fish Lake Trailhead on FR 2840) and have about the same elevation gradient (250 to 300 feet per mile). The Beaver Swamp Trail starts high (4,200 feet) and descends to Fish Lake while the Fish Lake Trail climbs to the lake, which means the Beaver Swamp Trail's season is shorter.

The main difference between the two paths is that the Fish Lake Trail gets to Fish Lake in 4 miles while the Beaver Swamp Trail gets there in 2. Granting that the Fish Lake Trail is beautiful throughout and well worth exploring, it's a mystery why it's so much more popular than its shorter counterpart, which is no slouch, scenery-wise, either (and also fairly popular).

Yielding to popular opinion, the Fish Lake Trail is the main route described here, with the Beaver Swamp Trail given as an option.

From the Fish Lake Trailhead, the Fish Lake Trail remains nearly level for 1.5 miles as it follows Fish Lake Creek through a beautiful forest with a moss-covered floor and moss-draped trees. The trees are a lot more

Fish Lake.

"Pacific Northwest" than forests at the same elevation in the Rogue River drainage, largely because of the presence of western redcedar (along with Douglas-fir and western hemlock). These three species comprise the "Big Three" of low-elevation Northwest forests. Look also for Pacific madrone (also a low-elevation species but extending clear to the lake), bigleaf maple, and vine maple. There are lots of rhododendron in the first mile, and tons of salal, trillium, vanillaleaf, and dwarf Oregon grape throughout. These species all love moist, closed-canopy forests and excellent soil.

The forest shows evidence of frequent burning, with scattered, large, fire-scarred conifers and much smaller conifers in between. Many upper hillsides appear to have burned quite severely 20 or 30 years ago, with stands of pole-sized conifers and grassy openings.

While the trail's elevation gradient of 250 feet per mile (1,000 feet in 4 miles) would put the Fish Lake Trail in the "easy" category, nearly all the gain comes between miles 1.5 and 3.5, where the gradient exceeds 500 feet per mile. That segment also contains two long, steep downhill pitches.

One and a half miles from the trailhead, the path swings away from the creek into a side valley, crosses a creek, and climbs steeply to a rocky ledge at the base of some vertical cliffs. Rounding a point, the route then turns into another side valley, crosses another creek and starts climbing yet again around another point hundreds of feet above the Fish Creek valley floor. There's an excellent vista of the Fish Lake basin with Highrock Mountain rising behind it.

The third and final side valley is Beaver Swamp, just inside the wilderness boundary. Beaver Swamp occupies a flat, grassy dale which in the spring of a wet year contains a large, shallow lake. You may see a lodge or other signs of beaver activity.

The path loses 100 feet in elevation as it drops into the little Beaver Swamp basin and crosses the stream inlet. It then climbs out and continues rising to the junction with the Beaver Swamp Trail, 0.5 mile past Beaver Swamp. Far below, between Beaver Swamp and the junction with the Beaver Swamp Trail, Fish Lake Creek is visible surging through narrow rock clefts and making a terrific din. There's a huge waterfall you can't see very well.

Beyond the trail crest at the Beaver Swamp Trail junction, the path drops sharply, then levels off as it enters the narrow gorge of the lake outlet.

The clear, emerald lake covers 90 acres with dense forest on all sides. Grasshopper Mountain's rocky, 5,523-foot flank rises to the southwest (right) while craggy Highrock Mountain (6,196 feet) soars abruptly to the southeast (left). The lakeshore is too steep for camping, except at the lake's far end where a delta of silt from various inlet creeks has created a grassy meadow and alder forest.

There's supposed to be a sunken airplane in the middle of the lake, the result of a crash many years ago. Local fishermen claim you can see it from a boat but the Forest Service insists this is only a rumor and there is no airplane.

Options: *Beaver Swamp Trail.* This path drops 600 feet from a ridgetop in 1.5 miles and doesn't follow a creek or pass a Beaver Swamp. It reaches the Fish Lake Trail in 1.5 miles and Fish Lake in 2 miles. The trailhead is on the same road as the Fish Lake Trailhead, only 4 miles farther up, with spectacular views of the South Umpqua Valley and surrounding mountains. The trailhead accommodates 15 to 20 cars.

Indian Trail. The Indian Trail (1573) begins at the outlet of Fish Lake into Fish Lake Creek, where the Fish Lake Trail arrives at the lake. The path breaks off to the right, crosses Fish Lake Creek over the top of a large log jam, parallels the lakeshore briefly, then climbs 800 feet in 2.5 miles, meeting the Lakes Trail from the Skimmerhorn Trailhead 0.5 mile before Buckeye Lake.

Upper Fish Lake Trail. The Fish Lake Trail parallels the lakeshore for 0.5 mile, then follows Highrock Creek for 3.5 miles to the Rogue-Umpqua Divide Trail, 8 miles from the Fish Lake Trailhead and 1 mile from the Hershberger Trailhead.

Lakes Trail. The Lakes Trail meets the Fish Lake Trail 0.5 mile beyond the end of the lake. Turn right for Cliff Lake, 3 miles away. It's possible to make a loop of the Indian Trail, Lakes Trail, and Fish Lake Trail, with either Fish Lake, Cliff lake, or Buckeye Lake as the base.

12 Rattlesnake Mountain

Highlights:	A remote dirt road takes you to a glorious meadowed valley bounded on both sides by wilderness and high peaks. At the end of the road, a grueling but beautiful hike leads to the summit of the Rogue-Umpqua Divide's second-highest peak.
Type of hike:	Day hike, out and back.
Total distance:	5.6 miles.
Difficulty:	Moderate.
Elevation gain:	300-foot loss, then a 1,700-foot gain.
Best months:	June–October.
Map:	USGS Fish Mountain quad.

Special considerations: There is no water once you leave the Rogue-Umpqua Divide Trail, and the route is steep and exposed.

Finding the trailhead: Take Oregon Highway 62 north from Medford past Union Creek. Where OR 62 swings right toward Crater Lake at milepost 57, continue straight (on Oregon Highway 230), toward Diamond Lake. Past milepost 12 on OR 230, opposite the Hamaker Campground turnoff, turn left onto gravel Forest Road 6560, where the sign says "Buck Camp." At the divide, FR 6560 becomes Forest Road 37. Turn left 0.5 mile beyond the divide onto Spur 800, continue 3.5 miles, past Lonesome Meadow, and turn left again onto Spur 870, the Fish Creek Valley Road.

It's 4 miles up Spur 870 to the trailhead over a fair gravel road (which gets muddy in spring). Follow the road for 1 mile past the deep draw where the Buck Canyon Trail crosses the road, to a little sign on the right denoting the Rogue-Umpqua Divide Trail (1470). If you pass the campsite on the left (Happy Camp), where Castle Rock comes into view, you've gone too far. Park on the shoulder or at Happy Camp.

Spur 800 is shown on the Forest Service map as a loop and signs at the turnoff say "Incense-cedar Loop." This is not a loop. There is a colossal washout just before the road rejoins FR 37.

Parking and trailhead facilities: The trailhead accommodates three or four cars along the shoulder. The walk from Happy Camp, which has a fire ring and parking for six cars, is less than 0.1 mile.

Key points:
0.0 Happy Camp Trailhead.
0.8 Whitehorse Meadow Trail junction (go left).
1.8 Windy Gap, Rattlesnake Way Trail (no sign, go right).
2.8 Summit of Rattlesnake Mountain.

The hike: One of the Cascade Mountains' great "secret places" lies immediately north of Crater Lake and west of Diamond Lake. Beautiful Fish Creek Valley contains broad floral meadows, dense forests, and an

Rattlesnake Mountain

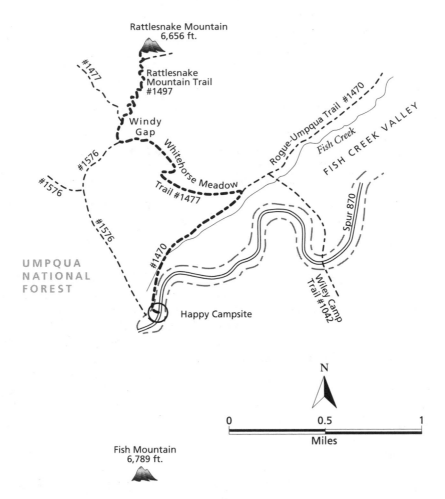

Rattlesnake Mountain
6,656 ft.

Rattlesnake
Mountain Trail
#1497

#1477

Windy
Gap

Rogue-Umpqua Trail #1470

Fish Creek

FISH CREEK VALLEY

#1576

Whitehorse Meadow

Trail #1477

#1576

#1576

Spur 870

#1470

UMPQUA
NATIONAL
FOREST

Wiley Camp
Trail #1042

Happy Campsite

N

0   0.5   1
Miles

Fish Mountain
6,789 ft.

enchanting stream meandering through the middle. Rocky crags and forested ridges rise sharply up the valley's sides. Since Fish Creek Valley Road penetrates the wilderness area, they may eventually close it to auto traffic. Meanwhile, despite a few rough spots, it's holding up remarkably well.

From the eastbound Rogue-Umpqua Divide Trailhead on Fish Creek Valley Road, the Rogue-Umpqua Divide Trail (1470) backtracks down the valley through a gorgeous meadow with 6,656 foot Rattlesnake Mountain rising directly overhead. The meadow is filled with corn lily, tower delphinium, and a myriad of other wildflowers. Look also for chokecherry. You'll find Pacific silver fir in the meadow not far from the trailhead. Largely absent in the Rogue drainage, the species abounds from the

Rogue-Umpqua Divide north. Noble fir, western white pine, mountain hemlock, and lodgepole pine also surround the meadow and form picturesque clumps in the meadow.

The path crosses the creek in the middle of the meadow, then dips into the woods. It's an easy, 0.8-mile hike, dropping 300 feet, on the Rogue-Umpqua Divide Trail to the junction with the Whitehorse Meadow Trail (1477). Turning left on the Whitehorse Meadow Trail, the path follows a pretty little side creek for 0.2 mile, then crosses some dry grassy openings before making several long switchbacks through the woods. After a 500-foot elevation gain, the path emerges at the Windy Gap saddle (5,600 feet).

Windy Gap itself is kind of boring. If you follow the Castle Creek Trail (1576) left from the gap for several hundred feet, you arrive at a small campsite with a view of Fish Mountain across the valley. Fish Mountain is the highest peak in the wilderness at 6,783 feet.

At the unsigned junction with the Rattlesnake Mountain Trail (1497) at Windy Gap, (it's called the "Rattlesnake Way Trail" on the wilderness map and the "Rattlesnake Mountain Trail" on road signs off of FR 37), the path to the summit takes off obviously on the right. The distance between the beginning of the Castle Creek Trail and Rattlesnake Mountain Trail is much less than shown on the wilderness map. The two paths meet the Whitehorse Meadow Trail almost directly opposite each other.

The hike's final mile is rather strenuous, climbing 1,100 feet through forested patches, grassy draws, and rock outcrops to the top of Rattlesnake Mountain. The trail, which is very faint in spots, actually misses the summit and continues for 2 miles past the trail's high point to an alternate trailhead described under "Options." The final uphill leg of the Rattlesnake Mountain Trail snakes, if you'll pardon the expression, past some impressive volcanic rock formations, some of which appear to have been painted yellow. The yellow is lichen.

A short unnumbered side trail at the trail crest (go left) leads to the actual summit, a flat expanse of rock with unbelievable views straight down into Fish Creek Valley and across to Fish Mountain, Hershberger Mountain, Mount Bailey, the Crater Lake summits, and the Umpqua Valley.

Options: *Castle Creek Trail.* The Castle Creek Trail (1576) begins 200 feet beyond the eastbound Rogue-Umpqua Divide Trailhead on Fish Creek Valley Road, at Happy Camp. Instead of dropping down into Fish Creek Valley, then climbing back up, this route contours across to Windy Gap. While you save 0.3 mile by following this route instead of the Rogue-Umpqua Divide/Whitehorse Meadows route, the path climbs a little too high and you end up having to drop back down into Windy Gap. Also, the Rogue-Umpqua Divide/Whitehorse Meadows route is prettier. The

Castle Creek route offers nice views of Castle Rock. It's best to make a loop out of it.

Rattlesnake Mountain Trail (or Rattlesnake Way Trail) from the eastern end. It's possible to climb Rattlesnake Mountain via the far end of the Rattlesnake Mountain Trail. The distance is about the same as the main hike described above, and the gradient is a little less strenuous (the path starts at 5,600 feet, the same elevation as Windy Gap). Neither the trailhead drive, the trailhead, nor the trail are as spectacular as the drive up Fish Creek Valley. The optional trail stays in the woods for much of the way and includes a steep, 0.5-mile side trip to Mosquito Lake, a 3-acre pool decorating an impressive little glacial cirque. The lake is well named.

To reach the Rattlesnake Way Trailhead from OR 230, continue on FR 37, past the Fish Creek Valley/Spur 800 turnoff, until you pick up the pavement. Look for Spur 200 1.2 miles later, on the right and a paved (for 200 feet) but unsigned turnoff on the left immediately after. If you pass Spur 100 and cross Rogue Creek, you've gone too far. From Roseburg, the turnoff is 5.5 miles up FR 37 from the Watson Falls parking area at milepost 61 on OR 138

A sign at the FR 37 turnoff to Rattlesnake Mountain gives both the road number and the mileage to the Rattlesnake Mountain Trailhead. Unfortunately, you can't see it from FR 37. The road is Forest Road 3702, which was somehow omitted from the Umpqua National Forest Map. Follow FR 3702 for 3.5 miles to Spur 500, then follow Spur 500 to the end, 5 miles later. The road is slow, with a few rough spots and dozens of waterbars which are readily negotiated.

Castle Rock from trail to Rattlesnake Mountain.

The trailhead sign is located at a little switchback, 0.3 mile from the road end. There is room for six cars. The gravel ends at the sign and the road becomes much steeper (rising 400 feet in 0.3 mile) but it is drivable. The trailhead itself consists of a logging landing (room for eight cars) overlooking beautiful Quartz Canyon, with views of Mount Bailey and Diamond Peak. The unmarked path heads up the ridge crest.

West on the Rogue-Umpqua Divide Trail from Fish Creek Valley. The westbound Rogue-Umpqua Divide Trail takes off at the end of Fish Creek Valley Road, 1 mile from the eastbound trailhead. It's 2 miles from the westbound trailhead to Hole-in-the-Ground, 3.2 miles to the upper end of the Fish Lake Trail, and 4 miles to the Hershberger Trailhead. This is a popular, mostly forested, ridgetop hike with many vistas of Fish Mountain and Highrock Mountain.

13   Abbott Butte

Highlights:	A mountaintop lookout tower (Abbott Butte) and an impressive rock formation (Elephant Head).
Type of hike:	Day hike, out and back, or shuttle.
Total distance:	About 6 miles (Huckleberry Gap to Abbott Butte and back).
Difficulty:	Moderate.
Elevation gain:	1,031 feet.
Best months:	Late May–October.
Map:	USGS Abbott Butte quad.

Special considerations: This hike consists of two trails, The Rogue-Umpqua Divide Trail (1470) and the CCC Trail, a closed road. The two paths closely parallel each other and cross twice on the way to Abbott Butte. Although they have separate trailheads, the routes are so interchangeable on portions of the hike that it was difficult to make one the main hike and the other an option. The described hike utilizes portions of both trails.

This chapter recommends the Huckleberry Gap Trailhead (RUD Trail) as the main entry, with the Spur 950 trailhead (CCC Trail) described under "Options." Above Windy Gap, the narrative recommends the RUD Trail on the way up and the CCC Trail on the way down. To climb Abbott Butte, you need to use the CCC Trail. To visit the base of Elephant Head Rock and continue on to the Yellowjacket Camp Trailhead, also described under "Options," use the RUD Trail.

All trails cross steep, mostly north-facing slopes with many lingering snowbanks early in the season. There are no creek crossings on the main route.

The map inset shown here includes both the RUD and CCC Trails. Because the CCC Trail is officially "unmaintained," it is not shown on

Abbott Butte

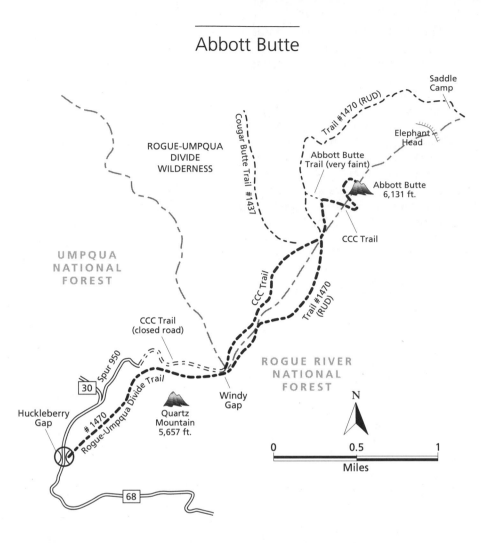

Forest Service maps, even though it receives 90 percent of the use. The CCC Trail is the only viable route on the final leg to the Abbott Butte summit. The RUD spur trail to the top of Abbott Butte is very faint and difficult to follow.

Finding the trailhead: Take Oregon Highway 62 from Medford, past Prospect and milepost 51, to the Woodruff Bridge (Abbott Camp) turnoff (Forest Road 68). Turn left and go 13 miles on FR 68, to the Rogue-Umpqua Divide at beautiful Huckleberry Gap. The eastbound Rogue-Umpqua Divide Trailhead is on the right, at Huckleberry Gap.

Parking and trailhead facilities: All three trailheads accommodate five cars each.

Key points (from Huckleberry Gap):
0.0 Huckleberry Gap Trailhead.
1.0 Wilderness boundary/Windy Gap.
2.0 Junction with CCC Trail to Abbot Butte (go right for summit, left for Elephant Head).
3.0 Abbott Butte summit.

The hike: From the Huckleberry Gap Trailhead (see the note about the Spur 950 trailhead under "Special Considerations"), the Rogue-Umpqua Divide Trail (1470) makes its way gently downhill, through a dense and gloomy woods on the north face of Quartz Mountain (5,657 feet), a rocky peak just west of Abbott Butte (6,131 feet). The highlight of this first mile is a huge outcrop of columnar basalt halfway along. Approaching Windy Gap, look for Alaska yellow cedar in the woods, along with Douglas-fir, white fir, noble fir, and western white pine. A brief glimpse of Abbot Butte turns up just before Windy Gap (not the same Windy Gap as in Hike 12).

At Windy Gap (5,310 feet), the RUD Trail meets the CCC Trail for the first time. A sign at Windy Gap informs hikers that horses should stay on the CCC Trail because the RUD Trail is not passable for hooved beasts. Beyond Windy Gap, the RUD Trail is much more dramatic than the CCC Trail. A nice loop is possible by taking the RUD away from Windy Gap and the CCC back to Windy Gap. Ninety percent of use appears to be on the CCC Trail.

The RUD above Windy Gap follows the south side of the ridge, which is very steep and open, with scree slopes and long vistas. The CCC contours up the ridge's north side, which is densely forested with no vistas. According to the map, the CCC route passes a junction with the Cougar Butte Trail (1437), but this intersection isn't really apparent and you may not be able to find it.

From the RUD side of the ridge, you can see the Crater Lake rim, Mount McLoughlin, and the Abbott Creek drainage. The RUD also offers a closeup view of a towering and impressive lava plug, proof that these are the Western Cascades and not the High Cascades. (A lava plug is a tower of lava that used to be an inner conduit in a volcano whose outer portions have eroded away. There are no lava plugs in the High Cascades because its volcanoes have not yet eroded away.) Much of this portion of the RUD is rocky and outsloped (tilted sideways), with sheer drop-offs.

The RUD trail touches the CCC Trail 0.5 mile beyond Windy Gap, then again 1 mile beyond Windy Gap (2 miles from the Huckleberry Gap Trailhead). At this third junction, a sign identical to the one at Windy Gap again informs visitors that horses should use the CCC Trail. If you wish to hike to the Abbott Butte summit,

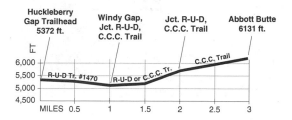

73

you must take the CCC Trail from here on. If you remain on the RUD Trail, you come to a junction sign on the right, after 0.2 mile, pointing to a side trail to Abbott Butte. This side trail is very faint and not recommended. The CCC route is far superior.

The 1-mile hike on the CCC Trail to the summit is lovely, with long vistas of the meadows on the north side of Abbott Butte, and views beyond into the South Umpqua drainage. Look for clusters of chokecherry on the way up and, at the top, stands of noble fir and mountain hemlock.

The lookout tower, which is beautiful from a distance, is actually quite dilapidated. The ladder is broken and the structure has been condemned. Since this is a wilderness area, the lookout will be demolished eventually.

Aside from the lookout and the ruins of an old outhouse, there's not much to see on the actual summit. The best vantage points lie just to the north and south of the summit. According to the map, it's possible to make your way cross-country from the summit to the top of Elephant Head Rock, a sheer, gray, 500-foot cliff. But there are a couple rock outcrops in between and many opportunities to get lost.

Options: *CCC Trailhead (Spur 950).* The hike from the Spur 950 trailhead to Windy Gap is 0.5 mile shorter than the RUD trail from Huckleberry Gap. Although this shorter distance looks very compelling on the map, the path is in terrible condition, trends steeply uphill, and is far less scenic than the RUD. Morever, the trailhead is unmarked, unmaintained, and not recommended by the Forest Service. To reach the Spur 950 trailhead, continue driving past the road summit at Huckleberry Gap on Forest Road 68,

Elephant Head, Abbott Butte.

which becomes Forest Road 30 at the gap. Follow the sign to Tiller. It's 0.5 mile to Spur 950, on the right, and another 0.5 mile up spur 950 to the trailhead at the road end. There are no signs as trail and trailhead are officially unmaintained.

Elephant Head and the Yellowjacket Camp Trailhead. If you're hiking through to the Yellowjacket Camp Trailhead or the base of Elephant Head, return to the Rogue-Umpqua Divide Trail when done climbing the mountain, and continue east (right), over a vast, grassy flat dotted with rock outcrops. A trail junction sign on the RUD, 0.2 mile past the CCC junction to the top of Abbott Butte, indicates a side trail to Abbott Butte.

Crossing the large meadow, the RUD rises to a crest, then drops steeply through the woods for 0.3 mile before leveling off as it approaches Saddle Camp, the closest you come via trail to Elephant Head. This north-slope route retains snow very late in the season.

Saddle Camp is situated just before the saddle between Abbott Creek, in the Rogue drainage, and another Abbott Creek, in the Umpqua drainage. Those Abbott boys had a talent for attaching their names to things.

From Saddle Camp, it's 1 mile on the RUD Trail to the junction with the Golden Stairs Trail (1092, Hike 14), over a path that contours high above the Abbott Creek Research Natural Area. Look for improving views of Elephant Head (behind you), the Abbot Creek basin (on the Rogue side), and Mount McLoughin, with magnificent old-growth stands alongside the trail.

At the Golden Stairs junction, where the RUD Trail crosses into the Woodruff Creek drainage, head uphill cross-country for 100 feet to a rock outcrop with yet another outstanding view. From the Golden Stairs junction, it's a fairly steep mile downhill on the RUD Trail to the Yellowjacket Camp Trailhead. One lengthy pitch near the trailhead is especially steep.

To get to the Yellowjacket Camp Trailhead, turn right (go straight, actually) onto Forest Road 6510, towards Hershberger Lookout just before Abbot Creek Campground, 2 miles up FR 68 from OR 62. After 2 miles, turn left on Spur 500, which ends at Spur 700 after 4 miles. Go straight on Spur 700 at the intersection with Spur 500. It's 1.5 miles farther to the RUD Trailhead, on the right (7.5 miles from the beginning of FR 6510). The trailhead is called "Yellowjacket Camp." Head west (left) on the trail for Elephant Head.

14   Golden Stairs

Highlight: An exhausting, low-elevation (at the beginning) trail, passing spectacular rock formations early on, with panoramas of the High and Western Cascades. The only trail into the Abbott Creek Research Natural Area.

Type of hike: Day hike, out and back, or shuttle.
Total distance: Up to 8.8 miles.
Difficulty: Moderate (strenuous first mile).
Elevation gain: 1,600 feet.
Best months: April–June, October–November.
Map: USGS Abbott Butte quad.

Special considerations: The first 2-mile section of this trail, from the Golden Stairs Trailhead, is a designated off-highway-vehicle (OHV) area, at least on a trial basis. The OHV season is July 1 to October 1. While one might argue that this trail is far too fragile to accommodate OHV use, according to the Forest Service, fewer than 15 hikers a year use the Golden Stairs Trail and nearly all of that is in spring and fall. The trail gets very hot in mid-summer due to the low elevation. The OHV clubs have agreed to maintain the trail, reinforce the fragile spots, and police use. Other designated OHV trails do not meet the standards for inclusion in this book.

Very steep first mile. No water.

Finding the trailhead: Lower: Take Oregon Highway 62 north from Medford, past Prospect, to the Woodruff Bridge (Abbott Camp) turnoff (Forest Road 68) past milepost 51. Proceed left and go 5 miles to the junction with Spur 550, which has a prominent "Golden Stairs Trail" sign. It's 2 miles up Spur 550 to the trailhead. Be careful after 1 mile, where the wide, gravel road goes into a gravel quarry and Spur 550 makes a hard left and becomes narrower. There's another ambiguous intersection 0.5 mile farther where you go straight and do not bear left. The trailhead turnoff is well marked on the left. An obvious but unmarked trailhead, passed en route, is not your destination.

Upper: Just before Abbot Creek Campground on FR 68, follow Forest Road 6510 right (straight, actually), toward Hershberger Lookout. After 2 miles, you come to Spur 500 (turn left), which ends at Spur 700 after 4 miles. Go straight at the 500/700 intersection. It's 1.5 miles up Spur 700 to the Rogue-Umpqua Divide Trailhead at Yellowjacket Camp and 1.8 miles farther to the unmarked upper Golden Stairs Trailhead. Look for a primitive road

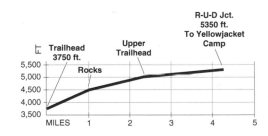

Golden Stairs

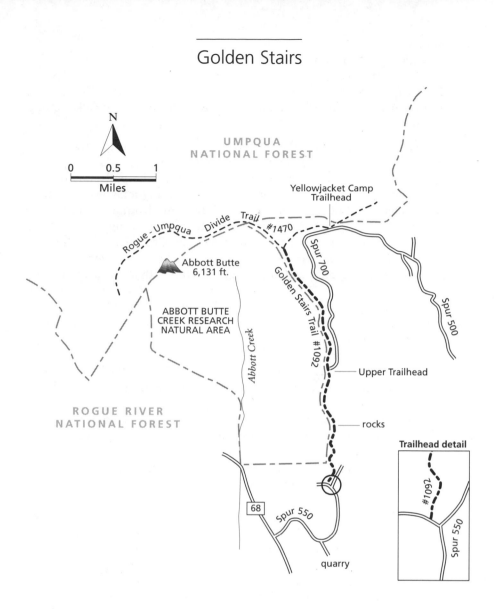

uphill to the right, with a short connecting trail taking off on the right 100 feet up the road.

The trail west from the Yellowjacket Camp Trailhead (Hike 13), leads to the upper terminus of the Golden Stairs Trail after 1 mile.

Parking and trailhead facilities: The lower trailhead holds six cars, with additional parking and an OHV alternate trailhead 0.2 mile down the road. There's parking for three or four cars on the shoulder of Spur 700 at the upper trailhead. Abbott Creek Campground is 4 miles from the lower trailhead, on FR 68.

Key points:

0.0 Golden Stairs Trailhead.
1.0 Rock formations.
2.2 Upper trailhead.
4.4 Rogue-Umpqua Divide Trail junction (go right for Yellowjacket Camp Trailhead).

The hike: It is unclear whether "Golden Stairs" refers to the trail's horrendous steepness or the sometimes yellowish rock formations it passes, each higher than the last. There are no actual stairs. The path may or may not represent a metaphoric "golden stairway" to a higher spiritual plane. Or, the "golden" part of the trail's name might come from a rumored gold mine owned by the Abbott brothers, after whom everything in the area is named. (There were no genuine gold mines in the Cascades, including the Western Cascades.) Whatever the name's origin, the trail is very nice.

Before setting out on the Golden Stairs Trail (1092), you should be aware of several options. If you have two cars and it's later than mid-May (when the snow at the far end of the road melts in most years), you can avoid the steep uphill direction of the trail's initial mile by leaving a car at the lower trailhead and starting at the upper trailhead, 2.2 trail miles from the lower trailhead. Or you can start at the Yellowjacket Camp Trailhead and hike 1 mile westward on the Rogue-Umpqua Divide Trail (1470), then 4.4 more miles in the downhill direction on the Golden Stairs Trail, it's entire length.

Since the prettiest spots on the Golden Stairs lie in the second mile from the lower trailhead, the best way to experience the path is with an out-and-back hike where you go as far as your endurance and interest permits, then turn around. While the lower trailhead is usually snow-free by mid-April or earlier, the route's upper 2 miles are often snowed over until May or June.

From the lower trailhead, the path begins inscribing steep switchbacks almost immediately. In 1999, the initial mile was impressively upgraded by the OHV people, with retaining walls and other fancy improvements. The switchbacks pretty much stop after 0.5 mile, and the path becomes even steeper, maintaining this grade until the upper trailhead.

For the most part, the path remains on the Abbot Creek side of the north-south trending ridge. Look behind you while on the Abbott Creek side for fantastic views of Mount McLoughlin and, faintly on the horizon to McLoughlin's right, Mount Shasta. Abbot Creek is an undeveloped research natural area adjacent to and south of the Rogue-Umpqua Divide Wilderness. The Golden Stairs Trail is its primary hiking access unless you enter cross-country.

The 2,600-acre Abbott Creek Research Natural Area was created in 1947 so the Oregon State University School of Forestry could study sugar pines there. No research has been conducted in the area since the 1950s. It is a beautiful roadless area and one of only three RNAs on the Rogue River National Forest. The others were created in 1970 and 1995.

The only time the Golden Stairs Trail hits the Woodruff Creek side of the ridge and looks east is when it comes to one of the three barren rock outcrops. The eastward views reveal the entire Crater Lake Rim, plus Mount Thielsen, Union Peak, and Devil's Peak.

The first open area, where the trail breaks out onto eastward-facing barren rock, is level and easy. Enjoy it while you can. The next breakout is steep and spectacular, with the trail running precipitously along the 2-foot-wide top of a steep, narrow ridge with rock outcrops on either end. At the third, most impressive and final rock area, the path runs just to the west of the narrow crest and you have to climb 10 feet uphill to get to the crest.

Beyond the rock outcrops, the gradient transitions from "strenuous" to "moderate" and the path largely stays in the woods except for a few small meadows. Approaching the upper trailhead, at 5,000 feet, the route finally levels off. The last 2 miles continue to hug the ridgetop, which is still pretty narrow, with views of Abbott Butte and Elephant Head to the northwest. While the path is strenuous at the beginning and easy at the end, the overall gradient (a 1,600-foot rise in 4.4 miles), comes to 364 feet per mile, which falls at the easy end of moderate.

Option: *Rogue-Umpqua Divide Trail.* From the Yellowjacket Camp Trailhead described in Hike 13, it's only 1 mile to the junction with the Golden Stairs Trail's upper end. From the same junction, it's 1 mile to Elephant Head on the RUD Trail and 3 miles to the top of Abbott Butte.

Upper Rogue Area

The Rogue River, southern Oregon's primary waterway, rises from a natural spring just inside Crater Lake National Park and flows 250 miles, through mountains, glacial valleys, farmland, cities, and whitewater canyons, to its rendezvous with the Pacific Ocean at Gold Beach. The river's first 50 miles cut across the Cascades, with lava flows continually attempting to obliterate the river and the river constantly reasserting itself. Nearly all of the 50 miles through the Cascades are lined with trail, with access roads every 2 to 8 miles. Nearly all 50 miles are gorgeous.

15 Upper Rogue Canyon

Highlights:	Fantastic, waterfall-laden canyon cut by the Rogue River into Mount Mazama ash.
Type of hike:	Day hike, shuttle.
Total distance:	About 8 miles.
Difficulty:	Easy.
Elevation loss:	1,070 feet.
Best months:	June–October.
Maps:	USGS Pumice Desert and Hamaker Butte quads.

Special considerations: Narrow side canyons may be clogged with snow long after the area appears to be snow-free. Plenty of water.

Finding the trailhead: Take Oregon Highway 62 north from Medford to Union Creek. Where OR 62 swings right towards Crater Lake, past milepost 57, continue straight on Oregon Highway 230 toward Diamond Lake. The northern trailhead is located at milepost 19, at the Crater Rim View Point parking area. For the southern (Hamaker Campground) trailhead, turn off OR 230 past milepost 12, onto Forest Road 6530. Continue straight on FR 6530 for 1 mile, past the Hamaker Campground turnoff, and proceed to the river crossing. The northbound trail takes off 0.1 mile before the bridge, uphill to the left, a few hundred feet beyond the southbound trailhead.

Parking and trailhead facilities: Northern: There is parking for 30 cars in a paved lot. Southern: Eight cars can park along the shoulder, with Hamaker campground 1 mile away by trail or road.

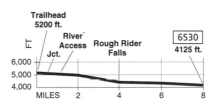

Upper Rogue Canyon

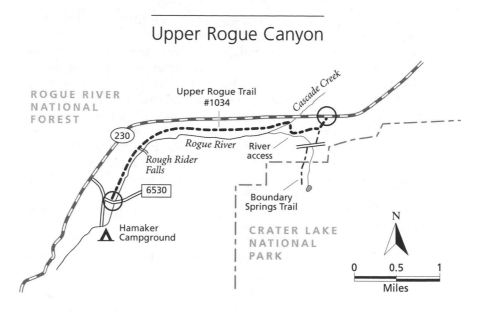

Key points:
  0.0 View Point Trailhead.
  0.5 Upper Rogue Trail junction (go straight).
  1.2 Rogue River access.
  2.3 Cascade Creek.
  4.0 Rough Rider Falls.
  8.0 FR 6530 (southern trailhead).

The hike: This route's first 4 miles, heading south from the northern trailhead, may be the most scenic of the entire 41-mile Upper Rogue Trail (1034). In addition, on warm days, the pine scent can be heavenly, as can the alternation between the river's crashing roar and the stillness of the side canyons.

The Upper Rogue Trail begins on a level plateau, beside an ever deepening side canyon, amid a stand of scrawny lodgepole pines. It's 0.5 mile from the View Point Trailhead to the Boundary Springs Trail junction. (The Boundary Springs Trail is unnumbered.) The main Rogue canyon, with a blue stream rushing along its floor, comes into view just before the junction. Bear right, along the ridgetop, for Hamaker Meadow, 7.5 miles distant.

Shortly beyond the junction, the trail manages to descend the steep ash slopes to the water's edge, just for a minute. It crosses a small creek with very steep banks, then chugs quickly back up to the high plateau.

The next mile is spectacular as the gray ash bluffs soon evolve into a memorable gorge. The loose, barren ash and pumice of the canyon walls shoot downward to a vertical drop-off above the water. A maze of pinnacles and eroded ridges jut from the bottom while the river courses through narrow crevices and over cascading waterfalls. All this occurs less than 4 miles from Boundary Springs, the source of the Rogue.

Just beyond a handsome waterfall, 2 miles from the trailhead, the path heads up an immense side canyon. It follows a flat-top bench for a while, then dips down to a wooded creek and up the other side. The north-facing side of the path down to Cascade Creek, and the canyon bottom, may remain under snow long after everything else has melted off. Even if the canyon bottom is full of snow, it's often possible to make your way across and locate the spot where the route emerges on the opposite slope.

For 2 miles beyond Cascade Creek, the path continues along a level bench far above the river, but the canyon slopes become densely forested and a little less steep. Shasta red fir joins the lodgepole pine, along with mountain hemlock and western white pine. All are middle- to upper-elevation species.

A long descent to Rough Rider Falls and the river's edge begins as you approach mile 4. The 60-foot-high Rough Rider Falls is a major highlight. The noise deafens, the spray exhilarates, and the scene enchants as a brilliant green mossy rock face frames the falling water. For a good look, you must leave the trail briefly. It's a wonderful lunch spot. If you can't arrange a pickup from Hamaker Campground, the hike from the View Point Trailhead to Rough Rider Falls and back offers an outstanding out-and-back trip, 4 miles in each direction.

Past Rough Rider Falls, the route follows a densely wooded, narrow canyon bottom. Douglas-fir, western hemlock, grand fir, white fir, incense cedar, and sugar pine begin to sneak in, along with evergreen chinkapin. Willow and alder brush line the stream banks, as they do from Boundary Springs to the ocean.

It's 2.5 miles (6.5 miles from the trailhead) along the water's edge from Rough Rider Falls to a smaller but still impressive, unnamed waterfall. Past this spot, the trail ascends the now much gentler hillside and makes its way through second-growth Douglas-fir and ponderosa pine. The valley has widened considerably, with the river scribing wide meanders through a flat, sometimes swampy bottom.

The trail hits FR 6530, 8 miles from the View Point Trailhead. For Hamaker Campground, turn right and follow the road a couple of hundred feet to the opposite trailhead. This gentle mile, following the river's wooded side, peers out on Hamaker Meadows on the opposite bank.

Options: *Boundary Springs Trail.* See Hike 27.

Upper Rogue Trail south from Hamaker Campground. See Hike 16.

16   Highway Falls

Highlights: Waterfalls, meadows, forests, and ash bluffs along the Upper Rogue River Trail.
Type of hike: Day hike, shuttle.
Distance: About 7 miles.
Difficulty: Easy.
Elevation loss: 400 feet.
Best months: June–October.
Map: USGS Hamaker Butte quad.

Finding the trailhead: Take Oregon Highway 62 north from Medford to Union Creek. Where OR 62 swings right towards Crater Lake, past milepost 57, continue straight on Oregon Highway 230, towards Diamond Lake. For the northern trailhead, turn right past milepost 12 onto the well-marked Hamaker Campground Forest Road 6530. From FR 6530, hang a right after 0.6 mile onto Spur 900 and proceed 0.5 mile through the campground to the closed bridge. The southbound trail begins just over the bridge.

For the southern trailhead, take the other end of FR 6530 (National Creek Road), off OR 230 past milepost 6. The trailhead is 1 mile up, at the far end of the bridge spanning the Rogue.

Parking and trailhead facilities: Parking at the Hamaker Campground (northern) trailhead is limited to 3 or 4 cars. The campground is very pretty. At the National Creek (southern) trailhead, there is room for 15 cars along the wide road shoulder.

Key points:
0.0 Hamaker Campground.
2.2 Hurryon Creek.
4.0 Highway Falls.
7.0 National Creek Road (southern trailhead).

The hike: Although just as scenic, this segment is very different from the adjacent View Point/Rough Rider Falls segment (Hike 15). The river is wider and the rock is older. The flirtation with OR 230, on the other side of the river, offers either annoyance or an ego boost as tourists, photographing the river from beside their cars, wonder how you got across.

For the first 2 miles from Hamaker Campground (heading south), the Upper Rogue Trail (1034) rides the side of a steep, log-strewn slope. Not far below, the river meanders through a flat-bottomed valley of open meadow

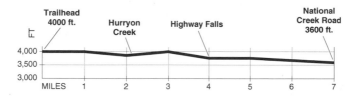

Highway Falls

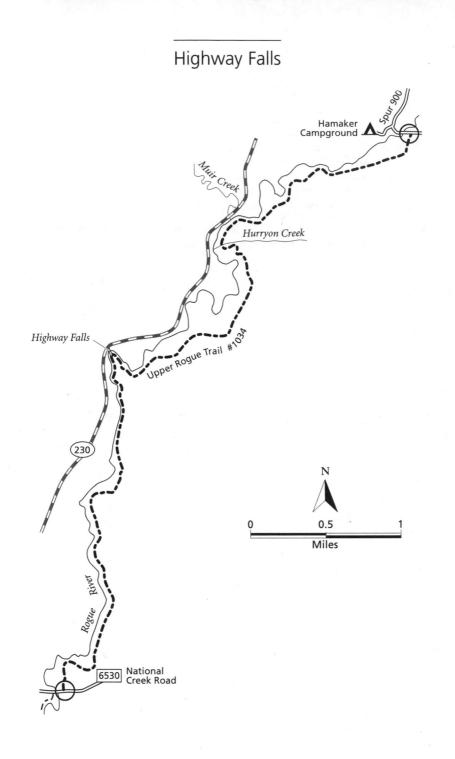

and marsh. Droopy, narrow-spired mountain hemlocks dot the grassy expanse. Occasionally, in these first 2 miles, the canyon narrows and the river speeds up. Once in a while, the path drops down to the water's edge, only to quickly resume its position several feet up the hillside.

This initial stretch is dotted with numerous side creeks, skunk cabbage bogs, and muddy spots. During the second mile, you can find a few Pacific silver firs hidden among the grand and white firs. Near Muir Creek, the trail skirts a vast green meadow with the Rogue's clear waters wandering through the middle.

Two miles from the trailhead, the Muir Creek bridge pops into view, on the opposite side of the Rogue on OR 230. From here to just below Highway Falls, you catche frequent glimpses of this busy thoroughfare. Shortly beyond the bridge, the trail crosses Hurryon Creek, spanned by several downed logs. Past Hurryon Creek, the path begins a series of winding, uphill pitches to the top of some extremely steep pumice bluffs. Look for vistas of river bends, the highway, and Rabbit Ears.

A series of tight switchbacks down to the water's edge signals the approach of Highway Falls at mile 4. The river here abruptly drops about 15 feet, then makes a right-angle bend immediately downstream. This is a good turnaround spot if you're unable to arrange a pickup at the trail's National Creek end.

Shortly after Highway Falls, the path ascends one last bluff, affording a tremendous view of a rocky river bend. From there on, the bluffs all rise from the opposite (north) side while the trail snakes through an endless maze of jackstrawed logs strewing the flats at the water's edge on the south bank. For the final 3 miles to National Creek Road, the remarkably

Highway Falls.

uniform canyon consists of level, parklike flats on one side and towering pumice bluffs on the other. The channel runs straight, for the most part, with fast-moving water coursing down the center.

A final bend in the Rogue, followed by a 0.5-mile, unobstructed view downriver, signals the hike's last leg. A log bridge across a small creek is not the anticipated crossing of National Creek. Not far from this lesser bridge, the trail cuts across some mossy rocks while a false trail continues straight. Be careful here.

Immediately after the massive, hand-railed log bridge over National Creek, the canyon widens and the river swings away from the trail. Finally, an immense highway bridge appears and the trail climbs the hillside to the road, 7 miles from the trailhead at Hamaker Campground.

Option: *National Creek to Foster Creek.* A hundred feet down the westbound continuation of the Upper Rogue Trail, on the other side of the National Creek Bridge from Highway Falls, look for some grossly out-of-place subalpine firs. At 3,600 feet, this is a surprisingly low elevation for this species, which indicates that the spot can get mighty cold. They normally aren't found below 5,500 feet in southern Oregon. According to the Forest Service, the species, though very infrequent, is scattered throughout the region between Boundary Springs and National Creek.

Beyond the subalpine firs, there's an exceptionally pretty little meadow just before the Rogue enters an impressive canyon. The trail bypasses the canyon by heading up and over some low hills before emerging at the Foster Creek parking area. This 2-mile trail segment is not described as a separate hike because it offers little of interest and there's a spot 0.2 mile down where folks invariably get lost (heading north to south), even if armed with careful trail descriptions.

17 River within a River

Highlights:	A very easy, pleasant stretch of the upper Rogue River.
Type of hike:	Day hike, shuttle.
Total distance:	About 4 miles.
Difficulty:	Easy.
Elevation gain:	Minimal.
Best months:	June–November.
Map:	USGS Union Creek quad.

Special considerations: High water in Foster Creek may block access in spring. River meanders occur along the entire route.

Finding the trailhead: Northern: Take Oregon Highway 62 north from Medford to Union Creek. Continue straight (on Oregon Highway 230), toward Diamond Lake, where OR 62 swings right towards Crater Lake

River within a River

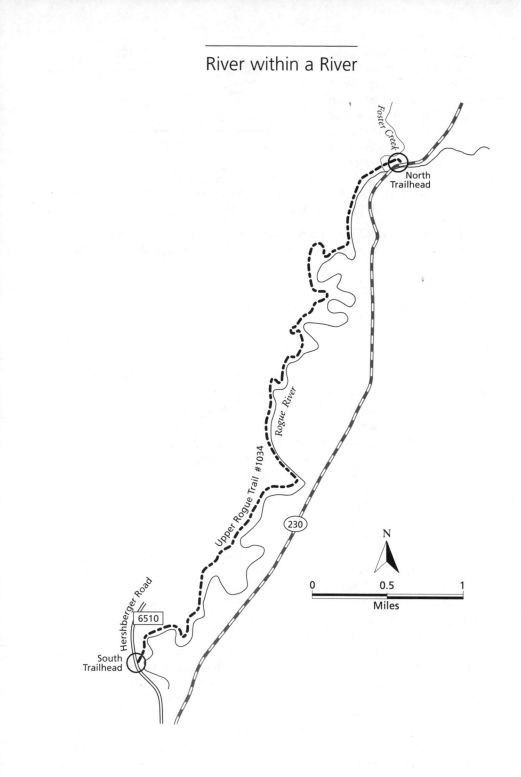

past milepost 57. At milepost 5 on OR 230, just past the bridge over the Rogue River, turn into a parking area on the left. The southbound trailhead is across the mouth of Foster Creek, where it meets the Rogue. Southern:

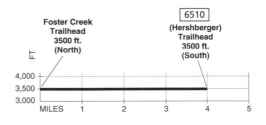

At milepost 1 on OR 230, turn left, across the Rogue River, onto the gravel Forest Road 6510. It's 0.1 mile to the trailhead, on the right. If you don't see a sign for the trail, just start walking north along the river.

Parking and trailhead considerations: Northern: The cramped parking area accommodates five cars. Southern: Ten cars fit on the shoulder and at turnouts.

Key points:
    0.0 Foster Creek Trailhead (northern).
    4.0 FR 6510 trailhead (southern).

The hike: The "River within a River" is the upper Rogue's gentlest segment. What it lacks in grandeur, it makes up in quiet beauty and geological interest.

Before starting on this segment of the Upper Rogue Trail (1034), some observations from the highway between the two trailheads may heighten the experience. Notice the steep, eroded bluffs of compacted volcanic ash. They are evident not only in road cuts but at gaps along the highway where you can pull off and observe the sweeping valley below. On the broad valley bottom below the road, a mature lodgepole pine forest is slowly yielding to western white pine and Douglas-fir. The Rogue River channel here is embedded in a much larger river of ash (hence the name "river within a river"), which spewed from Mount Mazama during the major eruption that resulted in Crater Lake. Across the valley, you can see Rabbit Ears, a large, two-pronged volcanic plug in the Western Cascades.

No matter which end of the segment you begin your hike on, stop at the Foster Creek Trailhead (northern) first to make sure Foster Creek is fordable. From the northern trailhead, Foster Creek is crossed after 0.1 mile. From the southern trailhead, it lies at mile 3.9. You're likely to get a little wet no matter what time of year you cross.

Once across Foster Creek (heading south from the Foster Creek Trailhead), scramble up the bank to a grassy flat where you may or may not locate the trail sign. It's impossible to get lost. As with the southern trailhead, simply follow the river and the trail will turn up.

The path follows one of the more relaxed river sections because the water has cut broad meanders in the flat ash beds. Since the topography offers little of interest except for a few low, undercut banks, the generally level path hugs the shore. The river has changed course frequently, so look for dry sections of riverbed called "oxbows," where the river has cut across a meander loop. Some may contain a little stagnant water.

18 National Creek Falls

Highlight:	Very short trail to a huge waterfall.
Type of hike:	Day hike, out and back.
Total distance:	About 1 mile.
Difficulty:	Moderate.
Elevation loss:	200 feet.
Best months:	May–November.
Map:	USGS Hamaker Butte quad.

Finding the trailhead: Take the paved Forest Road 6530 (National Creek Road), past milepost 6 off Oregon Highway 230. The trailhead is 4 miles up, on the right, with lots of signs. It's 0.1 mile up a spur road to the parking area.

Parking and trailhead facilities: There's room for ten cars in the gravel parking lot.

Key points:
0.2 Top of falls.
0.5 Bottom of falls.

The hike: Where Oregon Highway 230 passes National Creek Road, the area is densely wooded with canyons and hillsides all around. By contrast, National Creek Road, after 1 mile, dips down across the Rogue, then climbs onto an immense plateau, uncharacteristically flat even for an ash deposit, with high mountains rising in the background. 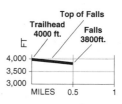 The arrow-straight road takes you to a parking area in the middle of the flat, where the sign says "National Creek Falls Trail—1053." Within a minute, you're walking down the steep sides of a narrow, shaded gorge. A glance at the USGS topo map shows that all streams in the vicinity flow through narrow, shaded, steep-sided gorges.

It takes two long switchbacks for the path to drop down through the dense woods to the top of the falls at National Creek, and two more longer switchbacks to reach the bottom of the 100-foot tumble. Since it's only 0.5 mile to the bottom, it would be hard to rate this trail as "strenuous" even if it were ten times steeper.

One thing to remember about this country, with its narrow canyons that receive little sunlight, is that the snow lingers in the canyons longer than it does on top. On June 12, 1999 (the snowiest year ever), there were huge snowbanks near and at the bottom. There were also a few snowbanks on top, and you had to walk the last 0.2 mile along the road to reach the trailhead.

National Creek Falls

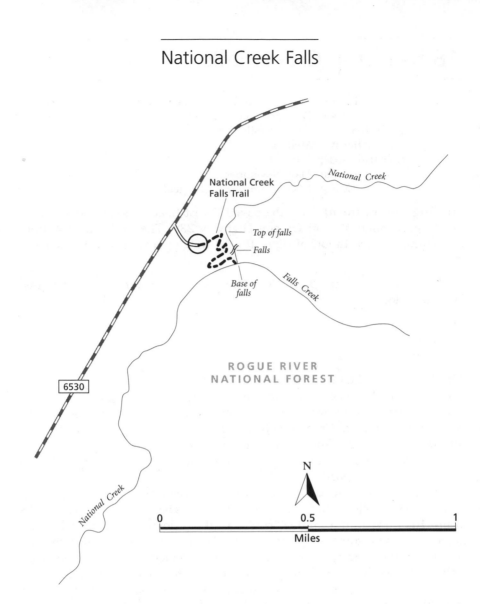

Late spring is a good time to visit because that's when the water is its most thunderous. However, it's also when the canyon has the most mosquitoes. The 80-foot falls fan out over a pyramidal rock face with a split flow in the middle, into a large collecting pool. In spring, you can't get very close to the falls because of wind and spray, but that dies down somewhat by late summer.

National Creek Falls.

19 Farewell Bend

Highlights:	Spectacular vistas and rock gorges along a secluded path across the river from heavily used areas. One of the best Upper Rogue segments.
Type of hike:	Day hike, shuttle.
Total distance:	About 6 miles.
Difficulty:	Easy.
Elevation gain/loss:	Minimal.
Best months:	May–November.
Map:	USGS Union Creek quad.

Finding the trailhead: Northern: Take Oregon Highway 62 north from Medford to Union Creek. Past milepost 57, where OR 62 swings right towards Crater Lake, continue straight (on Oregon Highway 230) toward Diamond Lake. One mile later turn left, across the Rogue, onto the gravel Forest Road 6510. It's 0.5 mile to the trailhead, on the left. A shortcut just over the bridge, uphill to the left at a small Forest Service bulletin board, cuts 0.5 mile off the hike. Southern: Take Oregon Highway 62 from Medford, past Prospect to the Natural Bridge Campground near milepost 54. Turn onto the campground road, bearing left after 0.3 mile toward the interpretive sign and parking area (0.2 mile). The northbound Upper Rogue Trail is located on the right just before the footbridge.

Parking and trailhead facilities: Northern: 10 cars can park along the road. The large and popular Farewell Bend Campground is 2 miles away, just before Union Creek on OR 62. Southern: There's a restroom and parking for 50 cars at the Natural Bridge Geological Area, with the Natural Bridge Campground adjacent.

Key points:
0.0 FR 6510 trailhead.
2.0 Farewell Bend Campground (across river).
4.5 Flat Creek.
5.2 Side trail and footbridge to Natural Bridge Campground.
6.0 Bridge to Geological Area parking area.

The hike: While this segment of the Upper Rogue Trail (1034) passes two of the upper Rogue River's most important formations, Rogue Gorge and Natural Bridge, the former cannot be seen from the trail and both can be visited by car. Natural Bridge is described in Hike 21. If you start this hike at the northern end, you hit the series of steep switchbacks in the down-hill direction.

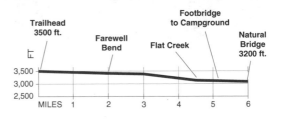

Farewell Bend

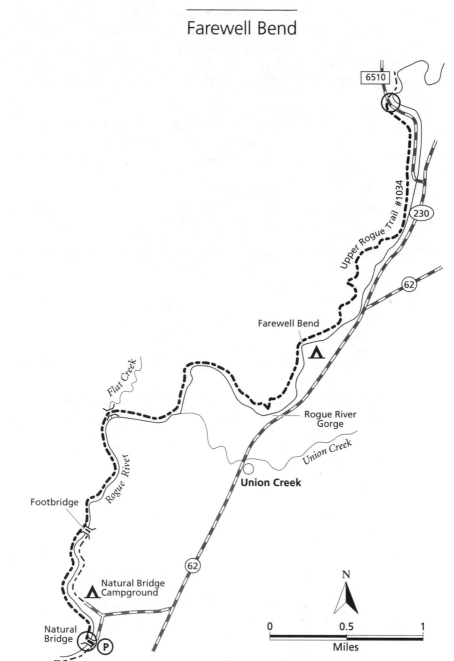

From the northern trailhead, you find yourself in a world of steep slopes, deep ravines, dense forests, little underbrush, numerous switchbacks, and only occasional glimpses of the river. The initial 2 miles contain the segment's only potentially drinkable water, as the trail crosses several streams, seeps, skunk cabbage bogs, and a couple of charming little springs.

After 2 miles, Farewell Bend Campground comes into view, on a flat across the river. At the actual bend (mile 2.8), the spectacular scene reveals a long view up the canyon and a profusion of outcrops, islands, and rapids. Shortly after, at mile 3, the path drops to the water's edge. There, the river surges through a narrow, rocky channel formed from a collapsed lava tube. This is a wonderful picnic spot.

The next mile wanders inland, away from the river, which is busy hurling itself through the Rogue Gorge. The gorge is best viewed from a parking area immediately north of Union Creek, on OR 62. Although the Upper Rogue Trail misses the gorge, the river's elevation drops noticeably beyond the formation. The path holds a fairly level contour but the river is now several hundred feet below the trail.

Eventually, the path twists and switches sharply back down to the water, paralleling the now placid stream for two miles (4 and 5). This pleasant, level section alternates between woods and meadows. Union Creek Campground and several summer homes adorn the opposite bank. At mile 4.5, the trail crosses the wide channel of Flat Creek via a sawed-flat fallen log.

A footbridge across the Rogue, 5.2 miles from the northern trailhead, leads to the Natural Bridge Campground. Crossing it cuts 0.8 mile off the route but misses the Natural Bridge Geologic Area. Should you continue straight ahead, another footbridge, leading to the parking lot, turns up at mile 6, just past the geological area.

20 Union Creek

Highlights:	An easy, pleasant walk with an extremely accessible trailhead. Beautiful in autumn, with aspen, cottonwood, and bigleaf maple sending out glorious aromas.
Type of hike:	Day hike, shuttle.
Total distance:	4.4 miles.
Difficulty:	Easy.
Elevation gain:	399 feet.
Best months:	May–November.
Map:	USGS Union Creek quad.

Finding the trailhead: Western: Take Oregon Highway 62 north from Medford to the town of Union Creek at milepost 56. The trailhead is just before the store, on the west side of Union Creek (the store is on the east

Union Creek

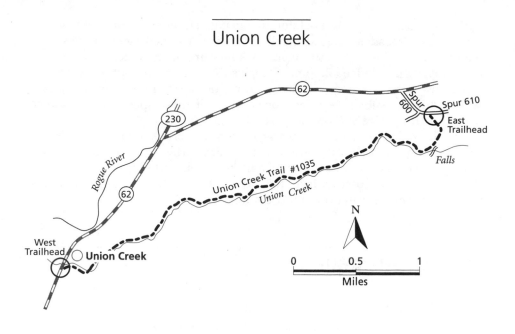

side). Eastern: Continue past the town of Union Creek to a well-marked turnoff on the right, near milepost 59, for the Union Creek Trail. The trailhead is 0.3 mile up the dirt side road (Spur 600). The highway sign claims it's 1 mile. Turn left on Spur 610 for the last couple of hundred feet.

Parking and trailhead facilities: Western: This is mostly private property, so park at your own risk. The nearest public parking is the Rogue Gorge area, 0.1 mile north on OR 62. Union Creek has a store, restaurant, campground, and tourist cabins, but no gas station or public restrooms. Eastern: A little gravel pad provides parking for six cars.

Key points:
0.0 Union Creek Store (western trailhead).
3.4 Gorge.
4.0 Waterfall.
4.4 Union Creek Trailhead (eastern trailhead).

The hike: This easy, pleasant, stroll though a botanically diverse terrain starts at the busy Union Creek Store on OR 62. The Union Creek Trail (1035) hugs the wide creek throughout, with many lovely picnic spots. It

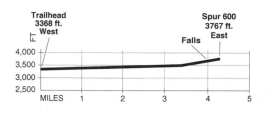

doesn't matter if you hike a few hundred feet, 1 mile, or all 4.4 miles, it's all pretty and mostly uniform, except for the last mile, where the wide, airy canyon narrows to a moss-covered rock gorge, with much denser woods. Look for quaking aspen (uncommon on the west side of the Cascades), bigleaf maple, red alder, Pacific dogwood, western white pine, white fir, western hemlock, mountain hemlock, ponderosa pine, sugar pine, lodgepole pine, Douglas-fir, Engelmann spruce, incense cedar and many other species in this transitional area between the montane and lower subalpine forest zones. Most of these species are evident from the Union Creek Store parking lot.

At mile 4, where the trail turns away from the creek towards the upper trailhead, you find a pretty little waterfall. From the waterfall to the eastern trailhead, the path cuts away from the creek and climbs a steep but short bank, then crosses a level flat. By starting at the eastern trailhead, you can reach the waterfall in just 0.4 mile.

21   Knob Falls

Highlights: A beautiful walk along the Upper Rogue River Trail, beginning at a fascinating geological site and traversing a narrow canyon with a nice waterfall.
Type of hike: Day hike, shuttle.
Total distance: About 3 miles.
Difficulty: Easy.
Elevation loss: 275 feet.
Best months: Generally snow-free year-round.
Maps: USGS Union Creek and Prospect North quads.

Special considerations: The trail lies at the lower end of the normal snow zone and may occasionally get snowed over. It is almost always clear from late March to mid-December. If you go in winter, call the Prospect Ranger District to check on conditions (see Appendix C).

Finding the trailhead: Northern: Take Oregon Highway 62 north from Medford, past Prospect to the Natural Bridge Campground near milepost 54. Turn onto the campground road, bearing left after 0.3 mile towards the interpretive sign and parking area (0.2 mile). The trail south is just before the footbridge, on the left. The interpretive trail exploring Natural Bridge crosses the footbridge and bends right. Southern: Take OR 62 past milepost 51 to Forest Road 68. The turnoff sign announces "Woodruff Bridge" in summer and "Abbott Camp" in winter. The trailhead lies 1.2 miles down, just before the bridge, at the river crossing. Walk through the picnic area on the right to the trailhead.

Parking and trailhead facilities: You'll find restroom, a campground, and parking for 50 cars at the Natural

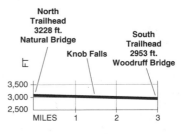

Knob Falls

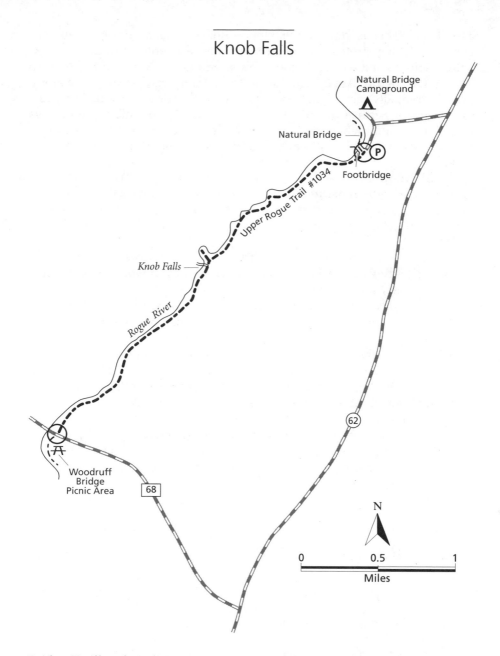

Natural Bridge
Campground

Natural Bridge

Footbridge

Upper Rogue Trail #1034

Knob Falls

Rogue River

62

Woodruff
Bridge
Picnic Area

68

N

0   0.5   1
Miles

Bridge Trailhead. A dozen cars can park at the Woodruff Bridge Trailhead, which has a charming little picnic area. Abbott Creek Campground is 2 miles farther down FR 68 from Woodruff Bridge.

Key points:
  0.0 Natural Bridge Geological Area.
  1.4 Knob Falls.
  3.0 Woodruff Bridge.

The hike: This is one of the Upper Rogue Trail's shorter segments, marked by long stretches of quiet water and a couple of dramatic highlights. Before heading out, spend a few minutes checking out the Natural Bridge Geological Area. The Rogue completely disappears at Natural Bridge, gradually reemerging several hundred feet downstream. According to the Forest Service, the river follows a network of underground lava tubes. Such tubes, which riddle volcanic areas, are formed when the outer surface of flowing lava hardens while the still-molten interior continues moving.

From Natural Bridge heading south, the Upper Rogue Trail (1034) looks back on one of the more impressive whitewater canyons. Things continue to be fairly exciting for the first mile, with surging rapids below a series of barren cliffs above the far bank. Look for a couple of immense, jutting rock formations.

The trail here is fairly level, if a little rocky in places, and offers multiple opportunities to peer into the chasm. Gradually, it works its way higher up the bank and the woods grow increasingly dense. A forest of old-growth Douglas-fir and western hemlock, with a sprinkling of western white pine, closes in. Oregon grape and little princess pine occupy the light-starved understory. Moss clings everywhere.

At mile 1.4, where the river makes a hard loop around a narrow, steep-sided peninsula, a short side trail follows the peninsula's crest to a vista point. From there, you can peer down into the narrow, collapsed lava tube through which Knob Falls, a steep cascade much like Rogue River Gorge at Union Creek, tumbles.

Below the falls, the river quiets down and the trail drops to a low bluff near the water's edge amid willow and alder thickets. Finally, the path emerges near a pretty little waterfall at Woodruff Bridge. From there, simply step across the road for Takelma Gorge and the next section.

22 Takelma Gorge

Highlights:	A spectacular rock gorge on the Rogue River.
Type of hike:	Day hike, shuttle.
Total distance:	About 4 miles.
Difficulty:	Easy.
Elevation loss:	Minimal.
Best months:	Any.
Map:	USGS Prospect North quad.

Special considerations: Stinging nettles along the trail. Filter all water.

Finding the trailhead: Northern: Take Oregon Highway 62 north from Medford, past Prospect, to the Woodruff Bridge (Abbott Camp) turnoff (Forest Road 68) near milepost 51. Proceed left for 1.2 miles to the river crossing. The southbound trailhead at Woodruff Bridge is well marked on

Takelma Gorge

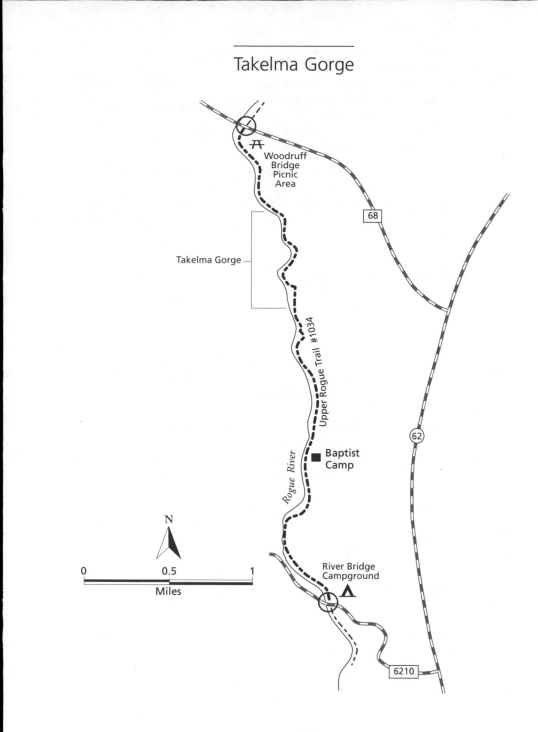

Woodruff
Bridge
Picnic
Area

68

Takelma Gorge

Upper Rogue Trail #1034

Rogue River

■ Baptist
Camp

62

N

0   0.5   1
Miles

River Bridge
Campground

▲

6210

the left, through the picnic site. Southern: To reach the far trailhead at River Bridge Campground, leave OR 62 past milepost 49, turning left onto Forest Road 6210, following the sign to "River Bridge," 0.5 mile away. The northbound trailhead is on the right just before the river crossing.

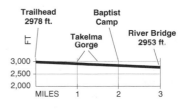

Parking and trailhead facilities: Northern: A dozen cars can park at the Woodruff Bridge Trailhead, which has a charming little picnic area. Abbott Creek Campground is 2 miles farther down FR 68 from Woodruff Bridge. Southern: The River Bridge Trailhead accommodates 8 cars and boasts a tiny campground.

Key points:
    0.0 Woodruff Bridge Trailhead.
    1.0 Beginning of Takelma Gorge.
    1.5 End of Takelma Gorge.
    2.0 Baptist Camp.
    4.0 River Bridge Trailhead.

The hike: The Indian tribe for which Takelma Gorge is named seems to spell their name *Takilma* in Josephine County and *Takelma* in Jackson County. No matter what the spelling this group has a lovely gorge named in its honor.

The first mile of the hike, on the Upper Rogue Trail (1034) south from the Woodruff Bridge Trailhead, hugs the river as it wanders through a second-growth forest of Douglas-fir, western hemlock, sugar pine, and ponderosa pine. Watch out for stinging nettles here (see "Plants to avoid" in the natural history section of the introduction).

After a placid initial mile, the river enters a narrow, black chasm that is deeper and more impressive than any encountered since the river's origin at Boundary Springs. A sign tacked to a tree announces that you've arrived at Takelma Gorge. The trail surface grows quite rocky here. Notice the bubbles petrified into the once boiling and gas-laden lava rock. And watch for a few spots of *pahoehoe,* also called ropey lava, a sign of fast-moving, highly liquid magma (as opposed to the more slow moving *aa* or blocky lava).

Takelma Gorge's far end offers the best views. A little point of land below the trail peers into the dark defile. Inside, water oozes out from between layers of basalt lava into the whitewater below.

Beyond the gorge, the river widens and slows, and the trail drops closer to the water. The rest of the walk to River Bridge, past the Rogue Baptist Camp, is pleasant and gentle, with a view of some nice riffles.

The hike ends at the River Bridge road crossing.

23   River Bridge to Prospect

Highlights: More gentle canyons and easy, placid river sections, beginning (or ending), at a tiny reservoir.
Type of hike: Day hike, shuttle.
Total distance: 4.5 miles.
Difficulty: Easy.
Elevation loss: Minimal.
Best months: Year-round.
Map: USGS Prospect North quad.

Finding the trailhead: Northern: Take Oregon Highway 62 north from Medford, past Prospect, to milepost 49, turning left onto Forest Road 6210. Follow the sign to "River Bridge," 0.5 mile away. The southbound trailhead is on the left. Southern: At milepost 43, just before the Prospect turnoff and immediately after a large canal running under the highway, look for a dirt road to the left. Follow it 0.5 mile to the PPL Recreation Site and reservoir, also known as North Fork Park. The trailhead is at the far end of the picnic area.

Parking and trailhead facilities: The River Bridge Trailhead accommodates 8 cars and boasts a tiny campground. Up to 15 cars can park at the PPL Recreation Site, which also offers several picnic tables.

Key points:
   0.0 River Bridge Trailhead.
   3.0 Trail leaves river.
   4.5 PPL trailhead.

The hike: This final segment of the Upper Rogue Trail (1034) offers an easy, quiet path along the Prospect Plateau, with some fine views of the Rogue. Among Rogue River segments with paralleling trails, this is the farthest upriver that appears to be negotiable by raft or kayak. The first 3 miles boast numerous riffles; the last mile lazes through the upper reaches of a little reservoir.

For the first 0.5 mile, heading south from River Bridge, the trail hugs the sandy riverbank at water level, working its way around rocks and willow thickets. The path bumps several dirt roads and occasionally seems to disappear. Keep to the water's edge, and you should have no problem.

Finally, the roads peter out and the trail takes over. For the next 1.5 miles, the route follows a lovely, shaded canyon, with numerous glimpses of the fast-moving river. Look for a couple of excellent views as the path repeatedly climbs the dirt and rock bluffs (no more than 20 or 30 feet high), then drops back to the water.

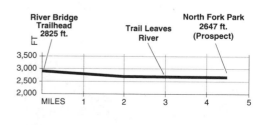

River Bridge to Prospect

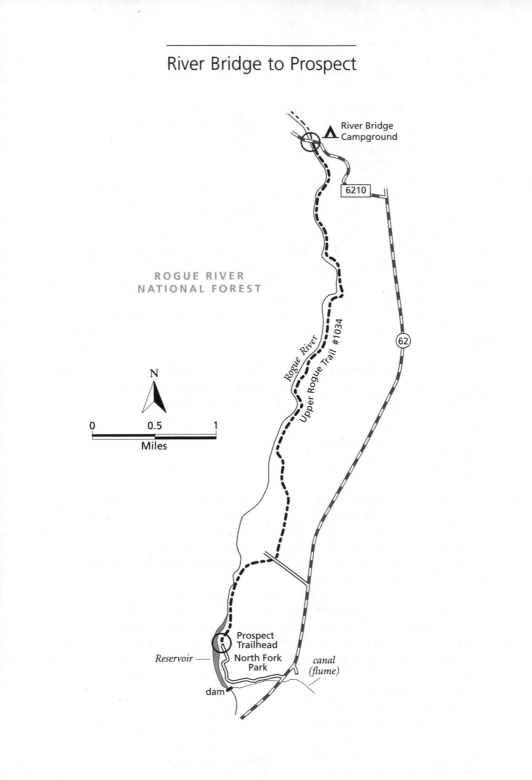

River Bridge
Campground

6210

ROGUE RIVER
NATIONAL FOREST

Rogue River

Upper Rogue Trail #1034

62

N

0   0.5   1
Miles

Prospect
Trailhead
North Fork
Park

Reservoir

canal
(flume)

dam

At mile 3, the path ascends the steep embankment for good, cutting inland for 0.5 mile, around a private inholding. The upland forest here consists of giant, old-growth Douglas-fir scattered through a managed forest of much smaller grand fir, Douglas-fir, ponderosa pine, sugar pine, and madrone.

Notice the flatness of the land away from the river. The Prospect Plateau, on which you're walking, is made of dammed-up lava which flowed down from the High Cascades. At one time, the flow continued to Bear Creek Valley but it has eroded back considerably. The Table Rocks (Hikes 56 and 57) are the only remnant of the flow's former extent in the valley. Barring further lava flows, the Prospect Plateau itself will eventually erode into isolated mesas.

The path rejoins the Rogue for the final mile, again atop a low bluff. This section is the upper reaches of a small reservoir. The river here moves slowly, with areas of inundated woods and grass on the far bank. The PPL Recreation Site looks out on the charming little impoundment. It's a perfect spot to fish, eat lunch, and explore the small dam—a fine ending to a long and wonderful journey.

Lost Creek Lake Area

Lost Creek Lake was created in 1977, mostly for flood control, with the completion of Lost Creek Dam on the Rogue River. The lake has a surface area of 3,430 acres and a mean water level of 1,874 feet above sea level. The dam is 3,600 feet long and 345 feet high. There's a restaurant at the lake, plus a marina, fish hatchery, power plant, beaches, picnic areas, campgrounds, boat launches, and miles of lakeshore trail. The little Spirit of the Rogue Nature Center, near the hatchery, is worth a visit. The lake contains rainbow trout, bass, crappie, bluegill, catfish, and German brown trout.

24 Mouth of South Fork

Highlight:	A gorgeous and mostly easy walk to the confluence of the main Rogue River and its combined Middle and South Forks.
Type of hike:	Day hike, shuttle.
Total distance:	4.8 miles.
Difficulty:	Easy north to south, difficult south to north.
Elevation loss:	422 feet.
Best months:	Any.
Map:	USGS Cascade Gorge quad.

Special considerations: If you start at the Peyton Bridge Trailhead, be aware that the barrier where the trail starts means you should not go that way due to a washout. Instead, walk down the road towards Oregon Highway 62 for 0.1 mile, until you see a small sign that says "Rogue River Trail." The rerouting is poorly marked at the trailhead and the washout is very dangerous.

Finding the trailhead: Northern: Take Oregon Highway 62 north from Medford to the beginning of Mill Creek Drive, near milepost 38. Bear right and continue 1.8 miles to a turnout that has been closed off with low wooden posts and boulders. The only sign says that mountain bikes aren't allowed. There is also a public trash can. The trail runs downhill to the left, along the old road. Southern: Just over the immense bridge past milepost 35 on OR 62 (spans the upper end of Lost Creek Lake) turn

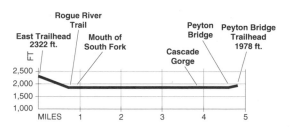

104

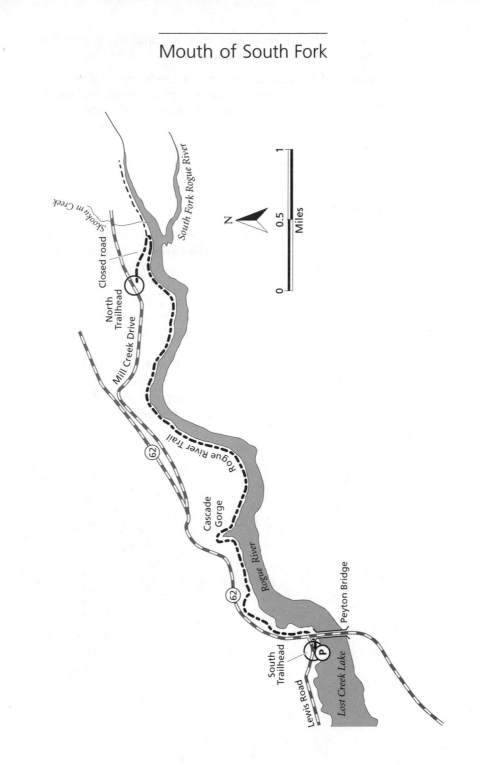

left onto Lewis Road. Immediately after, turn left into the Peyton Bridge Trailhead parking area (see "Special considerations").

Parking and trailhead facilities: Northern. There's room for two cars in the blocked-off driveway, plus two or three more cars on the shoulder. Southern: The parking area holds six cars and has a small solar outhouse.

Key points (north to south):
    0.0 Mill Creek Drive trailhead.
    0.7 Rogue River Trail junction (go right).
    0.9 Mouth of South Fork.
    3.8 Cascade Gorge.
    4.8 Peyton Bridge Trailhead.

The hike: The Rogue River's South Fork, which begins at Blue Lake in the Sky Lakes Wilderness, is actually longer than the main river above the confluence of the two streams. By the time the South Fork reaches the main river, it has been joined (4 miles upstream), by the mighty Middle Fork, which rises in the Seven Lakes Basin and flows through southern Oregon's most spectacular glacial canyon. In short, the confluence of the Rogue's South Fork and main river is an impressive spot and well worth a look.

The confluence is also just about where the Lost Creek Dam impoundment ends (most of the time). If you walk upstream from there, you'll find free-flowing river. If you head downstream, you are greeted by a placid lake. Impounded water fills the first 0.5 mile of the South Fork when water is high.

Mouth of South Fork from Rogue River Trail, above Lost Creek Lake.

From the northern trailhead, the access trail (unnumbered), a closed-off road, makes one of the steeper descents in this book—600 feet in 0.7 mile. That's why it's better to start there than end there. It's not that bad, though, if all you want is a quick gander, out and back, at the confluence.

The access trail ends at the river, 0.2 mile upstream from the confluence, at a lovely wooden footbridge over Skookum Creek. From the footbridge, the Rogue River Trail (unnumbered in the Lost Creek Lake area) takes off north. The Rogue River Trail southbound along the river, to the mouth of the South Fork and the Peyton Trailhead, comes in 200 feet before the bottom of the connecting trail, on the right.

The Rogue River Trail maintained by the Corps of Engineers and BLM above Lost Creek Lake is one of the prettiest and best-constructed paths around. The canyon wall is steep and densely wooded and the path is deeply cut, with lots of small rock outcrops and side creeks. Vegetation is profuse. The main trees are Douglas-fir, grand fir, sugar pine, ponderosa pine, and incense cedar, with madrone, bigleaf maple, and red alder thrown in. Look also for Pacific dogwood, oceanspray, and vine maple, with shade-loving underbrush of vanillaleaf and dwarf Oregongrape (among many others).

The mouth of the South Fork is very impressive but basically just a large confluence in the canyon. Below the mouth, the path continues along the river for 2.9 miles. The next highlight (mile 3.6) is a large "wow" through the rocky lava chasm of Cascade Gorge. Past Cascade Gorge, the forest thins out, with a lot more grass, ponderosa pine, and Oregon white oak. Look for white ash deposits at the river's edge at and below Cascade Gorge.

Finally, Peyton Bridge appears, 4.8 miles from the trailhead. The path goes under the bridge before arriving at the trailhead. This is a very photogenic spot.

Option: *North from the bottom of the north access trail.* This direction on the Rogue River Trail ends up at Barr Creek Falls and Mill Creek Falls after 3.5 miles (4.2 miles from the north trailhead). Both falls are impressive plunges over a lava bluff into the Rogue. Both are over 100 feet high.

25 Viewpoint Mike

Highlights:	A winter and spring hike with lots of wildflowers, leading to a vista point on a barren lava outcrop.
Type of hike:	Day hike, out and back.
Total distance:	About 5 miles.
Difficultly:	Strenuous.
Elevation gain:	950 feet.
Best months:	October–May.
Map:	USGS McLeod quad.

Special considerations: Because of its steepness and low elevation, plus its proximity to Lost Creek Lake, this trail gets very hot and humid in midsummer. It is not recommended if the temperature in Medford is over 90. There is no water.

Finding the trailhead: Take Oregon Highway 62 north to the bridge over the Rogue River, near milepost 29, just past the turnoff to the fish hatchery at Lost Creek Lake. The first paved side road, across the bridge on the right, is Crowfoot Road. The Viewpoint Mike Trail begins a couple of hundreds yards on the left, down Crowfoot Road.

Parking and trailhead facilities: A paved lot offers parking for 20 cars across the road from the trailhead. Stewart State Park, with its beach, store, restaurant, boat launch, restrooms, and campground, is 4 miles farther down OR 62 on Lost Creek Lake. The fish hatchery and the Spirit of the Rogue Nature Center are well worth a visit.

Key points:
0.0 Viewpoint Mike Trailhead.
0.7 First viewpoint.
1.0 Road crossing.
2.5 Summit, second viewpoint.

The hike: This unnumbered path offers an excellent workout and is snow-free nearly all year except after a major winter storm. It's in its glory in spring, when dozens of wildflower species bedazzle the grassy fields and airy woods. The only drawback is the path's affinity for OR 62, which it parallels along the tops of some deep road cuts for the first 1.5 miles. Eventually, the path swings away from the road.

The trail climbs steeply from the outset and rarely lets up as it ascends from an elevation equal to the base of the Lost Creek Dam (1,500 feet) to about 650 feet above the top of the dam. Much of the route traverses a grass and Oregon white oak association, indicative of low elevation and extreme summer heat and dryness. Oregon white oak is

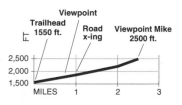

Viewpoint Mike

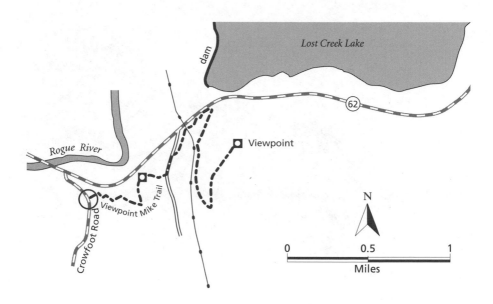

the state's least shade tolerant tree. It is even less shade tolerant than ponderosa pine.

Occasional wooded stands in the first 1.5 miles are open and brushy,
with small ponderosa pines, Oregon white oak, California black oak,
madrone, whiteleaf manzanita, buckbrush ceanothus (also called wild
California lilac), whitethorn ceanothus, birchleaf mountain mahogany, tall
Oregongrape, and wild grape. Look also for scattered Douglas-fir and
sugar pine. Like Oregon white oak, whitethorn ceanothus and birchleaf
mountain mahogany are indicators of low elevation and very hot, very dry
sites.

Many wildflowers flourish along the trail including cat's ear, wild iris,
Indian paintbrush, lupine, Indian pink, ookow, camas, erigonium, loma-
tum, and the magnificent balsamroot daisy.

Oh yes, poison oak also flourishes along the trail.

After 0.7 mile, you arrive at a park bench on the top of a deep road cut,
with an outstanding view of the dam, the fish hatchery, and the Rogue
River. Be careful of the poison oak growing out of the wall behind the
bench.

After 1 mile, the path emerges onto a dirt road, which it follows for 0.1
mile (turn left, then right). Past the road, the path continues to climb and
continues to parallel OR 62 for another 0.3 mile.

At mile 1.3, the route makes a 90-degree turn to the right, swings away
from the highway for good, and ducks behind a large hill. The highway
noises fade away and the forest becomes denser and cooler, with larger

Approaching Viewpoint Mike.

trees, more Douglas-firs and sugar pines and fewer ponderosa pines. This segment is long, steep, and unvarying but a welcome respite from the heat and dryness. Eventually, you come to a switchback with a wooden bench, which means you're only 0.3 mile from the end.

From the switchback the path climbs around some rock faces and crosses a ridge, where Lost Creek Lake and OR 62 come back into view, except you're now far above both. The path makes its way across a long, steep lava outcrop to the summit, which has a wooden bench, cliffs, and an outstanding vista. Look for a buzzard roost immediately east. All of Lost Creek Lake is visible from the vista point, along with the dam and Flounce Rock across the lake. On the eastern horizon, Union Peak blends into the Crater Lake rim and Hillman Peak.

Option: You can shave 0.8 mile off the hike by beginning at the dirt road which the trail crosses rather than at the trailhead. To find it, continue on OR 62 beyond the Crowfoot Road turnoff to the first side road on the right (about 1 mile) that has mailboxes and a locked gate. Park at the turnoff but don't block the gate. Walk 0.2 mile to the trail crossing and turn left.

26 Baker Cypress Botanical Site

Highlight:	A short hike to the northernmost stand of one of the rarest tree species in North America, with a spectacular vista point nearby.
Type of hike:	Day hike, out and back.
Total distance:	About 1 mile.
Difficulty:	Easy.
Elevation gain:	Minimal.
Best months:	April–December.
Map:	USGS Cascade Gorge quad.

Finding the trailhead: From Medford, take Oregon Highway 62 north to Ulrich Road, near milepost 38. Turn left onto Ulrich road, proceed 2 miles to Flounce Rock Road, and turn left again. It's 4 miles on Flounce Rock Road to the well-marked trailhead on the left.

Parking and trailhead facilities: The trailhead has room for six cars.

Key points:
0.0 Botanical Site Trailhead.
0.5 Baker cypress stand.

The hike: From the trailhead, follow the path for 0.2 mile until it makes a right-angle turn to the right, into a cleared corridor. Where the corridor and path end (at mile 0.3), double back to the left and continue until you come to a large clearing (at mile 0.4). The Baker cypress stand and an interpretive sign lie across the clearing to the right (mile 0.5). There is no obvious reason why the trail doubles back on itself since the terrain is nearly level.

Baker cypress (*Cupressus bakerii*) is one of the rarest trees in North America. The species is limited to 10 or 12 widely separated stands in the Siskiyou and Cascade Mountains, along the California-Oregon border. In the Siskiyous, the species is limited to serpentinite soils. In the Cascades, it occurs on recent lava flows with extremely thin soil. In both places, it inhabits the ecotone (transition) between a clearing and a normal forest stand.

The species was longed believed to be extremely short lived and fire dependent and that seedlings were only produced after an intense fire wiped out the parents. Over the years, many visitors to the Baker Cypress Botanical Site have been disturbed by this lack of reproduction, which brings up the fascinating question of whether or not it is ethical to burn down individuals of an endangered species—or allow them to be burned down—to generate the reproduction that saves the species from extinction.

Then, in 1996, a huge windstorm blew over and killed most of the larger cypresses. Within weeks, the area was overgrown with seedlings (which

Baker Cypress Botanical Site

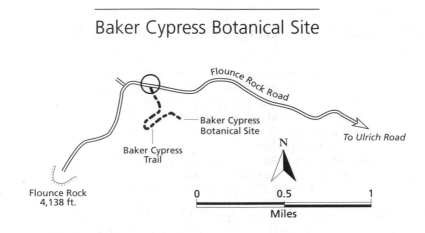

refuted the theory that a soil microbe prevents the cypress seeds from germinating and that reproduction occurs only when the heat of a fire wipes out the microbe).

Option: *Flounce Rock.* From the Botanical Site Trailhead, it's a 0.5-mile drive up the steep dirt road to the right, to the top of Flounce Rock. A "Flounce," is a fringe sewn onto the bottom of a skirt. How this relates to Flounce Rock is a mystery. A 0.2-mile trail leads from the microwave tower (with parking for four cars), to the rim. The views of Lost Creek Lake, the Cascades and the Rogue and Bear Creek Valley are breathtaking.

Crater Lake National Park

Crater Lake National Park was established in 1902 as America's, and the world's, fifth national park. The park's 183,000 acres are highlighted by soaring summits and a stunning 6-mile-diameter lake, thought until a few years ago to be the world's deepest. As recently as 30 years ago, the lake's exact depth was unknown. At an official depth of 1,932 feet (give or take a few feet because of fluctuations in the lake level), the lake now ranks as America's deepest and the world's sixth deepest lake. The lake is surrounded by sheer cliffs and gravel drop-offs and the shore has only a single access, Cleetwood Cove, where the boat tours dock. The conically shaped deep spot lies 1 mile off the eastern shore.

Park roads are opened to Rim Village year-round, although Rim Drive isn't usually plowed out until mid-June. Entrance fees are collected only after the Rim Drive opens. If you pass an open entrance station by car, it'll cost $10 in 2001. Some of the Crater Lake trails described in this book do not require passing an entrance station.

The park receives a spectacular amount of snow but most trails are usually passable by late June and remain clear until the snow begins to fly, usually in late November or early December.

---

27 Boundary Springs

Highlights:	A beautiful canyon, several magical springs, and the ultimate source of the Rogue River.
Type of hike:	Day hike, out and back.
Total distance:	About 5 miles.
Difficulty:	Easy.
Elevation gain:	Minimal.
Best months:	June–October.
Map:	USGS Pumice Desert West quad.

Special considerations: Since the trail originates outside Crater Lake National Park, there is no entrance fee.

Finding the trailhead: Take Oregon Highway 62 north from Medford to Union Creek. Where OR 62 swings right towards Crater Lake, past milepost 57, continue straight on Oregon Highway 230 towards Diamond Lake. The trailhead is located at milepost 19, the Crater Rim Viewpoint parking area.

To cut 1 mile off the hike, turn right off OR 230, 2 miles past the Viewpoint parking area, onto Spur 760, following the signs to Lake West. This is a rough dirt road. A cramped trailhead with limited parking is

Boundary Springs

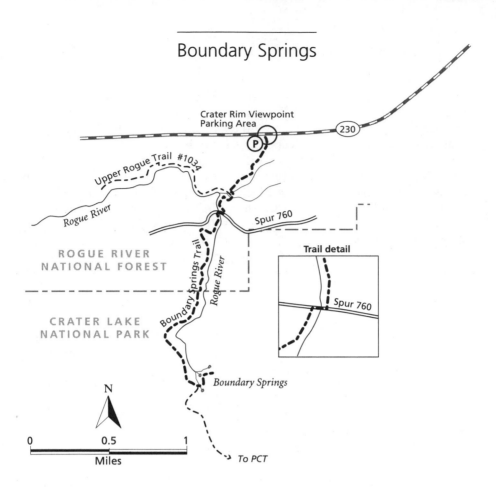

located 3.2 miles up, where the Rogue passes through a large culvert. Head left on the trail for Boundary Springs.

Parking and trailhead facilities: The paved Viewpoint parking area holds 30 cars.

Key points:
  0.0 Viewpoint Trailhead.
  0.5 Upper Rogue Trail junction (go left).
  1.0 Road crossing.
  1.8 National Park boundary.
  2.5 Boundary Springs.

The hike: It's not true that the Rogue rises from a hole in the Crater Lake rim's north side. The water feeding beautiful Boundary Springs, source

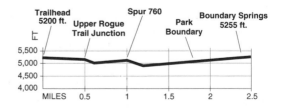

Heritage Institute class at Boundary Springs, source of Rogue River.

of the Rogue's main fork, comes instead from runoff and ground water on Crater Lake's outer slopes.

From the Viewpoint Trailhead, the path (which begins as the Upper Rogue Trail 1034), initially follows a level plateau through a stand of small lodgepole pine. It's 0.5 mile from the parking area to the junction. Turn left, downhill, for Boundary Springs on the unnumbered trail (see Hike 15).

Past the junction, the trail dips in and out of a steep ravine. The bottom may remain snow clogged—and therefore difficult or impossible to cross—until early July, long after the surrounding area clears. Climbing quickly out of the ravine, it's another 0.5 mile along a level plateau above the river to Spur 760.

After crossing the river via Spur 760, the trail rounds a small side creek, then gradually climbs to a bench high above the water and continues south towards the national park boundary. Steep slopes of loose ash border the rushing stream. The volume of water and the immensity of the canyon are surprising considering the nearness of the river's source.

The trail enters the park 1.8 miles from the trailhead. There, the path begins edging closer to the water and hikers are treated to a profusion of monkey flowers and red huckleberry. Approaching the springs, numerous moss-covered logs bridge the wide, shallow river.

Just past an open, marshy area marked by a "Boundary Springs" sign, the path swings away from the river and connects with a closed road leading to the Pacific Crest Trail and the park interior. To view the actual springs—there are three of them—make your way across the marshes along several faint way-trails. Do not walk on the mossy rocks in this fragile area.

The middle spring is the most impressive. From atop a small log, you see a dry hillside on one side and a full-blown river on the other. The newborn stream quickly fans out across a rock face as it begins its journey to the Pacific.

28 Sphagnum Bog

Highlight:	A mostly easy walk on a remote, little-used trail to a beautiful and fragile botanical area just inside Crater Lake National Park.
Type of hike:	Day hike, out and back.
Total distance:	About 4 miles.
Difficulty:	Easy to moderate.
Elevation loss:	350 feet.
Best months:	June–October.
Maps:	USGS Pumice Desert West, Crater Lake West, and Hamaker Butte quads.

Special Considerations: Since no National Park entrance stations are passed, there is no entrance fee. Also, even though the trailhead is well

Sphagnum Bog

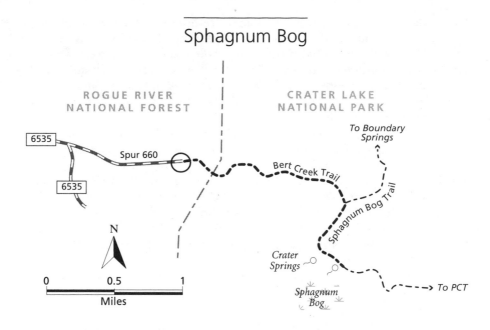

ROGUE RIVER
NATIONAL FOREST

CRATER LAKE
NATIONAL PARK

6535

Spur 660

6535

To Boundary
Springs

Bert Creek Trail

Sphagnum Bog Trail

Crater
Springs

N

0   0.5   1
Miles

Sphagnum
Bog

To PCT

maintained by Rogue River National Forest, it is not in the trailhead parking fee program because it enters the National Park after 0.3 mile.

Be prepared for mosquitoes early in the year. There is plenty of water.

Park Boundary

Trailhead
5626 ft.

Junction

Sphagnum Bog
5300 ft.

FT

6,000
5,500
5,000
4,500

MILES   0.5   1   1.5   2

Finding the trailhead: Take Oregon Highway 230 north past milepost 6 to the paved Forest Road 6530 (National Creek Road), on the right. It's 1 mile to the Rogue River crossing and 1.5 miles to the Forest Road 6535 turnoff on the right (FR 6535 is a loop—take the second, paved end of FR 6535). Follow FR 6535 for 5 miles, past the gravel quarries where the pavement ends, to Spur 660, which goes straight while FR 6535 veers right. It's 1 mile on Spur 660 to the trailhead at the road's end.

Parking and trailhead facilities: Four cars can park at the trailhead (barely). There is no trailhead bulletin board but there is a cattle gate, a drift fence, a small sign that says "trail" (two signs, actually—follow the one by the gate), and a truckload of gravel dumped on the parking area. The local trail riders association is involved with the maintenance of this trailhead.

Key points:
0.0 Bert Creek Trailhead.
0.3 National park boundary.
1.5 Sphagnum Bog Trail junction (go right).
2.0 Sphagnum Bog.

The hike: This is a beautiful, extremely remote trailhead. A logged area above the road has turned into a high, rocky meadow with a resident elk herd. The logging is a little difficult to understand since the only tree of significant commercial value at this 5,600-foot elevation is western white pine, which isn't nearly as valuable as Douglas-fir, sugar pine, or ponderosa pine. Shasta red fir and mountain hemlock, also in abundance, are of only marginal commercial value.

From the trailhead, the unnumbered Bert Creek Trail (a name which appears on exactly zero maps), wanders through a nondescript, mosquito-infested woods on rolling terrain for 0.3 mile to the park boundary. Once inside the boundary, it climbs gently to a ridgetop, then drops steeply down to what looks like a long, level section. This seemingly level section, however, actually rises, as the topo map shows. In mid-July of 1999, with the snow melt six weeks behind schedule, this "level" stretch gradually evolved from having no snow cover to being covered with heavy snow, so it's a safe bet you're headed uphill.

The Sphagnum Bog Trail (also unnumbered) turns up on a second ridgetop, 1.5 miles from the trailhead. Turn right onto the Sphagnum Bog Trail for Sphagnum Bog.

From the hilltop junction, the Sphagnum Bog Trail drops abruptly down for 0.5 mile through the woods and across a small meadow to Crater Creek. Just past the meeting with Crater Creek, the path climbs a short hill, then hits the end of a closed-off road with a turnaround. There are two hitching posts in the turnaround, plus a sign announcing that horses are not permitted beyond that point.

From the turnaround, following the old road through a stand of small lodgepole pines, the trail passes a pretty little spring, loops back down to the creek, and finally meets Sphagnum Bog. The path immediately above the bog is very faint, difficult to follow, and covered with fallen, jack-strawed lodgepole pines.

The discontinuous wetlands occupy the level creekbed downhill to the right of the trail. It is possible to walk down to the bog and examine the plant species but the site can be mushy early in the year and the ecosystem is fragile. The bog tends to dry up late in the season. There are no trails into the bog.

Sphagnum Bog is the most botanically diverse spot in Crater Lake National Park with 131 identified plant species. Technically, it is not a bog but a mire, because there isn't quite enough sphagnum moss. A mire is swampy while a bog is spongy. In a true bog, the dead layers of sphagnum moss (*sphagnum* is the Greek word for "moss") build up into peat, an important fuel in some parts of the world. In a floating bog, the sphagnum moss forms a dense mat over the surface of a lake. This is not a floating bog.

The Sphagnum Bog species list includes sphagnum moss and a myriad of water and acid-loving trees, shrubs, and wildflowers. There are 13 species of sedge, 4 species of bullrush, 3 species of monkeyflower, 4 species of violet, 3 species of daisy, and 3 species of huckleberry. The stars of the show are Mt. Mazama collomia, an endangered species found only in Crater Lake National Park, and two species of drosera, or sundew, insect-eating plants with a rosette of sticky leaves at the base.

While Sphagnum Bog is very pretty, and a remote, seldom-visited gem, it is also one of the most mosquito-infested places in the universe. As with other mosquito havens in the region, the situation improves later in the season.

The drive from the trailhead back to OR 230 offers an outstanding view of Rabbit Ears and Hershberger Mountain.

Options: If you head north (left) on the Sphagnum Bog Trail, you come to Oasis Spring after 2 miles and Boundary Springs (Hike 27) after 6 miles. If you continue south on the Sphagnum Bog Trail, the path dead-ends at the Pacific Crest Trail (2000) in 3 miles, near Red Cone Spring (basically in the middle of nowhere).

29 Cleetwood Cove

Highlights: The only access to the shore of Crater Lake. Also, the origin of the boat rides.
Type of hike: Day hike, out and back.
Total distance: 2.2 miles.
Difficulty: Moderate (steep but short).
Elevation loss: 642 feet.
Best months: Mid-June–October.
Map: USGS Crater Lake East quad.

Special considerations: There is no water on this trail and it can get very hot and humid; however, the hike isn't very long. Boat rides at midday and on weekends sell out quickly so you may have to wait a couple of hours. The tour lasts one hour and 45 minutes. Boats don't go if it's windy or raining. The trail is almost always crowded. Bring water, sunscreen, and a hat if you go in the boat. See Hike 30, for more about the boat rides.

Finding the trailhead: From the Rim Village at Crater Lake National Park, head north 8 miles on the Rim Drive to the junction with the North Entrance Road. Turn right at the junction, towards Cleetwood Cove, 5 miles away. Park at Cleetwood Cove.

Parking and trailhead facilities: A large, paved parking lot can accommodate up to 100 cars; it's often full on midsummer weekends. There are solar toilets at the end of the trail, near the boat docks.

Key points:
   0.0 Cleetwood Cove Trailhead.
   1.1 Lakeshore, boat dock.

Cleetwood Cove

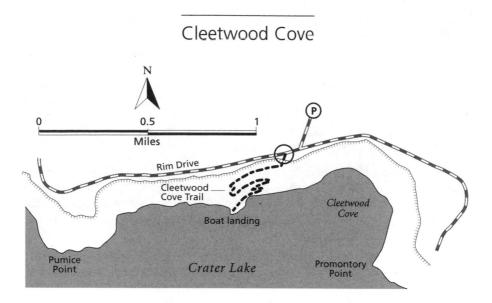

The hike: This is a hike everyone should take and everyone who lives in Oregon eventually does. The boat ride around the lake, with a stop at Wizard Island, is a great way to experience the most scenic attraction in a very scenic state.

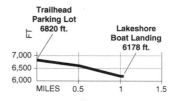

From the trailhead, the path drops relentlessly through several switchbacks and a high-elevation woods of lodgepole pine, western white pine, and mountain hemlock. You pass many people on their way up who are red in the face, perspiring, and breathing heavily. Don't worry, the path isn't that difficult and the trail isn't very long. It does attract many visitors who aren't used to hiking. There are wooden benches at regular intervals.

After 0.7 mile, the forest yields to bare rock, the lakeshore facilities come into view, and the path steepens as it negotiates the last long switchbacks. At the bottom, you find the boat dock, a ranger hut, and a solar toilet. There's room for a little exploring, but the shore is too steep to permit wandering very far from the dock area. The swimming is wonderful. Going up is much harder.

30   Wizard Island

Highlight:	A boat ride to an island in Crater Lake, followed by a trek to the summit of a 750-foot-high cinder cone. Regarded by some as Oregon's most spectacular and unusual hike.
Type of hike:	Day hike, out and back.
Total distance:	1.8 miles.
Difficulty:	Moderate.
Elevation gain:	755 feet.
Best months:	Late June–Labor Day (when the boats run).
Map:	USGS Crater Lake West quad.

Special considerations: Wizard Island hikers are completely dependent on the boat tours. If you get off your tour boat to hike on the island, you have to wait for the next boat that has room, which might not be until the last boat of the day. Boat rides may be canceled without notice due to bad weather or mechanical problems but the boat operators will pick up all hikers at the end of the day no matter what. Boat rides are $15 per person as of 2001.

Bring plenty of water as there is little tree cover on the trail and you might end up stranded for hours. There is no water on the island. Solar exposure on the boat can be intense, so wear a hat, sunglasses, and sunscreen.

Wizard Island from Rim Village, Crater Lake.

Wizard Island

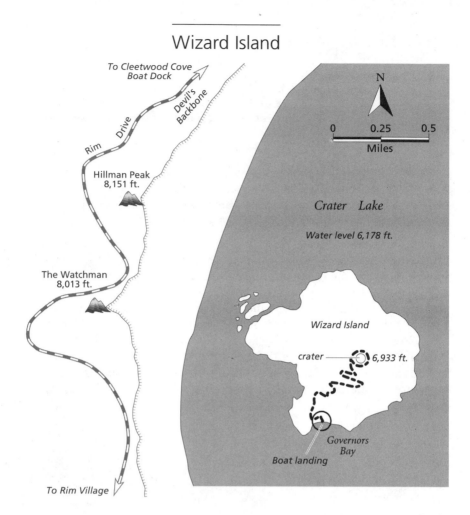

Finding the trailhead: See Hike 29, Cleetwood Cove. Wizard Island boat tickets are sold in the Cleetwood Cove parking lot. Take the boat tour from the Cleetwood Cove dock and get off at Wizard Island. The trailhead is well marked at the island's boat dock area.

Trailhead facilities: There are a few trees near the Wizard Island boat dock but the area is mostly jagged lava rock. There are solar toilets near the Wizard Island boat dock.

Key points:
0.0 Boat dock trailhead.
0.9 Summit.

The hike: The privately operated, ranger-guided boat ride to Wizard Island is a treat even if you don't take the hike. The boat leaves from the end of the Cleetwood Cove Trail and costs $15 (the price goes up frequently). It takes 40 minutes to reach the island and another hour to get back to Cleetwood Cove. Along the way, the boat visits the Devil's

122

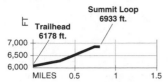

Summit Loop
6933 ft.

Trailhead
6178 ft.

7,000
6,500
6,000

MILES   0.5   1   1.5

Backbone, Llao Rock, an incredibly beautiful waterfall, the Phantom Ship, the lake's 1,932-foot "deep spot," and much more. Even up close, it's the bluest water you can possibly imagine.

The little harbor of jagged black lava rock at Wizard Island is gorgeous bordering on enchanted. Scattered mountain hemlock offers a modicum of shade while the nearly symmetrical, 764-foot cone rises abruptly in the background.

It's a 0.9-mile walk from the boat dock to the summit. That's a lot of trail, considering the island is only 0.6 mile across. The trail ascends the cone's south slope, which loses snow fastest in spring (snow on the cone's north side can linger to mid-July or later).

The cone's bottom third is thinly forested. Mountain hemlock is the most common tree up to the treeline, where scattered whitebark pine predominates. Trees on the recent lava flow, at the base of the cone on the island's west and north sides, are smaller and sparser than the trees on the cone and on the rest of the island. One would expect lodgepole pine on such a harsh site. Their absence might have to do with the fact that mountain hemlock also comprises 90 percent of the trees on the rim.

The Wizard Island lava flow represents the park's last-known volcanic activity. The flow at it's base probably emerged 200 years ago. Estimates are that the major eruption of Mount Mazama which created Crater Lake occurred about 7,000 years ago, and that the Wizard Island cone was formed 1,000 years ago.

There is an even larger cinder cone in Crater Lake, called Merriam Cone, not far from Cleetwood Cove, but it is completely submerged.

The Wizard Island Trail is reasonably gentle for the first 0.3 mile. Then the serious ascent begins. In a series of hot, dusty, exposed switchbacks, the path gains 764 feet in 0.9 mile. With the unbelievable scenery and relatively short distance, the climb goes pretty fast. A small loop runs around the 90-foot-deep crater at the summit. The unique perspective of the lake and surrounding cliffs from the summit is unforgettable and overwhelming.

Options: Believe it or not, there are options on this tight little island. If you end up with hours to kill waiting for your boat ride back, the hike around the island is 2 miles long. There is no trail for much of the way and some of the lava rock and gravel slopes can be miserable. It takes about two hours. A 0.5-mile way-trail, branching off near the beginning of the path up the cone, explores the recent lava flow and three small ponds around Fumarole Bay.

You can also go swimming, eat a picnic lunch, and commune with the magnificent solitude between boat arrivals (they show up every hour during the peak season and stay about 15 minutes).

31 Mount Scott

Highlights:	A splendid panorama of all of Crater Lake and much of southern Oregon from the highest point in Crater Lake National Park.
Type of hike:	Day hike, out and back.
Total distance:	About 5 miles.
Difficulty:	Moderate.
Elevation gain:	1,243 feet.
Best months:	July–October.
Map:	USGS Crater Lake East quad.

Special considerations: There is no water on this trail. It is almost entirely in the open and fairly steep but not very long. Sun can be intense because of the high elevation. Bring water and wear sunscreen.

Finding the trailhead: Take any Crater Lake National Park entrance (half the roads in southern Oregon lead there). The north entrance is closest to the Mount Scott Trailhead. From the north entrance, it's 10 miles on Oregon Highway 209 to the North Entrance/Rim Drive junction (8 miles from Rim Village). From the junction, head left (east) for 11 miles on the Rim Drive, past Cleetwood Cove, to a large switchback just before the Cloudcap turnoff. Look for the well-marked trailhead at the far end of the switchback.

Parking and trailhead facilities: Thirty cars can park along the shoulder and a couple of picnic tables offer a place to snack near the trailhead. The nearest camping is at Lost Creek, 7 miles away on the Pinnacles Road, inside the park.

Key points:
0.0 Mount Scott Trailhead.
2.5 Summit.

The hike: If Crater Lake is the scenic highlight of Oregon, the Mount Scott Trail is the ultimate hike in Crater Lake National Park (Hike 30, the Wizard Island cone, is the best hike in the park but not the ultimate hike). While not particularly difficult, the Mount Scott Trail offers the ultimate view of Crater Lake.

Perhaps 80 percent of the trees on Mount Scott are mountain hemlock, recognized by their bent or drooping tips. Look also for narrow, spirelike subalpine fir, along with Shasta red fir and lodgepole pine. The stunted little trees hugging the highest ridges are whitebark pine. Most of the trees are concentrated near the lower end of the

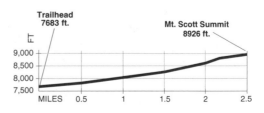

Mount Scott

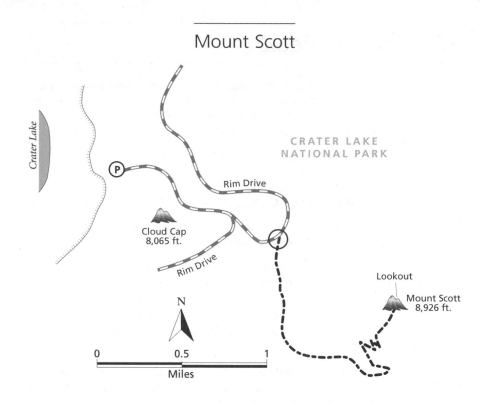

hike. Above that, they are widely scattered. The terrain along most of the trail consists of ash, pumice, and loose gravel.

The trail to the top of "Great Scott," the park's highest point at 8,926 feet, begins to the right of a little hillock. It stays fairly level for the first 0.7 mile as it passes an immense avalanche basin sweeping down from the summit. Reaching the peak's back side, it's pretty much a straight contour up the steep, fairly uniform, sparsely vegetated slope to the lookout on top. There's not much variation until you reach the crest. There are switchbacks along the way at mile 1.8 and 2.1, with the lake coming into view at mile 2.2. At mile 2.2, you reach the narrow, level, summit ridge, arriving at the lookout at mile 2.5 (which offers a great view but the viewing platform is usually locked).

Many landmarks may be seen from the Mount Scott summit (Mount Thielsen, Diamond Lake, Diamond Peak, the South Sister, the Klamath Basin, Mount McLoughlin, Mount Shasta), but the lake is so overwhelming you are hard pressed to notice them. As noted, this is the ultimate view of one of America's ultimate scenic wonders.

From the summit, the aforementioned avalanche basin, a long, unbroken sweep of ash and loose gravel, shoots straight down almost to the parking area. People occasionally use it as a shortcut down but the Park Service probably frowns on that. Besides, the shortcut only saves you about five minutes.

32 Garfield Peak

Highlights:	A gorgeous trail from the Crater Lake Lodge, up a narrow, rocky ridge with cliffs, dropping directly to Crater Lake. Outstanding vista from the summit.
Type of hike:	Day hike, out and back.
Total distance:	3.4 miles.
Difficulty:	Moderate.
Elevation gain:	984 feet.
Best months:	July–October.
Maps:	USGS Crater Lake West and Crater Lake East quads.

Special considerations: There is no water on the trail, but it isn't very long and there are plenty of shady spots.

Finding the trailhead: Take Oregon Highway 62, the Crater Lake Highway, to the south Crater Lake entrance past milepost 73. Proceed 6 miles on the South Entrance Road, past Mazama Campground and park headquarters, up the hill to the Rim Village. Continue past the gift shop for 0.3 mile, to the far end of the lodge. The trail begins behind the lodge, at the rim above the lake.

Parking and trailhead facilities: The paved parking lot near the trailhead offers parking for 20 cars and the lodge offers more parking for guests. The lodge also has restrooms and a gift shop. You can camp at Annie Springs, near the south entrance.

Key point:
0.0 Lodge trailhead.
1.7 Summit.

The hike: Garfield Peak is not named after a U.S. President or a cartoon cat. It is named for a former Secretary of the Interior.

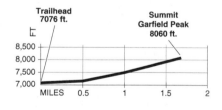

As you drive the winding road between Crater Lake's Park Headquarters and Rim Village, you should catch a glimpse of the Garfield Peak Trail. It is visible clinging to a mass of tortured pink lava above an immense drop-off.

The Garfield Peak Trail is one of the most accessible and spectacular within Oregon's only national park. While the park's Mount Scott is 900 feet higher, Garfield Peak is part of the actual lake rim while Mount Scott is set back from the lake. The Garfield Peak Trail is shorter and a little steeper than the Mount Scott Trail. The route is part of a longer trail paralleling the Rim Drive as far as Discovery Point, 3 miles from the lodge in the opposite direction from Garfield Peak.

Garfield Peak

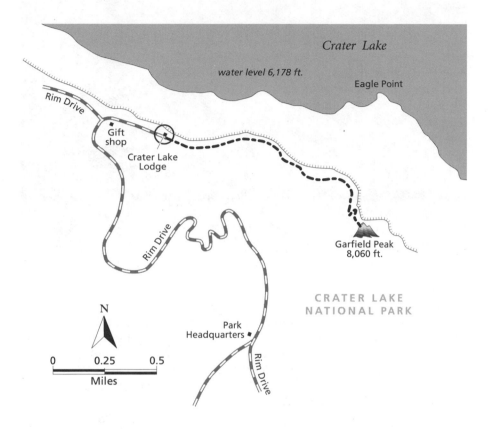

As the path to the Garfield Peak summit heads uphill from the lodge, snaking through enchanted forest pockets and peering over the rim's imposing crags, it passes high-elevation forests of whitebark pine, mountain hemlock, and subalpine fir. Clean and parklike, with picture-perfect vistas at every turn, the route brings to mind the idealized imagery of a nineteenth century landscape painting. It is, to quote Walt Whitman, a study in "pure luminous color." The rocks vary from orange to pink to purple to tan to gray to black and are splotched with Day-Glo yellow, red, and black lichen. Wildflowers of all hues and descriptions poke from between the rocks and carpet the occasional patches of grass and woods. The lake, of course, is a hundredfold bluer than the bluest sky. And the surrounding forests and meadows spread their iridescent greens, yellows, and blue-blacks to the horizon.

At the summit, a roomy flat with a smattering of windswept whitebark pines, cliffs shoot down 1,900 feet to the lake, near the Phantom Ship. If you dove off, you'd land in the water. Both the Rim Village and park headquarters can be seen far, far below.

Phantom Ship, Mt. Scott, Crater Lake from Garfield Peak.

This is an ideal spot for orienting yourself to local geography. Aside from old favorites such as Mounts Shasta, McLoughlin, and Thielsen, several other landmarks can be seen. Union Peak's jutting pyramid rises dramatically from the park's southwest corner. To the south and a little farther away, you see Devil's Peak, at the core of the Sky Lakes Wilderness. The Middle Fork of the Rogue flows northward off Devil's Peak, through the spectacular Seven Lakes Basin.

The rugged, summits to the northwest belong to the Rogue-Umpqua Divide range and are much older than other mountains in the vicinity. Fish Mountain is the highest peak in that group.

33 Annie Creek

Highlight:	A huge, steep-sided ash canyon near the Crater Lake National Park South Entrance.
Type of hike:	Day hike, loop.
Total distance:	1.7 miles.
Difficulty:	Moderate.
Elevation loss and gain:	200 feet.
Best months:	June–October.
Map:	USGS Crater Lake West quad.

Special considerations: There is lots of water, most of which comes from a huge spring less than 1 mile away, but don't drink it because of all the

Annie Creek

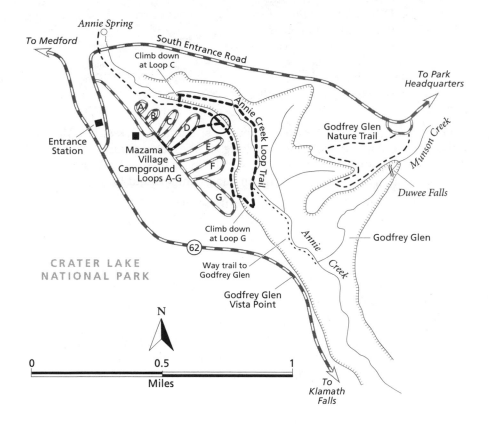

people and buildings nearby. The path contains two very steep pitches as the loop enters, then leaves the canyon. The steep, ashy north slopes retain snow in spring much later than the rest of the trail. Attempting to walk across these precarious snowbanks can be dangerous.

Finding the trailhead: Take Oregon Highway 62 north from Medford to the Crater Lake National Park South Entrance at milepost 73. Since every crossroads in southern Oregon has a sign directing you to that spot, it isn't hard to find. Immediately past the south entrance station, on the right, you find the turnoff to Mazama Village. Park at the store, continue through the parking lot on foot to the campground road, and turn right.

It's a five-minute walk to and through Loop D. The trail runs along the canyon rim at the far end of Loop D (also the far end of Loops C, E, F, and G). The actual trailhead is located at the amphitheater between Loops D and E. Go left at the trailhead for the quickest route into the canyon.

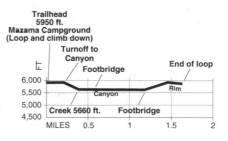

Parking and trailhead facilities: Your best bet is to park at the Mazama Village Store parking lot, since parking at the campground is for paid campers only. In addition to a store, you'll find gas, showers, cabins, and a laundromat. There are restrooms on each campground loop.

Key points (heading left from the amphitheater):
0.0 Amphitheater Trailhead.
0.2 Turnoff into canyon (go right).
0.4 Annie Creek.
0.6 Footbridge.
1.2 Footbridge.
1.4 Back on rim.
1.7 End of loop.

The hike: This little orphan of a hike (get it? Annie?) would be first on the list of magnificent trails at Crater Lake National Park, except that there are no views of the lake. Instead, it explores a spectacular and fascinating ash canyon.

Annie Creek Canyon is easy to find. Every loop in the Mazama Campground touches it. A popular vista point on OR 62, just east of the south entrance, provides an outstanding view of not only the Annie Creek Canyon but of an equally impressive side canyon, Godfrey Glen (see "Options").

The canyon is named for Annie Gaines, who visited Crater Lake in 1865 and reputedly was the first female to do so. The reason for the canyon's flat, parklike bottom is that the soft ash deposit into which the canyon is cut, fills an old, much wider, flat-bottomed glacial valley. The present valley bottom is the original, much harder valley floor before it filled up with ash.

Heading left (north) from the trailhead at the amphitheater, the path hugs the rim for 0.2 mile before making a sharp switchback and plunging into the gorge (do not try to follow any of the unmarked way-trails which also seem to lead into the gorge—they are extremely dangerous). Views along the rim reveal the steep bluffs and spires of the canyon walls and the grassy meadows of the canyon floor, with Annie Creek running down the middle.

The spires are caused by gas fumaroles that once made their way up through the compacted ash deposits. The minerals in the gas rendered those spots harder and slower to erode than the surrounding ash. The park's best spire formations may be seen off the Rim Drive at the Pinnacles.

(Note: If you continue hiking along the rim instead of taking the path down into the canyon, you come to Annie Springs, the source of Annie Creek. See "Options.")

Back at the start of the canyon climbdown, you can pick up an interpretive booklet for 75 cents. (It's free if you return the booklet when you're done.) The trail makes it to the canyon bottom in 0.2 mile and two steep switchbacks. The ashy hillside is very steep and loose but not as steep and loose as the hillside on the climb back up, 0.8 mile south.

Once at the bottom, the path follows the creek's southwest (campground) side, around the base of some ash slopes, for 0.2 mile. It then crosses a little footbridge to the more wooded northeast bank. Look for mountain hemlock, Shasta red fir, subalpine fir, and lodgepole pine. The scene soon opens out into an enchanted meadow that you won't want to leave. Buttercups, monkeyflower, Indian paintbrush, sedges, and horsetails thrive in the meadow. A highlight is Annie Creek Falls, a 15-foot vertical plunge that's just past where the trail crosses a little side creek.

After 0.3 mile, the path crosses another footbridge and returns to the southwest bank, continuing along the canyon bottom for another 0.3 mile.

Where the trail starts back up the hill, a faint, unoffficial way-trail continues straight ahead towards Godfrey Glen. The way-trail follows Annie Creek downstream for 0.3 mile but ends 0.3 mile short of Godfrey Glen. Hiking to Godfrey Glen involves either pushing through dense willow

Godfrey Glen.

brush or wading down the middle of Annie Creek in thigh- to waist-deep water. See "Options" for the Godfrey Glen rim trail.

Returning to the rim in a series of switchbacks, the Annie Creek Trail contours up a loose, steep, exposed ash slope, emerging at the far end of campground Loop G, 0.3 mile from the trailhead.

Options: *Annie Springs.* Instead of hiking down the north climb down into the canyon, continue north (straight) along the rim for 0.3 mile, to the South Entrance Road. Cross the road and follow the continuing trail for 0.1 mile to the source of Annie Creek. The spring is large and impressive but full of concrete, metal, and artificial impoundments.

Godfrey Glen. For an impressive view from the rim of Godfrey Glen, a large side canyon off Annie Creek, drive the South Entrance Road past Mazama Campground for 0.6 mile to the turnout for the Godfrey Glen Nature Trail. After walking 0.2 mile down the level trail, you come to the most spectacular-sounding waterfall you've ever heard, where Munson Creek courses through a narrow, vertical-walled ash gorge. While you can get tantalizingly close to the waterfall, you can't see it. A fantastic rim-top view into Godfrey Glen turns up soon after. Godfrey Glen is much like Annie Creek canyon: flat, meadowy, very pretty, and bordered by tremendous ash bluffs and spires. From the trail, the OR 62 Godfrey Glen vista point can be seen far in the distance.

If you're dying to see the Godfrey Glen Creek waterfall, called Duwee Falls, make the difficult side trip to Godfrey Glen described in the main hike, then bushwhack as far up Godfrey Glen Creek as you can. Or drive around to the Godfrey Glen vista point on OR 62 and get out your binoculars.

---

34 Union Peak

Highlights:	Spectacular panorama from the top of a steep-sided volcanic pyramid.
Type of hike:	Day hike, out and back.
Total distance:	About 11 miles.
Difficulty:	Easy for 5 miles, strenuous for 0.5 mile.
Elevation gain:	1,509 feet.
Best months:	Late June–October.
Map:	USGS Union Peak quad.

Special considerations: While this route lies entirely within Crater Lake National Park, no entrance stations are passed, so no fee is required. The last 0.5 mile to the summit may be impassable well into July. No water.

Finding the trailhead: Drive North from Medford on Oregon Highway 62 (Crater Lake Highway) to the well-marked spot inside Crater Lake

Union Peak

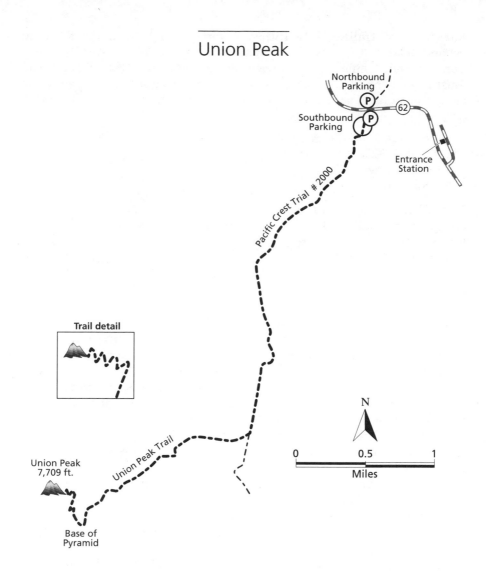

National Park where the Pacific Crest Trail (2000) crosses the highway at milepost 72. The crossing is located 1 mile before (west of) the turnoff to the park's south entrance station.

Look for a well-marked roadside turnout containing an interpretive sign for the Pacifc Crest Trail (PCT), on the north (left) side of the highway. This is the trailhead for the PCT northbound to Dutton Creek and Canada. The trailhead for the PCT southbound, to Union Peak and Mexico, is located opposite the interpretive sign on the south (right) side of the highway. An unnumbered, 200-foot dirt road leads to the southbound trailhead parking area.

Parking and trailhead facilities: A dirt parking lot at the trailhead accommodates 10 cars. The nearest camping is at Annie Creek Campground, 1 mile away. To reach the Annie Creek Campground, you must pay an entrance fee at the south entrance station, in addition to the campground fee. There is no water on this hike.

Key points:
0.0 Southbound PCT trailhead.
2.9 Union Peak Trail junction (go right).
4.9 Base of pyramid.
5.5 Summit.

The hike: Anyone who has approached Crater Lake National Park from the west has seen Union Peak. Just before the park boundary, at milepost 64 on Oregon Highway 62, an immense,

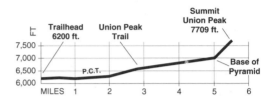

black, steep-sided volcanic mountain suddenly looms in front of you. Almost immediately, the highway curves away and the mysterious peak disappears from view. It is never seen again—not from the highway or any other road.

The mountain is Union Peak, the 7,709-foot sentinel of the park's south-west corner and one of Southern Oregon's more challenging hikes. The peak's 900-foot rock pyramid sticks out like a boil amid much more level surroundings. The horrendously steep, 0.5-mile final walk up the pyramid is immensely scenic, great fun (if exhausting), and well worth the lengthy trek to the base.

From the trailhead, the first 2 miles along the Pacific Crest Trail (2000) are relatively level and featureless as the path makes its way through a forest of mountain hemlock, Shasta red fir, and lodgepole pine. If you enjoy strolls through the woods, it's lovely; if not, the scenery gets much better farther up.

After 2 miles, the path begins a gentle rise out of the Union Creek drainage to the low divide with the Red Blanket Creek drainage. When you come to a long, level pumice flat covered with stunted lodgepole pines, 2.7 miles from the trailhead, you're at the Union Creek–Red Blanket divide and should start looking for the Union Peak junction.

In the 2.9 miles between the trailhead and the Union Peak junction, Union Peak is nowhere to be seen. Turning onto the well-marked but unnumbered Union Peak Trail (not shown on the Sky Lakes Wilderness map), the summit appears briefly, looking much closer than the 2.5-mile distance indicated on the trail sign. The peak then disappears for 1.5 miles, reappearing in a beautiful area of rolling hills with alternating forest stands and grassy openings. The problem is that the path keeps veering away from the summit cone, which it completely passes before finally doubling back. That's why it takes 2.5 miles to get there.

The pyramid's main feature is its steepness. At a trail gradient of 1,800 feet per mile, there isn't a steeper path anywhere in southern Oregon (the Mount McLoughlin Trail's final mile ascends 1,700 feet). There isn't a more beautiful trail, either. A profusion of wildflowers—penstemon, Indian paintbrush, lupine, and saxifrage—decorate the white, orange, purple, and black rock outcrops, creating memorable scenery. It's a well-engineered path too, except for the final 100 feet which scramble up a sharp, cindery rock face. Watch for loose boulders, slippery pitches, and steep drop-offs.

From the summit, you can't quite see into Crater Lake but you can see the cliffs of the far shore, with Mounts Thielsen and Bailey rising behind. To the south, much of the Sky Lakes Wilderness is visible, especially the Red Blanket Creek drainage.

The peak's geology becomes obvious at the summit. The mountain is a volcanic cone of cinder and ash, with much dense, pasty lava in the mix and spatter formations on top. It is not an ancillary cone to Mount Mazama, where Crater Lake is located, but a major summit in its own right.

It appears that a south-flowing glacier on Mount Mazama once flowed past Union Peak into Red Blanket Creek. The evidence was later obscured by tons of volcanic ash from the major eruption of Mount Mazama, 6,600 years ago, which ultimately formed Crater Lake. Many of the tons of ash burying Union Peak's base no doubt came from Mazama, although a huge amount also spewed from Union Peak itself.

Union Peak.

Option: *Union Peak from the Sky Lakes.* To reach Union Peak from the Sky Lakes Wilderness, follow the Pacific Crest Trail (2000) north into Crater Lake National Park. The shortest route follows the Red Blanket Trail (1090, Hike 36), to the Stuart Falls Trail (1087), to the PCT, to the Union Peak Trail, arriving atop Union Peak after 10.5 miles.

35 Pumice Flat

Highlights:	A geologically interesting shortcut to the Pacific Crest Trail, with highlights at Pumice Flat and the PCT junction.
Type of hike:	Day hike, out and back.
Total distance:	About 6 miles.
Difficulty:	Easy.
Elevation gain:	490 feet.
Best months:	June–October.
Map:	USGS Union Peak quad.

Special considerations: Although the trail lies entirely within Crater Lake National Park, no entrance stations are passed to reach the trailhead, so no fee is required. There is no water on this path.

Finding the trailhead: This may be the only roadside trailhead with no parking whatsoever. The trailhead is fairly well marked on the south side of Oregon Highway 62, 3 miles east of the turnoff to the south entrance station, near milepost 76. Park at the picnic area on the left side of the road and walk 0.2 mile east along OR 62 to the trailhead on the right. (Be cautious: there's very little road shoulder and fast traffic.) The trailhead sign is small and much easier to see heading west than east.

Parking and trailhead facilities: Park as close as possible to the east entrance of the Lodgepole Picnic Area, which has room for 20 cars and contains picnic tables and pit toilets.

Key points:
0.0 Pumice Flat Trailhead.
2.0 Pumice Flat.
3.0 Pacific Crest Trail (2000) junction.

The hike: This easy 3-mile trek is mainly used as a shortcut by southbound Pacific Crest Trail (2000) hikers wishing to save a mile. Early in the season, PCT through hikers often use the Pumice Flat Trail (unnumbered) and the Stuart Falls Trail (1087) as alternate routes because the highest elevation that way is 6,300 feet, versus 6,800 feet on the PCT. While possibly not as scenic as

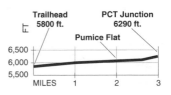

Pumice Flat

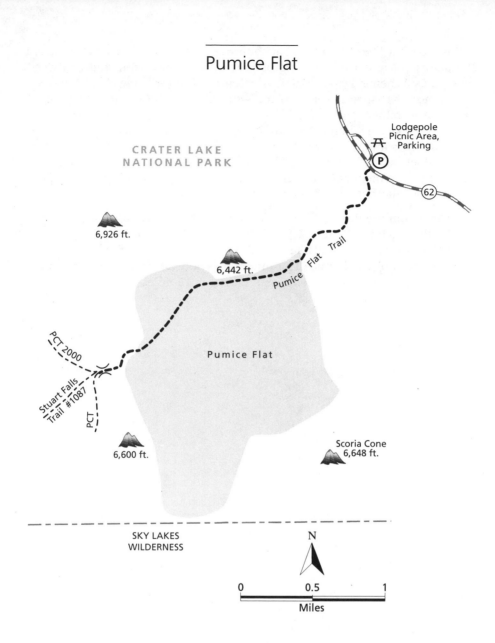

some other paths in this book, the Pumice Flat Trail boasts several interesting features.

From the trailhead, the path wanders through the woods for 1.5 miles, making its way around Bear Bluff, a handsome, steep-sided, 6,445-foot summit. Beyond Bear Bluff, the path levels off (it never was very steep), as makes its way onto Pumice Flat.

Pumice Flat lives up to the "flat" billing but is made of ash, not pumice. Pumice is volcanic froth. The flat is gray and covered with stunted lodgepole pines. When lodgepole pines, which are noted for being able to survive where no other species can, become stunted, you know you're looking at truly lousy soil.

For the hike's final mile, a row of impressive, white, unnamed, 6,900-foot peaks appears immediately to the west. The last 0.2 mile climbs gently over a 6,300-foot saddle on the same 6,900-foot ridge, meeting both the PCT and the east end of the Stuart Falls Trail at the Pumice Flat Trail's prettiest spot, a meadowy glade surrounded by white rock formations.

Option: From the Pumice Flat/PCT/Stuart Falls junction, it's 4 miles north on the PCT to OR 62 (Hike 34) and 2.3 miles straight ahead on the Stuart Falls Trail to Stuart Falls (Hike 36). The Stuart Falls Trail rejoins the PCT 6 miles south of the Pumice Flat junction. The PCT south from the junction encounters no major scenic highlights for 15 miles, until it enters the Seven Lakes Basin.

Sky Lakes Wilderness

The broad and majestic Sky Lakes Wilderness follows the crest of the High Cascades from the Crater Lake National Park boundary south for 30 miles. It culminates at Mount McLoughlin (9,495 feet), southern Oregon's highest peak and perhaps the most perfectly conical volcano in the United States. Spectacular Devil's Peak (7,582 feet), halfway between McLoughlin and Crater Lake, stands guard over the Seven Lakes Basin. Other highlights include the Blue Canyon Basin, the Sky Lakes Basin, the canyon of the Middle Fork Rogue, and Stuart Falls.

The 114,000-acre wilderness is unusual in that instead of a few trailheads leading to many destinations, it has many trailheads leading to a few destinations (the Forest Service has closed down a lot of the trails). Trails range from long and gentle, across ash fields, broad moraines, and glacial valleys, to steep and brutal on the major summits. Of the hundreds of named lakes, most are small, shallow ponds, some of which dry up in summer. The wilderness boasts 25 to 30 major lakes, ranging in size from a couple of acres to 40 acres. All lakes are quite shallow but many boast surprising purity and clarity. The major lakes are all worth a peek.

---

36 Stuart Falls

Highlights:	This trail begins in a low-elevation, old-growth forest, climbs along a steep, waterfall-laden gorge, and wanders past high-elevation meadows. It ends up at one of the prettiest waterfalls around. Options abound.
Type of hike:	Day hike or backpack, out and back.
Total distance:	About 10 miles.
Difficulty:	Moderate.
Elevation gain:	1,600 feet.
Season:	May–November.
Maps:	USGS Red Blanket Mountain and Union Peak quads.

Finding the trailhead: Take Oregon Highway 62 north from Medford to the Prospect turnoff past milepost 43. Turn right and proceed 1 block to Mill Creek Drive, then turn right again and continue for half a block to the Prospect–Butte Falls Road at the Prospect Hotel. Turn left towards Butte Falls and left again 1.5 miles later up Forest Road 6205, Red Blanket Road. Bear left at the fork after 0.3 mile, where the sign says FR 6205. Upper Red Blanket road is closed and gated in winter. Follow the dusty, occasionally rutted route 11 miles to the trailhead.

Parking and trailhead facilities: Fifteen cars can park at the trailhead.

Stuart Falls

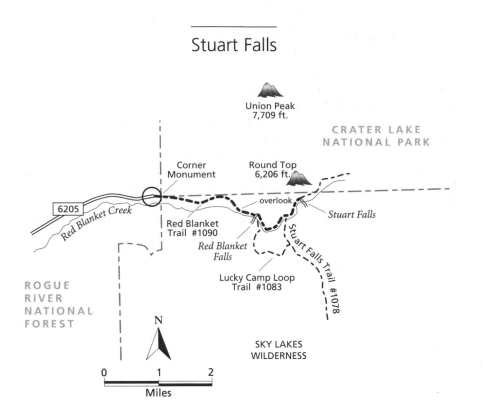

Key points:
0.0 Red Blanket Trailhead.
0.2 Crater Lake National Park corner monument.
2.2 Red Blanket Creek overlook.
3.2 Red Blanket Falls.
3.3 Lucky Camp Loop Trail junction.
4.5 Stuart Falls Trail junction (go left).
5.0 Stuart Falls.

The hike: This challenging, highly scenic trail leads to one of the region's prettier waterfalls. Beginning at the Sky Lakes' second lowest trailhead (3,800 feet), the route's lower portions open up fairly early. You can usually make it to Red Blanket Falls by mid-May and to Stuart Falls a month later.

Much of the path lies within 0.5 mile of the Crater Lake National Park boundary. Look carefully on the left at mile 0.2 for a concrete monument marking the park's southwest corner. It's 16 straight-line

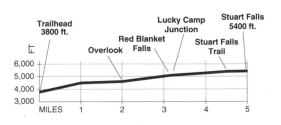

Stuart Falls.

miles from the monument to the park's southeast corner and 20 miles to the northwest corner.

After passing the monument, the Red Blanket Trail (1090), climbs steadily for its first 2 miles, with occasional level pitches, clinging to a sometimes steep, densely wooded hillside out of view of Red Blanket Creek, which it supposedly follows. The downed trees in the first 2 miles were knocked over during a huge storm in the winter of 1995–1996, which closed the trail for a season. The trees had been weakened by a seven-year drought.

Trees in this middle-elevation forest of Douglas-fir, white fir, sugar pine, and western hemlock are up to 100 years old and 36 inches in diameter. Look for an area where much of the forest burned down 30 or 40 years ago and was repopulated by scattered Douglas-fir mother trees, easily identified by their immense size and fire-scarred bases. Look also for shade-loving understory plants such as trillium, little princess pine (whose root is used in some brands of root beer), and dwarf Oregongrape (used for a yellow dye).

Eventually, trail meets creek at a narrow rock gorge with a huge side-creek waterfall on the opposite side. The next mile, sometimes muddy, continues at a fairly steep ascent, winding through a forest broken by wet seeps of willow and alder brush.

Red Blanket Falls turns up 3.2 miles from the trailhead. You catch glimpses of at least three waterfalls here as the trail quickly ascends, but you cannot see all of Red Blanket Falls unless you're adventurous to the point of insanity. Most readily visible is the upper falls, a 20-foot-high gush of log-strewn water. At the bottom, there's a second, 50-foot plunge that the trail goes nowhere near. Look for the far end of the Lucky Camp Loop Trail (1091) just above Red Blanket Falls.

Beyond Red Blanket Falls, the trail levels off, the creek slows down, and the valley opens out to a series of grassy, tree-lined flats. The still-lush forest has now evolved into an association of mountain hemlock, western white pine, Shasta fir, lodgepole pine, and a few Engelmann spruce. It's a good place to observe elk, if you're very quiet.

The wet meadows are fascinating. If rainfall has been above average, the meadow grows larger because conifer seedlings, which try to creep from the edges, are drowned and die back. If rainfall has been below average, the meadows get smaller as the seedlings encroach. On dry meadows, the opposite is true. There, seedlings that try to creep in from the edges die from lack of water during drought years and thrive during wet years.

When the path enters a narrow, green gorge along Red Blanket Creek, at mile 4.5, it means the Red Blanket Trail is about to end at the junction with the Stuart Falls Trail (1078), a remnant of the old Oregon Skyline Trail. Before the Pacific Crest Trail was built, the Skyline Trail was the main South Cascades pathway, entering Crater Lake National Park at Stuart Falls Camp, a popular overnight camping spot.

Magnificent Stuart Falls, at mile 5, fans out over a 60-foot chunk of lava like a Spanish fan, dropping into a clean, quiet pool. It's a terrific spot that can get a little crowded. Climb up the rocks on the north side for a fantastic wildflower display.

Options: *North on Stuart Falls Trail.* By continuing north from Stuart Falls, you'll hit the National Park boundary after 0.3 mile but won't enter the park for 0.6 mile. It's 2.3 miles from Stuart Falls to the junction with the Pumice Flat Trail (Hike 35) and the Pacific Crest Trail (PCT). Look for glimpses of steep-sided, flat-topped Bald Top Mountain (6,200 feet), towering overhead to the northwest as you leave the Stuart Falls area. From the Pumice Flat Trail (unnumbered) junction, it's 4 miles to OR 62 via the PCT, past the Union Peak Trail (Hike 34). It's 3 miles to OR 62 via Pumice Flat.

Lucky Camp Loop. On the return trek, consider taking a short loop trail by continuing south on the Stuart Falls Trail instead of returning to the Red Blanket Trail. You'll have to ford Red Blanket Creek to do this, through ankle-deep water with a silty bottom and no stepping stones. The Stuart Falls Trail meets the Lucky Camp Trail after a dull, if level mile. Things perk up during the Lucky Camp Trail's first mile, where a myriad of springs ooze out across moss-covered rocks. There's a fabulous view of Union Peak here. The Lucky Camp Trail's second mile wanders through a series of uninteresting wooded flats, before meeting Red Blanket Creek again, immediately above Red Blanket Falls. The creek crossing is not difficult most of the time.

37 Mudjekeewis Mountain

Highlights:	A fantastic panorama of the immense Middle Fork Rogue canyon and the Devil's Peak area. Continue to McKie Meadow and make a loop by returning via Tom and Jerry Mountain.
Type of hike:	Day hike or backpack, loop.
Total distance:	11.5 miles.
Difficulty:	Moderate to strenuous.
Elevation gain:	1,619 feet.
Best months:	June–November.
Maps:	USGS Devil's Peak, Red Blanket Mountain, and Imnaha Creek quads.

Finding the trailhead: Take Oregon Highway 62, Crater Lake Highway, north from Medford to the Prospect turnoff past milepost 43. Turn right, proceed for 1 block, then turn right again onto Mill Creek Drive and continue for half a block to the Prospect Hotel. At the hotel, turn left onto the

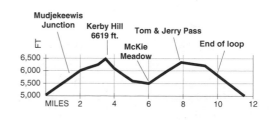

Mudjekeewis Mountain

Prospect–Butte Falls Road. Continue for 3 miles, then bear left onto Forest Road 37. Bear left again after 3 more miles on Forest Road 3795, toward Bessie Rock. It's 6 miles to the Tom and Jerry Trailhead.

Parking and trailhead facilities: The trailhead accommodates 20 cars.

Key points:
> 0.0 Tom and Jerry Trailhead.
> 1.5 Mudjekeewis Trail junction (go right).
> 3.5 Kerby Hill overlook.
> 6.0 McKie Meadow, end of Tom and Jerry Trail (go left).
> 7.8 Tom and Jerry pass.
> 10.0 Mudjekeewis Trail junction (completion of loop).
> 11.5 Trailhead.

The hike: The route begins at the Tom and Jerry Trailhead on the Tom and Jerry Trail (1084) and rises a fairly stiff 1,500 feet in the first 3 miles, remaining mostly in the woods. Although it's a nice woods, there's nothing remarkable until the summit meadow at 2.8 miles. At mile 1.5 from the trailhead, the Mudjekeewis Trail (1085) takes off uphill to the right. While both the Tom and Jerry Trail and the Mudjekeewis Trail end up at McKie Cabin, the Mudjekeewis is 0.5 mile farther and Tom and Jerry crests 300 feet lower. The view where the Mudjekeewis Trail crests compensates for the added distance and height.

Turning right onto the Mudjekeewis Trail, the summit, at Kerby Hill, 3 miles from the trailhead, reveals a glorious mountaintop wildflower meadow. The main wildflowers are phlox, heather, lupine, and Indian paintbrush.

The panorama is even more impressive than the wildflowers. To the south, Kerby Hill drops abruptly into the emerald gorge of the Middle Fork Rogue, then quickly rises up to Devil's Peak and the Seven Lakes Basin, with Mounts McLoughlin and Shasta tossed in for good measure. Look for a fantastic view of the Middle Fork Rogue cascading over Boston Bluff.

To the east, the view drops over a cliff into a lakeless glacial cirque, then across a broad, forested glacial valley to McKie Meadow, which you can't quite see. To the north, at the far end of the rim on which you're standing, 0.5 mile away, stands Mudjekeewis Mountain itself, four feet higher than Kerby Hill. Beyond Mudjekeewis Mountain lie Red Blanket Creek and the peaks of the Crater Lake rim.

An eastward-moving glacier probably originated at the base of Mudjekeewis/ Kerby Hill rim, which leveled the now flat expanse around McKie Cabin, then joined another glacier moving westward from the Cascade crest. The entire mass then flowed down Halifax Creek to merge with the huge Middle Fork glacier (which didn't have a name 10,000 years ago), coming in from the Seven Lakes Basin to the south.

From Kerby Hill, the trail plunges 1,000 feet in 2 miles to McKie Cabin, which lies smack in the middle of nowhere, at the bottom of a broad, densely forested glacial valley. The cabin site, campsite, and nearby meadow are a favorite destination of horse people.

At McKie Camp, you pick up the far end of the Tom and Jerry Trail for the return loop (go left). You also pick up the McKie Camp Trail (1889) described as an option. As noted, the Tom and Jerry Trail climbs to a 6,300-foot saddle 1.8 miles from McKie Cabin, then competes the loop back to the trailhead in a long walk through the woods with few landmarks.

Option: *McKie Camp Trail—northeast.* This path travels gently northeast from McKie Meadow, picking up the Stuart Falls Trail (1078) in 1.5 miles and the Pacific Crest Trail (2000) in 2 miles. Head south on the PCT for 0.2 mile for a look at a large ash flat called the Oregon Desert.

38 Middle Fork Rogue

Highlights: A one-way trek past a beautiful meadow with multiple springs, over a summit, down one of the steeper
trail segments in this book and out southern
Oregon's mightiest glacial valley.

Type of hike: Day hike or backpack, shuttle.

Total distance: 12.5 miles.

Difficulty: South to north—moderate to easy. North to south—
easy for 6 miles, strenuous for 2.5 miles, easy for 3.5
miles.

Elevation gain and loss: 1,082-foot gain, then 2,782-foot loss.

Best months: June–October for King Spruce/Alta Lake Trails. May
(or earlier)–November for the Middle Fork Trail.

Maps: USGS Imnaha Creek and Devil's Peak quads.

Special considerations: Hikers using the described route (Seven Lakes
Trail to King Spruce Trail to Alta Lake Trail to Middle Fork Trail), should
begin at the Seven Lakes Trailhead and finish at the Middle Fork Trailhead
to hit the segment that drops 1,800 feet in 2 miles in the downhill direction. In the opposite direction, the route from the Middle Fork Trailhead
to either the Halifax junction or the base of Boston Bluff, is a lovely, out-
and-back early season hike along the Middle Fork. The Halifax Trail is not
accessible before mid-July due to high water and may soon be abandoned.
The Seven Lakes Trailhead is normally under snow until mid-June while
the Middle Fork Trailhead usually opens up in mid-April.

Finding the trailhead: For the Middle Fork and Seven Lakes Trailheads,
take Oregon Highway 62, Crater Lake Highway, north from Medford past
milepost 43 to the Prospect turnoff. Turn right, proceed for 1 block, then
turn right again onto Mill Creek Drive. A half a block later, turn left at the
Prospect Hotel onto the Prospect–Butte Falls Road. Continue for 3 miles,
then bear left onto Forest Road 37 (paved and gravel).

For the Middle Fork Trailhead, it's 7.5 miles on FR 37 to Forest Road
3785. Follow FR 3785 left 3 miles to the trailhead.

For the Seven Lakes Trailhead, follow FR 37 for 12 miles to Forest Road
3780. The sign for the Seven Lakes Trailhead at the FR 37–FR 3780 junction is visible only in the
direction heading back
towards Prospect. Look for
FR 37 to make a right-
angle right turn, with a
wide gravel road taking off
to the left. Proceed 3 miles
to the end of FR 3780.

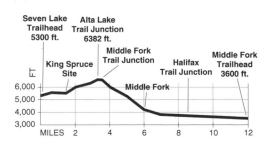

Middle Fork Rogue

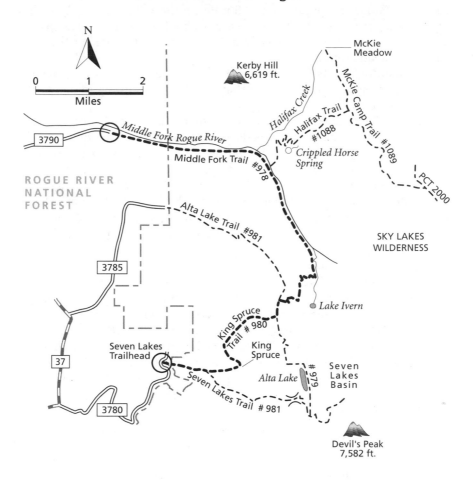

Parking and trailhead facilities: The Seven Lakes Trailhead holds 20 cars and has a horse ramp. The Middle Fork Trailhead accommodates 10 cars.

Key points:
- 0.0 Seven Lakes Trailhead.
- 0.6 King Spruce Trail junction (go left).
- 1.5 King Spruce Camp.
- 3.5 Alta Lake Trail junction (go left).
- 4.0 Middle Fork Trail junction (go right).
- 6.5 First glimpse of Middle Fork.
- 9.0 Halifax Trail junction.
- 12.5 Middle Fork Trailhead.

The hike: Most people who hike from the Seven Lakes Trailhead are more interested in the Seven Lakes Basin than anything else. They tend to regard the King Spruce junction, 0.6 mile up the path, as merely an indicator on the return trip that they are almost back to their car. The primary use of the King Spruce Trail is as an alternate route back to the Seven Lakes Trailhead from Alta Lake.

This hike highlights the beautiful King Spruce Trail and includes it as part of an unusual and fascinating route which has nothing to do with the Seven Lakes Basin.

From the Seven Lakes Trailhead it's a steady uphill climb on the Seven Lakes Trail (981), through the woods to the King Spruce junction. Turn left at the junction. Once on the King Spruce Trail (980), the path levels off, arriving at the King Spruce site in 1 mile.

King Spruce is a large wet meadow, with the trail contouring above mostly in the woods. The meadow is typical of the area, dominated by corn lily, butterweed, coneflower, Indian paintbrush, Queen Anne's lace, columbine, penstemon, and many other species. The map shows an established campsite.

As pretty as the place is, one wonders why they call it "King" Spruce. There are a few small Engelmann spruces scattered around but they are certainly not the king. The largest and most dominant trees are mountain hemlock and Shasta red fir, with lots of western white pine. This is, however, a typical spruce site: moist, high elevation, and fairly sheltered.

Immediately after the King Spruce meadow, the trail begins a moderate ascent, passing four springs in rapid succession, all with beautiful vistas westward. Every spring is larger and prettier than the last, culminating in a lovely cascading creek on the steep hillside. The springs all occupy open seep areas surrounded by willow and wildflowers, the showiest of which are Indian paintbrush and tower delphinium. The final spring is 2 miles from the Seven Lakes Trailhead and 1.5 miles from the King Spruce Trail's far end.

Beyond the four springs, the path becomes very rocky (and less interesting) as it continues to climb. It eventually crosses a false summit with a dry, grassy meadow, then starts downhill, only to begin climbing again. On August 14, 1999 (following one of the snowiest winters ever), there was an incredible amount of snow here, including a 6-foot-high drift. The ridgetop area lies between 6,300 and 6,400 feet, compared to the 5,300-foot trailhead.

Three and a half miles from the Seven Lakes Trailhead, the King Spruce Trail ends at the Alta Lake Trail (979) junction (6,387 feet). Turn left (north) and follow the Alta Lake Trail for 0.5 mile to the upper end of the Middle Fork Trail, which takes off to the right. (Or turn right onto the Alta Lake Trail and hike for 1.5 miles to visit Alta Lake, a fabulous camping spot.) The 0.5 mile on the Alta Lake Trail, left from the King Spruce Trail, is densely wooded and slightly downhill, crossing a couple of level glades. Were you to remain on the Alta Lake Trail in this direction instead of turning onto the Middle Fork Trail, you'd arrive at the Alta Lake Trailhead 4 miles away, at 4,900 feet.

The initial 2 miles on the Middle Fork Trail, from the Alta Lake/Middle Fork junction, drops 1,800 feet in 25 switchbacks and ranks among the steeper extended-trail segments in the Sky Lakes Wilderness. From the steepness, and the presence nearby of names such as "Boston Bluff," one would expect this segment to cross an area of rock outcrops and scree slopes. It does not. Instead, it remains in the woods for almost the entire length. Near the top, you are briefly greeted with a panorama of the Middle Fork Canyon but the route quickly settles down to serious descending, leveling off briefly one-third of the way down at a small, wet meadow. Do not take the trail through the meadow but stay to the left.

Two-thirds of the way down, you arrive at the highlight: a fantastic view of part of Boston Bluff, which from this angle is seen as an immense, narrow, pointed monolith soaring 1,500 feet overhead. The Boston Bluff formation is almost a mile long and you're only seeing the very end. It gets much higher. At 0.3 mile past the Boston Bluff view, the Middle Fork Trail offers a dizzying peek into the churning, eroded canyon of Lake Ivern Creek. Lake Ivern is described in Hike 40.

Where the Middle Fork Trail finally begins to level off, it's still 0.5 mile before you catch sight of the Middle Fork of the Rogue River. But the stream eventually shows up, 2.5 miles from Halifax Junction and 6 miles from the Middle Fork Trailhead. The river is fast, beautiful, and lined with white cobbles and boulders.

The Middle Fork here flows down an immense glacial valley, the largest and deepest in Oregon, marked by steep, even sides and a flat bottom. Since the river has cut a small canyon into the larger valley, the trail's designers chose to locate the path away from the river, on a more level bench. Hence, the scarcity of river approaches.

The elongated ridge rising above the river's opposite bank prior to Halifax junction is part of Bareface Mountain. Farther down the path, after the Middle Fork Trail (and the river and the canyon); makes a 90-degree turn from north to west, Mudjekeewis Mountain (elevation 6,623 ft.) becomes the canyon's north face.

The trail along the river above Halifax Junction remains mostly in view of the water but a fair distance away. The river here is lined with low dirt bluffs. This is the best river access you're going to get. Below Halifax Junction, you can't see the river at all and reaching it involves pushing through jackstrawed trees and dense brush. Above Halifax Junction, the forest understory is much less cluttered.

A dominant understory species in the path along the Middle Fork, is little princess pine, a member of the wintergreen family. A few years ago, little princess pine officially replaced sassafras as the root of choice in natural root beer. The species is clonal, which means individual plants are connected underground to other plants through root runners. Whatever is harvested, within reason, will grow back within a couple of weeks (although it's illegal to pick little princess pine without a permit).

The Halifax Trail (1088) takes off to the right, 9 miles from the Seven Lakes Trailhead. It's 0.2 mile on the Halifax Trail to a beautiful wooded glade on the river, offering the best river access and the prettiest spot on the Middle Fork Trail. If you can get across the river, which you often can't, you can climb to Crippled Horse Spring in just 1 mile. To reach Crippled Horse Spring, the Halifax Trail fords the Middle Fork. As long as significant snow remains in the high country, the river will be impassable due to high water.

Below Halifax Junction, the species composition of the forest changes dramatically. The woods here consist mostly of small Douglas-fir, sugar pine, grand fir, and incense cedar. The once ubiquitous mountain hemlock has disappeared, replaced by western hemlock. Pacific yew abounds in the understory, along with little princess pine, trillium, dwarf Oregongrape, whortleberry, Pacific dogwood, and varnishleaf ceanothus. Look for a bunch of bunchberry dogwood near mile 3. While common farther north, the species is rare in the Rogue drainage.

Between Halifax Junction and the trailhead, there's not a hill, side creek, or clearing, and only three brief glimpses of the river. If you've hiked in from the Middle Fork Trailhead, after 3 miles of sensory deprivation, the spot where the trail swings south is a major highlight. The good news is that at 3,600 feet, the Middle Fork Trailhead is the lowest in the Sky Lakes and accessible in April.

Options: *Alta Lake Trail.* From the junction with the King Spruce and Alta Lake Trails, it's 1.5 steepish miles (right) to Alta Lake (6,800 feet) and another 1 mile back to the Seven Lakes Trail. Alta Lake is among the prettiest and most unusual lakes in the Sky Lakes (Hike 39). The primary use of the King Spruce Trail is as part of a (beautiful) loop that follows the Seven Lakes Trail to the Alta Lake Trail to the King Spruce Trail and back to the Seven Lakes Trail.

Halifax Trail. Presuming you make it across the Middle Fork, the seldom-used Halifax Trail rises 1,000 feet in 1 mile to Crippled Horse Spring. The path starts to level off at the spring. It's 3 miles on the Halifax Trail from the Middle Fork junction to the aptly named Solace Camp, then 2 more miles (heading north) to McKie Camp. As of 1999, the Forest Service had not decided whether to keep the Halifax Trail open or abandon it.

39 Seven Lakes Basin

Highlights:	A hugely popular trail into the magnificent Seven Lakes Basin, with side trips to Devil's Peak, Alta Lake, and Lake Ivern. This may be southern Oregon's most scenic hike, especially when combined with Devil's Peak Trail.
Type of hike:	Day hike or backpack, out and back.
Total distance:	About 10 miles.
Difficulty:	Strenuous.
Elevation gain and loss:	1,600-foot gain, 800-foot loss.
Best months:	Late June–October.
Maps:	USGS Imnaha Creek and Devil's Peak quads.

Special considerations: The Seven Lakes Trail and the Pacific Crest Trail from Devil's Peak both follow steep north-slope routes into the Seven Lakes Basin and may contain impassable snowbanks well into July. The density of mosquitoes can be astonishing in the basin in June and July. The situation gets better in August and much better in September. There is adequate water along most routes, except for the Devil's Peak Trail, but also much horse traffic.

Finding the trailhead: For the Seven Lakes Trailhead, take Oregon Highway 62 north from Medford to the Prospect turnoff past milepost 43. Follow signs to the town of Prospect. From OR 62, turn right on First Street and right again on Mill Creek Drive. At the Prospect Hotel, turn left onto the Prospect–Butte Falls Road. After 3 miles, bear left onto Forest Road 37 and follow it 13 miles to Forest Road 3780. The sign for the Seven Lakes Trailhead is at the FR 37–FR 3780 junction but can be seen only in the direction heading towards Prospect. Look for FR 37 to make a right-angle turn right with a wide gravel road talking off left. Proceed 3 miles up FR 3780 to the trailhead.

Parking and trailhead facilities: The Seven Lakes trailhead accommodates 20 cars and has a horse-loading ramp. The nearest Forest Service Campground is Big Ben, on Forest Road 37, 2 miles past the FR 3780 turnoff.

Key points:
- 0.0 Seven Lakes Trailhead.
- 2.0 Frog Lake.
- 3.5 Summit and Devil's Peak Trail junction.
- 3.7 Alta Lake junction (0.7 mile to Alta Lake).
- 4.3 South Lake.
- 4.5 Cliff Lake.
- 4.7 Pacific Crest Trail junction.
- 5.0 Middle Lake.

Seven Lakes Basin

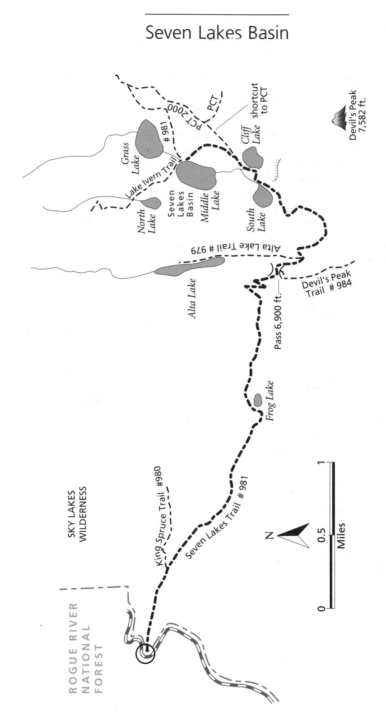

Grass Lake

981

Lake Ivern Trail

North Lake

Seven Lakes Basin

Middle Lake

Cliff Lake

shortcut to PCT

PCT 2000

PCT

South Lake

Devil's Peak 7,582 ft.

Alta Lake Trail # 979

Alta Lake

Pass 6,900 ft.

Devil's Peak Trail # 984

Frog Lake

King Spruce Trail #980

Seven Lakes Trail # 981

SKY LAKES WILDERNESS

ROGUE RIVER NATIONAL FOREST

N

0   0.5   1
Miles

The hike: From the Seven Lakes Trailhead it's a fairly relentless 2-mile uphill trek on the Seven Lakes Trail (981) to Frog Lake, through a middle-elevation, second-growth forest of white fir, sugar pine, lodgepole pine, and western white pine. While a few brushy areas adorn this segment, a large burn a decade ago has nearly grown back.

Frog Lake is the forest canopy's first real opening. The charming, 2-acre pool signals the start of the real scenery, with impressive lava cliffs just to the east. The camping ban at Frog Lake has recently been lifted and the site is now officially "rehabilitated." Let's hope it stays that way.

Beginning 1 mile beyond Frog Lake, the steepening path surmounts a series of switchbacks. Three and a half miles from the trailhead, the trail emerges at a wooded, 6,900-foot saddle overlooking the Seven Lakes Basin. The view is breathtaking, especially shortly after you start down.

At the Seven Lakes saddle, the Devil's Peak Trail (984) takes off on the right. If you have a hankering to climb Devils Peak and visit the Seven Lakes Basin on the same trip, do Devil's Peak first. That way, you can make a spectacular loop of the Pacific Crest Trail's steep plunge into the basin in the downhill direction. See Hike 41, the Devil's Peak climb, for a description of the Seven Lakes Basin's geology.

Whatever else you do, be absolutely sure to make the short side trip to Alta Lake, the largest, most unusual, and probably the prettiest of the Seven Lakes, and the only one not inside the basin. The Alta Lake Trail (979) lies 0.2 mile beyond the Devil's Peak Trail junction, to the left off the Seven Lakes Trail. It's a level, 0.5-mile hike to the lake. See "Options."

After the tantalizing preview from the saddle and a 1-mile descent with a 550-foot elevation loss, you reach the basin proper. The descent winds through a forest of Shasta fir, lodgepole pine, subalpine fir, and mountain hemlock, with several small wildflower meadows breaking the monotony. Much of the terrain is open, offering frequent barren hillsides and long vistas.

The magnificent basin contains forests, many moist grassy openings, springs, marshes, bluffs, and rocky crests. The first lake, South Lake, is a clear, steep-sided tarn surrounded by an airy woods of mostly lodgepole pine. The lake is unstocked and few campsites are available.

Cliff Lake, 4.5 miles from the trailhead, is among the Sky Lakes' most beautiful. The deep blue pool hugs the base of a tortured, 1,000-foot lava wall which looks like it might have been coughed up from Hell. The cliff is not part of Devil's Peak but belongs to a rocky dome that juts up in the middle of the basin. While Cliff Lake is the most coveted camping spot because of its beauty and forested shore, there is little level space except near the outlet.

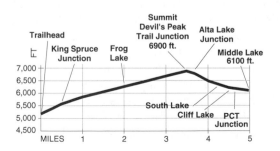

Beyond Cliff Lake, 4.7 miles from the trailhead, you arrive at the junction with Trail 900 (heading right), a shortcut spur to the Pacific Crest Trail (2000), which heads south towards Devil's Peak.

Continuing past the Trail 900 shortcut spur on the Seven Lakes Trail, you quickly arrive at another junction, with the Pacific Crest Trail heading right and the Seven Lakes Trail continuing straight. The PCT here is actually another shortcut spur. If you follow it, you will have 0.3 mile to decide whether to head north towards Canada or south towards Mexico.

With all those junctions and shortcuts behind you, it's 0.3 mile to Middle Lake and the Lake Ivern Trailhead, 5 miles from the Seven Lakes Trailhead parking area. Middle Lake is the basin's second largest after Alta Lake. While not quite as pretty as Cliff Lake, there is plenty of camping and an awesome view of Devil's Peak towering immediately south. From Middle Lake, you can see the Devil's Peak Trail on the ridge just to the right of Devil's Peak. At Middle Lake, camp in designated areas only and tether your horses in designated areas.

Although the official hike for this chapter ends at Middle Lake, the Seven Lakes Trail continues for another 0.8 mile, inscribing a wide arc around Grass Lake and crossing two large, fast-flowing creeks (the trail runs slightly uphill from Grass lake), before ending for good at it's third encounter with the PCT (go left at this last PCT junction for the Sevenmile Marsh Trailhead and right for Devil's Peak).

Grass Lake is stocked with brook trout. Much of the lake is surrounded by a vast marshy meadow where horses are not allowed. Camping is permitted at the better-defined and more wooded west shore. Several side trails, marked "camping" and "horse camp," lead there.

Options: *Sevenmile Trail.* The popular Sevenmile Trail (3703), reaches the Seven Lakes Basin in the same distance as the Seven Lakes Trail, and it doesn't climb a 6,900-foot saddle to get there. The route offers the best early-season entry into the area. The 5,500-foot trailhead, at a small campground, may be the Sky Lakes' prettiest.

The Sevenmile Trail is easier but less scenic than the Seven Lakes Trail. The basin somehow feels more special if you first view it from a 6,900-foot saddle, with immense, craggy mountains all around, and then climb down into it. On the Sevenmile route, you merely hike through the woods for a long time and end up at a bunch of pretty lakes.

To reach the Sevenmile Trailhead, follow the directions to the Cold Springs Trailhead, except continue on OR 140 past the Cold Spring turnoff to Westside Road, near milepost 43. Take the paved Westside Road left for 17 miles, to where it becomes Sevenmile Road and swings sharply east (right). The gravel Forest Road 3300 takes off there. After 3 miles, FR 3300 arrives at a complex junction with a sign directing you to the Sevenmile Trailhead in 6 miles. Follow Forest Road 3334 through old-growth forest to the trailhead and campground. The trailhead elevation is 5,500 feet while the elevation at Middle Lake, 5 miles away, is only 6,100 feet.

The Sevenmile Trail spends its early portion passing Sevenmile Marsh.

The marsh consists mostly of flat, grassy areas alongside a creek, downhill from the gently climbing trail. At mile 0.8, the marsh widens considerably, with the abrupt, forested wall of Klamath Point (7,210 feet), rising on the creek's far side. Then the marsh ends. For the last mile to the PCT junction, the path climbs for brief stretches and stays level for long stretches.

At the PCT junction at mile 1.8, go left (south) for the Seven Lakes Basin, in the Devil's Peak direction. The opposite direction on the PCT (north), takes you to the McKie Camp Trail in 2 miles and Crater Lake National Park in 10.5 miles.

Beyond the junction, heading south on the PCT, after 1.2 miles of gentle downhill hiking (and occasionally not so gentle), the PCT hits the edge of a rim high above the spectacular Middle Fork Canyon, Oregon's largest glacial valley. The view is partly obscured by trees and not nearly as impressive as the view of the same canyon from Lake Ivern. But it's pretty impressive. The reddish bulge on the ridgetop to the northeast is Mount Maude (7,184 feet).

Forests along the way alternate between small lodgepole pines on the dusty, ashy areas and mixed middle-elevation forests on the better-developed soils. The mixed forests consist of lodgepole and western white pines, subalpine and Shasta red firs, mountain hemlock, and Engelmann spruce. You pass many small, grassy, marshy areas, as well as dryer open areas of red huckleberry, red heather, and pinemat manzanita.

Beyond the rim encounter, the path starts seriously uphill, crossing Honeymoon Creek. Two and a half miles from the Sevenmile junction, the PCT meets the far end of the Seven Lakes Trail. Follow the Seven Lakes

Alta Lake.

Trail 0.4 mile to Grass Lake and 0.8 mile to Middle Lake and the Lake Ivern Trailhead.

Lake Ivern Trail. The 2.2-mile Lake Ivern Trail (994) from Middle Lake takes you past North Lake to the remote and isolated Lake Ivern, with a spectacular view of the Middle Fork Canyon and points north. See Hike 40.

Alta Lake Trail. This is hard to explain but if you count only the lake itself and not the cliffs and mountains around them, Alta Lake becomes the prettiest of the Seven Lakes group. It's also the largest. The lake's serene beauty is enhanced by mysterious and unusual geology. Unlike every other lake in the region, or anywhere else, Alta Lake perches atop a dome-shaped mountain whose summit appears to have been whacked with a giant hatchet. For the best perspective on Alta Lake's weird setting, hike 1 mile up the Devil's Peak Trail from the Seven Lakes summit and look back. The steep-sided lake is 0.5 mile long but only a few hundred feet wide, with a precipitous creek outlet (and a continuation of the trail) leading north into the Middle Fork.

According to Dr. Monty Elliott, chair of Southern Oregon University's Geology Department, Alta Lake is the result of a "normal fault," a big crack where one side slipped downward, the other side slipped upward and the up side does not overhang the down side. At Alta Lake, the east side is the down side. Normal faults result from tension, or pulling apart of the land, rather than compression or squeezing together. In the Cascades, you're much more likely to find evidence of compression than of tension. Compression is characterized by folding and "reverse faulting." In a reverse fault, the up side overhangs the down side. Much of the Alta Lake Fault has been obliterated by glacial action and erosion. The Alta Lake Fault is shown on State of Oregon geological maps.

Alta Lake has lots of fish and many fewer mosquitoes than the six lakes in the basin. To get to Alta Lake follow the directions given under the main hike for this section.

40 Lake Ivern

Highlights:	An easy, pleasant hike to the smallest and most remote lake in the Seven Lakes Basin, with a stop at North Lake. A spectacular panorama of the Middle Fork Canyon from the lake outlet.
Type of hike:	Day hike, out and back from the Seven Lakes Basin.
Total distance:	4.4 miles (14.4 miles from the Seven Lakes Trailhead and back).
Difficulty:	Easy.
Elevation loss:	400 feet.
Best months:	July–October.
Map:	USGS Devil's Peak quad.

Lake Ivern

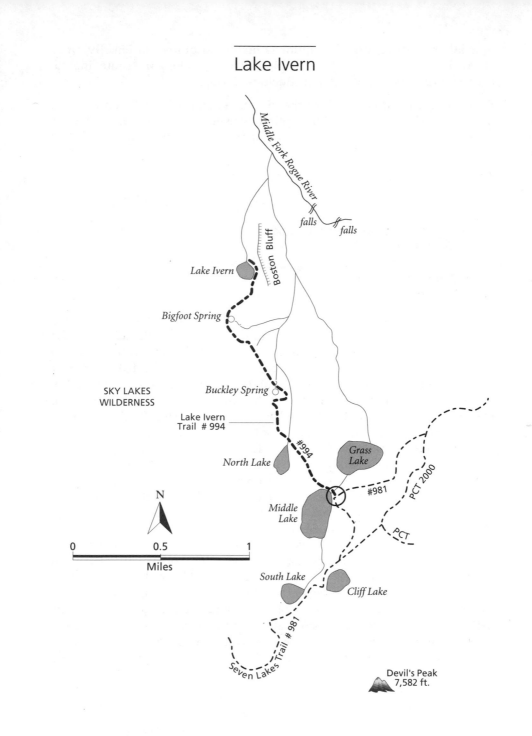

Middle Fork Rogue River

falls *falls*

Boston Bluff

Lake Ivern

Bigfoot Spring

Buckley Spring

SKY LAKES
WILDERNESS

Lake Ivern
Trail # 994

#994

North Lake

Grass Lake

#981

N

0   0.5   1
Miles

*Middle
Lake*

PCT 2000

PCT

South Lake

Cliff Lake

Seven Lakes Trail # 981

Devil's Peak
7,582 ft.

Special considerations: Not quite as many mosquitoes at Lake Ivern as at Middle or Grass Lakes. There is plentiful water along the route, including some fine-tasting water from Buckley Spring.

Finding the trailhead: Follow the directions under Hike 39, either from the Seven Lakes Trailhead or the optional Sevenmile Trailhead, for 5 miles to the Lake Ivern Trail, which begins at the Seven Lakes Trail at Middle Lake.

Trailhead facilities: Camping is permitted in designated campsites at Middle Lake.

Key points:
0.0 Lake Ivern Trail junction on Seven Lakes Trail.
0.5 North Lake.
1.3 Buckley Spring.
1.8 Bigfoot Spring junction.
2.2 Lake Ivern.

The hike: Lake Ivern, the Seven Lake Basin's smallest and most remote lake, sits precariously on a ledge 2.2 miles from the trailhead at Middle Lake, in the middle of the drop-off into the Middle Fork Canyon at the end of a cul-de-sac trail. There is no direct trail from the Seven Lakes Basin to the Middle Fork Canyon, into which all the basin's lakes drain, due to an imposing, waterfall-laden series of cliffs called "Boston Bluff." The main reason for visiting Lake Ivern is to have a look at Boston Bluff and obtain a unique panorama of the Middle Fork Canyon, 1,000 to 2,000 feet below.

From the trailhead, the Lake Ivern Trail (994) crosses the Middle Lake outlet, then wanders gently downhill through the woods, passing North Lake after 0.5 mile. There is no trail to North Lake and it cannot be seen from the Lake Ivern Trail. Look for a small creek crossing with a sign to the right that says "horse feed." Go left there, up the creek for a few hundred feet. The creek soon opens to a large wet meadow with North Lake in the middle and the yellow rock of the Alta Lake ridge directly overhead.

The Lake Ivern Trail's steepest downhill pitch comes shortly beyond North Lake when the path inscribes a wide switchback through the deep woods. It then levels off high up a steep hillside that plummets down to the Middle Fork. The hillside is densely forested and you can't see very far. The path crosses several rocky scree slopes and, overall, is very pleasant. Buckley Spring emerges at the base of a scree slope rock pile at mile 1.3.

At mile 1.8, a trail takes off downhill to the right, with a sign that says "Bigfoot Spring—¼ mile." The map shows at least two springs in the vicinity. However, the side trail peters out after 0.2 mile without passing any springs (well, maybe a very small one). It is not a good place to get lost. The Forest Service

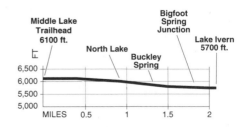

158

Outcrop at Lake Ivern.

plans to abandon the Bigfoot Spring Trail. Buckley Spring is much more productive as a water source and is on the main trail.

At mile 2, the path enters a small forested bench, crossing a low saddle soon after. For the best view down Boston Bluff, head right at the saddle to a nearby rock outcrop. The campsite area at Lake Ivern, well away from the lake, also offers a view down Boston Bluff.

Beyond the bench and saddle, the path contours slowly down through the woods to the lake, with the Middle Fork Canyon dominating the panorama in the distance. The lake itself isn't much, but it is stocked with brook trout. The trail ends at the lake outlet. The outlet creek immediately drops straight down over a huge cliff.

For the best view of the Middle Fork Canyon, cross the Lake Ivern outlet creek and climb up the rocks on the other side. You can see, from left to right, the Alta Lake Ridge (with the Alta Lake outlet creek less than 0.2 mile away), Gopher Ridge, the Middle Fork Canyon, Kerby Hill, Mudjekeewis Mountain, Tom Mountain, Jerry Mountain, Union Peak in Crater Lake National Park, Halifax Ridge, and Maude Mountain.

41 Devil's Peak

Highlights:	From the pass above the Seven Lakes Basin, this hike scales the summit of Devil's Peak. When combined with the Seven Lakes Trail, this is the most scenic route in the Sky Lakes.
Type of hike:	Day hike, out and back. Backpack if combined in a loop with the Seven Lakes Basin.
Total distance:	About 5 miles (12 miles from Seven Lakes Trailhead and back).
Difficulty:	Strenuous.
Elevation gain:	682 feet.
Best months:	July–October.
Map:	USGS Devil's Peak quad.

Special considerations: The Devil's Peak Trail becomes passable two weeks after the Seven Lakes Trail opens. Unlike the Seven Lakes Trail, there is no water on the Devil's Peak Trail except for melting snowbanks, which can persist into August.

Finding the trailhead: The trailhead for the Devil's Peak Trail is located on the right at mile 3.5 on the Seven Lakes Trail (See Hike 39).

Key points:
    0.0 Devil's Peak junction on Seven Lakes Trail.
    1.3 Pacific Crest Trail junction (go left).
    2.3 Devil's Peak way-trail (go left).
    2.5 Devil's Peak summit.

Devil's Peak

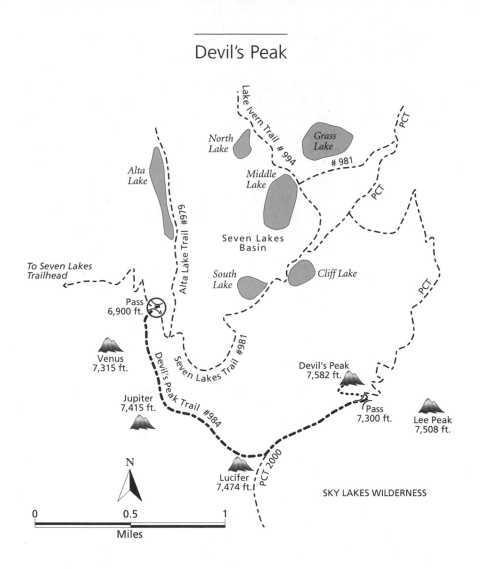

Map labels:

Lake Ivern Trail #994

PCT

North Lake

Grass Lake #981

Alta Lake

Middle Lake

PCT

Alta Lake Trail #979

Seven Lakes Basin

To Seven Lakes Trailhead

South Lake

Cliff Lake

PCT

Pass 6,900 ft.

Venus 7,315 ft.

Seven Lakes Trail #981

Devil's Peak Trail #984

Devil's Peak 7,582 ft.

Jupiter 7,415 ft.

Pass 7,300 ft.

Lee Peak 7,508 ft.

N

Lucifer 7,474 ft.

PCT 2000

SKY LAKES WILDERNESS

0   0.5   1
Miles

The hike: The Devil's Peak Trail (984) is deceptively gentle (at first), and a welcome respite for travelers who've climbed 3.5 steep miles up the Seven Lakes Trail to reach it. The juncture of the two trails is at a 6,900-foot summit. The level first half

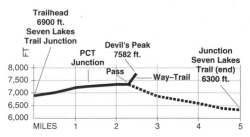

Elevation profile labels: Trailhead 6900 ft. Seven Lakes Trail Junction; PCT Junction; Devil's Peak 7582 ft.; Pass; Way–Trail; Junction Seven Lakes Trail (end) 6300 ft.; FEET 8,000 7,500 7,000 6,500 6,000; MILES 1 2 3 4 5

of the 1.3-mile Devil's Peak Trail, between this summit and the Pacific Crest Trail (2000), wanders through a beautiful woods and past an exquisite pond before steepening considerably and making its way onto the talus slopes just below the looming cliffs of Mount Lucifer (7,474 feet).

The Mount Lucifer traverse is the route's most impressive, with vistas of Devil's Peak; South, Middle, and Grass Lakes; and an astonishing view of Alta Lake.

The PCT turns up at a treeline saddle offering the hike's first view southward. Turn left on the PCT for Devil's Peak and right for Mount Luther (Hike 50). For the next mile, the PCT climbs moderately as it makes it's way around Devil's Peak's steep south flank. Immediately past Devil's Peak, the PCT arrives at another saddle, then plunges into the Seven Lakes Basin towards Middle Lake, losing 800 feet in 1 mile.

From the saddle where the PCT begins its descent into the Seven Lakes Basin, a primitive, 0.2-mile way-trail takes off left, up the barren, rocky upper slopes of 7,582-foot Devil's Peak. In contrast with the trailhead's dense forests, only a few brave, windswept, whitebark pines and mountain hemlocks, along with widely scattered lupine and saxifrage, dot the alpine expanse.

From the little rocky knob atop Devil's Peak, North, Grass, and Middle Lakes are easily visible to the north in the Seven Lakes Basin (Alta and South Lakes have now disappeared). So are Union Peak, Crater Lake's south rim, the Rogue-Umpqua Divide range, and the immense glacial canyon of the Rogue River's Middle Fork. Bear Creek Valley, containing Medford and Ashland, can be seen to the east while the Klamath Basin and Upper Klamath Lake dominate the west.

The view north from Devil's Peak reveals the Seven Lakes Basin as a large, complex glacial cirque. The glacier responsible was a substantial valley glacier rather than the more common small, hanging, mountain glacier.

Pacific Crest Trail at Devil's Peak into Seven Lakes Basin.

The Middle Fork canyon, leading out of the basin, presents a wide, U-shaped profile typical of the work of a valley glacier. The glacier ended where the valley reverts to a V profile, beyond the Middle Fork Trailhead and just before the river crosses Forest Road 37. This means the glacier was about 12 miles long.

Mount McLoughlin, Southern Oregon's premiere peak, dominates the view south, as does the high, rocky, yellowish crest that radiates from Mount Lucifer to Mount Luther (7,163 feet). Between Mount Luther (Hike 50) and the wide dome of Pelican Butte (8,036 feet), lies the (apparently) flat, forested expanse of the Sky Lakes Basin (Hike 49), sloping gently off to Cherry Creek to the east. If you look carefully, you can see a couple of the larger Sky Lakes. West of Mount Luther, the Blue Canyon Basin forms a glacial valley from Mount McLoughlin to the South Fork Rogue.

Day hikers return to the Seven Lakes Trailhead the way they came. Backpackers should avail themselves of the opportunity to spend time in the magnificent Seven Lakes Basin by completing a 14-mile loop (measuring from the Seven Lakes Trailhead parking area), involving the Seven Lakes Trail, the Devil's Peak Trail, and the PCT. See "Options."

Options: *Loop through Seven Lakes Basin.* To complete the 14-mile loop which visits both Devil's Peak and the Seven Lakes Basin, after climbing Devil's Peak, return to the beginning of the short way-trail to the Devil's Peak summit. From there, the northbound PCT (left) plummets into the Seven Lakes Basin, with the far end of the Seven Lakes Trail showing up in 2.5 miles. From the Seven Lakes/PCT junction in the basin, head left (west) on the Seven Lakes Trail. It's 0.5 mile on the Seven Lakes Trail to Middle Lake, 2 miles back to the saddle where the Devil's Peak Trail starts (completing a 7 mile loop) and 6 miles back to the Seven Lakes Trailhead.

Pacific Crest Trail, south. From the junction with the Devil's Peak Trail, the southbound PCT reaches Mount Luther in 2.5 miles and the upper Sky Lakes Basin in 4 miles.

42   Blue Canyon Basin

Highlights:	A beautiful, easy, hike past numerous lakes. Magnificent trailhead drive.
Type of hike:	Day hike or backpack, out and back.
Total distance:	About 6 miles.
Difficulty:	Easy to moderate.
Elevation loss:	547 feet.
Best months:	June–October.
Map:	USGS Rustler Peak quad.

Special considerations: Lots of mosquitoes before mid-July. The uphill direction is on the return hike. Plenty of water.

Blue Canyon Basin

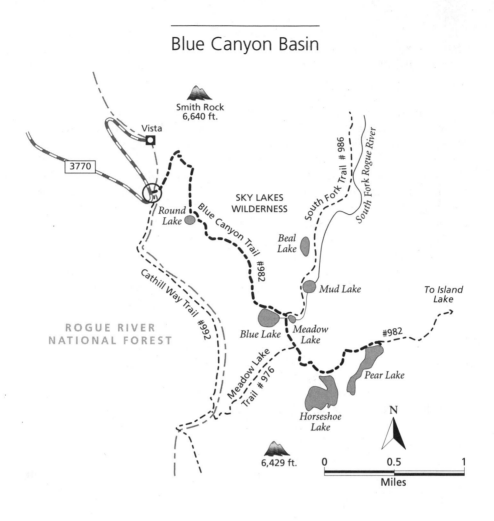

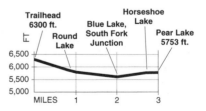

Finding the trailhead: Take Oregon Highway 62 north from Medford to the Butte Falls turnoff near milepost 16. Turn right and drive 17 miles to the town of Butte Falls. Continue past Butte Falls on the same road, for 1 mile, to the Prospect turnoff. Cross the bridge and proceed 2 miles to the gravel Rancheria Road. Stay on Rancheria, which becomes Forest Road 32, for 15 miles. FR 32 eventually merges with Forest Road 37. After less than 1 mile on FR 37, a red gravel road, Forest Road 3770, takes off right. Follow FR 3770 for 6 miles to the elaborate Blue Canyon Trailhead.

Watch for impressive vistas of Devil's Peak and Mount McLoughlin from FR 3770. If you drive past the trailhead for 1 mile, there's a mountaintop vista point.

Parking and trailhead facilities: There is parking for 20 cars at the beautifully landscaped trailhead.

Key points:
0.0 Blue Canyon Trailhead.
0.8 Round Lake.
2.0 Blue Lake, junction with South Fork Trail.
2.2 Meadow Lake Trail junction.
2.7 Horseshoe Lake.
3.0 Pear Lake.

The hike: The Blue Canyon area is exciting and accessible. Unfortunately, too many people feel that way. In summer, it tends to be crowded and horses kick up a lot of dust. September and October are better times to visit. There are fewer visitors and mosquitoes then, and you can enjoy the fall colors around Butte Falls (though there may be occasional mountain storms).

From the trailhead, the Blue Canyon Trail (982) drops gently but steadily through a beautiful forest of Shasta red fir, mountain hemlock, and western white pine. The path skirts around Round Lake after 0.8 mile, then passes two or three smaller lakes. At mile 1.5, as you approach Blue Lake, look for a few Engelmann spruce. This mountain dweller is fairly rare in Southern Oregon. It thrives in cold, moist, thick-soil areas. In the central Rockies, Engelmann spruce occupies an entirely different niche, being the region's dominant upland north slope species, with quaking aspen the dominant upland south slope species.

Blue Lake, the prettiest (and bluest) lake in the Blue Lake Basin, sits 2 miles down the trail at the base of a towering cliff headwall. The seasonal Meadow Lake lies near Blue Lake, in a large meadow fringed with subalpine fir, mountain hemlock, and lodgepole pine. Blue Lake is currently unstocked while Meadow Lake contains brook and rainbow trout.

Beyond Blue Lake at mile 2.2 you pass the Meadow Lake Trail (976), which connects to the Cathill Way Trail 992. Horseshoe Lake turns up a half mile later, then Pear Lake, 3 miles from the trailhead. Both are gentle, shallow giants with sinuous shorelines nestled against low headwalls.

In the vicinity of Horseshoe and Pear Lakes, the path crosses areas of jumbled rock, ripped from the mountainside by glaciers and deposited in mounds called moraines. Look on the larger boulders for gouged, smooth-sided facets. The gouges, called "striations," result from the glacier passing directly over the rock. Look also for rocks full of tiny bubbles formed when gas escaped from the molten lava as it cooled.

Options: *The Cathill Way Trail.* For a loop through the Blue Lake Basin offering still closer closeups of McLoughlin, try the Cathill Way Trail (992), which takes off (right) from the Blue Canyon Trail a few hundred feet from the trailhead. Heading south along the gentle crest of Cathill Ridge, the occasionally faint path peers into Blue Canyon's wide glacial valleys but offers no lake views. After 1.5 miles, you arrive at the steep, 1-mile

Meadow Lake Trail (975) into the basin. The Meadow Lake Trail emerges at the Blue Lake Trail between Blue Lake and Horseshoe Lake. If you stay on Cathill Way, you meet the PCT (2000), 3 miles from the Blue Canyon Trailhead. From the PCT/Cathill junction, it's 4 miles to Four Mile Lake.

Island Lake. Island Lake, the biggest lake in the wilderness, lies 2 miles beyond Pear Lake on the Blue Canyon Trail, 5 miles from the Blue Canyon Trailhead. See Hike 43.

---

43 Island Lake

Highlights:	An easy hike to Island Lake, the largest lake in the Sky Lakes Wilderness, plus two other large and beautiful lakes.
Type of hike:	Day hike, out and back.
Total distance:	About 8 miles (14 miles from the Blue Canyon Trailhead).
Difficulty:	Easy.
Elevation gain:	347 feet gain, then 280 feet loss.
Best months:	June–October.
Maps:	USGS Rustler Peak and Pelican Butte quads.

Special considerations: This hike describes the Forest Service's "preferred" route to Island Lake via the Blue Canyon Trail, which gets you there in 5 miles (7 miles to Red Lake) from the Blue Canyon Trailhead. See "Option."

Lots of mosquitoes early in the season.

Finding the trailhead: Follow directions to the Blue Canyon Trailhead given in Hike 42. Hike the Blue Canyon Trail to Pear Lake. The description in this chapter follows the Blue Canyon Trail beginning at Pear Lake.

Parking and trailhead facilities: See Hike 42.

Key points:
    0.0 Blue Canyon Trail at Pear Lake.
    2.0 Island Lake.
    2.5 Junction with Red Lake Trail (go left).
    4.0 Red Lake.

The hike: Island Lake, at 40 acres, is very pretty, amazingly clear considering how shallow it is, and the largest lake in the Sky Lakes Wilderness. Beginning the hike at Pear Lake on the Blue Canyon Trail (982), 3 miles from the Blue Canyon Trailhead, continue through the woods and over glacial moraines for 2 miles, to the south end of Island Lake. The

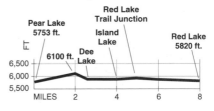

Island Lake

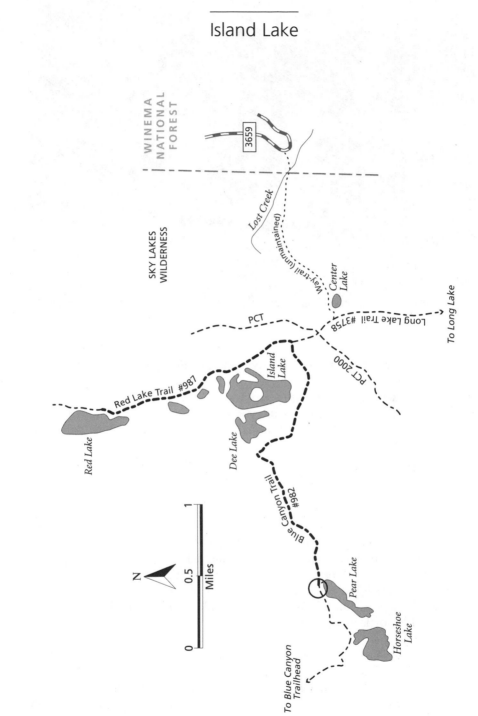

Red Lake.

south end offers the best perspective on the lake's size and is the best place to view the island.

If you make your way off trail, around to Island Lake's western shore, then head west through the woods, you quickly arrive at the much more secluded, 14-acre Dee Lake. The Blue Canyon Trail passes fairly close to Dee Lake, 1 mile before the trail ends at the Red Lake Trail junction.

Beyond Island Lake's south end, it's 0.5 mile to the junction with the Red Lake Trail (987). Turn left (west) and walk for 0.3 mile for a view of Island Lake that has Mount McLoughlin rising in the distance, the only real highlight of the topography here. Island Lake doesn't appear as large from the north end because the island blends in with the shore and most of the lake's expansive south end can't be seen.

Look for lots of Engelmann spruce at Island Lake, along with mountain hemlock, western white pine, and Shasta red fir. Subalpine fir, which abounds at Horseshoe and Pear Lakes, is not present at Island Lake.

Continuing past Island Lake on the Red Lake Trail, the path passes three smaller lakes (or larger ponds), then drops down several glacial moraines before meeting the extremely shallow, teardrop-shaped Red Lake (7 miles from the Blue Lake Trailhead and 1.5 miles from the Blue Canyon/Red Lake junction). Red Lake is among the largest in the Sky Lakes but doesn't look it, partly because a goodly portion is filled with marsh grass. The topography here offers little of interest except for some low, forested ridges.

Option: *Lost Creek Trail From the Blue Canyon Trailhead.* The unofficial Lost Creek Trail reaches Island Lake in 1.5 miles. The Lost Creek Trail also leads to Long Lake (second largest in the wilderness) in 2 miles, versus 3.5 for the "preferred" route to Long Lake (the Badger Lake Trail from Four Mile Lake (Hike 45).

The Lost Creek Trail is unmaintained, the trailhead is unmarked, and the path is not shown on any current Forest Service map. According to the Forest Service, the Lost Creek Trail makes it so easy to reach Island, Red, and Long Lakes that overuse becomes a problem. While the Lost Creek Trail is not closed, the Forest Service urges hikers to consider other routes. This is not the only book that describes the Lost Creek Trail, which appears on most non-Forest Service maps. Since the Lost Creek Trail is "unofficial," there is no parking fee at the trailhead.

To reach the unsigned Lost Creek Trailhead, follow the directions to the Coldsprings Trailhead (Hike 48). Follow Forest Road 3651 for 8.5 miles to Forest Road 3659, on the left. It's 1.2 miles to a sharp uphill switchback. Look for a small parking area immediately past the switchback curve. There's parking for four cars at the trailhead turnout, plus a few more along the road shoulder.

From the trailhead, the Lost Creek Trail climbs very gently for 1 mile, through a woods of lodgepole pine, western white pine, mountain hemlock, and Shasta red fir, until it meets Center Lake, a large grassy opening that often has no water. There are a few small logs across the unmaintained trail but the route is easy to follow. At Center Lake, the path climbs steeply but briefly, meeting the Red Lake Trail from Long Lake, then the Pacific Crest Trail (2000) in short order. Turn right onto the Red Lake Trail for Island and Red Lakes.

Cresting a low ridge, the Red Lake Trail quickly starts back down and soon passes the far end of the Blue Canyon Trail. For the best view of the island in sprawling Island Lake, and to fully grasp the lake's size, follow the Blue Canyon Trail (left) for 0.5 mile. For a great view of Mount McLoughlin rising above Island Lake, continue on the Red Lake Trail. The Red Lake Trail takes you to the north end of Island Lake after 0.3 mile, then to Red Lake in 1.5 miles.

Back at the junction with the Lost Creek and Red Lake Trails above Center Lake, it's 1.2 easy miles to Long Lake (2.2 miles from the Lost Creek Trailhead). Just turn left instead of right. Long Lake is very long and pretty, with more dramatic surrounding topography and denser forests than Island Lake. It isn't as blue, though.

44 Squaw Lake

Highlights:	The closest lake to Mount McLoughlin, with a trail that crosses a huge terminal moraine at the base of a giant glacial cirque on McLoughlin.
Type of hike:	Day hike, out and back.
Total distance:	4 miles to Squaw Lake and back. 5 miles to PCT and back.
Difficulty:	Easy.
Elevation gain:	Minimal.
Best months:	June–October.
Map:	USGS Mount McLoughlin quad.

Special considerations: Lots of creeks and ponds but most are dried up by August. Mosquitoes are abundant in early season.

Finding the trailhead: Take Oregon Highway 140 east from White City, near Medford, and drive to the Four Mile Lake turnoff (Forest Road 3661), near Lake of the Woods at milepost 37. Proceed 6 miles up the heavily used gravel road to the trailhead parking area in the Four Mile Lake Campground. The sign at the trailhead says "Badger Lake, PCT." It's also the Squaw Lake Trailhead.

Parking and trailhead facilities: Fifteen cars fit in the trailhead parking area. The campground has pit toilets.

Key points.
0.0 Four Mile Lake Trailhead.
0.1 Badger Lake/PCT junction (go straight).
2.0 Squaw Lake.

The hike: The huge avalanche basin on Mount
McLoughlin's east face,
extending from near the
summit down to Four Mile
Lake, looks for all the
world like a crater left by a

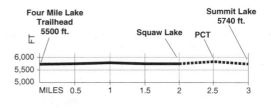

lateral volcanic blast, with an immense rubble field at the bottom. Only from the Squaw Lake Trail, which crosses the "rubble field," is it obvious from the rounded rocks that this is a terminal glacial moraine. From Squaw Lake's unique angle, one can see that the avalanche basin is actually two side-by-side glacial valleys.

From the trailhead at the Four Mile Lake Campground, it's an easy 2 miles on the Squaw Lake Trail to Squaw Lake. Signs and paths at the trailhead are a little confusing. For Squaw Lake, at the junction 0.1 mile from the trailhead, take the direction straight ahead, where the sign says "To PCT." (You will be on Trail 993 which is also the Twin Ponds Trail, described in Hike 46.)

Squaw Lake

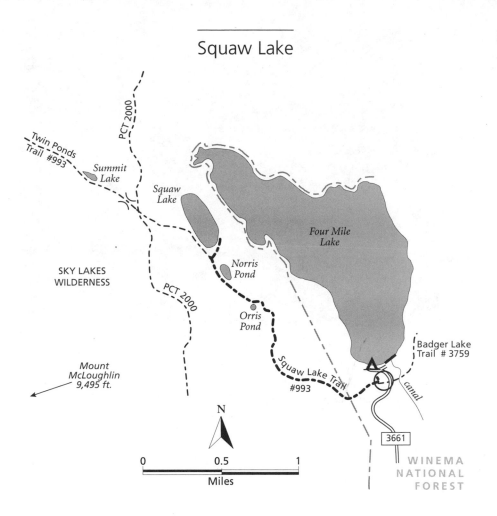

The route wanders through a lodgepole pine forest and over rolling moraines, with glimpses of Mount McLoughlin popping up after 1 mile. The trail then passes Orris and Norris Ponds, the former a large pool surrounded by a small meadow and the latter a small pool surrounded by an immense meadow. Shortly after Norris Pond, Squaw Lake appears, big, shallow, clear, and surrounded by dense forest. For a knockout view of McLoughlin, make your way around to the lake's eastern shore.

Option: *Twin Ponds Trail.* If you continue on the trail past Squaw Lake, it's 0.5 mile, up a gentle grade through the woods, to a low saddle and the Pacific Crest Trail. If you continue straight and don't turn onto the PCT, the trail ends at the Twin Ponds trailhead, 4.8 miles from Four Mile Lake (Hike 46).

Pacific Crest Trail. A popular 13-mile, two-day loop follows the Squaw Lake Trail from Four Mile Lake to the PCT to the Cathill Way Trail to the

171

Squaw Lake.

Meadow Lake Trail into the Blue Canyon Basin. It then follows the Blue Canyon Trail past Island Lake to the Long Lake Trail, which returns to Four Mile Lake.

45 Badger Lake

Highlights:	Long Lake (second largest in the wilderness), Badger Lake, and an impressive view of Mount McLoughin rising out of Four Mile Lake make for an exquisite journey.
Type of hike:	Day hike, out and back.
Total distance:	7.4 miles.
Difficulty:	Easy.
Elevation gain:	306 feet.
Best months:	June–October.
Map:	USGS Lake of the Woods North quad.

Special considerations: The Badger Lake Trail spends the first 0.5 mile from the Four Mile Lake Trailhead making a wide, confusing loop around the campground. To eliminate that 0.5 mile, consider turning right at the campground entrance instead of left, and parking by the little dam, near the gate with the "Road Closed" sign. From the gate, follow the closed dirt road on foot, across the white footbridge at the spillway, to another short

Badger Lake

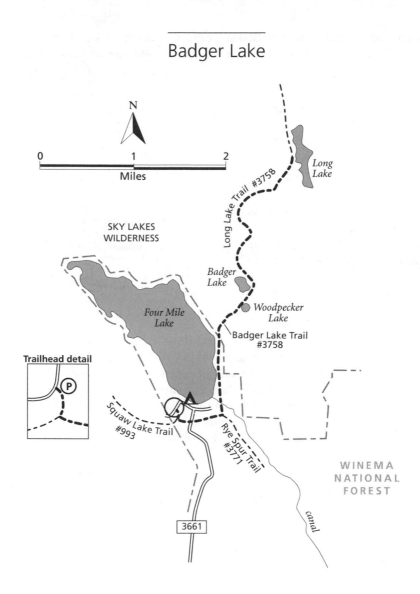

road, then to a narrow way-trail connecting with the Badger Lake Trail. Turn left on the Badger Lake trail.

Finding the trailhead: Take Oregon Highway 140 east from White City, near Medford and drive to the Four Mile Lake turnoff (Forest Road 3661), near Lake of the Woods at milepost 37. Proceed 6 miles up the heavily used gravel road to the trailhead parking area in the Four Mile Lake Campground. The sign at the trailhead says "Badger Lake, PCT." If you hike 0.1 mile down the trail from the Four Mile Lake Trailhead, a junction points to (left) Badger Lake and (straight ahead) the PCT, which is actually the Squaw Lake Trail.

Parking and trailhead facilities: There's room for 15 cars at the Four Mile Lake Trailhead, in the middle of a large campground. There are pit toilets in the campground.

Key points:
    0.0 Four Mile Lake Trailhead.
    0.5 Four Mile Lake.
    1.3 Leave Four Mile Lake.
    1.8 Woodpecker Lake.
    2.0 Badger Lake.
    3.7 Long Lake.

The hike: Another highly recommended trail from Four Mile Lake (besides the Squaw Lake Trail) is the Badger Lake Trail (3758), which becomes the Long Lake Trail (3759) beyond Badger Lake (and Trail 987, the Red Lake Trail, beyond Long Lake). The

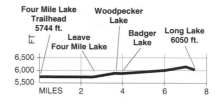

Badger Lake route follows the driftwood-lined shore of Four Mile Lake for nearly a mile, and offers outstanding vistas of the intensely blue lake and of Mount McLoughlin's overwhelming presence not far away.

One and a half miles from the trailhead, the Badger Lake Trail climbs a small rock outcrop. It then cuts inland, away from the lake, and climbs steeply for 0.2 mile, up the route's only upgrade, with an elevation gain of maybe 100 feet. The forest here become much greener and denser as you move away from the recent volcanic deposits at the lake, with their predominantly lodgepole pine forests. The trail also becomes less dusty and looks like real dirt instead of volcanic ash.

You arrive first at Woodpecker Lake, a charming, green-water pool. Badger Lake lies 10 minutes away. Badger Lake, despite the green water, is one of the more lush and verdant spots in the Sky Lakes.

Beyond Badger Lake, the path winds gradually and uneventfully upward through the woods for 1.7 miles, to the aptly but unoriginally named Long Lake, a lovely, elongated blue gem nestled (not surprisingly), in a long, narrow valley. Long Lake, at 37 acres, is the second largest lake in the Sky Lakes Wilderness.

Option: You can also reach Long Lake via the unofficial Lost Creek shortcut (see Hike 43). From the Lost Creek parking area, it's 2 miles to Long Lake instead of 3.7 miles.

46 Twin Ponds

Highlight:	The closest trailhead to Mount McLoughlin (including the McLoughlin Trailhead), followed by a pleasant walk on a historic trail along a creek.
Type of hike:	Day hike, out and back.
Total distance:	5.6 miles.
Difficulty:	Easy.
Elevation gain:	1,000 feet.
Best months:	June–October.
Map:	USGS Mount McLoughlin quad.

Special considerations: Prior to mid-July, this trail can be very muddy and crosses much water, especially after a wet winter.

Finding the trailhead: Take Oregon Highway 140 east from White City, near Medford, to Forest Road 37 (paved) near milepost 29. Turn left and continue for 9 miles. Just before Willow Lake, FR 37 cuts sharply east and the pavement ends. Continue for 1.2 miles to where, FR 3760 takes off to the right. Follow it 4 miles to the Twin Ponds Trailhead. The Forest Service recreation map shows FR 3760 as "3670."

Parking and trailhead facilities: A former logging landing 200 feet from the trailhead and road end has room for eight cars.

Key points:
0.0 Twin Ponds Trailhead.
0.8 Twin Ponds.
2.5 Summit Lake.
2.8 PCT junction.

The hike: The Twin Ponds Trailhead is the closest trailhead to the Mount McLoughlin summit, closer even than the Mount McLoughlin Trailhead. Located well up McLoughlin's northwest flank, the trailhead offers a rare closeup view of the majestic mountain. The vistas continue for the path's first 0.2 mile as you traverse an old clearcut and make your way towards the low, forested divide between McLoughlin and the Blue Canyon Basin. The vista away from McLoughlin offers an impressive panorama of the valley surrounding the town of Butte Falls, with Cat Hill rising to the east.

The clearcut is a forester's nightmare, an excellent example of a worst-case regeneration scenario. Every brush species imaginable chokes the site, including varnishleaf ceanothus, green manzanita, bittercherry; and in the woods, serviceberry, whortleberry, red and green huckleberry, and dwarf Oregongrape. The few scattered ponderosa pines are probably the remnants of a failed planting. Among native conifers, there are widely scattered white fir, Shasta red fir, western white pine, and mountain hemlock.

The Twin Ponds Trail (993) to Summit Lake and Squaw Lake is among the oldest trails in the region. It was built in 1863 as part of the Rancheria

Twin Ponds

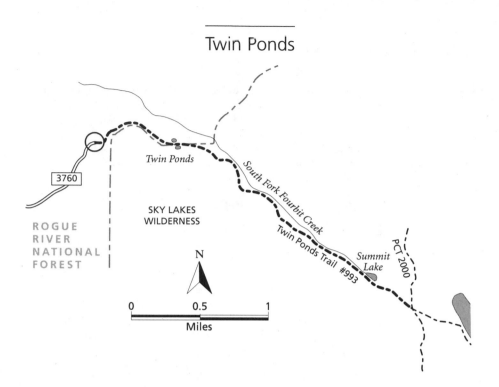

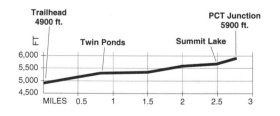

Trail, a military wagon road that went from the gold mines at Jacksonville (near Medford) to Fort Klamath.

Unfortunately, the panoramas and silvicultural interest don't last. The instant the path enters the woods and starts climbing up Four Bit Creek, the vistas cease. The trail's destinations, Twin Ponds and Summit Lake, are well worth missing, although the hike along the creek is pleasant and easy. Twin Ponds, Summit Lake, and Fourbit Creek can go bone dry. They were in September, 1998.

Had it been July instead of September, however, the trail would have presented quite a challenge. In many places, it looked as though running water regularly flowed down the path. In some places, the path ran (unnecessarily) straight up the wide Fourbit Creek bed, crossing the stream six times in 2 miles.

From the trailhead, the path is reasonably level for 0.5 mile. It then abruptly shoots steeply uphill, ending at Twin Ponds 0.8 mile from the trailhead. It's interesting to note that one of The Twin Ponds lies inside the Sky Lakes Wilderness and the other doesn't. Above Twin Ponds, the path rises gently, with many level areas, until reaching a gentle divide in the woods, just past Summit Lake, at the Pacific Crest Trail (2000) crossing.

Option: *Squaw Lake:* It's 2.5 miles from the Twin Ponds Trailhead to Summit Lake, 2.8 miles to the PCT crossing, 3.3 miles to Squaw Lake, and 4.8 miles to Four Mile Lake.

47   Puck Lake

Highlights:	A beautiful, out-of-the-way trail to a large, clear lake.
Type of hike:	Day hike, out and back.
Total distance:	4.4 miles.
Difficulty:	Easy to moderate.
Elevation gain:	500 feet.
Best months:	June–October.
Maps:	USGS Pelican Butte and Devil's Peak quads.

Special considerations: Mosquitoes abundant in early season.

Finding the trailhead: From Oregon Highway 140 at White City, near Medford, proceed east, past Lake of the Woods to Westside Road near milepost 43. Turn left and drive 12 miles to the well-marked Nannie Creek turnoff (Forest Road 3484), on the left. It's 6 miles up the excellent gravel road to the trailhead.

Parking and trailhead facilities: The trailhead accommodates ten cars.

Key points:
    0.0 Nannie Creek Trailhead.
    2.2 Puck Lake

The hike: The Nannie Creek Trail (3707) and Puck Lake boast two of the most fun names in any wilderness. Puck Lake ranks among the Sky Lakes' most

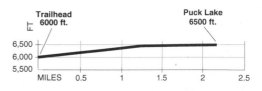

isolated, blue, and serenely beautiful bodies of water. The drive to the trailhead offers majestic panoramas of Upper Klamath Lake (Oregon's largest natural lake), the flat ranchlands above Upper Klamath Lake, and the high peaks of the Cascades immediately west. Much of the Sky Lakes, the Mountain Lakes basin, and the Crater Lake rim are visible from Westside Road.

The forests along the Nannie Creek Trail are very "east side," with smaller trees and less underbrush than their west-side counterparts due to less precipitation (Devil's Peak and Mount McLoughlin form a rainshadow blocking weather systems from the west). Although the trailhead elevation

Puck Lake

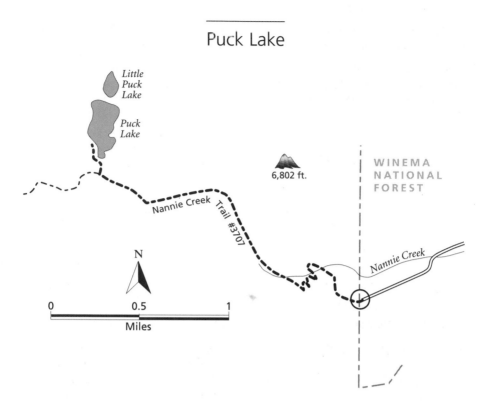

is 6,000 feet, the access road opens up about the same time as west-side trailheads 1,000 feet lower. Trees along the access road are mostly lodge-pole and ponderosa pine. On the trail, Shasta red fir, western white pine, and mountain hemlock predominate.

From the trailhead, the Nannie Creek Trail winds through the woods for 1 mile, climbing a moderately steep series of switchbacks to a hilltop. The path then levels off and heads up a long, narrow, shaded draw, meanders around a large ridge, drops slightly, and crosses a second draw before reaching the exquisite and surprisingly large lake at mile 2.2.

The lake turnoff is unmarked but the lake is easily visible from the main trail so the route is obvious. Though relatively large at 24 acres, Puck Lake is extremely shallow (10 feet deep). At 6,450 feet, it is second only to Alta Lake in elevation in the Sky Lakes. There are no major peaks visible from its shoreline. What makes the lake so gorgeous is the amazing clarity of its water. The lake drains into Threemile Creek, located 4 miles south of Sevenmile Creek. The lake's biggest drawback is the abundance of mosquitoes. They say fishing is fantastic.

North Puck Lake can be reached by walking to Puck Lake's north shore and heading off through the woods for a few hundred feet.

Option: *The rest of the Nannie Creek Trail.* If you continue on the Nannie Creek Trail past Puck Lake for 1 mile, the path emerges at a white rock scree slope with a stunning panorama of the Sky Lakes Basin, Mount Luther, the Cherry Creek Canyon, and Pelican Butte. It's 2 miles on the Nannie Creek Trail from Puck Lake to the junction with the Snow Lakes Trail. Turning left there, it's another 2 miles to Trapper Lake, 6 miles from the Nannie Creek Trailhead (see Hike 50).

48   Lower Sky Lakes Basin

Highlights:	Easy hike to numerous large lakes in the lower portion of the Sky Lake Wilderness's principal basin and namesake.
Type of hike:	Day hike or backpack, out and back.
Total distance:	7 miles.
Difficulty:	Easy.
Elevation gain:	200 feet.
Best months:	June–October.
Map:	USGS Pelican Butte quad.

Special considerations: The Sky Lakes Basin is famous for its mosquitoes before mid-July. Most creeks dry up by mid-July. After that, the only water is in the lakes.

Finding the trailhead: From White City, near Medford, take Oregon Highway 140 east towards Klamath Falls. At milepost 41, past Lake of the Woods, a gravel road (Forest Road 3651), leads to the left. It's 10 miles up the gravel road to the Cold Spring Trailhead.

Parking and trailhead facilities: There's parking for 20 cars at the popular trailhead, with a couple of primitive campsites. Cold Spring's water is very cold but probably not safe to drink due to the many horses.

Key points:
0.0 Cold Spring Trailhead.
0.5 Wilderness boundary.
0.6 South Rock Creek Trail junction.
2.4 Sky Lakes Trail junction (go right).
2.8 Isherwood Loop junction (go left).
3.2 Sky Lakes Trail junction (go right).
3.3 Big Heavenly Twin Lake.
3.5 Little Heavenly Twin Lake.

The hike: The Cold Spring Trail (3710) to Isherwood and Heavenly Twin Lakes, largest in the lower Sky Lakes Basin, may not be quite as scenic as some other trails in the wilderness. On the other hand, many hiking devotees swear by this level, easy, lake-filled pathway into the Sky Lakes Basin, after which the wilderness was named. An extra 2 miles will land you at Trapper Lake (Hike 49), in the upper basin, the most beautiful of the Sky

Lower Sky Lakes Basin

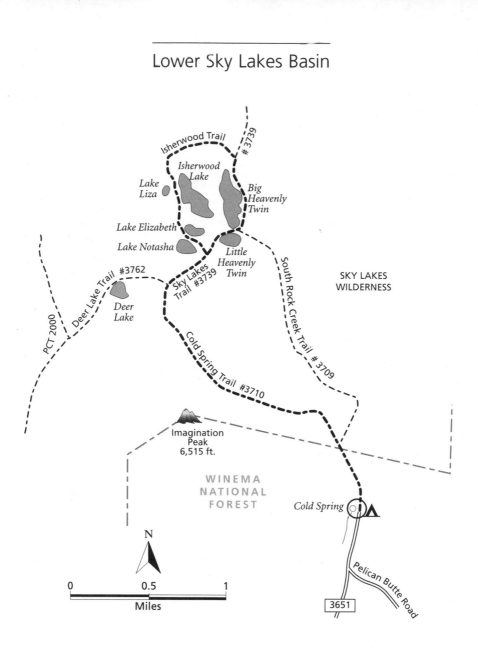

Lakes Basin lakes. Rest assured, there are many gorgeous spots before Trapper Lake. Swimming and picnicking are excellent, although fishing is only fair.

When viewing this part of the wilderness as a distant panorama from the top of Devil's Peak (Hike 41) or the Pelican Butte lookout (a fantastic drive up a steep dirt road which begins just before the Cold Spring trailhead), there appears to be little of interest in the area's topography. But while there are many level stretches and little elevation gain or loss, the

Pat Bernstein, Cold Spring Trail.

path rises and falls with surprising frequency. Between miles 1.0 and 2.0, the path skirts the base of Imagination Peak. Farther on, the route crosses numerous glacial moraines (rubble piles bulldozed up by glacial movement).

The smaller lakes in the wide lower basin are mostly tarns. The larger lakes (Isherwood and the Heavenly Twins) are glacial lakes caused by moraine impoundments but without the obvious cliff headwalls that indicate the source of the glacier.

In the upper basin, the lakes' glacial origins are much more obvious. Lakes Margurette and Trapper hug the base of impressive headwalls. The broad glacier in the lower basin began at Lost Peak and the Cascade crest south of Mount Luther and flowed east into Buck Creek. The glacier in the upper basin began at Mount Luther and Devil's Peak and flowed into Cherry Creek. At some point, the upper-basin and lower-basin glaciers probably merged.

The Cold Spring Trail trails off through a woods of mountain hemlock,

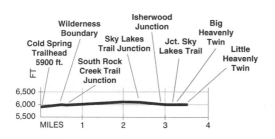

lodgepole pine, and Shasta fir. After 0.6 mile, just past the wilderness boundary, the South Rock Creek Trail (3709) enters stage right. Stay on the Cold Spring Trail for now.

It's 2.4 miles from the trailhead to the junction

with the Deer Lake Trail (3762) and Sky Lakes Trail (3739). Follow 3739 to the right, then turn left onto the Isherwood Loop Trail at mile 2.8 (unless you're not interested in Isherwood Lake). Almost immediately, you'll pass two small but pretty lakes, Notasha and Elizabeth. Soon after, Isherwood Lake pops into view. It's a short, steep scramble downhill to the shore. The trail then loops past a couple of ponds near the head of Isherwood Lake, then rejoins the Sky Lakes Trail at Big Heavenly Twin Lake, largest in the Sky Lakes Basin at 25 acres. Hang a right at the Isherwood/Sky Lakes far junction to make a loop that returns to the trailhead. A left takes you to Trapper and Margurette Lakes after 2 miles. The Isherwood/Sky Lakes far junction, heading north towards Lake Margurette, is the beginning of Hike 49.

Heading right from the Isherwood far junction, the southbound Sky Lakes Trail runs alongside Heavenly Twin, past a skunk cabbage seep. It then swings right, onto the narrow isthmus between Big Heavenly Twin Lake and Little Heavenly Twin Lake. From the isthmus, the lake cluster's only panorama can be seen—a fine view of Devil's Peak a few miles north. The isthmus is the lower basin's prettiest spot.

Options: *Pacific Crest Trail.* If you turn left instead of right where the Cold Spring Trail meets the Sky Lakes Trail, you'll come to the PCT (2000) after 1 mile. The nearest highlight on the PCT is the top of Mount Luther, 4 miles north. Hike 50 offers a better route to the top of Mount Luther.

South Rock Creek Trail. The South Rock Creek Trail begins (or ends) where the Sky Lakes Trail swings onto the isthmus between Little and Big Heavenly Twin Lakes. The path is an alternate to the Cold Spring Trail. The rockier tread skims the edge of an old clearcut before returning to the Cold Spring Trail after 2 miles. The path offers a pretty good view of Pelican Butte and is a little shorter and more level than the Cold Spring Trail.

49   Upper Sky Lakes Basin

Highlights:	Gorgeous big blue lakes and high mountains in the Sky Lakes' namesake basin.
Type of hike:	Backpack, out and back.
Total distance:	4 miles (11 miles via Cold Spring Trailhead).
Difficulty:	Easy.
Elevation gain:	Minimal.
Best months:	June–October.
Map:	USGS Pelican Butte quad.

Special considerations: Two of the lakes on this hike are Mosquito Lake and No-See-Um Lake. What more is there to say? June to mid-July are the worst.

Upper Sky Lakes Basin

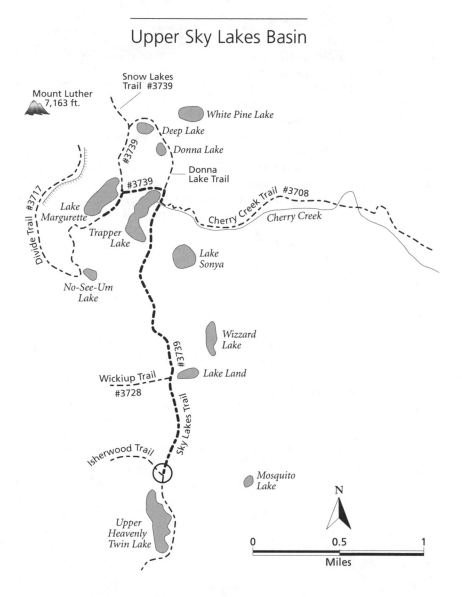

Finding the trailhead: This is a continuation of Hike 48, the Lower Sky Lakes Basin. The hike begins 3.5 miles from the Cold Spring Trailhead, at the far end of Upper Heavenly Twin Lake, where the Sky Lakes Trail meets the Isherwood Trail for the second time.

Key points:

    0.0. Sky Lakes Trail at second Isherwood junction.

    0.7 Land Lake.

    1.6 Trapper Lake, Cherry Creek Trail junction.

    1.7 Donna Lake Trail junction.

    2.0 Lake Margurette.

The hike: For the Sky Lakes Basin's most scenic and lake-filled area, continue on the Sky Lakes Trail (3739) north from Upper Heavenly Twin Lake. The mostly level path winds through a hemlock and lodgepole pine

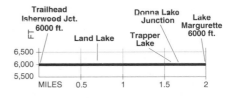

forest, over moraine boulder fields and past the oddly named Lake Land, with a couple of impressive glimpses eastward into Wizzard Lake and Cherry Creek. After 1 mile or so, Mount Luther (7,163 feet) pops briefly into sight, then disappears, only to return as Trapper Lake is approached.

Trapper Lake is easily the basin's prettiest and among the most scenic in the wilderness. It's also among the basin's larger lakes, about the same size as Isherwood and Margurette.

Trapper Lake is blue and big and clear, with lots of level campsites and many side trails nearby. To the north rises Devil's Peak while the Mount Luther complex swoops abruptly up from the lake's western shore (actually, a black cliff headwall rises out of the lake's western shore, with the yellow rock mountain set back above). To the southeast, Pelican Butte dominates the horizon.

As it turns out, the black cliff and yellow mountain do not rise from Trapper Lake. It's hard to believe, but Lake Margurette lies between Trapper Lake and the cliff. Lake Margurette is almost as big as Trapper Lake and much deeper. If you look very closely to the west from Trapper Lake towards Mount Luther, you'll notice a low moraine at the base of the

Trapper Lake.

black cliff, with Lake Margurette, 80 feet higher than Trapper Lake, hiding on the other side.

Cliff and mountain rise directly from the western shore of Lake Margurette, which isn't quite as pretty as Trapper Lake. From Lake Margurette, you can see only the black cliff, not the yellow mountain above.

If you head due east, cross-country and downhill from the extreme south end of Trapper Lake, you'll end up at Lake Sonya (off to the right), after 0.2 mile. Lake Sonya is fairly impressive considering there's no trail access. The perfectly round pool is 60 feet lower than Trapper Lake and stocked with brook and rainbow trout.

Options: *Donna Lake Trail.* The Donna Lake Trail is unmarked at Trapper Lake but hard to miss 0.1 mile beyond the junction with the Cherry Creek Trail. The route passes Donna Lake and Deep Lake in 0.5 mile, before joining the Snow Lakes/Sky Lakes (3739) Trail from Lake Margurette. It is 2 easy and scenic miles via the Donna Lake and Snow (or Sky) Lakes Trails, past Martin and Snow Lakes, from Trapper Lake to the junction with the Nannie Creek Trail (3707). See Hike 50. The view of Mount Luther from Donna and Deep Lakes is incredible.

Snow Lakes Trail. Heading right (north), from the junction with the Snow Lakes (or Sky Lakes) Trail at Lake Margurette, where the Divide Trail (3717) heads south (left), it's 0.5 mile to the far end of the Donna Lake Trail and 2 miles farther to the junction with the Nannie Creek Trail. Again, see Hike 50.

Cherry Creek Trail. The Cherry Creek Trail (3708) leads from the Cherry Creek Trailhead to Trapper Lake in 4.5 miles, versus 5 miles via the Cold Spring and Sky Lakes Trails. The bad news is that the trailhead elevation is 1,600 feet lower than the Cold Spring Trailhead. The path's first 3.5 miles are fairly level as the route makes it's way along the creek, up a wide, forested canyon carved by the former Cherry Creek Glacier. The last mile rises 1,000 feet. The trail crosses Cherry Creek twice and may be impassable in spring when water is high.

To reach the Cherry Creek Trailhead, follow the trailhead directions for Puck Lake (Hike 47). On Westside Road, 1.1 miles before the Nannie Creek turnoff, Forest Road 3450 (left) leads to the Cherry Creek trailhead after 1.8 miles.

Divide Trail. Beginning at Lake Margurette, the southbound Divide Trail (3717) climbs 800 feet in 2 miles to the pass immediately south of Mount Luther, where it ends at the Pacific Crest Trail (2000). From the pass, it's a technically easy but very steep off-trail hike (rising 363 feet in 0.2 mile) to the Mount Luther summit. See Hike 50.

50 Mount Luther

Highlight:	A stunning, seldom-visited gem, with panoramic views of the Sky Lakes Basin. The trail passes dozens of small lakes as it explores the magnificent white escarpment connecting Devil's Peak and Mount Luther.
Type of hike:	Backpack, loop.
Total distance:	7.2 miles (plus 10 additional miles from the Cold Spring Trailhead to the beginning of the loop, then back to the trailhead).
Difficulty:	Moderate.
Elevation gain:	900 feet.
Best months:	July–Oct.
Maps:	USGS Pelican Butte and Devil's Peak quads.

Special considerations: While the hike passes dozens of small lakes, and some larger ones, most creeks dry up by mid-summer and most lakes are brown and stagnant. The best bet for drinking, if you absolutely must, is to take water out of one of the clearer lakes (Trapper, Margurette, Donna, Deep, or a small lake on the Snow Lakes Trail, 0.5 mile before the PCT junction). No matter how clear the water looks, it should always be purified before drinking.

The Sky Lakes Basin is a mosquito paradise until mid-July or later, depending on the snow pack. Once you get up on the ledge, the situation improves dramatically. Morning is worst.

Finding the trailhead: This is a continuation of Hike 49. The described loop begins at Trapper Lake, at the junction of the Donna Lake Trail and the Sky Lake Trail. The turnoff to the Donna Lake Trail from the Sky Lakes Trail is unmarked but obvious, 0.1 mile north of the junction of the Sky Lakes Trail with the Cherry Creek Trail. The spot can be reached either from the Cold Spring Trailhead (5 miles, 200-foot elevation gain) or the Cherry Creek Trailhead (4.5 miles, 1,800-foot elevation gain).

You can also enter via the Nannie Creek Trail (4 miles, minimal elevation gain but lots of ups and downs and too much uphill hiking on the way out). The Nannie Creek route picks up the loop 2 miles north of Trapper

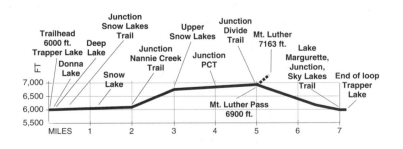

186

Mount Luther

Shale Butte
7,367 ft.

To Devil's Peak

PCT

Snow Lakes Trail #3739

Nannie Creek Trail #3707

PCT

Snow Lakes

Martin Lake

Wind Lake

Snow Lake

Luther Mountain
7,163 ft.

Deep Lake

Divide Trail
#3717

Donna Lake

Donna Creek Trail

PCT 2000

#3739

Lake Margurette

Trapper Lake

#3717

No-See-Um Lake

Sky Lakes Trail #3739

N

0   0.5   1
Miles

Lake. See Hike 47 for a description of the Nannie Creek Trail and beautiful Puck Lake.

Key points:
0.0 Trapper Lake.
0.2 Donna Lake.
0.4 Deep Lake.
0.5 Snow Lakes Trail junction (go right).
1.2 Lower Snow Lakes.
2.0 Nannie Creek Trail junction.
3.0 Upper Snow Lakes.
4.0 PCT junction (go left).
5.0 Mount Luther pass, Divide Trail junction (go left).
7.0 Lake Margurette.
7.2 Trapper Lake, end of loop.

The hike: The reason for describing this hike in the counter-clockwise direction is because it hits the steepest segment, between Lake Margurette and the Mount Luther pass, in the downhill direction. With an elevation differential of 800 feet in 2 miles, the segment could easily be done in the opposite direction.

Beginning at Trapper Lake, the most beautiful Sky Lakes Basin lake (see Hike 49), in the shadow of 7,163-foot Mount Luther, at the junction of the Sky Lakes Trail (3739) and the Donna Lake Trail (unnumbered and unsigned), the Donna Lake Trail heads north, passing a trio of exquisite tarns in 0.5 mile. Technically, a "tarn" is a lake that occupies a depression left by a detached chunk of glacial ice deposited as the main glacier retreated. In common usage, it refers to any small lake of glacial origin.

Donna Lake and Deep Lake are both in view of Mount Luther and both lovely. White Pine Lake is a little bigger than Deep Lake but isn't stocked and has no trail access. To reach White Pine Lake, hike through the woods due east from Deep Lake for 0.2 mile.

The Donna Lake Trail meets the Snow Lakes Trail (3739, the same number as the Sky Lakes Trail) from Lake Margurette immediately beyond Deep Lake. Turn right at the junction to continue the loop. Soon after, the Snow (Sky) Lakes Trail crosses the low rise of a forested arm radiating off the base of Mount Luther. This low rise is the reason the incredible panorama of the Sky Lakes Basin, from atop the white ledge farther up the Snow Lakes Trail, doesn't include views of Trapper, Margurette, Deep, or Donna Lakes.

The first and largest of the Snow Lakes shows up 0.7 mile beyond the Donna/Snow (Sky) junction. Snow Lake is the largest and most impressive of the Snow Lakes cluster, which consists mostly of small, stagnant, brown-water pools. Snow Lake abuts a barren scree slope at the very foot of Mount Luther and is stocked with brook trout. The other lakes in the vicinity, including Martin, Wind, and several ponds, are unstocked and also small and stagnant.

It's 2 miles from the beginning of the loop to the junction with the Nannie Creek Trail (3707), 0.5 mile past Martin Lake through the woods in gently rising terrain. A sign at the Nannie Creek junction claims that it's 3 miles to the junction with the Pacific Crest Trail (2000). On the map it looks more like 2 miles and feels like 2 miles on the trail.

For the first mile past the Nannie Creek junction, the path steepens considerably while remaining in a forest of smallish mountain hemlock, Shasta red fir, western white pine, and lodgepole pine. Look for the trail to gradually approach the huge, white, north-south escarpment running just to the west and connecting Mount Luther and Devil's Peak. The trail is shortly going to climb the escarpment.

Devil's Peak (7,582 feet), the region's highest summit, comes into view to the north, 0.5 mile past the Nannie Creek junction. Devil's Peak is on the left. The peak immediately to the right of Devil's Peak, which appears larger and higher, is Lee Peak, 75 feet lower. If you look closely at Devil's Peak, you can see the Pacific Crest Trail.

The Snow Lakes Trail now climbs a series of glacial moraines left by what was once a huge valley glacier emanating from Devil's Peak, Mount Luther, and the base of the white escarpment. The ice mass flowed across the upper Sky Lakes Basin and out Cherry Creek to the east. All these places can be seen as you continue up the path.

Things get interesting when the trail passes a largish (1 acre maybe), pretty but brown-water lake pressed against the base of the white escarpment. Immediately beyond this lake, the path inscribes a series of short switchbacks (seven of them) in the woods beside a steep scree slope. The

Mount Luther from Snow Lakes Trail. Snow Lakes at base.

route ends up on a rocky subledge on the white escarpment, below the main ledge.

There is a lake on this ledge-below-the-ledge. It is unnamed, unstocked, and covers only 1.5 acres. It is one of the most beautiful lakes in the world. On one end of the lake's white-rock shore, a white scree slope and cliff rise up to the main ledge. On the other end, the white rock (which close up is a grayish lava called "andesite"), drops abruptly down to the Sky Lakes Basin. The lake itself, in contrast to every other lake in the vicinity, is a brilliant, clear blue. The panorama from the lake, of Mount Luther, the Sky Lakes Basin, Pelican Butte, Mount McLoughlin, the Mountain Lakes formation, and the Klamath Basin, is awesome. The little lake is the loop's only reasonable water source.

The next 0.5 mile from the beautiful blue lake, along the white ledge's upper rim, is by far the most gorgeous segment on the entire loop. First you cross a rocky scree slope (it feels like you're walking on broken pottery). Then you enter a fairyland of white-rock ledges and subledges dotted with ponds. The cliff above the scree slope is highly convoluted, with the rock layers twisted into fantastic shapes and swirling patterns.

The unfolding view of Mount Luther is fascinating. Your destination is easily visible: the gap between Mount Luther and a slightly lower summit immediately east. The ledge you're following makes its way around the rim above a small but deep valley off the Sky Lakes Basin. The valley cuts into the Mount Luther formation northwest of the main summit.

The valley is reminiscent of Mount St. Helens. A ring of volcanic peaks forms a horseshoe-shaped basin (or crater), with one side either blown out by volcanic eruption or carved out by a glacier. In the crater's center, a large and obvious lava dome, where pasty lava oozed up following the eruption, can be seen both at Mount St. Helens and Mount Luther. One side of the lava dome below Mount Luther has been eaten away by glacial action.

The junction with the PCT marks the end of the white-rock ledges. Turn left for the Mount Luther pass, 1 mile away (you've come 4 miles). Most of this mile on the PCT follows the crest of a narrow, forested ridge which drops into the Upper Sky Lakes Basin to the east (and ultimately into the Klamath Basin) and into the Rogue River drainage to the west. Long views may be had in both directions and this is truly the "Pacific Crest." Look for lots of subalpine fir, joining the mountain hemlock and Shasta red fir. Look also for a wildflower called *dicentra* or Oregon bleeding heart.

At the PCT segment's low spot, 0.2 mile south of the Snow Lakes Trail junction, a side trail supposedly takes off right, to a place called Hemlock Lake (about 5 acres) after 0.8 mile and 500 feet lower down. Don't count on this as a side trip, however; you may not be able to find the trail.

The final approach to the Mount Luther pass runs along the top of yet another steep scree slope.The pass is fantastic, with rock outcrops perfect for sitting and pondering even though you can't yet see Trapper Lake or Lake Margurette. The off-trail climb to the summit of Mount Luther from the pass looks technically easy and short but is very steep (0.2 mile with an elevation gain of 363 feet). Most of the route to the top follows a grassy slope, with a series of jagged but easily climbed rock outcrops capping the forested summit.

To return to the loop's starting point, turn left onto the Divide Trail (3717) at the pass. From there, it's 2 miles and an 800-foot drop down to Lake Margurette. The Divide Trail is straight and relatively level for 0.6 mile from the pass. It then inscribes a series of short, steep switchbacks as it descends to a forested, pond-dotted bench. The path makes its way to the drop-off at the edge of the bench, then follows the top of a black-rock cliff, with Lakes Margurette and Trapper coming into view directly below. The cliff gets gradually lower and lower before fading away. By No-See-Um Lake (2 acres, unstocked), 1.5 miles from the pass, you're off the bench and the only things between you and Lake Margurette are 0.5 mile of woods and a couple more ponds.

At Lake Margurette, at the intersection of the Divide Trail and the Sky Lakes Trail, follow the Sky Lakes Trail right for 0.2 mile to the starting point at Trapper Lake.

Options: *PCT north and south.* If you head north on the PCT from the end of the Snow Lakes Trail, it's 2 miles to the junction with the Devil's Peak Trail (984) at Mount Lucifer and 3 miles to the pass between Devil's Peak, Lee Peak, and the Seven Lakes Basin. This is an outstanding and not too difficult side trip (see Hike 41). There is no water except for lingering snowfields.

If you head south on the PCT from the Mount Luther Pass, it's 8 mostly boring miles to the Red Lake Trail to Island and Red Lakes (see Hike 43).

---

51 Mount McLoughlin

Highlight:	A magnificent hike up southern Oregon's mightiest peak.
Type of hike:	Day hike, out and back.
Total distance:	About 11 miles.
Difficulty:	Extremely strenuous.
Elevation gain:	3,895 feet.
Best months:	July–October.
Map:	USGS Mount McLoughlin quad.

Special considerations: There is no water or any good place to camp on the trail. Horse travel is not allowed.

Finding the trailhead: Take Oregon Highway 140 east from White City, near Medford, to the Four Mile Lake turnoff (Forest Road 3661), near milepost 37. Turn left and proceed 3 miles to the roomy trailhead parking area, up a short side road (3650) on the left.

Mount McLoughlin

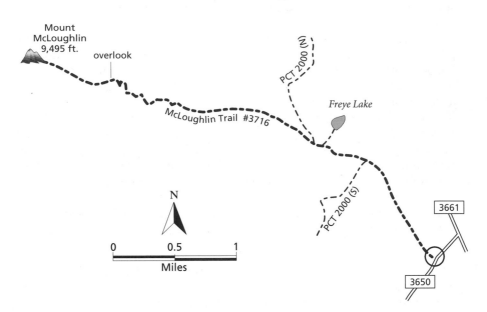

Parking and trailhead facilities: There's room for 30 cars at the trailhead.

Key points:
- 0.0 McLoughlin Trailhead.
- 1.0 Pacific Crest Trail junction (southbound).
- 1.4 Freye Lake Trail (unsigned).
- 1.5 PCT junction (northbound).
- 4.5 Overlook.
- 5.5 Summit.

The hike: The ascent of southern Oregon's Fujiyama is a major undertaking. The McLoughlin Trail (3716) rises 3,900 feet in 5.5 miles. Soaring altitude and a final mile that climbs 1,700 feet over arduous terrain make McLoughlin far more difficult than other hikes with a similar gradient and elevation gain.

McLoughlin's first 3 miles ascend only about 800 feet, gently exploring a deep woods of white fir, Shasta red fir, white pine, and mountain hemlock. It joins the Pacific Crest Trail (2000) from the south after 1 mile. At the end of the path's only long, level stretch, the PCT peels off northward. In between, the short Freye Lake Trail takes off to the right. It's five minutes to Freye Lake but why waste the energy when there's a mountain to climb?

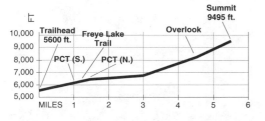

Between miles 2.0 and 3.0, increasingly steep and rocky treads with areas of loose gravel begin to show up. The gradient grows serious between mile 3.0 and mile 4.5; you climb 1,000 feet. The now tedious pathway slowly leaves the forest behind and enters open, rocky areas, dotted with brush and clumps of stunted whitebark pine. Vistas of Klamath Lake, Four Mile Lake, and Lake of the Woods emerge.

If you thought the trail was strenuous up to now, you'll think the lower portion was a piece of cake after the final mile. Don't feel compelled to climb the final mile, however. An overlook at mile 4.5 is worth the trip in itself. At the overlook, the trail finally hits the main ridge, unveiling a spectacular vista of the Crater Lake rim and the Sky Lakes to the north. The main summit comes into view for the first time here, as does an immense, barren avalanche basin careening down to Four Mile Lake. Overhead, a giant orange lava plug juts from the sweeping basin's upper end.

The avalanche basin is actually a giant, lakeless, glacial cirque. The rubble pile at the base is a terminal moraine and the lava plug does not rise from the basin but from a narrow ridge between two glacial cirques. (See Hike 44.)

Snow fields often dot the upper peak even in August. When we climbed McLoughlin in 1989 and 1998, there was far more snow than normal because of late springs and cool weather, but there was none near the trail either time. Snow melts on the ridge much sooner than on either side of the ridge.

Past the overlook, the route holds a level contour for a few hundred feet. It then takes off straight up a seemingly endless rock and ash fall, marked only by paint blazes. When you finally reach the ridge, the trail largely disappears. Widely scattered blazes mark the summit route along several interwoven paths.

In following the obvious ridge line to the summit, you are faced with some choices. A wall of rock extends along much of the ridge. On its south side, hikers must pick their way among large, often cindery, boulders. To the north, the top of the avalanche basin's scree field looks a little more trail-like but footing is poor in the loose sand and ash. Most hikers end up alternating between the two sides.

It takes three to five hours to reach the summit, depending on your level of conditioning. The peak is topped by a stone wall which used to be the base of a fire lookout.

The summit view is commanding. To the north, Broken Top, the South Sister, and Diamond Peak cap the horizon. You can also see Mount Thielsen, Mount Bailey, the summits of the Rogue-Umpqua Divide Wilderness, and the Crater Lake rim including Mount Scott. You cannot see Crater Lake, though. Closer in, the Sky Lakes Wilderness can be seen,

Mount McLoughlin, Four Mile Lake, from Badger Lake Trail.

especially Devil's Peak and the Blue Canyon, Seven Lakes, and Sky Lakes Basins. Among the Sky Lakes, only Island Lake is visible.

To the east lies Upper Klamath Lake, Yamsay Mountain, Pelican Butte, and the caldera of the Mountain Lakes Wilderness. Southward, Mount Shasta dominates, along with Lake of the Woods, Fish Lake, Howard Prairie Lake, Hyatt Lake, Pilot Rock, and the Marble Mountains.

To the west, the mountains are much farther away. Willow Lake is located easily enough, plus Mount Ashland, Table Rock, the Bear Creek Valley, and the Rogue canyon between Gold Hill and Grants Pass. Far in the distance, one can make out Eight Dollar Mountain near Selma and Preston Peak south of Cave Junction.

Just below the summit, there's a compelling shortcut back to the overlook that involves sliding down a steep scree slope. The Forest Service discourages this route because some people end up lost. While the Forest Service is correct, most people don't get lost. Still, in 1975 the author took a fake trail here and ended up descending the mountain off trail for 3.5 miles.

In its fine pamphlet on climbing the mountain, the Forest Service warns against false trails, and recommends following the blazes on rocks and trees as well as the actual trail, especially on the way down. This is VERY good advice.

Near the Sky Lakes

There are surprisingly few trails immediately adjacent to the Sky Lakes Wilderness. Here is a real charmer:

52 South Fork Trail

Highlight: A beautiful, easy path through the deep woods along a magnificent, wild trout stream.
Type of hike: Day hike, shuttle.
Total distance: 1.5 miles.
Difficulty: Easy.
Elevation gain: Minimal.
Best months: Late April–mid-December.
Map: USGS Rustler Peak quad.

Finding the trailhead: For the trailhead on Forest Road 37, take Oregon Highway 62 north from Medford to the Prospect turnoff past milepost 43. Follow signs (right) to the town of Prospect, located a block off OR 62. Turn right on Mill Creek Road. In Prospect, turn left at the Prospect Hotel onto the Prospect–Butte Falls Road. After 3 miles, bear left onto Forest Road 37 and follow it 13 miles to Forest Road 3780, the turnoff for the Seven Lakes Trail. Continue another 0.5 mile on FR 37 to the junction with Forest Road 3775. There's a parking area on the left on FR 37, immediately past the junction and just before the junction with FR 34.

For the upper trailhead, proceed up FR 3775 (right) for 1.2 miles, to a sign that says "Giant Sugar Pine." Park along the shoulder. The trailhead for the South Fork Trail is on the south side of the road, directly opposite the Giant Sugar Pine Trail.

Parking and trailhead facilities: Ten cars can park at the lower trailhead, five cars at the upper trailhead.

Key points:
- 0.0 Giant Sugar Pine Trailhead.
- 0.2 Junction of access trail and South Fork Trail (go left).
- 1.4 Footbridge.
- 1.5 Trailhead on FR 37.

The hike: This is the best segment of a 10-mile trail exploring the South Fork of the Rogue just outside the Sky Lakes Wilderness.

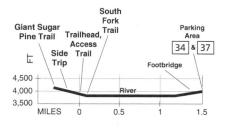

South Fork Trail

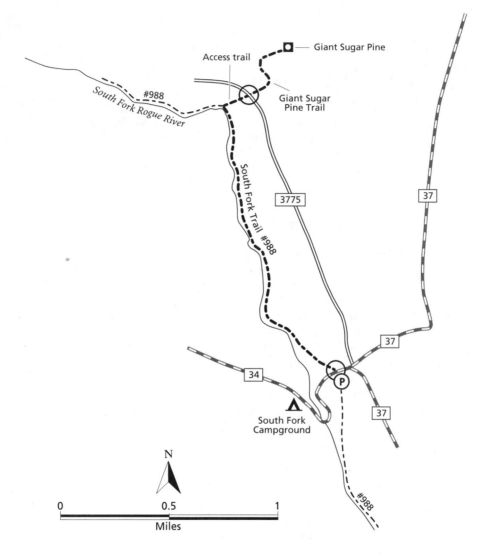

Giant Sugar Pine

Access trail

Giant Sugar
Pine Trail

#988

South Fork Rogue River

South Fork Trail #988

3775

37

37

34

37

P

South Fork
Campground

#988

N

0   0.5   1
Miles

Toss in some fishing and the short Giant Sugar Pine Trail (see Options), and you have an excellent outing.

From the upper trailhead, a 0.2-mile access trail (unnumbered) leads down to the relatively new and well-constructed South Fork Trail (988). Hang a left on the South Fork Trail for the Forest Road 37 trailhead, 1.3 miles away.

The path is fairly uniform, with pleasant views of the river and a beautiful middle elevation forest of Douglas-fir, Western hemlock, sugar pine, and incense cedar. Areas of blowdown from the horrendous 1995 storms are impressive.

Eventually, the land flattens out and wanders away from the river, crossing a side creek, a couple of skunk cabbage bogs, and a little footbridge. These are all signs that FR 37 is not far off.

Options: *Giant Sugar Pine Trail.* This 0.3-mile path leads uphill to a giant sugar pine, 5 feet in diameter and 275 feet high. Note the fire scarring on the tree's bark and the huge mound of old, shed bark scales at the base. Such bark mounds are typical of sugar and ponderosa pine.

The rest of the South Fork Trail. If you turn right (west) instead of left (east) on the South Fork Trail at the junction with the upper-access trail, and keep walking, you'll end up 4 miles farther up FR 3775 (downriver).

From the FR 37 trailhead, if you continue east on the South Fork Trail, you'll come out 5.5 miles upriver, at the bridge where FR 37 crosses the Rogue near Parker Meadows Campground. These are both fine paths. The 5.5-mile upper segment runs through a narrower canyon that abounds with side creeks and is generally farther from roads than the two other segments. The described hike is best.

Mountain Lakes Wilderness

The first thing everybody notices on being shown a map of the Mountain Lakes Wilderness is that the wilderness is square. It covers one township, 6 miles by 6 miles, 36 sections, which should be 23,040 acres but is actually 23,071 acres. It turns out that of all the federal wilderness areas in the United States, this is the only square one. Nature does not normally lend itself to such even measurement.

An explanation for the squareness might be that the Mountain Lakes is one of the Pacific Northwest's oldest wilderness areas. It was among the original three primitive areas set aside by the Forest Service in 1930, along with the Eagle Cap and Mount Jefferson, also in Oregon. In those days, people preferred squares to natural contours. It was easier to map squares and back then, the empty corners weren't likely to infringe on anybody, which is not the case today. For the same reason, nearby Crater Lake, one of the five original U.S. National Parks, established in 1902, is a nearly perfect rectangle.

Geologically, the Mountain Lakes Wilderness has a history nearly identical to Crater Lake, 40 miles north. Both are large volcanoes which, after disgorging their inner magma, caved in on themselves, forming crater-like basins called "calderas." In addition to Crater Lake and the Mountain Lakes, there are two other calderas in the region: Newberry Crater, near Bend (with two lakes inside); and the Medicine Lake Highlands, near Lava Beds National Monument near Klamath Falls. The Medicine Lake Highlands is the largest volcano in basal area in the United States. The Medicine Lake system is highly eroded despite erupting as recently as 1875.

Unlike Crater Lake, the Mountain Lakes caldera developed outlets, as Crater Lake eventually will. The Mountain Lakes developed the outlets as a result of heavy glacial activity. This has not happened (yet) at Crater Lake because the Crater Lake caldera was formed after the end of the last ice age, 10,000 years ago. The Mountain Lakes volcanic activity is older.

The Mountain Lakes caldera is breached at Varney Creek, Moss Creek, and South Pass Creek. Seldom Creek (route of the Mountain Lakes Trail) and Clover Creek were once the site of glaciers which did not breach the caldera rim. The formation is crowned by a ring of five towering, barren, often jagged peaks, between 7,600 and 8,200 feet.

It is unclear whether any vestige of an internally drained basin remains in the Mountain Lakes formation. According to topographic maps, every spot in the wilderness has external drainage. And yet, looking northwest from the saddle above Lake Harriette, it certainly appears as though the area around Whiteface Peak and Eb and Zeb Lakes is an enclosed basin.

53 Lake Harriette

Highlights:	A fascinating trail to one of Oregon's largest and most beautiful alpine lakes.
Type of hike:	Backpack, out and back.
Total distance:	13.4 miles.
Difficulty:	Moderate.
Elevation gain:	1,400 feet to the Lake Harriette saddle, followed by a 150 foot loss.
Best months:	June–October.
Maps:	USGS Aspen Lake and Pelican Bay quads.

Special considerations: Mosquitoes are horrible before mid-July.

Finding the trailhead: Take Oregon Highway 140 east towards Klamath Falls from White City, near Medford. Between milepost 47 and 48, near the Odessa Creek Campground, a road sign points to the right, up Forest Road 3637, to the Varney Creek Trail (You want Odessa Creek Road. Do not take Forest Road 3610–Varney Creek Road). Follow FR 3637 for 2 miles to Forest Road 3664. Turn left on FR 3664 and follow it 2 more miles to the trailhead, 4 miles from OR 140.

Parking and trailhead facilities: The roomy trailhead holds 30 cars. Camping is available at Lake of the Woods and the Odessa Creek Campground.

Key points:
  0.0 Varney Creek Trailhead.
  1.0 Bridge over Varney Creek.
  4.5 Mountain Lakes Loop junction (go left).
  5.5 Lake Como.
  6.5 Lake Harriette saddle.
  6.7 Lake Harriette.

The hike: Even though it's 6.7 miles to Lake Harriette, this most popular of all routes into the Mountain Lakes Wilderness goes by quickly. Each of the first 4 miles is different from the last, and they're all interesting, unusual, and beautiful.

The first mile follows the east side of Varney Creek and ends at the creek crossing. The second mile follows the steep slope on the west side

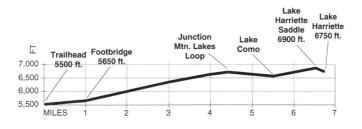

Lake Harriette

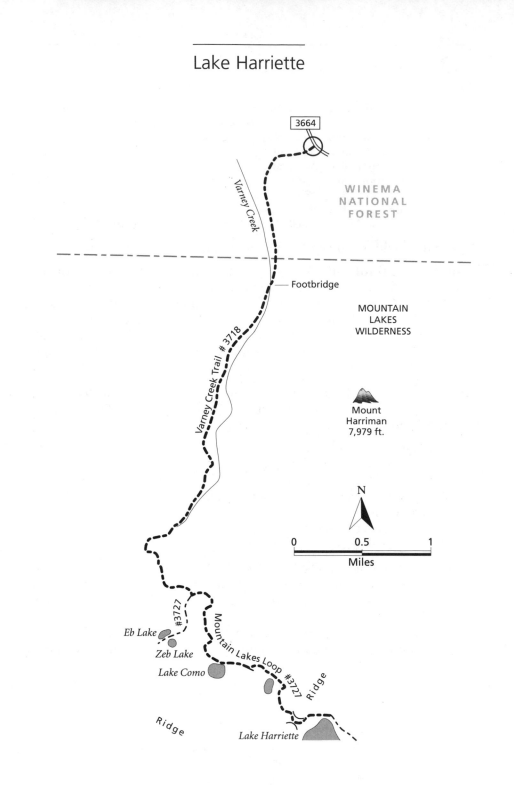

3664

WINEMA
NATIONAL
FOREST

Varney Creek

Footbridge

MOUNTAIN
LAKES
WILDERNESS

Varney Creek Trail # 3718

Mount
Harriman
7,979 ft.

N

0   0.5   1
Miles

#3727

Eb Lake

Zeb Lake

Lake Como

Mountain Lakes Loop #3727

Ridge

Ridge

Lake Harriette

of Varney Creek, through more open country, with Mount Harriman (7,979 feet) rising opposite. In the third mile, you reach the glaciated area, the valley widens out, and the trail starts crossing glacial moraines. The fourth mile, while somewhat similar to mile 3, is a little steeper, and during this segment the barren scree slopes of the high peaks come into view. During the last 0.5 mile before the junction with the Mountain Lakes Loop Trail (4.5 miles from the trailhead), the path crosses a low summit and descends into the forested basin.

Technically, you entered the Mountain Lakes caldera in the second mile when you passed Mount Harriman. Varney Creek, however, has eroded well into the formation so the present actual basin, or what's left of it, is quite small and marked only by a barely noticeable divide at the head of Varney Creek. Similarly, the glacier that formed Lakes Como and Harriette ate clear though the massive ridge between Mount Harriman and Mount Carmine so that Como and Harriette now drain into the Klamath Basin via Moss Creek.

From the trailhead, it's 1 mile through the woods on the Varney Creek Trail (3718) to the wilderness boundary just before the creek crossing. It used to be 0.2 mile but they relocated the trailhead in 1982. During this initial mile, the view from the heavily wooded path evolves from the Klamath Basin and Mount McLoughlin to the opposite side of Varney Creek, far below.

There's an interesting vegetational transition as you hike up Varney Creek, from a land of middle-elevation Douglas-fir and sugar pines to upper-elevation Shasta red fir, mountain hemlock, and western white pine, with millions of lodgepole pines at all elevations. Look for a few Engelmann spruce near the Varney Creek crossing.

The fireweed along miles 2 and 3 and the delphinium (larkspur) at the end of mile 3 are noteworthy. Fireweed grows in extremely hot and open but fairly moist areas that have burned within the last 10 or 20 years. The high, purple (tower) delphinium grows in moist seeps and no doubt denotes the elusive springs shown on the wilderness map.

The Varney Creek Trail ends 0.2 mile beyond the trail summit, at the junction with the Mountain Lakes Loop Trail (3727). Head left on the MLLT for Lakes Como (1 mile) and Harriette (2.2 miles) and right on the MLLT for Eb and Zeb Lakes (0.5 mile). Past the junction, in the Lake Como direction, the trail enters an enchanted land of lakes, cliffs, yellow scree slopes, lingering snowfields, and subalpine forests.

Beautiful, shallow Lake Como is nestled at the foot of a low headwall. Past Lake Como, the trail begins a steep rise through a jumble of boulder fields and ridges, passing a lovely unnamed lake almost as large as Lake Como that is set in a wider, more open basin.

At 6.2 miles from the Varney Creek Trailhead and 1.7 miles from the Varney Creek junction, the path bumps into a wall. To surmount it, the trail takes a steep, if blessedly short, uphill pitch with outstanding views of the basin and a small, lakeless glacial cirque.

Soon after, 6.5 miles from the end of the trailhead, the path emerges at a narrow, rocky saddle atop the headwall above Lake Harriette, the Mountain Lakes' largest and most beautiful body of water. Lake Harriette is the largest glacial lake described in this book and the second largest lake that is a hike destination (after Fish Lake, Hike 11). A vertical cliff rises up from the 6,900-foot saddle above Lake Harriette to a 7,500-foot summit (see Hike 54). A massive slope of pure white boulders begins at the saddle and tumbles from the base of the cliff down to the lake.

From the saddle, the view southwest peers over another, much wider saddle, across the South Pass basin to Aspen Butte. At 8,208 feet, Aspen Butte is the highest peak in the wilderness. It is a treeless, blocky, wedding-cake formation with sheer cliffs peeking over the ridge. The actual summit lies just to the right of the blocky part. (See Hike 54 for instructions on climbing Aspen Butte.)

In the opposite direction, looking northwest from the saddle away from Lake Harriette, most of the Mountain Lakes Basin and its encircling ring of peaks can be seen. Although the view of the basin can only be described as gorgeous, you can't see any of its lakes from here.

The saddle above Lake Harriette, impressive though it is, offers a foreshortened view of the lake that doesn't really give an accurate sense of its sprawling size. For a less dramatic but more accurate vista, continue on the Mountain Lakes Loop for 2.5 miles past Lake Harriette to the pass above Mystic Lake (Hike 54), where you turn off to climb Aspen Butte.

Lake Harriette, 0.2 mile from the saddle and 6.7 miles from the trailhead, is not only the prettiest of the Mountain Lakes, it's the prettiest lake

Delphinium along Varney Creek Trail, Mountain Lakes Wilderness.

in Southern Oregon and perhaps all of Oregon. At 70 acres, it is huge for an alpine glacial cirque lake. White and gray cliffs and talus slopes drop straight into Harriette's deep, intensely blue waters to the south and west. A beautiful little flat, with an open forest stand and green grass underneath, lines the northwest shore. To the east, the lake is held in place by a large glacial moraine which drops off into the immense Moss Creek glacial valley.

Options: *The rest of the Mountain Lakes Loop Trail.* The MLLT from Lake Harriette south to the Aspen Butte turnoff, and from the Varney Creek Trail west and south to the Clover Creek Trail, is described in the Mountain Lakes Loop chapter (Hike 55). The MLLT from Aspen Butte west to the Clover Creek Trail is described in the Aspen Butte chapter (Hike 54).

54 Aspen Butte

Highlight:	A magnificent 8,206-foot summit, highest in the Mountain Lakes Wilderness. Fantastic views of Lake Harriette and other alpine lakes.
Type of hike:	Day hike or backpack, out and back.
Total distance:	About 13 miles.
Difficulty:	Moderate.
Elevation gain:	2,458 feet.
Best months:	July–October.
Maps:	USGS Aspen Lake and Lake of the Woods South quads.

Finding the trailhead: Take Oregon Highway 140 east from White City to the Dead Indian Memorial Road turnoff at milepost 38, just past the Lake of the Woods turnoff. Turn right and drive 8 miles to Clover Creek Road (County Road 603), which ultimately meets Oregon Highway 66 near Keno. Turn left onto Clover Creek Road. A well-marked gravel side road, Forest Road 3852, begins just past milepost 5 on Clover Creek Road and ends at the trailhead, 3 miles up.

Parking and trailhead facilities. The Clover Creek Trailhead, among the prettier in this book, boasts a small campground (no restrooms or water) and parking for eight cars.

Key points:
- 0.0 Clover Creek Trailhead.
- 2.0 Clover Lake.
- 3.5 Mountain Lakes Loop Trail junction (go right).
- 5.5 Aspen Butte Trail junction (go right).
- 6.5 Summit of Aspen Butte.

The hike: Aspen Butte is a handsome peak by any standard and not that difficult a climb. The north side of this proud volcanic summit was rudely torn away by a glacier, leaving cliffs and rock slopes

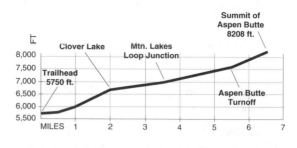

that tumble 1,000 feet to the aptly named Mystic Lake.

The shortest route to the Aspen Butte summit is via the Clover Creek Trail (3722) and the Mountain Lake Loop Trail (3727). Until 10 years ago, the route was 2 miles shorter than it is now. It was rerouted due to erosion problems. It is now 6.5 miles from the trailhead to the top of Aspen Butte.

From the trailhead, the path takes off through the woods, crosses the wilderness boundary almost immediately, and doesn't start uphill or meet Clover Creek for 0.5 mile. The initial 0.5 mile alongside Clover Creek is the steepest pitch on the entire route although it contains a few welcome level spots.

Clover Creek is very pretty, running through deep woods, narrow canyons, and wet meadows rife with wildflowers. Look for wildflowers that like wet feet: tower delphinium, butterweed, Queen Anne's lace, corn lily, grass, sedge, and white-topped clover. The only unusual forest denizen is Pacific silver fir, which is rare south of the Rogue-Umpqua Divide. Other than that, the usual gang of trees can be found: lodgepole pine, Shasta red fir, western white pine, mountain hemlock, and white fir.

At mile 1.5, the path crosses Clover Creek, levels off, and winds around in the woods for 0.5 mile, passing a tiny, stagnant pond. The valley widens here, from a narrow, V-shaped canyon to a flat expanse filled with glacial moraines, just below Clover Lake. That means you've entered an area formerly occupied by a small glacier, the only southward flowing glacier in the Mountain Lakes. The Clover Creek Glacier began just south of Whiteface Peak and moved to the southeast.

At mile 2.0, Clover Lake shows up. For as small and shallow as it is, and for a green-water lake, it is surprisingly pretty. You can fish for brook trout here and enjoy your first views of the caldera rim.

Above Clover Lake, the path continues uphill through the woods at an easy grade. It crosses a number of moraines, necessitating a couple of steep but short downhill pitches. According to the Forest Service and the USGS map, there are 36 "glistening" lakes in the vicinity, all tiny, stagnant, seasonal ponds, collectively known as the Clover Creek Lakes. All you see from the trail are Clover Lake and the aforementioned stagnant pond.

Finally, 3.5 miles from the trailhead, in a nondescript spot in the woods, the Clover Creek Trail ends at the Mountain Lakes Loop Trail. The elevation here is 7,000 feet. Hang a right for Aspen Butte and a left for the upper end of the Mountain Lakes Trail, 2 miles away.

Aspen Butte

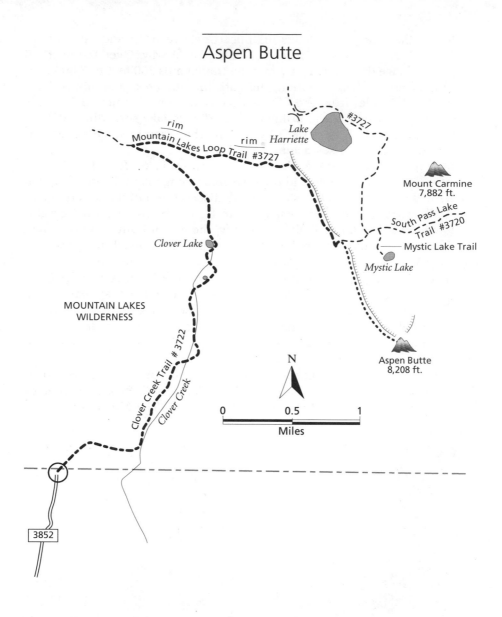

Shortly beyond the junction, heading right, the path starts to get inter-esting. The top of the caldera rim comes into view, 500 feet straight up, with rock falls and talus slopes tumbling down to the trail. The rock is mostly pink and tan. The trail tries to stay below the rock but doesn't always succeed. Forests here are much more open than down on Clover Creek and the trail tread, generally, is very rocky with many faint spots. It may be necessary to follow tree blazes in places to be sure where the trail goes.

While the caldera rim looks disconcertingly high up and far away at first, never fear. You don't have to climb all that way. Over the next 1.5 miles, the ridge drops 200 feet while the trail climbs 300 feet to 7,300 feet.

Finally, after a long flirtation, the path hits the crest high above Lake Harriette, 1.5 miles from the Clover Creek junction. The next 0.5 mile is glorious, with views of the brilliant blue, 70-acre lake sprawling 600 feet below, at the foot of the series of cliffs on which you're standing. Mount Carmine (7,882 feet) rises behind Lake Harriette.

Making its way along the edge of the rim above Lake Harriette, the trail climbs 300 feet in 0.5 mile and presents many long vistas. Eventually, you come to a large rock duck (a stone pile that serves as a trail marker) where the path starts downhill. The Aspen Butte Trail takes off here, on the right, following the ridgeline uphill. Technically, the Aspen Butte Trail is a way-trail, unmarked, unnumbered, and faint in places, although it appears on some maps.

Before starting up Aspen Butte, continue on the Mountain Lakes Loop Trail downhill for a few hundred feet. Mystic Lake quickly appears in the basin below, with mysterious Aspen Butte, one of the most magnificent peaks you'll ever see, rising up behind it like a silent, hooded, druid priest. As impressive as Aspen Butte is, it doesn't photograph well. You have to be there to grasp its full impact.

Still on the Mountain Lakes Loop Trail, it's 0.2 mile from the Aspen Butte turnoff to the South Pass Lake Trail (3720). South Pass Lake, 2 miles away, is also visible near the Aspen Butte turnoff. The Mystic Lake Trail

Lake Harriette from Aspen Butte turnoff on Mountain Lakes Loop. Mount Harriman in background.

begins 0.1 mile down the South Pass Lake Trail from the Mountain Lakes Loop Trail. (See Hike 55.)

The rocky crest of Aspen Butte lies 1 mile (right) from the Aspen Butte turnoff at the crest of the Mountain Lakes Loop Trail. The route ascends 600 feet and is very bouldery. Also, the path tends to braid and there are rock ducks where there shouldn't be. No matter, just follow the sharp ridgeline. It shouldn't take more than an hour, if that, to get from the turnoff to the summit, even though you're slowed down by a couple of large boulder fields, especially near the top. Look for windswept whitebark pines, a treeline species, near the summit.

The view from the craggy summit is predictably outstanding. The huge cirque basin with Lake Harriette in the distance to the north is the most impressive. You can also see most of the caldera basin and rim, Mount McLoughlin, and a big chunk of the Klamath Basin. The large body of water at the base of the main slope to the southeast is Aspen Lake.

Options: *West on the Mountain Lakes Loop.* See Hike 55.
The South Pass Lake Trail. See Hike 55.
Lake Harriette. See Hike 53.

55 Mountain Lakes Loop

Highlight:	Two lovely little lakes and the portions of the Mountain Lakes Loop Trail that are not described in other chapters.
Type of hike:	Backpack, loop.
Total distance:	8.2 miles.
Difficulty:	Moderate to strenuous.
Elevation gain:	1,050 feet.
Best months:	Late June–October.
Maps:	USGS Aspen Lake and Lake of the Woods South quads.

Special considerations: There is some confusion about trail distances for both the Mountain Lakes Loop Trail (MLLT) and the Mountains Lakes Trail (MLT) (which is described in "Options"). The Forest Service map of the Mountain Lakes Wilderness gives the MLLT at 8.2 miles, which is about right. The same map lists the MLT at 6.2 miles, which is more than a mile too long. On the other hand, the Recreational Opportunity Guide for the Mountain Lakes Wilderness, put out by Winema National Forest, shows the MLLT at 10.3 miles, which is 2 miles too long, and the MLT at 5.1 miles, which is dead on.

Finding the trailhead: For the Mountain Lakes Loop Trail, follow directions to the Varney Creek Trailhead (Hike 53) and hike 4.5 miles to the end

Mountain Lakes Loop

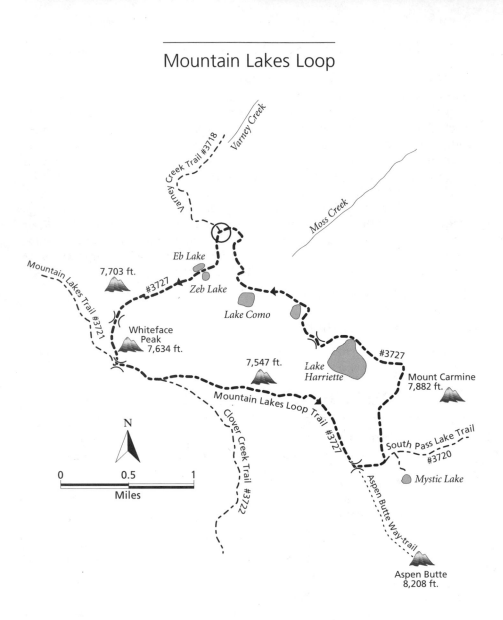

of the Varney Creek Trail. For the hike described in this chapter, turn right onto the Mountain Lakes Loop Trail at the Varney Creek junction, toward Eb and Zeb Lakes. The loop is described in a counter-clockwise direction beginning at the end of the Varney Creek Trail.

Parking and trailhead facilities. See Hike 53.

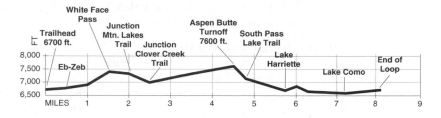

Key points:

0.0 End of Varney Creek Trail.

0.5 Eb and Zeb Lakes.

2.0 Mountain Lakes Trail junction.

2.5 Clover Creek Trail junction.

4.5 Aspen Butte Trail junction.

4.7 South Pass Lake Trail junction.

5.7 Lake Harriette.

7.2 Lake Como.

8.2 End of loop.

The hike: This chapter describes two noncontiguous segments of the Mountain Lakes Loop Trail not described in Hikes 53 and 54. They are the 2.5-mile segment from the Varney Creek Trail (3718) to the Clover Creek Trail (3722) and the 1.2-mile segment from the Aspen Butte Trail (unnumbered) to Lake Harriette.

Varney Creek Trail to Clover Creek Trail

The first highlight you arrive at, heading west (right) on the Mountain Lakes Loop from the end of the Varney Creek Trail, is Eb and Zeb Lakes (elevation 6,750 feet, about 1 acre each). These tiny, amazingly clear pools, sit on either side of the trail, 0.5 mile from the junction. Eb is the one nestled against the mountainside, which is a part of Whiteface Peak. Zeb sits out in the middle of the flat. These are surprisingly deep and pretty lakes, considering their minuscule size and terrible names. The lakes are unstocked.

From Eb and Zeb, it's a steep but impressive 1-mile hike, through forest and across rock fields, to the 7,400-foot saddle just north of Whiteface Peak (7,634 feet). The barren yellow peak is visible to the south. It's a fairly easy climb to the summit for the saddle.

At the saddle, you can see westward for the first time, with a view down the Seldom Creek glacial valley, route of the Mountain Lakes Trail, to Lake of the Woods. (See "Options.") The loop trail then contours through the woods for 0.5 mile, dropping to a second, 7,300-foot saddle, where it meets the upper end of the Mountain Lakes Trail.

The 7,300-foot saddle is interesting because two glaciers emanated from the spot, each flowing in opposite directions. The Seldom Creek glacier flowed northwest while the much smaller Clover Creek Glacier flowed southeast. A steeply downhill 0.5 mile leads from the saddle to the 7,000-foot junction with the Clover Creek Trail at mile 2.5. See Hike 54 for a description of the 2-mile hike on the Mountain Lakes Loop Trail from the Clover Creek junction to the Aspen Butte junction.

Aspen Butte junction to Lake Harriette

Beyond the Aspen Butte junction, you discover why the Forest Service recommends hiking in a counterclockwise direction. The trail drops 300 feet in 0.2 mile in a large switchback as it descends into the magnificent glacial cirque of Mystic Lake and South Pass Lake, with the foreboding Aspen Butte, highest point in the wilderness, towering 8,208 feet overhead just to the south. This is spectacular country. Both Mystic Lake and South Pass Lake are visible from the Mountain Lakes Loop Trail near the Aspen Butte junction. It's 0.2 mile from the Aspen Butte junction to the South Pass Lake Trail (3720) junction at a low saddle (7,300 feet) between Mystic lake and Lake Harriette. Follow the South Pass Lake Trail (right) for 0.1 mile to the 0.2 mile long Mystic Lake Trail (left). Also, it's 1.5 miles on the South Pass Lake Trail from the Mountain Lakes Loop to South Pass Lake (see "Options").

Beyond the South Pass Lake Trail junction, the loop trail drops rapidly into the Lake Harriette basin. It's a very rocky, up-and-down (mostly down) 1 mile from the South Pass Lake Trail to Lake Harriette. From Lake Harriette, it's 1.2 miles to Lake Como (over a short, steep, rocky pass) and 2.2 miles to the end of the loop at the Varney Creek junction.

See Hike 53 for a description of the Mountain Lakes Loop Trail from the Varney Creek junction to Lake Harriette.

Options: *The Mountain Lakes Trail.* This path is amazingly popular, considering it's the longest and least-interesting route into the Mountain Lakes. Clover Creek reaches the Mountain Lakes Loop after 3.5 miles while Varney Creek does it in 4.5 miles. The MLT takes 5 miles to reach the loop and 6 miles to get anyplace significant (Eb and Zeb Lakes). The Mountain Lakes Trail (3721) begins at the lowest elevation (5,200 feet) and crests at the highest elevation (7,300 feet) of any of the three Mountain Lakes entries. It is fairly popular due to it's proximity to Lake of the Woods.

From the trailhead, the path climbs gradually through the usual mixed-conifer forest. Just about where the path enters the wilderness, at mile 1.5, the terrain opens out from a narrow V canyon following Seldom Creek, to a wide glacial valley with scree slopes and peaks in the distance. The valley contains several small lakes, only one of which, Lake Waban (about 2 acres), has a trail access (right at mile 3.2). The 500-foot Lake Waban Trail is unsigned near a large meadow.

The first mile past Lake Waban is fairly level as it crosses a series of moraines and outcrops. The path steepens considerably for the final mile as it ascends to a saddle just south of Whiteface Peak, where it meets the Mountain Lakes Loop Trail. You can't see Lake of the Woods from the saddle but you can see Brown Mountain and Mount McLoughlin.

To reach the Mountain Lakes Trailhead, turn right off Oregon Highway 140 onto Dead Indian Road at milepost 37, then immediately turn left onto

Forest Road 3610, then Forest Road 3660. It's 4 miles to the trailhead, which accommodates eight cars alongside the road.

South Pass Lake Trail. The South Pass Lake Trail (3720) explores a beautiful glacial basin between Aspen Butte and Lake Harriette. The trail leads to Mystic Lake in 0.1 mile, Paragon Lake in 0.8 mile, and South Pass Lake in 2 miles. South Pass Lake occupies a steep-walled, flat-bottomed, densely forested glacial valley.

Bear Creek Valley

The huge, highly developed valley containing Medford and Ashland is named for Bear Creek, a once pretty stream that flows into the Rogue River at the valley's north end. The Bear Creek Greenway, a series of trails, bike paths, and jogging paths that follow the creek from Ashland to the town of Gold Hill, is not included in this book because some of it is paved, most of it lies within view of Interstate 5, and long stretches of the creek are badly polluted and unpleasant. Still, the Greenway has its nice spots and they're working on the rest of it.

56 Lower Table Rock

Highlights:	A steep hike up a spectacular flat-topped mesa with rare plants and an outstanding view.
Type of hike:	Day hike, out and back.
Total distance:	About 4 miles.
Difficulty:	Moderate.
Elevation gain:	800 feet.
Best months:	All.
Map:	USGS Sam's Valley quad.

Special considerations: While rated a "moderate," the trail contains some very steep pitches. In summer, because the route is at a low elevation, exposed, and humid until the top, it can be very hot and uncomfortable. In winter, the path becomes extremely muddy. Late winter and spring are the best times for viewing rare wildflowers around the seasonal ponds.

Finding the trailhead: From Medford, take Table Rock Road north past White City. The route makes a left turn and a right turn before it intersects with Wheeler Road, 4 miles beyond TouVelle State Park. Follow Wheeler Road 2.5 miles (left) to the trailhead area. From Grants Pass, take Sams Valley Road (left) to Tresham Lane. Turn right on Tresham and right again on Wheeler.

Parking and trailhead facilities: The trailhead parking area accommodates 20 cars.

Key points:
    0.0 Lower Table Rock Trailhead.
    0.5 Alternate trail junction (go left).
    1.0 Rim.
    2.0 Overlook above Rogue Valley.

Lower Table Rock

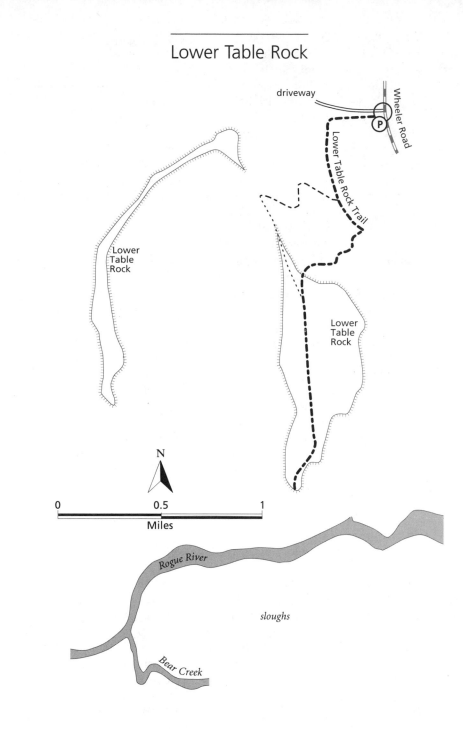

The hike: This "mighty fortress," with the look of a flat-topped desert mesa, is one of the prominent landmarks along the middle Rogue River. The formation is fascinating in its geology, botany, and history. The trail makes a pleasant afternoon

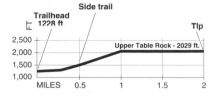

jaunt in winter or spring. March and June are best for wildflowers. Beautiful gold fields of flowers blanket the top in March while a myriad of wildflowers bloom in June. The trailhead compound was built by the Nature Conservancy, which also maintains the trail and owns a piece of the rock. They've done a commendable job.

The unnumbered path parallels a driveway at first, then turns off into a scrubby, low-elevation woods of white oak, madrone, and ponderosa pine. Poison oak abounds, along with several ceanothus species. This part of the trail cooks in summer, as confirmed by the dry-site vegetation, so bring water in warm weather. The route has some steep spots, a few dusty areas, and places which become quite muddy in wet weather. It reaches the top in 1.5 miles, ascending a talus slope with no view of the cliffs.

The path forks at mile 0.8. To easily reach the good vista points and cliff tops, bear left at the fork. Once on top, it's another mile to the mesa's southern tip above the Rogue. The surface is amazingly flat. You can walk and walk towards objects appearing a short way off and it takes a very long time before they start looking closer.

Table Rock is the farthest outrider of a still-eroding lava flow from ancient Crater Lake (Mount Mazama). It rises 800 feet above the surrounding valley. Once on top, look for "patterned ground," gravel mounds unique to level volcanic surfaces and largely unexplained. The species of wildflowers growing on the mounds are different from those growing between them.

The Table Rock surface is mostly covered with grass. In late summer, it is a mass of cured-out foxtails and star thistles. On the other hand, a spring visit reveals a breathtaking carpet of yellow goldfield flowers, rippling in the breeze as far as the eye can see.

Formerly (and briefly) the Takelma Indian Reservation, the site boasts several rare wildflowers. Look for Brewer's rock cress, scarlet fritillaria, and three-bract onion. Nearly the entire earthly range of a plant called dwarf meadowfoam is confined to the tops of Upper and Lower Table Rock around the vernal pools which form in winter and spring. The pools are also home to several species of waterfowl (mostly mallards).

At the far end of an abandoned landing strip, continue straight but bear slightly right, towards the clump of trees. You end up on a high point of rock overlooking the Rogue. You may scare off 10 or 20 buzzards from a nearby roost so don't panic if one swoops 10 feet over your head. They don't eat live humans. Rattlesnakes may be another worry. You hear stories of them up here (the author has never seen any).

Lower Table Rock from Upper Table Rock.

Option: If you turn right instead of left at the junction at mile 0.8, you arrive at a narrow saddle in 0.6 mile. For an interesting little loop, head left, cross country, up the ridgeline from the saddle. There's some easy rock climbing, and poison oak and ticks to look out for, but it's great fun. You'll rejoin the main trail in 0.5 mile.

57 Upper Table Rock

Highlights:	A steep hike up a spectacular flat-topped mesa with rare plant species and an impressive view. The cliffs aren't as high as at Lower Table Rock, but the surface is larger and there's much more trail on top.
Type of hike:	Day hike, out and back.
Total distance:	3.2 miles.
Difficulty:	Moderate.
Elevation gain:	750 feet.
Best months:	All.
Map:	USGS Sams Valley quad.

Special considerations: The trail starts a little higher than at Lower Table Rock and isn't quite as steep or as hot in summer. Winter and spring are best for viewing the rare wildflowers around the seasonal ponds.

Upper Table Rock

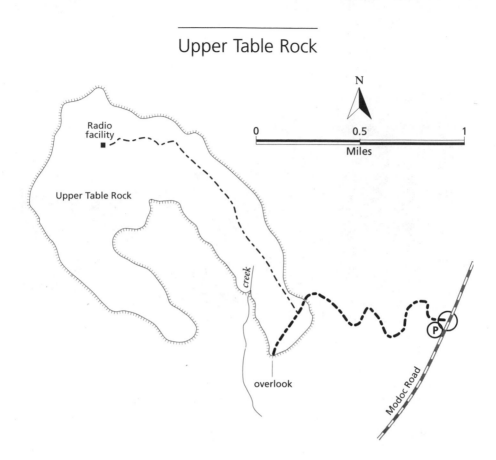

Finding the trailhead: From Medford, take Table Rock Road north, past White City and turn right on Modoc Road, 1 mile past TouVelle State Park. Modoc Road winds for 2 miles through pear orchards and past some old military barracks. Just past the high point, you'll see a Pacific Power transformer on the right and an enclosed parking area on the left.

Parking and trailhead facilities: The trailhead parking area accommodates 20 cars and has a pit toilet.

Key points:
0.0 Upper Table Rock Trailhead.
1.2 Rim.
1.3 Trail junction (go left).
1.6 Overlook above Rogue.

The hike: Upper Table Rock is a fascinating afternoon diversion for those who have conquered Lower Table Rock but have not had their fill of flat-top rocks. The trail is shorter and less steep than its lower counterpart and a little more open, with better views. The top of Upper Table Rock is 30 feet higher than Lower Table Rock but the trailhead is 150 feet higher. The

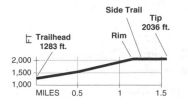

Side Trail
Tip
2036 ft.
Trailhead
1283 ft.
Rim
2,000
1,500
1,000
MILES   0.5   1   1.5

Upper Table Rock Trail (unnumbered) switches back and forth across grass, patches of ceanothus and manzanita, and clumps of oak and madrone. Like its sister (or brother) trail, the rim is visible from the trailhead but not from most of the trail until near the top.

At 0.3 mile, after climbing a couple of switchbacks beyond a house-sized boulder, you come to a little wooden bench. Intended for sitting and contemplating the view of the Bear Creek Valley, the bench is used extensively as a boot scraper. The path can get pretty muddy in winter.

After 1.2 miles, past another bench and a talus slope, the trail gently meets the top of the mesa. It's another 0.4 mile to the formation's southern tip with an overlook above the Rogue. The cliffs aren't quite as high as on Lower Table Rock because there's more talus (debris) at the base. But the upper rock has more flat surface and forms a tighter horseshoe. The center of the Upper Table Rock horseshoe is a spectacular rock gorge (see "Option"). Look for a huge, detached monolith just off the rock's southern tip.

The view from the southern tip, 1.6 miles from the trailhead, is similar to that from Lower Table Rock, with a panorama of the Rogue Valley, Medford, the Siskiyous, and Cascades. The seasonal wetlands on Upper Table Rock dry up in summer to form shallow, flower-filled depressions. Dwarf meadowfoam, found only atop the Table Rocks (and at the Agate Desert near White City), grows at their edges. In winter, collected water is

Cliffs—Upper Table Rock. View of Bear Creek Valley.

extensive enough to attract hundreds of ducks. If you scare them off, the sky becomes black with waterfowl.

Spring, of course, is the best time to visit as the rock is home to many rare, and some not-so-rare, wildflowers. Still, even at Christmas, one can find tiny yellow flowers scattered among the mosses and weeds.

Option: A trail that bears exploring takes off northward (right) 0.1 mile onto the rim. From the junction, it looks like the path leads to a small monument a few minutes away. The monument is actually a radar installation 2 miles away and three stories high. The route visits both the head of the canyon forming the middle of the horseshoe and the mesa's north rim.

58 Roxy Ann Peak

Highlight:	This hike climbs the brushy little dome-shaped mountain that rises directly behind the city of Medford.
Type of hike:	Day hike, out and back.
Total distance:	About 3 miles.
Difficulty:	Moderate.
Elevation gain:	573 feet.
Best months:	Any.
Map:	USGS Medford East quad.

Special considerations: No water, very hot in midsummer, very muddy in winter, plentiful poison oak. This trail is in a Medford City Park.

Finding the trailhead: In Medford, go east on Jackson Street (the street on which the Medford Center is located), which eventually dead ends at Hillcrest Road. Turn left onto Hillcrest. Past milepost 3 on Hillcrest, a gravel road turnoff to the left has a sign that says "Prescott Park." It's 2.3 miles to the loop road around the summit, where you turn left again. After 0.4 miles on the loop road, you arrive at a small picnic site (the North Side Picnic Area) and trailhead.

Parking and trailhead facilities. There's parking for six cars at the North Side Picnic Area. If you're there for a picnic, there's a larger, nicer picnic area on the loop road on the south side of the peak. To get there, go right on the loop road instead of left.

Key points:

0.0 North Side Picnic Area.

1.3 Road (go right).

1.5 Summit.

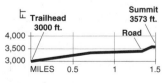

Roxy Ann Peak

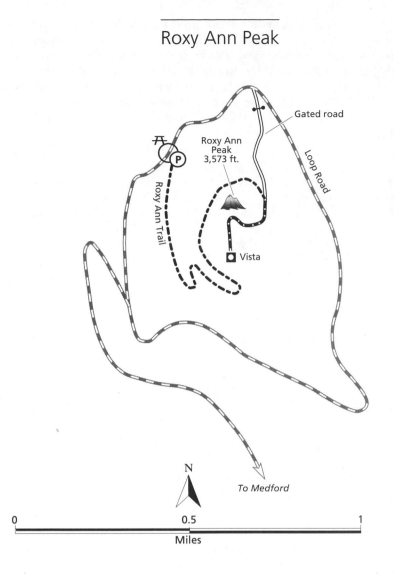

The hike: Driving up Hillcrest Road, with Roxy Ann Peak rising immediately above, it's hard to figure how a 1.5-mile trail and loop road could fit unto such a tiny area. When you get on the trail and look up at the peak, however, it suddenly looks very, very big.

This sometimes steep (unnumbered) path begins in a little glade of oak and pine and makes it's way to the summit in a series of long switchbacks. The low-elevation dry-site vegetation here is virtually identical to that described under Viewpoint Mike Trail at Lost Creek Lake (Hike 25). The forest is confined to the peak's north side and the summit while the south side is hot and grassy. Douglas-fir begins to show up as you approach the top.

After three long, zig-zag switchbacks amid rock falls, brush, and poison oak, all on the peak's west face, the path swings around to the north face (after 0.9 mile), then the east face. The west face offers views of Medford, the north face reveals the Table Rocks and farmland, and the east face offers glimpses of Mount McLoughlin peeking through the oaks and pines.

After 1.2 miles, the path emerges onto a very steep road on the peak's west face. Turn right, uphill. Follow the road for 0.1 mile to the summit and continue following it (bear to the left) until it ends.

The summit is rather busy, with five small cinderblock buildings and two communications towers. At the road's end, there are two green, side-by-side buildings. If you walk between them, a short trail leads to the summit's only real vista point, a rock platform with a view southward of Mount Ashland and Grizzly Peak (Hike 61). It's much hotter on the rock platform than back in the woods.

Soda Mountain Area

The Soda Mountain area is an east-west range connecting the Siskiyou Mountains to the Cascades and forming the 6,200-feet-high head of Bear Creek Valley. The range begins at Siskiyou Summit (the 4,300-foot pass into California on Interstate 5), and ends with the merger into the Cascades' main north-south spine. This is the only point where the Siskiyou/Klamath mountain system is connected to the Cascades. That might explain why the Pacific Crest Trail uses Soda Mountain to get out of its side trip through the Trinity Alps, Marble Mountains, and Siskiyous and return to the main mountain range.

The 7 miles of Pacific Crest Trail from Pilot Rock to Soda Mountain Road is not particularly recommended. While it contains a few pleasant meadows and views of Soda Mountain, Grizzly Mountain, and the Buckhorn Creek valley, much of the trail follows a maze of still-open jeep roads. The path misses the main highlight, the Soda Mountain summit. You can drive to the summit.

Pilot Rock, Soda Mountain, Hobart Butte, Grizzly Mountain, and Roxy Ann Butte, all belong to the Western Cascades, not the High Cascades. The Soda Mountain area has been a small (7,000 acres) BLM wilderness study area since 1987. In 1999, it was designated as Cascade-Siskiyou National Monument, due to its botanical diversity at the boundaries of several major forest regions and mountain ranges, with both high-desert and high-mountain influence. The summit of Soda Mountain, which is full of radio repeaters, is not part of this newly designated monument, which is as yet undeveloped.

---

59 Pilot Rock

Highlight:	A very steep trail to the top of a famous pioneer landmark.
Type of hike:	Day hike, out and back.
Total distance:	2 miles.
Difficulty:	Strenuous.
Elevation gain:	808 feet.
Best months:	May–November.
Map:	USGS Siskiyou Pass quad.

Special consideration: This is a strenuous route with no water and many vertical drop-offs. People have been killed falling off Pilot Rock. Avoid this hike in wet weather or if there's snow on the peak.

Pilot Rock

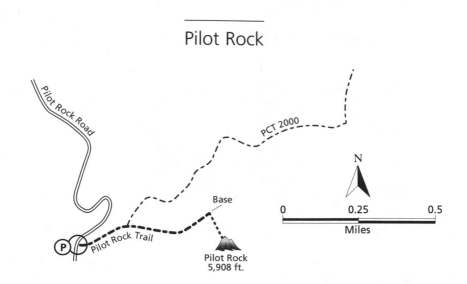

Finding the trailhead: Take Interstate 5 south from Ashland and get off at exit 5, the Mount Ashland exit. After leaving the freeway, the Mount Ashland Road takes off to the right after 0.5 mile. If you continue straight instead of turning towards Mount Ashland, the paved road crosses under the freeway, goes over a pass, and enters California.

Two miles from the freeway exit, a dirt road left bears a BLM sign denoting Pilot Rock Road. Proceed up this road for 2.5 miles, bearing right at the gravel pit. There are several side roads but you should meet your objective simply by heading towards Pilot Rock. Park at the PCT trailhead at the summit of Pilot Rock Road.

Parking and trailhead facilities: There's room for ten cars at the trailhead.

Key points:
    0.0 Pilot Rock Trailhead (PCT).
    0.2 PCT and Pilot Rock Trail junction (go right).
    0.6 Base of Pilot Rock.
    1.0 Top of Pilot Rock.

The hike: The sentinel guarding Oregon's border against invaders from the south has long been a landmark to pioneers. Hence it's name. Visible for miles from the south and east, it is the first Oregon landmark people notice as they head up Interstate 5 from California (except for Mount McLoughlin).

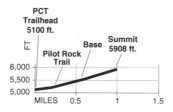

Pilot Rock.

The rock is an immense volcanic plug, a cylindrical tower of lava, the innermost remnant of an old volcano. There are other such plugs in southern Oregon (Rabbit Ears comes to mind, in the Rogue-Umpqua Divide). All lie within a fragmented mountain system called the Western Cascades. Much older than the more extensive High Cascades, the Western Cascades have experienced several million more years of erosion.

Pilot Rock measures 500 feet in diameter and 400 feet in height. From a distance, its sides appear nearly perpendicular and the structure seems uniformly round and insurmountable. That is not actually the case, although the hike up is strenuous.

The trek to the base begins inauspiciously enough, on the reasonably level Pacific Crest Trail (2000). The easy travel is short-lived as the Pilot Rock Trail breaks off to the right after 0.2 mile. The Pilot Rock Trail is unsigned and unnumbered but obvious. It is also extremely steep. Dirtbike activity has made the soil compacted and slick. As you approach the bottom of the main wall, the indistinct, braided trail trends along the base of the rock's north side.

At mile 0.6, there is a huge talus slope emerging from a little canyon, forming a natural entry into the fortress. The talus is made of loose rock at a slope of 70 percent. It's a grueling climb but not very far.

You eventually find yourself at a tiny notch, perhaps 6 feet wide (one foot wide at the bottom), with a rock overhang at about eye level. If you're fairly agile, this should pose no barrier. If not, get a leg up from a friend.

Above the overhang, the route emerges into a tiny basin. From there, simply pick your way to the top. You shouldn't have much difficulty. It's steep in spots and you may find yourself using hands and feet to make your way up. But you won't need climbing gear.

The summit is remarkable for its profusion of survey markers, the view of the Shasta Valley and Mount Shasta, and the exhilaration of a successful outing.

Options: *Side Trail.* A side trail on the right, halfway up, follows a narrow and precipitous ledge that dead ends after 0.2 mile.

Pacific Crest Trail. It's 6 miles east along the PCT from the Pilot Rock Trailhead to the Soda Mountain Trailhead. In the opposite direction (west), the PCT mostly follows roads under the freeway and past the Mount Ashland turnoff. The PCT west pretty much parallels the Mount Ashland Road for 20 miles, to a point well past Mount Ashland.

---

60 Hobart Bluff

Highlight:	An easy path into the Western Cascades, not far from Ashland. Terrific vistas.
Type of hike:	Day hike, out and back.
Total distance:	About 3 miles.
Difficulty:	Mostly easy.
Elevation gain:	502 feet.
Best months:	May–November, or when snow-free.
Map:	USGS Soda Mountain quad.

Finding in the trailhead: Take Interstate 5 to the second Ashland exit (exit 14) and follow Oregon Highway 66 towards Klamath Falls. Proceed 15 miles, past Emigrant Lake, to Soda Mountain Road, just before Green Springs Summit. Take Soda Mountain Road right for 3.5 miles to the second powerline crossing at a grassy meadow, which is also the Pacific Crest Trail crossing. Look for a PCT marker. The described hike goes left (east).

Parking and trailhead facilities: There's room for ten cars along the shoulder near the Pacific Crest Trail emblem.

Key points:
0.0 PCT trailhead.
1.1 Hobart Bluff Trail junction (go left).
1.5 Summit.

The hike: The natural inclination, upon reaching the PCT crossing on Soda Mountain Road, is to hike in the opposite direction on the PCT, away from Hobart Bluff, south toward Soda Mountain's

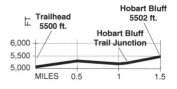

Hobart Bluff

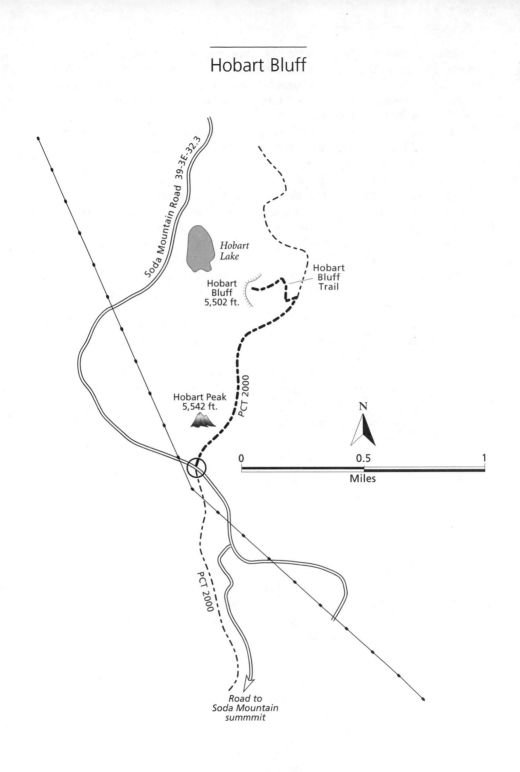

Soda Mountain Road 39-3E-32.3

Hobart Lake

Hobart Bluff
5,502 ft.

Hobart Bluff Trail

PCT 2000

Hobart Peak
5,542 ft.

N

0   0.5   1
Miles

PCT 2000

Road to Soda Mountain summmit

6,200-foot summit. While that is not a bad hike for a while, the route miss-es the summit and ends up following old jeep roads. Besides, 0.2 mile far-ther up the road from the trailhead, a side road scales Soda Mountain in 1.5 miles. The top is festooned with antennae, satellite dishes, and other communications equipment.

The trek eastward towards Hobart Bluff is not only far easier and less snowbound but impressive in its own right. Some consider it more scenic than the Soda Mountain direction.

After crossing a little grassy flat, the PCT heading east (left) towards Hobart Bluff (left/north) winds through alternating wooded patches of white fir and Douglas-fir, and grassy openings dotted with scrub white oak, mountain mahogany, and elderberry. They are all drought-loving species, especially the scrub white oak. Look also for rabbitbrush, a high-desert shrub related to sagebrush. Forested stands tend to be sparse, espe-cially on south-facing slopes.

After 0.5 mile, Hobart Bluff's stone precipice briefly appears in the dis-tance, then quickly vanishes as the trail cuts behind it to the right. After 1 mile from the trailhead, a well-marked (but unnumbered) side path takes off uphill to the left, attaining the level bluff top in 0.5 mile. Though fair-ly steep, the side path isn't very long.

On the side path, the scenery changes dramatically, with elegant stone outcrops and windswept junipers decorating the landscape. The route soon attains an impressive, rocky summit. That, however, is not the end of the trail. The actual overlook lies a precarious few hundred feet away, at the tip of a narrow, rocky finger protruding west from the main forma-tion, with vertical drop-offs on three sides. It's 300 feet to the bottom.

Look as you hike out the finger here for tilted rock strata. A primary sign that you're in the Western Cascades and not the High Cascades is that all the bedded rock formations are tipped 18 degrees, with the low end to the southeast and the high end to the northwest. In the High Cascades, bedded lava flows are all horizontal.

Option: *PCT to Green Springs Summit.* Soda Mountain Road begins at Green Springs Summit, where the PCT crosses Oregon Highway 140. It's possible to make Hobart Bluff a shuttle hike by parking a car at the upper trailhead (described above), and another car at the Greens Springs Trailhead. The hike would be 3.5 miles long. The best scenery lies in the mile leading up to Hobart Bluff, but it's all nice.

61 Grizzly Peak

Highlight:	A stunning panorama from the highest point on the east side of the valley surrounding Ashland, 3,000 feet above the valley floor.
Type of hike:	Day hike, out and back.
Total distance:	About 4 miles.
Difficulty:	Moderate.
Elevation gain:	700 foot gain, then 100 foot loss.
Best months:	May–November.
Map:	USGS Grizzly Peak quad.

Special considerations: This is a popular trail only 11 miles from downtown Ashland. Lower portions are very slippery when wet or foggy, as is often the case in spring and fall. No water. The BLM plans to extend the Grizzly Peak Trail into a loop trail.

Finding the trailhead: From Ashland, take Siskiyou Boulevard (Oregon Highway 66) east to Dead Indian Memorial Highway, just past the city limits. (Siskiyou Boulevard is exit 14 on Interstate 5.) Turn left onto Dead Indian Road. Between milepost 6 and 7 on Dead Indian, turn left onto Shale City Road (paved) and proceed 3.1 miles to the Grizzly Peak Trail sign (BLM Road 38-2E-9.2). Turn left at the sign and follow the gravel road. It's 0.7 mile to a complex intersection (take the uphill road on the left) and 1.7 miles to the trailhead.

(Note: The name "Dead Indian Road" is an embarrassment to most Ashlanders. It sounds very racist. Actually, the Dead Indian Plateau was named for two deceased Native Americans encountered by some pioneers, who sincerely intended the naming to honor the unfortunate gentlemen.)

Parking and trailhead facilities: The trailhead at the end of the road holds ten cars.

Key points:
0.0 Grizzly Peak Trailhead.
1.5 Side trail to Emigrant Lake vista point.
2.0 Summit.

The hike: Grizzly Peak was named in honor of a famous bear named "Old Reelfoot," the last known southern Oregon grizzly, who roamed the region for 50 years before being shot by a 17-year-old hunter in 1890. The nickname had to do with the animal, at some point, losing several toes in a leghold trap. The beast's stuffed body resided in a local museum for many years but has long since disappeared. Grizzly Peak and the Ashland High School football team, the Grizzlies, are named for Old Reelfoot.

One interesting feature of this gorgeous little chunk of the Western Cascades, in addition to the proximity to downtown Ashland and the

Grizzly Peak

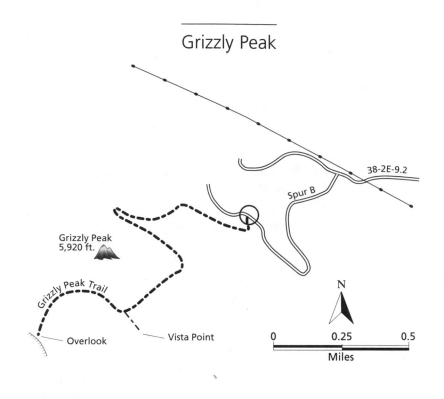

Grizzly Peak
5,920 ft.

Grizzly Peak Trail

Spur B

38-2E-9.2

Overlook

Vista Point

N

0   0.25   0.5
Miles

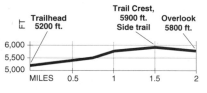

knockout view at the end, is the coastal feel of the forest. The feel is partly because the forest has a dense canopy and little underbrush, and the trees are large (although not immense—up to 30 inches in diameter). Also, the predominant tree species is grand fir, which is far more prevalent in the Coastal Ranges than the Cascades.

From the trailhead, the Grizzly Peak Trail (unnumbered) immediately enters the aforementioned dense forest, with only a few low, scattered trillium flowers occupying the understory (there are other understory species but trillium is the showiest). As you approach the summit, 2 miles later and 700 feet higher, the forest composition is almost identical. Other trees include occasional Douglas-fir (at an unusually high elevation), and incense cedar, with more and more white fir as you approach the summit.

There are many meadow openings along the way, which unlike the forest, change in species composition as you approach the summit. Hikers are treated to wave after wave of wildflowers as the season progresses.

After much winding through the woods, around a sharp switchback (mile 1) and up many upgrades, the path emerges at the first of three false summits (mile 1.3), a grassy meadow with rock outcrops. The first two false summits, in June, are covered with fawn lilies, a beautiful little nodding flower notable for blooming immediately after the snow melts.

After the initial false summit, which is the trail's high point, the path starts downward slightly but remains generally level. Since the top of Grizzly Peak is a broad plateau, the true summit is difficult to pinpoint. The trail does not cross the true summit, which lies northwest of the trail's upper portion and lacks a vista point or overlook.

At mile 1.5, you come to a side trail to the left (the main trail goes to the right), leading to an opening, after several hundred feet, with a sharp, rocky drop-off and a view of Emigrant Lake and Mount Ashland. Look for soaproot plants in the forest understory.

You'll know when you're approaching the end of the main trail at mile 2.0. The path gets steep again, briefly, and there are jagged rock outcrops everywhere. Instead of fawn lily, the predominant wildflower is Menzies delphinium, a low, dry-site species sometimes also called "larkspur" for the little spur on the back of each blossom. It's as though someone put the stem in the wrong place, on the side of the flower instead of at the end.

The summit is predictably glorious, with a walk across a meadow, over the top and slightly down to a rocky ledge. A recently burned forest lies immediately north. To the west, the scenery plummets 3,000 feet to Interstate 5, Ashland, and Emigrant Lake, with Mount Ashland and Wagner Butte (Hike 65) rising on the other side of the valley. You can also see Mounts Shasta and McLoughlin.

The east side of the valley around Ashland, of which Grizzly Peak is the highest point, is very interesting. It's totally different than the valley's west side. Mount Ashland, on the west side, is 2,000 feet higher than Grizzly Peak and belongs to the Siskiyous rather than the Cascades. While

Grizzly Peak Trailhead in fog.

the west side is densely forested, the east side contains vast mountainsides of open grassland (the forests of Grizzly Peak notwithstanding). The rock on the valley's east side, including Grizzly Peak, is Colestin sandstone, the region's only sandstone. It is considered part of the Western Cascades (look for the telltale Western Cascades slant in the rock strata at the trail end).

Part II

The Siskiyous

Western Jackson County

Western Jackson County is as different from Eastern Jackson County as white bread is from pumpernickel. Eastern Jackson County is entirely occupied by the Cascades while the western half is home to a large chunk of the Siskiyous. Included in the Siskiyou chunk is the range's highest peak, Mount Ashland (7,495 ft.), a major river canyon (the Applegate River canyon), and one of the country's more beautiful small wilderness areas (the Red Buttes Wilderness Area). If Western Jackson Country were located anywhere else, it would be hailed as a scenic wonder, but eastern Jackson County happens to have Crater Lake and the Sky Lakes, which are pretty hard to top.

---

62 Stein Butte

Highlight: A challenging hike to a low mountaintop with outstanding views of Applegate Lake, Elliott Creek Canyon, and the Red Buttes Wilderness. A good off-season outing.

Type of hike: Day hike, out and back.

Total distance: About 9 miles.

Difficulty: Moderate.

Elevation gain: 2,400 feet.

Best months: April–December.

Maps: USGS Squaw Lakes and Carberry Creek quads.

Special considerations: No water along entire route. The steep 2.5-mile segment of the Stein Butte Trail (929), from the summit down to Elliott Creek, shown on many maps, has been deactivated due to logging at the trailhead. For those desiring a one-way shuttle hike, the segment has been replace by the 3-mile New London Trail (928), which isn't quite as steep or scenic as the old route. The new route meets Elliot Creek Road 4 miles from the junction of Forest Road 1040 and 1050.

Finding the trailhead: Take Oregon Highway 238 south from Jacksonville or Grants Pass to the town of Ruch and turn right onto the Applegate Lake Road (County Road 859). The trailhead is at the Seattle Bar Picnic Site at the upper end of Applegate Lake, 4 miles past Applegate Dam. Park at the picnic site, walk across the road and follow the gravel side road for 100 feet. The trailhead is on the right.

Parking and trailhead facilities: The Seattle Bar Picnic Site holds 20 cars.

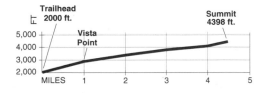

Stein Butte

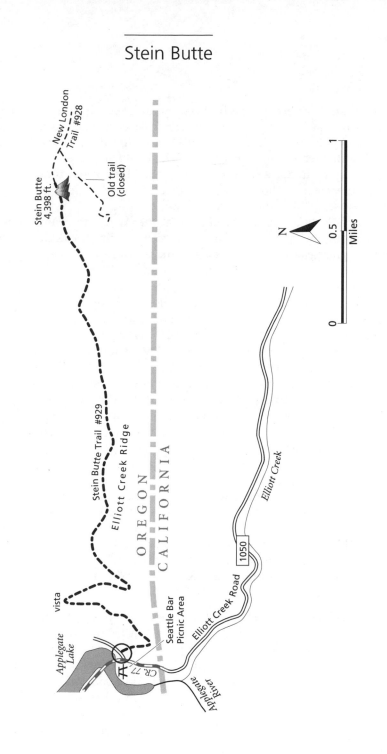

Key points:
   0.0 Seattle Bar Trailhead.
   1.0 Vista point.
   4.5 Summit.

The hike: For perhaps the best panorama of Applegate Lake and the high peaks of the Red Buttes Wilderness, this easily accessible trail (929) is unmatched. Early winter is the ideal viewing time, when the mountains are highlighted by snow. Portions of the trail's upper end, cresting at 4,398 feet, may be under a little snow as well. Most of the time, this enhances the experience, although it's prudent to avoid Stein Butte if it snowed down to 2,000 feet the previous day.

On the way to the trailhead, stop at the Applegate Dam vista point and check out the sign identifying the surrounding peaks, including Stein Butte. The peak doesn't look like much from there, just a small outcrop amid a jumble of higher, forested summits. The mountain's south side, from Elliott Creek, is much more impressive.

One thing to notice about the Applegate Lake area is the extreme difference in vegetation between the north and south slopes. Views north reveal peak after peak whose south-facing aspects are covered with little besides grass and brush. Southward views show lush, north-slope forests reaching to the mountaintops.

From the Seattle Bar Trailhead, the path winds steeply upward through forest and a few grassy openings. After 1 mile, it passes some rock formations, a quarry, and a rock outcrop with a commanding view of the lake. Beyond the quarry, the path levels off as it winds around the densely forested summits. The route crosses over to the Elliott Creek side, then back to the Applegate side several times before settling on the Elliott Creek side for its final 1.5 miles.

It's 4.5 miles to the trail crest and summit. Where the path cuts north, hits its high point, and starts back down, turn off the trail (right) for the summit. It's a steep but easy and open 0.1 mile to the old lookout site. From there, you see the lake, the Elliott Creek canyon and the Butte Fork canyon. Rising in the distance (counter-clockwise from the northwest), are Grayback Peak, Whiskey Peak, Kangaroo Mountain, the Red Buttes, and Condrey Mountain.

Option: *New London Trailhead.* To reach the New London Trailhead (Trail 928), which leads to the Stein Butte summit from Elliott Creek Road, drive past Seattle Bar and the end of the pavement into California. Turn left onto Elliott Creek Road and proceed 4 miles to the New London Trailhead sign, on the left at the junction with Forest Road 1065. There's parking for six cars on the road shoulder. This route is 1.5 miles shorter, a little steeper, and a little less scenic than the route from Seattle Bar. Better scenery and the convenience of the Seattle Bar Picnic Site make that the recommended route.

63 Middle Fork Applegate

Highlight: A pleasant and interesting walk to an old cabin along a National Recreation Trail.
Type of hike: Day hike, out and back.
Total distance: About 3 miles.
Difficulty: Easy.
Elevation gain: 300 feet.
Best months: April–December.
Maps: USGS Kangaroo Mountain quad.

Special considerations: Water is abundant but should be purified before drinking. The trail is entirely in California but reasonably accessible only via Oregon.

Finding the trailhead: Take Oregon Highway 238 south from Jacksonville or Grants Pass to the town of Ruch. At Ruch, turn up the Applegate Lake Road (County Road 859) towards Applegate Lake. Past the state line (4 miles beyond the dam), where the pavement ends, turn right onto Forest Road 1040. Follow it 5 miles to where Forest Road 1040 curves sharply uphill left and Forest Road 1035 goes straight. Proceed straight, not left, another 0.2 mile to where FR 1035 curves uphill right. The trailhead is well marked near the river, just before the uphill curve right.

Parking and trailhead facilities: Five or six cars can fit at the trailhead.

Key points:
0.0 Middle Fork Trailhead.
0.2 Trail meets river.
0.3 First cabin, swimming hole.
0.7 River crossing.
1.5 Second cabin.

The hike: Among devotees of peaceful ambles along gurgling mountain streams, the Middle Fork of the Applegate River (Trail 950) is a favorite—so much so that it has been included in the National Recreational Trail system. While the path

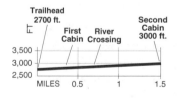

lies entirely in California, it is an honorary "Oregon" path because the only reasonable access to the trailhead is in Oregon and the trail is located in the Rogue River National Forest, headquartered in Oregon.

From the trailhead the path begins as a wide gravel road at the river's edge. After 0.2 mile, the road dead-ends at the river while a small path, the actual trail, heads up the bank, following the river through a majestic forest of old growth Douglas-fir, white fir, sugar pine, and ponderosa pine. Soon after (mile 0.3), you find yourself looking across the river to the first

Middle Fork Applegate

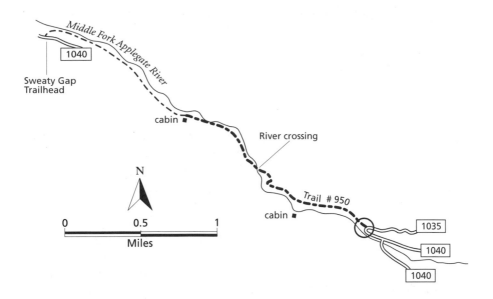

cabin. A little footpath descends to the river there, where you may take a dip in the swimming hole. At 0.7 mile, trail again meets river at a log-bridge river crossing.

From the bridge on, amid ferns and mosses, the area begins to feel like a rain forest out of the Olympic Peninsula. The old-growth stand is a spotted owl management area. After 0.8 mile on the south side of the river, you come to a second log cabin by a little spring, a perfect place for a picnic lunch and a good turnaround point.

Option: *Frog Pond/Sweaty Gap Trail.* The Middle Fork Trail ties in with the Frog Pond and Sweaty Gap Trails 1.5 miles beyond the second cabin. The Frog Pond and Sweaty Gap Trails lead into the Red Buttes Wilderness. For a one-way, 3-mile shuttle hike from the Middle Fork Trailhead, leave a second car at the Frog Pond/Sweaty Gap Trailhead. To reach the Frog Pond/Sweaty Gap Trailhead, continue uphill on FR 1040 instead of taking FR 1035. Follow FR 1040 for 11 miles to the well-marked trailhead.

64 Tunnel Ridge

Highlight:	An unusual, low-elevation, year-round hike following a historic mining ditch. Magnificent spring wildflowers.
Type of hike:	Day hike, out and back.
Total distance:	About 2 miles.
Difficulty:	Easy.
Elevation gain:	521 feet.
Best months:	Year-round.
Maps:	USGS Sterling Creek quad.

Special considerations: Many hiking options and alternate trailheads. No water. Poison oak abounds.

Finding the trailhead: Take Oregon Highway 238 southwest from Jacksonville to the town of Ruch. From there, follow the Applegate Lake Road (County Road 859) south to Little Applegate Road. Turn left on Little Applegate Road and proceed east 10 miles, past the Bear Gulch trailhead, to the Tunnel Ridge trailhead.

Parking and trailhead facilities: A turnout opposite the trailhead can accommodate eight cars.

Key points:
    0.0 Tunnel Ridge Trailhead.
    1.0 Tunnel.

The hike: This short, lovely hike through the brushy foothills of the little Applegate is ideal for a sunny afternoon in summer, or winter, with a picnic basket and all the kids you can round up. Wildflowers abound in spring. The described route,

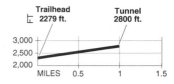

the Tunnel Ridge Trail, is a connecting link to the Sterling Mine Trail, a 26-mile path under development along an old mining ditch. From the 1870s to the 1930s, the ditch channeled water to the gold mines on Sterling Creek. The highlight of the 26-mile engineering feat is the 100-foot tunnel through Tunnel Ridge.

At the trailhead, be sure to walk down to the creek before heading up the path. It's particularly pretty. On the trail, it's an easy 1-mile walk up a sheltered draw to the ditch and tunnel. Most of the route runs through a forest of young white oak and ponderosa pine, a typical low-elevation, south-slope forest. The last 0.2 mile becomes rather steep as the route loops up an open, grassy area with excellent views of the Little Applegate canyon and 7,140-foot Wagner Butte. Look for scarlet fritillary, Oregon shooting star, and many other wildflowers in spring.

Tunnel Ridge

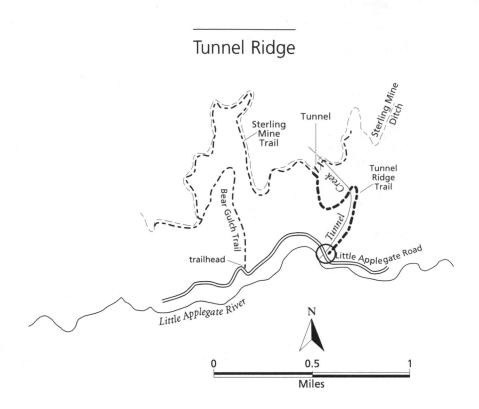

The trail passes over the top of the tunnel. The grassy lawn above, surrounded by oaks, makes a fine picnic site. From the tunnel, the Sterling Mine Trail can be followed in either direction. It's 2 miles west to the turnoff to the Bear Gulch connecting trail and 5 miles east to the Sterling Mine Trailhead (see "Options").

Options: *Bear Gulch Trail.* To complete a loop with the Bear Gulch Trail, follow the ditch trail (Sterling Mine Trail) left for 2 miles, then turn left where the Bear Gulch Trail joins in. It's 1 mile on the Bear Gulch Trail back down to the road, then 0.7 mile along the road back to the Tunnel Ridge Trailhead. The Bear Gulch Trail is a little less scenic than the Tunnel Ridge Trail but also less steep. An outstanding view of the Little Applegate canyon and Wagner Butte may be had where the Bear Gulch Trail meets the ditch trail.

Sterling Mine Trailhead. A third trailhead, 1.7 miles past the Tunnel Ridge Trailhead on Little Applegate Road, also connects to the Sterling Mine Ditch Trail after 1 mile. It's 5 miles from that trailhead to the tunnel, partly over private land. The BLM plans to relocate this part of the route away from the private inholding. This third connecting trail, at the Little Applegate Recreation Site, is steeper than the other two.

65 Wagner Butte

Highlight: The highest hikeable mountain overlooking Bear Creek Valley.
Type of hike: Day hike, out and back.
Total distance: About 8 miles.
Difficulty: Strenuous.
Elevation gain: 2,140 feet.
Best months: June–October.
Map: USGS Siskiyou Peak quad.

Finding the trailhead: From U.S. Highway 99 between Medford and Ashland, follow the signs to the Talent business district, then head up Main Street. Main Street becomes Wagner Creek Road. The road is narrow, steep, and winding beyond the end of the pavement and a little slippery in wet weather. Be extremely alert for oncoming log trucks.

At the top of the hill, bear left where the dirt road ends, a paved road takes off to the right (Forest Road 2250, the upper end of the Little Applegate Road), and a gravel road (Forest Road 22) takes off left. Follow the gravel exactly 2 miles, past the cattle grate at Wagner Gap, to the trailhead. Look for a large parking area on the right and a trailhead sign on the left.

Parking and trailhead facilities: There is space for 15 cars at the parking area.

Key points:
0.0 Wagner Butte Trailhead.
0.1 Side trail junction.
0.8 Slide.
1.2 Corral Creek.
2.4 Wagner Glade Gap.
3.5 Cold Spring.
4.0 Summit.

The hike: Wagner Butte towers directly above the Bear Creek Valley immediately west of Medford and Ashland. At 7,140 feet, it's right next to and only 200 feet lower than Mount Ashland, the Siskiyous' highest peak. If you've ever wished there were a wilderness trail to the top of Mount Ashland·instead of a network of roads, consider tackling Wagner Butte. The trailhead lies just 10.5 miles from downtown Talent.

From the trailhead, the path (1011) snakes through the woods for 0.1 mile, then hits a trail junction and a closed-off logging road. Follow the logging road to the

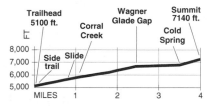

Wagner Butte

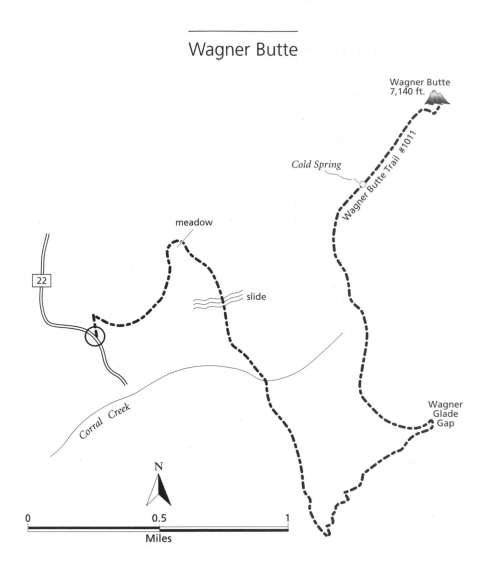

right, up some moderately steep pitches, to a little meadow 0.5 mile from the trailhead. The meadow offers good views of the Red Mountain area west of Mount Ashland. Note the meadow's misplaced sagebrush. Note also the arrow at the far end indicating the trail route.

At mile 0.8, beyond the meadow, through some woods, across a creek and past some more woods, the trail enters a large grassy area, cut by steep gullies. This is the infamous 1984 landslide which wiped out 0.2 mile of the trail. The slide is 3 miles long and reaches from almost the top of the mountain to well below the road. The trail was repaired in 1987.

Beyond the slide, the path skirts a small marsh as it reenters the woods. For 1.3 miles beyond the slide, the trail is pleasantly level, with a few

240

Lookout Base, Wagner Butte Summit, Bear Creek Valley, Mt. McLoughlin.

steeper pitches. It alternates between woods of Douglas-fir, white fir, ponderosa pine, and a little Shasta fir, and open grassy areas. Corral Creek, at mile 1.2, is icy cold and is extremely welcome on the way down.

At mile 1.8 the route breaks out into the open and takes off sharply uphill for 0.5 mile. Soon after, at Wagner Glade Gap (mile 2.4), the trail curves sharply north.

The last 1.6 miles, with the trail running just west of the crest, are stunning. The route is fairly level, with vistas everywhere. This area is mostly brush, broken by picturesque tree clumps. Look for mountain mahogany, sagebrush, and some lovely aspen groves. At Cold Spring (mile 3.5), a long, wet seep (possibly with grazing cattle), you find muddy spots, willow brush, abundant widlflowers, and an icy pipe spring.

Beyond Cold Spring, the trail begins a steep ascent up a boulder strewn, wildflower-covered hillside to the ridge top. It ends at the base of the little rock outcropping which constitutes the ultimate summit. It's a 5-minute climb up the rocks to an old lookout base, with views of Mount Ashland, Mount McLoughlin, Soda Mountain, the Marble Mountains, Ashland, and Medford.

Red Buttes Wilderness

This 20,300-acre chunk of mostly serpentinite magnificence (a black rock that weathers to orange) strides the California-Oregon border in the Siskiyou Mountains west of Mount Ashland, between the Applegate and Klamath Rivers. Trails are steep and the few alpine lakes are small. But you're not going to find scenery much prettier than Azalea Lake, Kangaroo Basin, Red Butte, and Upper Devil's Peak. Two rare tree species call the Red Buttes home, Baker cypress and Brewer spruce.

Some hikes described in this section are located either partly or entirely in California, even though this is supposedly a book about trails of Oregon. But they are in Rogue River National Forest, headquartered in Oregon. Hikes into the Red Buttes Wilderness that are most easily accessible via California are not included. The decision to include Hike 69, to Red Butte, was difficult. Most of the path lies in California's Klamath National Forest, but the trailhead is in Rogue River National Forest and easily reached from Oregon's Upper Applegate area. The hike explores the wilderness area's namesake mountain and is too good to leave out.

66 Tannen Lake

Highlight: Two small glacial-cirque lakes amid the prettiest of the Siskiyou high country.
Type of hike: Day hike, out and back.
Total distance: About 2 miles.
Difficulty: Easy.
Elevation gain: Minimal.
Best months: June–October.
Map: USGS Oregon Caves quad.

Special considerations: No drinkable water.

Finding the trailhead: Take U.S. Highway 199 south 30 miles from Grants Pass to Cave Junction. Turn up the Caves Highway (Oregon Highway 46) at Cave Junction, toward Oregon Caves National Monument. Two miles up Caves Highway, turn right on Holland Loop and continue for 1.5 miles, than go right on Bridgeview-Takilma Road. After 4 miles, turn left onto Happy Camp Road (County Road 5828, becoming Forest Road 48). At the summit of Happy Camp Road (milepost 13), turn left on Forest Road 4812 and follow the signs to Bolan Lake, then Tannen Lake. Stay right at the Bolan Lake turnoff (Spur 041). It's 8 miles from the summit to the Tannen Lake Trailhead. The trailhead is well marked.

Tannen Lake

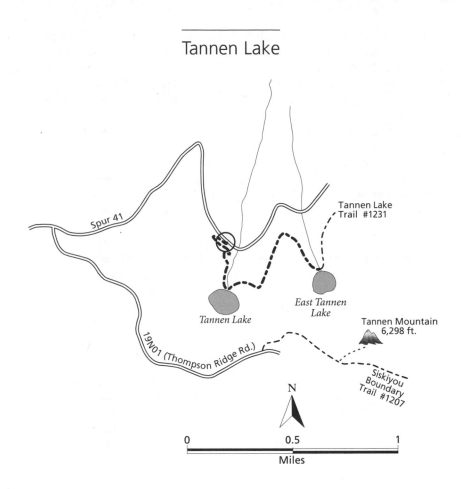

Parking and trailhead facilities: There is parking for ten cars along the road shoulder at the Tannen Lake Trailhead.

Key points:
    0.0 Tannen Lake Trailhead.
    0.4 Tannen Lake.
    1.0 East Tannen Lake.

The hike: The prettiest alpine lakes in the Oregon portion of the Siskiyous are Tannen and Bolan Lakes. Bolan has road access and a developed campground while Tannen lies at the end of a short, lovely hike. Glacial-cirque lakes such as these are infrequent in southern Oregon

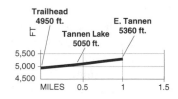

and hardly compare to the hundreds of lakes which nestle in the Marble Mountains and Trinity Alps just to the south. Still, the area is extremely scenic and well worth the drive and hike.

The road between the Bolan Lake turnoff and the Tannen Lake Trailhead boasts what may be Josephine County's best alpine scenery. The road is usually not passable until mid-June, however. Its unpaved, often bumpy surface snakes around the craggy ridges of Bolan and Althouse Mountains and peers down on Thompson Creek, the Klamath River, and the Marble Mountains.

The Tannen Lake Trail is short, easy, and interesting, and it's only 0.4 mile to the lake. Look for a profusion of wildflowers, rhododendron, and Sadler oak. The latter resembles a rhododendron except that its large, evergreen leaves, in a whorled arrangement, have sawtoothed edges. Sadler oak grows only in moist, high-elevation areas of the Siskiyou and Marble Mountains. Though considered rare, it is abundant within its narrow range.

Tannen Lake occupies a small, high-walled cirque with a creek outlet at one end. It has a steep, willow-choked shore with little access other than the campsite near the outlet. Swimming is difficult because covering the bottom is a mushy silt that gives way when stepped on to a maze of submerged logs. Fishing is supposed to be good.

East Tannen Lake lies 0.6 mile beyond Tannen Lake at the base of Tannen Mountain. It's a little smaller, with an even steeper shore, denser willow brush, and a mushier bottom. Fishing is good there, too.

Option: *Tannen Mountain.* To climb Tannen Mountain via the Siskiyou Boundary Trail (1207), turn right (south) at King's Saddle, an open, clearcut area, 1 mile before the Tannen Lake trailhead. You end up on Thompson Ridge Road. Look for the Boundary Trail 2 miles down, possibly marked by a square post but no sign. There's parking for four cars along the shoulder.

From the trailhead, the path ascends through a forest of western white pine, white fir, mountain hemlock, and incense cedar. For the expert, both Shasta red fir and the virtually identical noble fir may be found. This is unusual because the two species interbreed in the Siskiyous. A side trail left, near the trailhead, leads down to Tannen Lake. Stay right for Tannen Mountain.

At mile 0.5 from the trailhead, the route comes out on a grassy knoll. There it begins a long, steep downhill pitch, joining the Tannen Lake Trail 1 mile later. The Tannen summit can be seen 0.2 mile away from the knoll, on the left, peering above the grass. Since there's no trail to the summit, simply walk towards the peak and follow the ridgeline up. You should be perched atop the gray outcrop in ten minutes.

From the summit, which boasts a cozy little nestlike depression, the view is awesome. You can see most of the north half of the Marble Mountains as well as much of the Siskiyou Wilderness and the Klamath Canyon. The California state line lies 0.2 mile south of Tannen Mountain. There is a spectacular marble cavern 1 mile down the Boundary Trail from the summit, but you're not likely to find it, and there is a locked gate across the entrance. The opening is supposedly a 50-foot vertical drop.

67 Azalea Lake

Highlight:	The most spectacular trail in the Red Buttes Wilderness.
Type of hike:	Day hike or backpack, out and back.
Total distance:	About 12 miles.
Difficulty:	Moderate.
Elevation gain:	300 foot loss, 1,100 foot gain, then 600 foot loss.
Best months:	June–October.
Maps:	USGS Grayback Mountain and Figurehead Mountain quads.

Special considerations: Lots of water and lots of options. There are several trail routes to Azalea Lake but the described hike is the shortest, easiest, and most scenic. The trail crosses into California after 0.2 mile.

Finding the trailhead: Take Oregon Highway 238 out of Jacksonville or Grants Pass to the town of Applegate. In Applegate (just west of the bridge), follow Thompson Creek Road (County Road 10) south 12 miles to the summit. Turn left at the summit, towards Applegate Lake. It's 4 miles on County Road 777 to the gravel Steve's Fork Road (Forest Road 1040), on the right. Take the Steve's Fork 5 miles to Spur 400, on the left. Cross the bridge onto the steep but wide dirt road and continue 5 miles to the summit. Take the first side road on the right, just over the summit. The roomy Azalea Lake (Fir Glade) Trailhead lies 1 mile up this last dirt side road.

Parking and trailhead facilities: There is room for eight cars at the trailhead.

Key points:
  0.0 Azalea Lake Trailhead.
  0.2 State line.
  1.5 Fir Glade.
  2.6 Steve's Fork Trail.
  3.8 Thompson Creek Pass.
  4.7 Azalea Lake Pass.
  6.0 Azalea Lake.

The hike: The Azalea Lake Trail (955) may be the most scenic pathway into the Red Buttes Wilderness. While fairly lengthy at 6 miles, and while it traverses extreme-

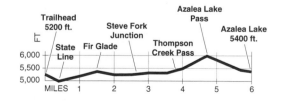

ly steep terrain, the miles disappear quickly on this surprisingly level path.

The Azalea Lake Trail, the Steve's Fork Trail, the Butte Fork Trail, and

Azalea Lake

1030

1040

Spur 400

OREGON

CALIFORNIA

Steve's Fork Creek

Fir Glade

Steve's Fork Trail # 905

Sucker Gap Trail # 906

Middle Fork Applegate River

Pyramid Peak
6,451 ft.

Azalea Lake Trail # 955

RED BUTTES WILDERNESS

Buck Mountain
6,200 ft.

5,876 ft.

Phantom Meadows

Azalea Lake

Thompson Creek Pass

Butte Fork Applegate River

Azalea Lake Pass

Butte Fork Trail #957

Lonesome Lake Trail #956

N

Figurehead Mountain
6,374 ft.

0   0.5   1

Miles

the Sweaty Gap Trail all lead to Azalea Lake (see "Options"). The Azalea Lake and Steve's Fork Trails begin in Oregon while the Sweaty Gap and Butte Fork Trails begin in California.

From the Azalea Lake Trailhead, it's an easy, 1.5-mile walk to Fir Glade, a vast meadow with an old cabin and a profusion of wildflowers. The path, which has been following an old road, cuts sharply left just before Fir Glade, at an easily missed turnoff. The Steve's Fork junction lies 1.1 miles beyond, on the right.

The 3 miles past Fir Glade are surprisingly level, holding a contour high above the Middle Fork Applegate River. The path crosses patches of dense forest, areas of more open woods and shrubs, and countless meadows and small springs. Wildflowers (Indian paintbrush, penstemon, monkshood, and others) abound. The black, craggy face of Buck Mountain is the most visible landmark, rising to the south on the other side of Phantom Meadow and the Middle Fork Canyon. The Steve's Fork Trail enters stage right at mile 2.6 (see "Options").

The route steepens considerably at the Thompson Creek Divide at mile 3.8, a pass between the Middle Fork Applegate and Thompson Creek, a tributary of the Klamath River. Look for views of Whiskey Peak back towards the trailhead, and towering Preston Peak in the distance to the west. Brewer spruce adorns the pass, along with some of the Siskiyous' highest-elevation knobcone and sugar pine.

After another 0.9 mile, the trail reaches a second, higher pass, then descends sharply, for 1.3 mile, to the lake, at mile 6. Coming into view at the second pass, the lake nests inside a small glacial cirque near Figurehead Mountain's sheer cliffs. The view down the Butte Fork to the aptly named Red Buttes is memorable.

The lake itself is beautiful and the area around it is botanically interesting. True to its name, azalea bushes line its banks. The lake is surrounded by lodgepole pine. While lodgepole abounds in the Cascades and Marbles, it is extremely rare in the Siskiyous.

The lake boasts a firm gravel bottom (which becomes a little silty in the center), and clear, shallow, warm water. Swimming is excellent but fishing, they say, is only so-so.

Beyond Azalea Lake, the path turns into the Butte Fork Trail. If you follow the Butte Fork Trail from the lake for 0.6 mile, you pass the precipitous wall of Figurehead Mountain and arrive at the Lonesome Lake turnoff. Another 0.6 mile on the Butte Fork Trail (1.2 miles from Azalea Lake), leads you to the upper end of the Sweaty Gap Trail. All these places are described under "Options."

Options: *Steve's Fork Trail.* The Steve's Fork Trail (905) to Azalea Lake is magnificent and about the same length as the route from the Azalea Lake Trailhead. It begins at an elevation 900 feet lower than the Azalea Lake Trail. To find the Steve's Fork Trailhead, continue on FR 1030 (Steve's Fork Road) to its end (milepost 10.5) instead of turning up Spur 400 for the Azalea Lake Trailhead.

From the trailhead (0.2 mile from the state line), the path winds through the woods above the creek for 0.7 mile, then hits a junction (go left), and crosses Steve's Fork Creek immediately after. After another 0.7 mile, the trail begins a series of moderate switchbacks through a forest of Douglas-fir, mountain hemlock, white fir, Shasta fir, sugar pine, and Brewer spruce. The path joins the Azalea Lake Trail after 4 miles at a junction 2.6 miles from the Azalea Lake Trailhead.

The Steve's Fork Trail features outstanding views of the looming rock face of Pyramid Peak across a small cirque basin. At certain times of the year, a creek runs down the entire face of the mountain, summit to base. The vista compensates for the route's steepness compared to the Azalea Lake Trail.

(Note: The Steve's Fork Trailhead is not in quite the same place as it was 10 years ago, when the state line ran right through it. Also, much of the lower trail system has been rerouted in the last few years.)

Lonesome Lake Trail. For Lonesome Lake, continue past Azalea Lake for 0.6 mile on the Butte Lake Trail, then turn right onto the Lonesome Lake Trail (956) and continue for 1.1 miles. The lake isn't much—1 acre—but the rocky basin and soaring peaks are stupendous.

Sweaty Gap Trail. The steepest and least-scenic route by far to Azalea Lake is the Sweaty Gap Trail (954). Use it only if you're in excellent shape. The path climbs from 4,200 feet to 5,600 feet in 1.5 miles, then drops down to 4,800 feet in the final 1.5 miles before ending at the Butte Fork Trail. The Sweaty Gap Trailhead is also the Frog Pond Loop Trailhead (see Hike 68).

Azalea Lake Trail, Pyramid Peak.

Butte Fork Trail. The Butte Fork Trail reaches Azalea Lake in 8 miles and runs along the bottom of a densely wooded canyon. It's very pretty but a little monotonous and visits to the creek are few and far between. The route is a favorite among riders. The best way to access the Butte Fork Trail is to follow the directions to the Frog Pond Loop Trailhead (Hike 68), and use the shortcut trailhead near milepost 2 on FR 1040.

68   Frog Pond Loop

Highlight:	A charming, somewhat steep hike into the Red Buttes Wilderness. Opens up earlier in the season than other mountain trails. Historical and botanical interest.
Type of hike:	Day hike, loop, or out and back.
Total distance:	7 mile loop.
Difficulty:	Strenuous.
Elevation gain:	1,600 feet.
Best months:	May–November.
Map:	USGS Kangaroo Mountain quad.

Special considerations: Trail is entirely in California and reasonably accessible only via Oregon's Applegate Valley. Lots of water.

Finding the trailhead: From Grants Pass or Jacksonville, take Oregon Highway 238 to Ruch. From there, follow the Applegate River Road (County Road 859) south for 15 miles, past the dam and reservoir to the state line, turning right onto the Middle Fork Road (Forest Road 1040) just past the state line. After 5 miles on FR 1040, swing left where the road makes a hard turn uphill and Forest Road 1035 continues straight. Stay on FR 1040. The first Frog Pond Trailhead is located 11 miles from the state line (6 miles from the uphill turn). The second Frog Pond trailhead, on the same road, lies 2 miles past the first trailhead. The second trailhead is also the Sweaty Gap Trailhead and the far terminus of the Middle Fork Trail.

Parking and trailhead facilities: Ten cars can park along the shoulder at the second trailhead. The first trailhead accommodates five cars.

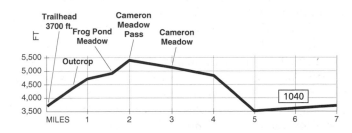

Frog Pond Loop

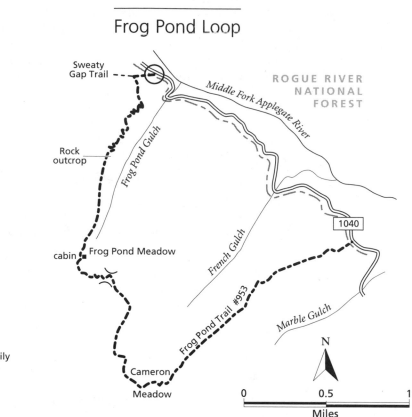

Mount Emily
6,100 ft.

RED BUTTES WILDERNESS

Key points:
   0.0 Sweaty Gap Trailhead.
   0.7 Rock outcrop.
   1.6 Frog Pond Meadow.
   3.0 Cameron Meadow.
   5.0 FR 1040, first trailhead.
   7.0 End of loop.

The hike: This exquisite path with floral meadows, looming cliffs, botanical oddities, and stunning vistas of the Red Buttes, boasts all the trappings of a nearly perfect day hike. Before elaborating on its wonders, however, readers are warned of a couple of less-than-sublime aspects, with suggested ways to minimize them.

The Frog Pond Trail may be reached via two trailheads, 2 miles apart on the same road. Although the actual path is only 5 miles, you have to walk 7 miles to complete the loop, including 2 miles along the road. From either trailhead, it's a fairly steep 2 miles to the journey's best stretch, the mile between McCloy Cabin and Cameron Meadow.

Even though the entire loop is described here, it's probably best to start at the second trailhead, hike 3 miles to Cameron Meadows, then double back. That not only reduces the trek by 1 mile, it avoids the rather annoying 2 miles between Cameron Meadow and the first trailhead.

Although both entry points offer a stiff uphill cardiovascular workout, the route from the first trailhead is much steeper and less scenic. Follow it only if you enjoy beating through a jungle of insects, vegetation, and spider webs. Higher up, this segment repeatedly disappears across a series of meadows and life becomes a constant search for rock piles, blazes or (ha!) signs. At one point, the route is signaled only by a 3-inch square flasher tacked to a tree 500 feet beyond where the path peters out. If you employ this portion of the trail, make it the downhill leg.

The second trailhead offers a less-steep (but still nowhere near level) ascent up a wooded, ridgetop hillside, initially through a forest of Douglas-fir and white fir. Farther up, western white pine, Shasta fir, and the rare and elegant Brewer spruce shade the route.

After 0.7 mile, shortly after a large rock outcrop, the pitch eases as the trail negotiates an opening overgrown with wall-to-wall bear grass. In May or June, when this spectacular lily species blooms, the display is staggering.

Soon after, at mile 1.6, the landscape opens out to the emerald expanse of Frog Pond Meadow. The cabin, built in the 1930s by a gold miner named John Calvin Knox McCloy, incorporates seven live incense cedars into its frame. The large, lilypad-choked pond, with its convoluted shoreline, provides an exquisite centerpiece to the meadow, the upper end of which is guarded by the soaring cliffs of Mount Emily. Look for bears in the meadow.

McCloy Cabin, Frog Pond Meadow.

Above the cabin, the path winds along the meadow's periphery, then disappears into a sea of wildflowers. Look for, among others, tiger lilies, spirea, corn lilies, Indian paintbrush, daisies, monkshood, penstemon, and cinquefoil.

Although the trail vanishes for 100 feet or so here, the route is obvious. The large black-on-white X, where the path resumes, is difficult to miss.

As the path leaves the Frog Pond area, it passes a smaller meadow at the base of an immense rock outcrop. The droopy-looking trees there comprise an extremely rare stand of Alaska cedar. Common in the northern Cascades, the species is confined in the Siskiyous to six or seven tiny, stunted, widely scattered clumps.

Beyond the Alaska cedars, the trail climbs several hundred feet to a boulder strewn ridgetop. This 1-mile segment, largely in the open, offers marvelous panoramas of the region's heights. Look for Whiskey Peak (opposite), Pyramid Peak (to the rear), and the immense, orange, double-humped Red Butte (dead ahead).

The path eventually drops into the Cameron Meadow basin at mile 3. Higher and less lush, but no less impressive than the Frog Pond Meadows basin, the surrounding rock faces are broken by patches of wildflowers, grass, and picturesque conifer clusters. Spend your time exploring, or perhaps scaling the ridgetop, instead of trying to sleuth out the continuing trail, which disappears at the meadow's edge.

In fact, it doesn't pay to venture too far past Cameron Meadows even if you do locate the continuing path. Beyond a charming little pond 0.1 mile down, the scenery quickly deteriorates.

If you do continue the loop, it's 2 steep, downhill, brushy miles back down to the road and 2 more miles along the road, slightly uphill with a very nice creek crossing in the middle, to the second trailhead.

69   Red Butte

Highlight:	Close-up exploration of the beautiful namesake peak of the Red Buttes Wilderness.
Type of hike:	Day hike, out and back.
Total distance:	7.6 miles.
Difficulty:	Easy.
Elevation gain:	1,200 feet.
Best months:	May–November.
Map:	USGS Kangaroo Mountain quad.

Special considerations: The trail is entirely in California. The total distance given presumes you hike on the PCT from Cook and Green Pass. You can shorten the hike 2.3 miles each way by driving an extremely low-quality road from the pass to the base of Red Butte.

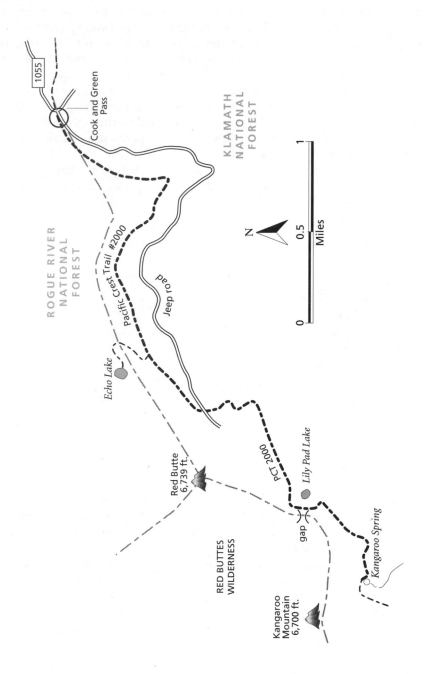

Red Butte

ROGUE RIVER NATIONAL FOREST

KLAMATH NATIONAL FOREST

1055

Cook and Green Pass

Pacific Crest Trail #2000

Jeep road

Echo Lake

Red Butte 6,739 ft.

RED BUTTES WILDERNESS

PCT 2000

Lily Pad Lake

gap

Kangaroo Mountain 6,700 ft.

Kangaroo Spring

N

Miles

0   0.5   1

There is excellent water where the road crosses the trail at the base of Red Butte and at Kangaroo Spring. As always, it should be purified.

Finding the trailhead: Take Oregon Highway 238 from Jacksonville or Grants Pass to the town of Ruch. From there, follow County Road 859, the Applegate River Road, south up the Applegate River for 15 miles, past Applegate Lake, to where the pavement ends at the state line. Immediately beyond, turn left onto Elliott Creek Road (Forest Road 1050), then turn right (east) 1 mile later onto the very steep Cook and Green Pass Road (Forest Road 1055). At Cook and Green Pass, 9 miles up, park and hike the Pacific Crest Trail to the right (west). A side road to the right will take you to the base of the Red Buttes but it's extremely poor. You can also hike the PCT eastward (see "Options").

Notes: The turnoff from FR 1050 to FR 1055 is currently unmarked. Also, a landslide at mile 3 on FR 1055 may require high clearance and four-wheel drive to get across. The spot was scheduled for repair in summer 2000.

Parking and trailhead facilities: There is parking for 15 cars at Cook and Green Pass.

Key points:
    0.0 Cook and Green Pass.
    2.0 Echo Lake overlook.
    2.4 Upper road crossing.
    3.0 Lily Pad Lake.
    3.8 Kangaroo Spring.

The hike: The Red Buttes pop up now and then on many southern Oregon back roads, usually just for a second. Their double-humped camelback outline is an instant giveaway. Also, they are red (orange actually).

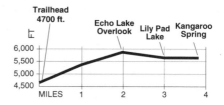

Trails converge everywhere at Cook and Green Pass. It's probably best to take the Pacific Crest Trail (2000) to the Red Buttes, although you can also walk or drive up the old road. While the latter has remained open, it's in very poor condition.

The PCT was rather ruthlessly gouged into the mountain just above the road, breaking the hillside's clean, majestic sweep and marring the area's beauty. It's a lovely walk, however.

If you choose to take the PCT, it's 2 miles to the Echo Lake overlook. Echo Lake is a small (3 acres), unstocked, perfectly formed glacial-cirque lake. The overlook is impressive but the hike down to the water probably isn't worth the effort.

At mile 2.4, the PCT crosses the upper end of the old road. This spot is as close to Red Butte's massive orange summit as the trail gets. If you have a hankering to climb Red Butte, this is the place to start. It doesn't look that difficult. The road continues for another mile to an old chrome mine.

Immediately beyond where the trail crosses the road, a wonderful little pipe spring emits the most delicious water you'll ever taste. Lily Pad Lake turns up 0.6 mile later, in a huge meadow with a tremendous view of the Seiad Creek Valley and the Devil's Peaks, both to the south. Lily Pad Lake covers 1 acre and is filled with pond lilies.

Beyond Lily Pad Lake, the PCT rounds a rocky point and enters the magnificent cirque of Kangaroo Spring at mile 3.8. The sheer, brilliant orange cirque walls are made even more stunning by a band of white marble that runs through the formation. There is no obvious spring or lake but there is lots of clear running water in the basin's meadows.

Beyond Kangaroo Spring, you can follow the PCT to the three Devil's Peaks (Upper, Middle and Lower), then hike down to the Klamath, or you can continue along the Siskiyou Crest and the Boundary Trail to Rattlesnake Mountain, Azalea Lake, and points west.

Options: *East on the Pacific Crest Trail.* Heading east from Cook and Green Pass, away from the Red Buttes, the PCT stays in the woods for 1.5 miles, then crosses the rocky summit of Copper Butte (elevation 6,194 feet) . From there, it's 6 more miles, over two more summits including 7,112-foot Condrey Mountain, to a trailhead on an incredibly long, winding road up from the village of Klamath River in California.

Devil's peaks. If you stay on the PCT past Kangaroo Spring, it's 0.5 mile to the junction with the Siskiyou Boundary Trail, 1.5 miles to Upper Devil's Peak (elevation 6,041 feet, with the trail missing the summit by 0.1 mile and 200 feet of elevation), 2.8 miles to Lower Devil's Peak, and 7.8 miles to the Klamath River Road, near the California town of Seiad Valley.

Josephine County

Josephine County, Oregon, one county west of Jackson County, boasts many unique scenic qualities. The Rogue River's Wild and Scenic section starts here, the eastern half of the vast Kalmiopsis Wilderness is accessible only from here, the largest serpentinite formation in North America is located here, and the county contains some of the highest and prettiest peaks of the Siskiyou range. The county's highest point is Grayback Mountain (Hike 74), rising to just over 7,000 feet.

Josephine County is also the locale of Oregon Caves National Monument which, in case you haven't figured it out, is why the Grants Pass High School football players are called the "Cavemen."

Not surprisingly, the county is rich with magnificent trails.

---

70 Taylor Creek

Highlight:	A pleasant hike along a beautiful creek, with many access points.
Type of hike:	Day hike, shuttle.
Total distance:	6.5 miles.
Difficulty:	Easy.
Elevation loss:	1,400 feet.
Best months:	Any.
Maps:	USGS Onion Mountain, Chrome Ridge, and Galice quads.

Special considerations: The description assumes a one-way hike in the downhill direction. If you only have one car and don't like hitchhiking, you need to do the route as an out-and-back hike. The path has numerous access points and can be hiked piecemeal. There is plenty of water but it should be purified.

Finding the trailhead: Leave Interstate 5 at Merlin. Follow Merlin-Galice Road 9 miles to (paved) Forest Road 25, known as Briggs Valley Road or Taylor Creek Road. Numerous well-marked trailheads begin at English

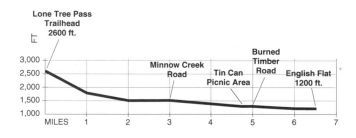

Taylor Creek

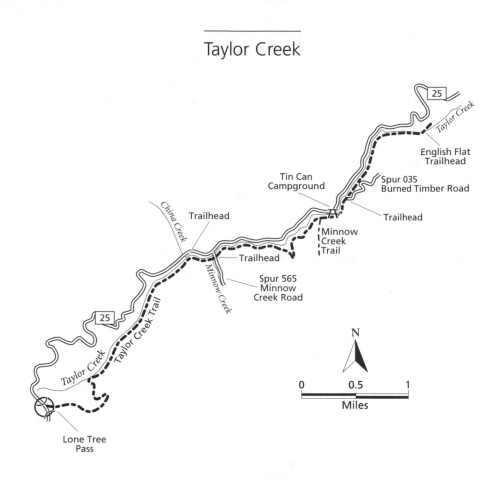

Flat at mile 3.5 on FR 25, a large meadow downhill from the paved road. Park at the gated turnoff. Other major trailheads can be found at Burned Timber Road (Spur 035, mile 4.5), Tin Can Campground (mile 5), Minnow Creek Road (Spur 052, mile 6.5, which becomes Spur 565 after 0.2 mile), and Lone Tree Pass (FR 2509, mile 9). The described hike begins at Lone Tree Pass and ends at English Flat.

Parking and trailhead facilities: There's parking for six cars at Lone Tree Pass, three cars at Minnow Creek and Burned Timber Roads, five cars at Tin Can Campground, and four cars at English Flat. There are pit toilets at Tin Can Campground.

Key points:
0.0 Lone Tree Pass Trailhead.
3.0 Minnow Creek Road.
4.7 Tin Can Campground.
5.0 Burned Timber Road.
6.5 English Flat.

The hike: The Taylor Creek Trail actually extends 10 miles, from Sam Brown Campground to English Flat. Of these, the 6.5 miles from Lone Tree Pass to English Flat are the most interesting. While the trail parallels FR 25 with uncomfortable proximity, the designers attempted to keep it as far from the pavement as possible. They came up with a beautiful, easy, well-constructed route visiting some magnificent pools, rock outcrops, waterfalls, and other scenic features.

Since the trail hits either a side road or FR 25 every mile or so, options are myriad. The shortest segment is the 0.3 mile from Burnt Timber Road to Tin Can Campground. Other segments run 1 to 2 miles between trail-heads. This is a wonderful route to explore piecemeal with children, a segment at a time.

For the most part, the trail is gouged into an extremely steep, densely forested, goat slope of a hillside. An abundance of canyon live oak, which loves steep, shallow-soiled, shady, low-elevation slopes, tells you much about the area's ecology. Canyon live oak has the hardest wood of any North American tree species.

The trail's initial mile, down from Lone Tree Pass, hugs the creek well away from the road. The road is busy descending a steep mountain slope just below the pass. This is the trail's steepest segment, especially the first 0.5 mile, which drops down from the pass in a long, north-slope switchback.

The trail's bypassing of Tin Can Campground, at mile 4.7, is an especially nice design feature. Located high above the creek, the path is held in place by retaining walls. The initial construction of these walls was

Taylor Creek Bridge at Tin Can Campground.

258

unsuccessful as they collapsed during a storm in 1993 and had to be rebuilt. Below Tin Can Campground, the route alternates between dense woods, rocky outcrops, and grassy meadows. Above, it's mostly dense woods.

Also in 1993, the log bridge spanning the creek at English Flat, where the trail ends at mile 6.5, was washed out in a storm. It was pretty scary looking at the time but has since been repaired. In summer, it's just as easy to wade the creek.

Option: *Minnow Creek Trail.* For excellent panoramas of the Taylor Creek basin, follow the Minnow Creek Trail, which meets the Taylor Creek Trail 500 feet west of Tin Can Campground. This new section of the Minnow Creek Trail makes a couple of wide, steep switchbacks, uphill and through the brush and hardwood, to a forested ridgetop, linking up with the old Minnow Creek Trail after 0.5 mile.

The old Minnow Creek Trailhead is reached by driving up Minnow Creek Road, the next left off FR 25 after Tin Can Campground. Follow the main road through two left turns to a well-marked trailhead.

The 0.2-mile path linking the old trailhead to the new path up from Tin Can Campground is among the steeper in these parts. It's so steep, in fact, that it's actually more stressful going down than up. Do this path three times a week and you'll always be in shape.

The bulk of the Minnow Creek Trail follows a dry, densely wooded ridgetop, with panoramas in two directions. The second-growth stand offers an excellent lesson in natural succession. The forest consists of large hardwoods (black oak, live oak, tanoak, and madrone) that invaded after logging 30 or 40 years ago. The scattered larger conifers are either pines, which also invaded after logging, or defective residuals left as seed trees. In between these larger trees, thousands of young Douglas-firs are slowly working their way from the understory, up through the hardwood and pine foliage, on their way to eventual dominance.

In a couple of places the path emerges at grassy openings that offer excellent views in both directions but particularly of the Taylor Creek drainage, with Mount McLouglin on the eastern horizon. The trail connects, after 3 miles, to a road spur in the vicinity of Onion Mountain.

71 Briggs Creek

Highlight:	A pleasant, short, easy creekside hike to an old gold mine.
Type of hike:	Day hike, out and back.
Total distance:	About 4 miles.
Difficulty:	Easy.
Elevation gain:	Minimal.
Best months:	April–November.
Map:	USGS Chrome Ridge quad.

Special considerations: There is plenty of water in Briggs Creek and side creeks but it should be purified. The described hike begins at an access point 1 mile down the trail from the main trailhead at Sam Brown Campground. See "Options" for directions to the main trailhead.

Finding the trailhead: Leave Interstate 5 at Merlin and follow Merlin-Galice Road 12 miles to Forest Road 25, which locals call Taylor Creek Road and the Forest Service calls Briggs Valley Road. Continue on FR 25 for 14 miles, past Big Pine to Sam Brown Campground, on the left. Turn right onto Forest Road 2512 just before the campground. At the first left beyond Sam Brown Campground (0.3 mile), turn onto a wide, steep, gravel and dirt road and follow it to the bottom of the hill. Then bear left and follow the road along the creek to the end. This side road may be gated, in which case, begin your hike at Sam Brown Campgound.

Parking and trailhead facilities: Three cars can park at the end of the road (15 at Sam Brown Campground).

Key points:
0.0 Side road trailhead.
2.0 Elkhorn Mine.

The hike: The Briggs Creek Trailhead at Sam Brown Campground is large, well groomed, and filled with amenities. After such an auspicious beginning, the path wanders through old clearcuts for 0.5 mile, then follows a perfectly drivable road for 0.5 mile. The described hike begins at the end of that road, where the real trail starts.

The road ends at a deep side creek which may not be crossable in winter. Immediately after, the trail passes an old hydraulic gold mining area. The site's steep banks, with overhanging tops, are characteristic of hydraulic mining. Soil was washed from the hillsides with a giant nozzle. It was then run

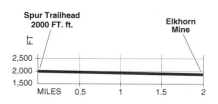

Briggs Creek

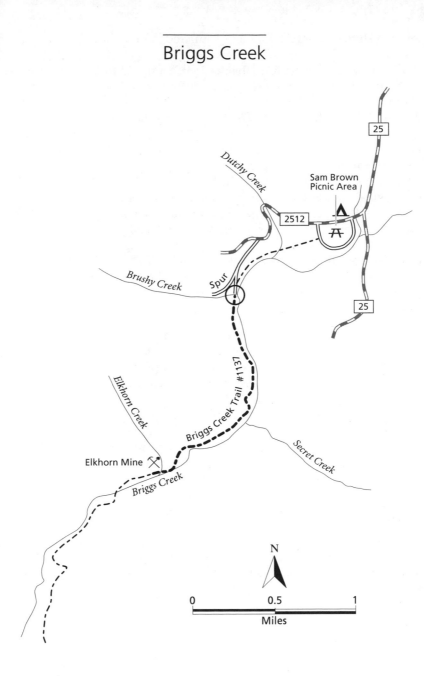

Dutchy Creek

Sam Brown
Picnic Area

25

2512

Brushy Creek

Spur

25

Briggs Creek Trail #1137

Elkhorn Creek

Secret Creek

Elkhorn Mine

Briggs Creek

N

0   0.5   1

Miles

through a sluice to extract gold and returned, laden with much silt, to the creek.

Trees growing in the mined banks look to be 50 to 60 years old. This just about corresponds to when gold mining petered out as a major industry (1940s and 1950s).

The initial mile beyond the creek crossing—the first mile of real trail—is gorgeous as the path winds 50 to 100 feet above the river through a majestic old-growth stand. The creek becomes rockier, wider, and ever more enchanting as you progress.

Autumn is the best time to visit, when the vine maple, bigleaf maple, and dogwood change color, but the trail is often open year-round. At 2,100 feet, the Big Pine area rarely has lingering snowpack. However, the creeks at the road's end and Elkhorn Mine can get nasty in winter and early spring, Elkhorn Mine makes a wonderful turnaround spot. The 1933 enterprise, according to the Forest Service, was a major employer during the Depression. All that remains are hydraulic mining scars, gravel tailings, bits of rapidly deteriorating litter, and an outhouse. Several more mines dot the path below Elkhorn.

Options: *The Sam Brown Trailhead.* For the Sam Brown Trailhead, turn left into Sam Brown Campground (the second Sam Brown entrance) and drive a third of the way around the loop. There are pit toilets, picnic tables, and parking for at least 15 cars. The trailhead is near the creek, just before the group picnic shelters.

Presuming you begin at the campground, the trail's first mile follows the creek through young forest stands and logging clearcuts. Of interest is the proliferation of Christmas tree-sized Douglas-fir. Such vigorous regeneration isn't that common in interior southwest Oregon and it's a pleasure to behold. Most of the trees were planted.

The rest of Briggs Creek. The route follows Briggs Creek for 5.5 miles beyond Elkhorn Mine. Around Swede and Onion Creeks, beginning 1.5 miles past Elkhorn Mine, the trail winds over some deep rock canyons. It makes three major creek crossings in the same vicinity, which are normally knee-deep but which can be impassable.

The path ends at a place called Brushy Bar, 4 miles short of the Illinois River Trailhead near the mouth of Briggs Creek.

72 Kerby Peak

Highlight:	Very steep, very scenic trail to the top of one of
	Josephine County's dominant peaks.
Type of hike:	Day hike, out and back.
Total distance:	About 7 miles.
Difficulty:	Strenuous.
Elevation gain:	2,602 feet.
Best months:	May–November.
Maps:	USGS Kerby Peak quad.

Special considerations: The White Creek Trailhead to the Kerby Peak Trail was almost impossible to find prior to 1998, partly because the trail was not maintained for 20 years. In 1998, the path was brushed out and rerouted slightly. And the sign at the trailhead, which had been knocked over and had scrub grown up around it, was repaired. There is no water on the trail and it is very steep.

The Rabbit Lake route to the top of Kerby Peak, described in other hiking guides, was much shorter and easier than the White Creek route. The Rabbit Lake route is no longer considered viable due to deterioration of Rabbit Lake Road.

Finding the trailhead: Take U.S. Highway 199 south from Grants Pass for 20 miles to the town of Selma. In Selma, turn left onto Deer Creek Road (County Road 5070). Proceed 8 miles to White Creek Road (38-6-18)

Kirby Peak Saddle.

Kerby Peak

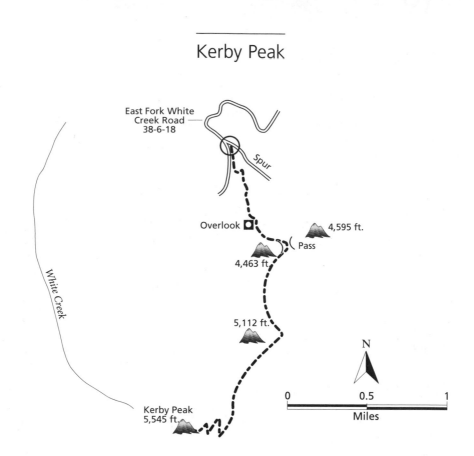

and turn right. After 0.3 mile, turn left onto the East Fork of White Creek Road (the second left) and continue 2 miles to the trailhead. Look for a side road on the left, with the trailhead just to the right of the side road. There should be lots of survey flagging in case you miss the sign.

Parking and trailhead facilities: A large flat on the left side of the road can accommodate ten cars.

Key points:
  0.0 White Creek Trailhead.
  1.0 Overlook.
  1.5 Pass.
  3.5 Summit.

The hike: Used to be, if you wanted to climb Kerby Peak, it was an easy, 1-mile trek from the end of Rabbit Lake Road, 14 miles up Deer Creek Road. Unless you have a high-clearance four-by-four vehicle, those days are long gone because the end of Rabbit Lake Road is rapidly returning to

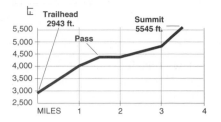

nature. Too bad, because in the 1970s, it was one of Josephine County's prettier drives.

Not to worry! Even with the new trail three and a half times as long and starting 2,000 feet lower, Kerby Peak is a great hike. The 5,545-foot mountain, one of Josephine County's prominent summits, towers above Lake Selmac, south of U.S. Highway 199 near Selma.

When the new Kerby Peak Trail above White Creek was constructed by the Young Adult Conservation Corps in 1978, the project drew lots of attention. But the trail attracted little use because the old Rabbit Lake route was so much easier. Over 20 years, the trailhead sign fell over, brush grew up around the trailhead and the last 0.5 mile became completely obscured. The path's first 0.2 mile was so steep and slippery, you couldn't walk on it in wet weather.

The White Creek–Kerby Peak Trail's Sleeping Beauty era ended in1998. The most noticeable improvement was the rerouting of the initial 0.2 mile, which now makes a long, reasonable switchback instead of charging up a slick, compacted goat slope.

The path's initial mile is uniformly steep as it inscribes dozens of switchbacks through a middle-elevation forest of Douglas-fir, white fir, incense cedar, and sugar pine, with the usual black oak and madrone hardwood cohorts. It's not an old-growth forest but it is a beautiful, closed-canopy second-growth forest.

The rock overlook at mile 1 offers an excellent hiking destination any time of year. The west-facing perch provides a fine panorama of the Deer Creek Valley and the trail's first view of Kerby Peak.

Beyond the overlook, the path steepens slightly as it continues its relentless upward march through the woods. Approaching mile 1.5, the route breaks out of the woods onto a large rock outcrop. Soon after, the trail hits a pass, with a rocky knob just to the left. The path here swings sharply right along the ridgetop, levels off for a while, climbs a short ways, then levels off again as it cuts around from the mountain's north face, to its east face, to its south face.

On the dry and fire-prone south face, the vegetation changes dramatically from forest to a bramble of low, dense brush. The main species are pinemat manzanita, green manzanita, and squawcarpet ceanothus. The path makes it way up through the steep, brushy slopes in a series of switchbacks before finally attaining the summit at mile 3.5.

The summit is gorgeous, with green meadows, brown-rock outcrops, a tremendous panorama, and a sheer cliff dropping off to the northwest. Look for the rare and beautiful Brewer spruce growing just over the cliffs.

As always, bring a map and lunch. Thus supplied, one can sit on the summit, munch a sandwich, pick out such landmarks as Murphy Mountain, Lake Selmac, and Grayback Peak, and be at peace with the world.

73 Bigelow Lake

Highlight:	A pretty, easy, meadowy hike into the high Siskiyous directly above Oregon Caves National Monument.
Type of hike:	Day hike, out and back.
Total distance:	About 4 miles.
Difficulty:	Moderate.
Elevation gain:	790 feet.
Best months:	June–October.
Map:	USGS Oregon Caves quad.

Special considerations: You might keep company with cows in the high meadows.

Finding the trailhead: Take Williams Highway (Oregon Highway 238) south from Grants Pass 12 miles to Water Gap Road. Bear right (straight, actually) onto Water Gap and continue 4 miles back to Williams Highway, following signs to Williams. Turn right onto Williams Highway and proceed 1.5 miles to the town of Williams. Go through Williams, ending up on Kincaid Road. Turn left onto Cedar Flat Road after 0.8 mile and left again onto Caves Camp Road 2 miles later. Caves Camp/Low Divide Road winds into the mountains around the base of Grayback Peak, Josephine County's highest. The road is unpaved after the first 3 miles but it's not difficult driving. Bear left at the major forks (Forest Road 4611 and Spur 070). After 16 miles (from Cedar Flat Road), you arrive at a cattle grate, with the trailhead just before it on the left.

Parking and trailhead facilities: There's parking for 15 cars along the shoulder.

Key points:
    0.0 Bigelow Lake Trailhead.
    0.5 Bigelow Lake.
    1.5 Bigelow Saddle, Boundary Trail, Lake Mountain Trail.
    2.0 Mount Elijah.

The hike: Two of the prettiest high-country locations in Josephine County are Bigelow Lake and Mount Elijah. The trail to both ends at Oregon Caves National Monument. It's 4.5 miles from the caves to Mount Elijah. However, it's only 2 miles from Bigelow Lake to Mount Elijah. The Bigelow Lake Trailhead is only a 15-minute drive from the monument, if you know the secret shortcut.

It's 0.5 mile up the Bigelow Lake Trail to Bigelow Lake, a shallow, 2-acre, lily pond in a meadow, with white cliffs rising overhead. The lake is off the trail, 0.1 mile to the right. The surrounding meadow is

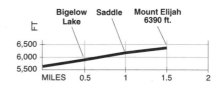

Bigelow Lake

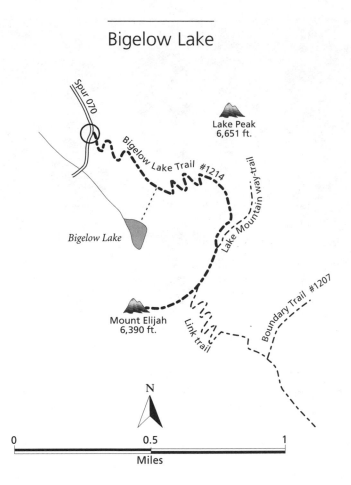

particularly beautiful in spring when water and wildflowers abound. The Forest Service lists 14 sensitive species growing near Bigelow Lake, including the rare and beautiful Mendocino gentian.

Be prepared to share this beauty, and the sensitive wildflower species, with grazing cows. Many high-mountain meadows in this area are open to grazing. The drift fence near the road serves only to keep them out of the national monument.

Above the lake, the trail twists upward, past more meadows, to a small saddle. There, a trail to the left leads to Lake Peak. The Lake Peak route is poorly marked and difficult to follow. To the right, the trail quickly forks. The downhill fork (left), connects to the Siskiyou Boundary Trail after 0.2 mile. The Boundary Trail is a 27-mile walk connecting Tannen Mountain and Grayback Peak. You're standing about halfway between the two.

The uphill fork (right) at the saddle, goes to the top of Mount Elijah after an easy 0.5 mile. From there, you can look down on Bigelow Lake or across to Whiskey Peak and the Red Buttes. It's a spectacular maze of

Jenny O'Leary and Sara Bernstein at Bigelow Lake.

looming mountaintops, made more impressive by the fact that almost none of the peaks are visible from paved roads. Mount Elijah itself, despite having Oregon Caves within its bowels, cannot be seen from anywhere in the national monument.

Option: *Lower Bigelow Lake.* Before starting up the Bigelow Lake/Mount Elijah Trail, you may wish to visit Lower Bigelow Lake, which occupies a tiny glacial cirque nearby. Walk down the road until you come to a second creek. Make your way up the creek to the left, through the brush, until you find a lake set in a small but deep basin. Along the way, look for Shasta fir, mountain hemlock, Douglas maple, and other high-elevation species.

74 Grayback Mountain

Highlight:	A beautiful hike to the highest point in Josephine County.
Type of hike:	Day hike, out and back.
Total distance:	About 6 miles.
Difficulty:	Moderate.
Elevation gain:	2,055 feet.
Best months:	June–October.
Map:	USGS Grayback Mountain quad.

Grayback Mountain

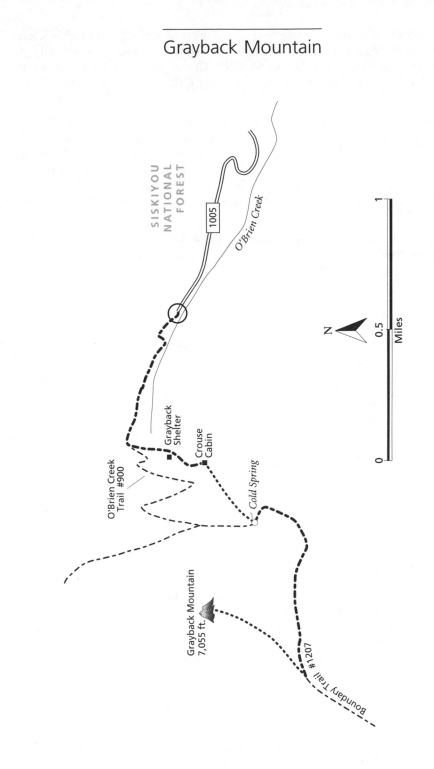

SISKIYOU NATIONAL FOREST

1005

O'Brien Creek

O'Brien Creek Trail #900

Grayback Shelter

Crouse Cabin

Cold Spring

Grayback Mountain 7,055 ft.

Boundary Trail #1207

N

0   0.5   1
Miles

Special considerations: The sign on Forest Road 10, where O'Brien Creek Road begins, says "O'Brien Creek Trail 2 Miles." It's actually 4 miles. It's 2 miles to the Lower O'Brien Creek Trail, which you do not want. There is water on the trail near Crouse Cabin and sometimes at Cold Spring.

Finding the trailhead: At the town of Applegate, from Jacksonville or Grants Pass on Oregon Highway 238, turn south up Thompson Creek Road (Forest Road 10), at the west end of the bridge, and proceed 12 miles to O'Brien Creek Road (Forest Road 1005). The latter comes in on a hilltop amid a maze of side roads but is clearly marked on the right. Take O'Brien Creek Road to the end. The last 0.5 mile is steep, rocky, and narrow.

Parking and trailhead facilities: There is parking for six cars at the trailhead. There is no room for a trailer turnaround and barely room for an auto turnaround.

Key points:
    0.0 Upper O'Brien Creek Trailhead.
    1.1 Grayback Shelter.
    1.2 Crouse Cabin (The Forest Service map says "Krause").
    2.3 Cold Spring.
    3.0 Pass.
    3.5 Summit.

The hike: Mighty Grayback Mountain, at 7,055 feet, is the highest summit in Josephine County. It is one of five Siskiyou peaks over 7,000 feet. While Grayback is no Shasta, Grants Pass residents feel a certain fond-

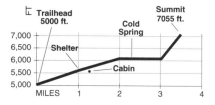

ness for the old gray mound, so aptly named and looking like a beached whale. A trip up Grayback won't guarantee membership in the Explorers Club, but it will provide a workout and some pleasant scenery.

    The trail (900) begins at the road end. It starts out by winding through the woods for 1 mile, mostly uphill but not killingly so. After crossing a tiny creek, the path emerges in a large meadow containing two rustic cabins. One is a Forest Service structure, the other was built by some people who graze cattle in the area.

    The meadow shoots up almost to the summit and is very steep at the far end. There used to be a series of markers leading across the meadow to Cold Spring on the Boundary Trail. The path has since been rerouted and is now longer but less steep, following the edge of the trees to the right.

    At Cold Spring (mile 2.3), (actually a pretty little creek), take the Boundary Trail (1207) left. After 0.7 mile (mile 3), you arrive at a saddle with a sharp ridge rising to the right. To attain the summit, merely walk up the ridge. There is no trail. It's like climbing stairs. Lots of stairs.

It's 0.5 mile from the saddle to the hogback summit. About one-third of the way up the ridge, you find another overlook of the meadow and cabin below. You can get down quickly by lighting out here and heading towards the cabin. It's fun, if a little muddy certain times of year. Don't try to go up this way.

According to a Forest Service inventory, there is supposed to be Baker cypress on the south face of Grayback, near the trail. I've never seen them and couldn't find anyone at the Forest Service who has. Many sensitive plant species adorn Grayback, including Lee's lewisia, Mendocino gentian and several lilies—if the cows haven't eaten them.

75 Miller Lake

Highlight:	A sometimes nice little lake, a loop trail, and some botanical oddities in a pretty cirque basin.
Type of hike:	Day hike, out and back with loop option.
Total distance:	1.6 miles.
Difficulty:	Moderate.
Elevation gain:	300 feet.
Best months:	June–October.
Map:	USGS Grayback Mountain quad.

Special considerations: A sign near the beginning of Forest Road 1020 warns that the road is closed due to washouts. In spring, 2000, there were two major washouts, all easily passable, if a bit rough. The road was repaired in summer, 2000.

Miller Lake is stagnant and has widely fluctuating water levels. Water from the creek should be purified.

Finding the trailhead: At the town of Applegate, from Jacksonville or Grants Pass on Oregon Highway 238, turn south up Thompson Creek Road (Forest Road 10), immediately west of town, at the west end of the bridge, and proceed to the summit. At the summit, bear right on Forest Road 1020, where the sign says "Miller Lake Trail 9 Miles" (it's actually 8 miles). Follow FR 1020 for 4.5 miles to Spur 400 (the sign was down in spring 2000; you want the road left toward Miller Lake, not FR 1020 right towards Sturgis Creek). The trailhead is at the end of Spur 400.

Parking and trailhead facilities: The large trailhead can accommodate ten cars. Note the spectacular view of Grayback Mountain, Josephine County's highest peak, at the trailhead.

Key points:
0.0 Miller Lake Trailhead.
0.8 Miller Lake.

Miller Lake

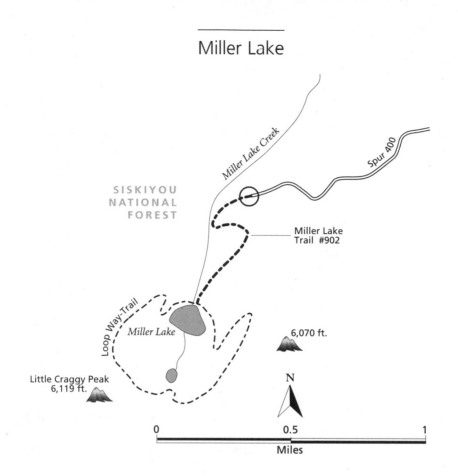

The hike: This interesting little dam-enhanced lake in the upper Applegate area boasts a 0.8-mile path from the trailhead, plus a wonderful (unofficial) 2-mile loop trail from the lake, up into the surrounding peaks and back (see "Options"). Also, within 0.5 mile of the lake, back in the woods away from the trails, stands one of Oregon's more fascinating botanical oddities.

Miller Lake Creek received a major overhaul in the notorious 1997–98 New Year's Eve flood, the same storm that took out parts of the road. Coming up from the trailhead on the Miller Lake Trail (902), after 0.2 mile, just beyond an impressive look at the flood-reamed canyon, the path crosses an older trail that was deactivated in 1990. The latter is a steep, closed-off logging road. The new route, straight ahead, is a little longer and less steep than the old route. It's best to hike to the lake on the new trail and return via the old trail. The old trail offers better creek views then the new trail. On the return trip, return to the new trail at mile 0.2.

Look for white fir and Douglas-fir along the trail, with lots of rhododendron and Sadler oak. Sadler oak, a low understory shrub, is a sure sign

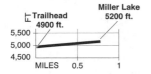

that you're in the Siskiyous and is always found with rhododendron, which it superficially resembles.

Though popular and offering good fishing, Miller Lake is rather foul. "Enhanced" by a small dam, the 5-acre pool has very steep banks and the water level is subject to great seasonal fluctuation. When the water level is down, the bank is muddy and unappealing. On the other hand, the glacial cirque in which the lake is nestled is lovely, with much rock and falling water. The main lake inlet flows downward in a photogenic staircase cascade.

Option: *Miller Lake Loop Way-Trail.* At the lake, a 2-mile loop way-trail commences with long uphill treks to the left or right. If you begin by going right, don't accidentally take the lower shoreline trail, which peters out after 0.1 mile.

Presuming you start by going left, the trail makes a long upgrade above the water to a rock outcrop, then inscribes a very long switchback in the opposite direction to another outcrop with a vista point, at the edge of the recently created Oliver Matthews Research Natural Area, which supposedly contains the world's largest Baker cypress tree (although Baker cypresses are extremely small and short-lived). The path then reverses direction and follows the mountain crest above the lake and back around past a little pond, before winding back down, in one last, long switchback, to the lake's east side.

In case you're wondering who Oliver Matthews is, the scientific name of the extremely rare subspecies of Baker cypress (which is also extremely rare), that grows at Miller Lake, is *Cupressus bakerii ssp. matthewsii.*

In compliance with legal requirements, the loop trail at Miller Lake is not numbered and is not considered part of the Forest Service's "official" trail system. At their request, the accompanying map shows only the general route.

Neither the Miller Lake Trail nor the loop way-trail passes the main Baker cypress stand, located 0.5 mile from Miller Lake. The Forest Service isn't thrilled with the idea of visitors to that extremely sensitive site.

76 Black Butte

Highlight:	High-mountain scenery, glorious panoramas, mighty glacial canyons, forest, meadows, and serpentinite ecology in the Siskiyou Wilderness.
Type of hike:	Day hike, out and back.
Total distance:	About 9 miles.
Difficulty:	Moderate.
Elevation gain:	500 feet.
Best months:	June–October.
Map:	USGS Polar Bear Mountain quad.

Special considerations: The trailhead and trail are entirely in California but the route is most easily reached via Oregon's Illinois Valley. For a one-way shuttle hike, see "Options" for directions to the Young Valley Trailhead, 2 miles beyond the far end of the described hike. Plenty of water.

Finding the trailhead: Take U.S. Highway 199 to Cave Junction and turn up Caves Highway (Oregon Highway 46). Turn right onto Holland Loop after 2 miles and right again on Bridgeview-Takilma Road (County Road 5820) after 2 more miles. Proceed on Takilma Road 4 miles past the Happy Camp turnoff, then 1 more mile through Takilma village. The road eventually becomes Forest Road 4904. Bear left where the centerline ends. Turn right 1.8 miles past the end of the centerline (pavement), over Dunn Creek, onto Forest Road 4906 (there is a sign in the opposite direction only), which becomes Spur 053. Proceed 10 miles to the trailhead, on the right.

Parking and trailhead facilities: The trailhead is on a pretty little open flat with room for ten cars and excellent views of the rocky south face of Black Butte and the canyon of the East Fork of the Illinois River.

Key points:
  0.0 Polar Bear Trailhead.
  1.8 Twin Valley Trail junction (go right).
  3.0 Junction (go right).
  4.0 Illinois River Trail.
  4.5 Young's Valley Trail (go right for Young's Valley Trailhead).

The hike: This trail penetrates the snow-capped crags that pop into view as you enter the Illinois Valley from Grants Pass. The group of summits rise

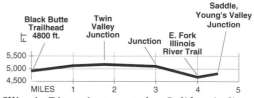

above the head of the East Fork Illinois River, just past the California line. Major summits include Young's Peak, Preston Peak, El Capitan, Black Butte, and Polar Bear Mountain.

Black Butte

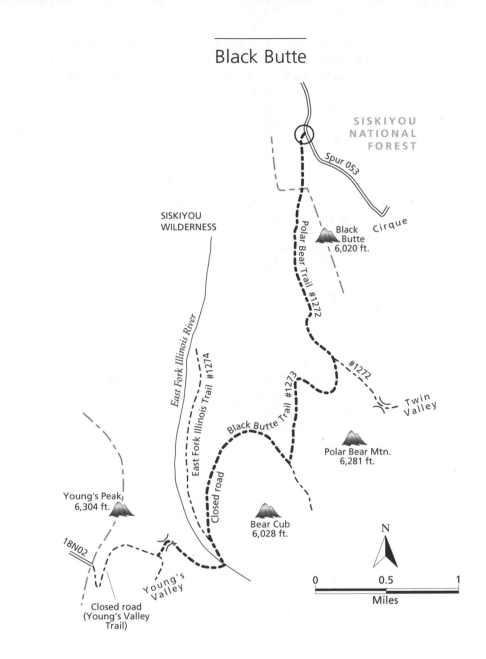

There's no mistaking Black Butte, a narrow, pointed projection towering above the trailhead area. If you have a little time, continue down the road, 1 mile past the Black Butte (Polar Bear) Trailhead to the first creek, noting the Brewer spruce along the way. The creek flows out of a small, steep-walled glacial cirque which bears exploring. Follow the creek through a narrow canyon into the cirque. Instead of a lake inside, there's a little marsh. Look for insect-eating darlingtonia plants.

The first part of the trail, which here is called the Polar Bear Trail (1272), circles around Black Butte's mysterious, rocky crest across a serpentine-soil area in an open, parklike forest of Jeffrey and western white pine. The view of the East Fork Illinois, far below, is spectacular.

After 1.8 miles, you come to a side trail that drops steeply downhill to the right, into a grassy basin. For the described hike route, turn right. By continuing straight (along the Polar Bear Trail), you end up in Twin Valley (see "Options").

Technically, the Black Butte Trail (1273) begins at this junction. It's much rougher than the more established Polar Bear Trail. Despite a few steep ups and downs, however, it's surprisingly level, considering the terrain. This is a beautiful area of meadow, forest, creek, and an occasional Port Orford cedar stand.

At mile 3, the Black Butte Trail emerges onto an old, closed-off jeep road. Go right. If you go left, the path ventures into a lovely cirque, then becomes horrendously steep. To the right, the trail contours high above the valley, with a view of a sheer, glacially polished rock face.

At mile 4, you find yourself stepping across a 4-foot-wide trickle of water surrounded by dense brush. This is the headwaters of the Illinois River's East Fork. Look for the upper end of the East Fork Trail (1274), on the right just before the crossing.

At mile 4.5, just beyond a small saddle, you finally reach the closed-off road into Young's Valley. Turn right and follow it 2 miles to the road end at the wilderness boundary. Alternately, you could turn around and return to your car, hike 1 mile to the left for Young's Valley, or explore some of the options below.

Options: *Young's Valley.* For a one-way shuttle hike, here's how to reach the trail's Young's Valley end by car: Continue southwest on US 199, past Cave Junction toward Crescent city. Seven miles into California, turn left up Knopke Creek Road (18N07). Follow it 14.5 miles to the T-junction with Forest Road 18N02, just before Sanger Lake. Turn right onto FR 18N02 and proceed 1.5 miles up the narrow, gravel road to the trailhead at the wilderness boundary. There's room for 10 cars. The Young's Valley Trail follows the old road, over the two orange berms (dirt piles). Another obvious trail at the parking area ends after a couple of hundred feet. It's a 2-mile walk down the Young's Valley Trail to the saddle at the far end of the Black Butte Trail.

The access road and trailhead offer one of the region's more impressive mountain panoramas, with views of El Capitan, Preston Peak, Young's Peak, Broken Rib Mountain, and the glacial cirque which is the source of the Smith River. One and a half miles down the Young's Valley Trail, Young's Valley Meadow comes spectacularly into view at the base of El Capitan.

Twin Valley. From the junction with the Black Butte Trail, it's 1.5 miles, on the Polar Bear Trail through the woods and over a low pass, to Twin Valley. The pass runs between Lookout Mountain and Polar Bear

Mountain. Twin Valley contains a pair of wet, floral meadows with some nice campsites and a views of Polar Bear and Lookout Mountains.

77 East Fork Illinois River

Highlight:	A magnificent, glacier-carved river canyon surrounded by high mountains and lined with old-growth forest. Interesting to observe the recovery from a major forest fire in 1987.
Type of hike:	Day hike or backpack, shuttle.
Total distance:	9.5 miles.
Difficulty:	Easy to moderate (south to north) moderate to strenuous (north to south).
Elevation loss:	2,800 feet.
Best months:	May–November.
Map:	USGS Polar Bear Mountain quad.

Special considerations:

1. The lower/northern (Hogue Pasture) trailhead is located just past Takilma Village. There are no services. Takilma gained a reputation in the late 1960s as a counterculture haven. It remains largely unchanged except that the population has aged a little. Many small, odd-looking houses line the East Fork of the Illinois River around Takilma. Residents are reasonably friendly as long as you don't "gawk."

2. The Hogue Pasture Trailhead is located near a favorite sunbathing spot on the river. Residents frequently remove trailhead markers so the trailhead may be difficult to find. Parking a car there overnight may be slightly risky because of heavy pedestrian traffic.

3. An alternate lower trailhead accessing the Osgood Ditch Trail, which joins the East Fork Trail after 1.5 miles, is described under Options.

4. This chapter's described hike starts at the East Fork Illinois Trail's upper (southern) terminus, in the Siskiyou Wilderness, at the junction with the Black Butte Trail, which is described in Hike 76. See Hike 76 for directions to the Polar Bear–Black Butte Trailhead and the optional Young's Valley Trailhead.

5. The East Fork Trail probably has more excellent, drinkable water than any other path in this book. Because of horse traffic, water should be purified.

6. The Hogue Pasture Trailhead, and the trail's final 0.2 mile, is in Oregon. Everything else is in in California.

Finding the trailhead: Upper/southern (Siskiyou Wilderness): The described hike begins at mile 4 on the Polar Bear–Black Butte Trail (Hike

East Fork Illinois River

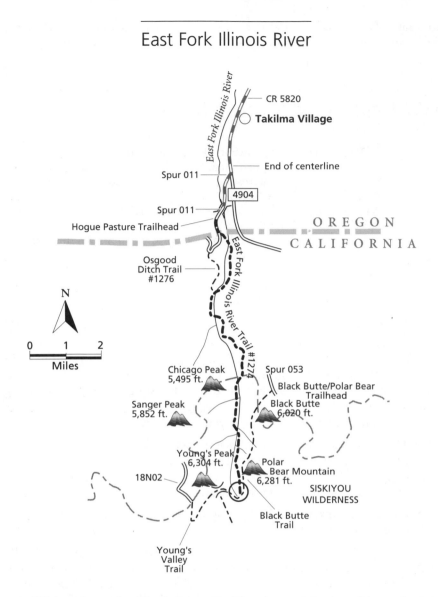

East Fork Illinois River

CR 5820

Takilma Village

Spur 011

End of centerline

4904

Spur 011

Hogue Pasture Trailhead

O R E G O N

C A L I F O R N I A

Osgood
Ditch Trail
#1276

East Fork Illinois River Trail #1274

N

0   1   2
Miles

Chicago Peak
5,495 ft.

Spur 053

Black Butte/Polar Bear
Trailhead
Black Butte
6,020 ft.

Sanger Peak
5,852 ft.

Young's Peak
6,304 ft.

Polar
Bear Mountain
6,281 ft.

18N02

SISKIYOU
WILDERNESS

Black Butte
Trail

Young's
Valley
Trail

76). Hiking from the Black Butte Trailhead, go right (north), at the junction with the East Fork Illinois Trail. If you start at the optional Young's Valley Trailhead, you can reach the beginning of the described hike in 2 miles instead of 4. But that involves a long, complicated drive over gravel roads entirely in California (see Hike 76, "Options").

Lower/northern (Hogue Pasture): Take U.S. Highway 199 to Cave Junction and turn up Caves Highway (Oregon Highway 46). Turn right onto Holland Loop after 2 miles and right again on Bridgeview-Takilma Road (County Road 5820) after 2 more miles. Take Takilma Road for 7 miles, through Takilma Village. Bear right on Spur 011 (where the centerline ends). Proceed 0.5 mile to the bridge over the East Fork, where the blacktop ends. Turn left and go 0.3 mile to a boulder-lined turnout and parking area on the left (which may or may not be marked as a trailhead). The trail is the old, narrow, dirt road.

Parking and trailhead facilities: The Hogue Pasture Trailhead has room for 10 or 12 cars. There's a beautiful swimming hole 0.2 mile before the trailhead, towards the bridge.

Key points (south to north):
    0.0 Beginning of East Fork Trail on Black Butte Trail.
    2.0 First river crossing.
    3.5 Second river crossing, begin uphill segment.
    6.0 Rejoin river, third river crossing, wilderness boundary.
    7.0 Osgood Ditch junction.
    7.2 Fourth river crossing.
    8.5 Fifth river crossing.
    9.3 State line.
    9.5 Lower (Hogue Pasture) trailhead.

The hike: The bad news is that for the most part, the beautiful high peaks surrounding the upper end of the Illinois River's East Fork can't be seen from the trail paralleling the river, except for a glimpse now and then. You cannot see that the path's initial 2 miles follow the bottom of a spectacular glacial valley. You can't see the hanging side valleys, colorful alpine meadows, or snow-covered, black-rock summits.

But don't worry. The reason you can't see all this is because the massive old-growth trees get in the way. Alas, hikers are forced (for the most part) to settle for peaceful, shady, close-up views of the river and its numerous cascading side creeks.

If you arrived at the upper trailhead via the Polar Bear–Black Butte Trail, you have already seen the glacially carved walls of the upper valley, the surrounding rocky peaks and all that good stuff. You can see most of it driving to the Black Butte/Polar Bear Trailhead.

Where the East Fork Illinois Trail (1274) begins, at the junction with the Black Butte Trail (1273), 4 miles from the Black Butte Trailhead, the river is about 4 feet wide and 6 inches deep. From there, the path quickly enters the deep woods, in a beautiful Port Orford cedar grove, as it plunges downward for 2 miles to the first of five river crossings.

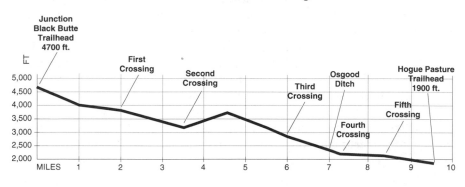

East Fork Illinois Trail, fourth crossing.

Each river crossing, not surprisingly, is wider and deeper than the last. All involve wet feet. However, even at the last crossing, 8.5 miles down, the river is only about 2 feet deep and 30 feet across. None of the crossings should pose a problem, unless you hike during the spring runoff in April or May, in which case you're unlikely to make it to the Black Butte Trailhead because of snow.

The 1.5 miles between the first and second river crossings (miles 2 to 3.5), are the route's most idyllic. The path levels off a little, the trees are the biggest, and you're still inside the wilderness.

At mile 3.5, you cross the river a second time, leave the wilderness, then leave the river and climb far up the mountainside, ascending 500 feet in 1 mile as the Illinois, far below, makes it's way through a narrow, rocky gorge.

At mile 6, after a descent just as steep as the ascent, the path rejoins, then crosses the river. The white fir, white pine, and Brewer spruce of the upper trail have been replaced by lower elevation Douglas-fir, sugar pine, ponderosa pine, and madrone. Port Orford cedar and incense cedar are found at all elevations.

Very much in evidence throughout the hike is the Longwood Gulch Fire of 1987 which destroyed 50,000 acres of forest. Note the mosaic pattern of the burn, with some areas devastated and other areas completely bypassed. Along most of the trail, except for the devastated areas around Hogue Pasture near the lower trailhead, you will see only an occasional charred tree. In such areas, the burn was fairly "cold," taking out hardwood and underbrush and charring tree trunks but killing only a few conifers. The path's final mile is riddled with logging roads and thousands of acres of burned trees. Some of the roads access salvage timber sales from the 1987 fire.

At mile 7.0, after running a couple of hundred feet uphill from the river, the path crosses Trail 1276, the Osgood Ditch Trail. (See "Options" for a description of this route, which returns you to Spur 011 a mile sooner than the main trail and eliminates two river crossings.)

The sign at the Osgood Ditch junction says it's 6.5 miles to the Young's Valley Trail, 3.5 miles to the Hogue Pasture Trailhead, and 2 miles to the Osgood Ditch Trailhead. However, distances given here are different: 7.5 miles to the Young's Valley Trail, 2.5 miles to the Hogue Pasture Trailhead, and 1.5 miles to the Osgood Ditch Trailhead.

Beyond the Osgood Ditch junction, the trail shoots steeply down to the river, where it makes its fourth crossing (mile 7.2). For the next 1.3 miles, to the fifth crossing, the terrain gradually widens out and levels off as the river emerges from the canyon into an area of low, mostly burned-over hills. With the more intense burn comes much brush, in addition to the usual dense riparian brush. Look for tanoak, bigleaf maple, red alder, deerbrush ceanothus, varnishleaf ceanothus, oceanspray, green manzanita, willow, Douglas maple, thimbleberry, red huckleberry, evergreen huckleberry, and lots of poison oak (especially away from the river).

The final mile, from the fifth river crossing (mile 8.5) to the Hogue Pasture Trailhead, can be confusing because the route follows a network of dirt roads, some of which are still opened to vehicles. Stick to the river and you can't go wrong. The unmarked state line is crossed at mile 9.3. At mile 9.5, you're done.

Options: *Starting at the Lower Trailhead.* The East Fork Illinois Trail can be hiked north to south, starting at Hogue Pasture, but it's almost entirely uphill with a 2,800-foot elevation gain. In summer, the Hogue Pasture area gets very hot. Also, the first mile from the Hogue Pasture Trailhead can be confusing because the path follows a maze of roads. It's much easier in the other direction.

A better bet for those wishing to explore the East Fork Trail's lower end, is to begin at the Osgood Ditch Trailhead and follow the Osgood Ditch Trail to the East Fork Trail. You can then either turn left and exit via Hogue Pasture or turn right and head south towards the Siskiyou Wilderness.

Osgood Ditch Trailhead. The Osgood Ditch Trailhead is located on Spur 011, 1.6 miles past the Hogue Pasture Trailhead. It's on the left, where the road makes a sharp switchback north. There's parking for one car at the trailhead (the spot is quite steep so set your emergency brake and block your tires). An additional two cars can park on the shoulder 100 feet up the road.

The 1.5-mile Osgood Ditch trail meets the East Fork Trail 2.5 miles from the Hogue Pasture Trailhead (the sign says 3.5 miles). In addition to cutting a mile off the East Fork hike, the Osgood path starts 300 feet higher and avoids the aforementioned road maze. Additionally, the trailhead is located in a much less trafficked spot. A nice downhill loop is possible by starting at Osgood Ditch and coming out at Hogue Pasture. You can then either walk or hitchhike back to the Osgood Ditch Trailhead.

The Osgood Ditch Trail follows an old canal used at the turn of the century to channel water from the East Fork to various gold mines. Because the ditch tends to trap water, vegetation is lush despite the surrounding forest-fire destruction. The path offers excellent views of the valley from far up the hillside. The crossing of Bybee Creek, near the trailhead, is lovely.

Turn left at the junction with the East Fork Illinois Trail to return to the Hogue Pasture Trailhead. It's a steep, 0.2 mile from the junction to a pretty river crossing.

---

78 Rogue River Trail (Grave Creek to Marial)

Highlight:	With Hike 79, this is the best hike in the Oregon Siskiyous. The path follows a world-famous whitewater gorge as it cuts through the Siskiyou Mountains and Coastal Range to the Pacific.
Type of hike:	Backpack, shuttle.
Total distance:	23.2 miles.
Difficulty:	Easy.
Elevation loss:	Minimal.
Best months:	Any.
Map:	USGS Mount Reuben quad.

Special considerations: The trail is usually snow-free all year. In winter, it is cold and rainy, side creeks are high, and campsites may be soggy. In midsummer, the canyon can be hot and humid in the afternoon. Neither of these conditions are deal-killers, however, and this is always a fantastic hike. Water abounds.

The description here is cursory and for trip planning only. The BLM puts out a detailed, 36-page pamphlet on the Rogue River Trail that is indispensable. Supplemental maps are also essential.

Finding the trailhead: Grave Creek Trailhead: Take the Interstate 5 Merlin exit, 3 miles north of Grants Pass, and follow Merlin-Galice Road for 23 miles past Galice to the Grave Creek Bridge. The trail begins at the far end of the boat launch area. Overnight hikers should park on the road, above the landing area.

Marial Trailhead: See Hike 79.

Parking and trailhead facilities: There are porta-potties and parking for 25 cars at the Grave Creek boat launch.

Rogue River Trail (Grave Creek to Marial)

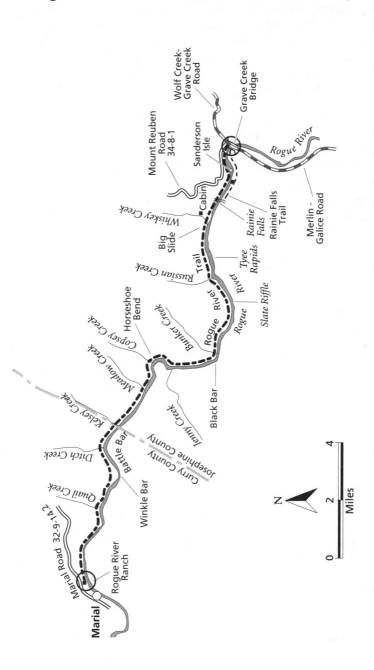

Key points (including all campsites):
0.0 Grave Creek Trailhead.
0.6 Sanderson homesite.
1.8 Rainie Falls (camp).
2.1 Cabin.
3.1 Whiskey Creek.
3.7 Big Slide (camp).
4.8 Tyee Rapids (camp).
5.8 Russian Creek (camp).
6.6 Slate Creek (camp).
9.1 Bunker Creek (camp).
9.6 Black Bar Lodge.
10.9 Jenny Creek (camp).
11.1 Horseshoe Bend.
12.3 Copsey Creek (camp).
13.6 Meadow Creek (camp).
15.4 Kelsey Creek (Camp).
16.6 Battle Bar.
16.6 Ditch Creek (camp).
17.5 Winkle Bar.
19.4 Quail Creek (camp).
23.0 Rogue River Ranch/Museum.
23.2 Marial Road.

The hike: One of this country's most famous river gorges may be seen from this trail. The route passes Rainie Falls, one of the Rogue River's scenic highlights and the only spot on the Wild and Scenic section of the lower Rogue which forces rafters and boaters out of the water.

There's a chance you'll come away from your hike smitten by the whitewater bug. Should that occur, check at the Rand Recreation Site to find out about permit requirements and when and where it's OK to go on the river. Or stop by any of the numerous raft rental and car shuttle services in Merlin or Galice.

The boat ramp at the foot of the Grave Creek Bridge, where the trail begins, is the river's most used. It is cramped for space and the short road down is very steep. In summer, it can be mobbed, necessitating parking on the road and walking down. The 2-mile Rainie Falls Trail begins on the

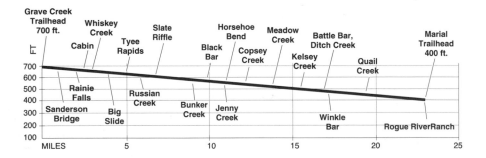

other side of the bridge, offering a better view of the falls than the Rogue River Trail but dead-ending there (see "Options").

The main trail (1160) begins at the boat launch area. It is well marked, mostly level, and usually cool and shaded. Kids love it. It's 1.8 miles to Rainie Falls and 3.1 to the Whiskey Creek footbridge.

Rainie Falls are more like rapids but are impressive, nevertheless. There's a developed campground with pit toilets there. To view the falls, hike down through the campground and climb out on the rocks. Boaters feed their crafts ropes through a narrow side channel bypassing the rapids.

Continue 1.3 miles beyond Rainie Falls and up a 0.1-mile side trail immediately beyond the Whiskey Creek footbridge, and you come to Whiskey Creek Cabin. Occupied from 1880 to 1977, it's now a registered national landmark and museum maintained by the BLM. They say fishing in Whiskey Creek is excellent.

Rainie Falls and Whiskey Creek make excellent out-and-back day hike destinations. For the perfect day hike, continue for 0.6 mile beyond Whiskey Creek, to Big Slide, a lovely, parklike basin on a shaded bluff above the river. The name comes from a huge, 100-year-old slide, barely visible through the trees. Big Slide supposedly marks the boundary between the Siskiyou Mountains geological province and the Coast Range geological province. Look for the crumbly metavolcanic greenstone rock to gradually give way to sandstone. The boundary is not distinct and Siskiyou rock formations turn up several times farther down the trail.

Beyond Big Slide, there are lots of things to see: old gold mines, delightful little side creeks, beautiful campsites. The next major landmark is

Rainie Falls, Rogue River Trail.

Black Bar Lodge, at mile 9.6. If you're not up to sleeping on the ground, they'll rent you a room if you call ahead. The lodge was built in 1932 and is open from mid-April to mid-November.

At Horseshoe Bend, mile 11.1, the river makes a huge curve. The curve must have reminded some creative individual of a horseshoe.

At mile 16.6, you come to Battle Bar, visible on the south side of the river (the trail is on the north side). Battle Bar is the site of skirmishes between the U.S. Army and the Takelma Indians in 1855 and 1856. The cabin at Battle Bar was built in 1947. The owner, Bob Fox, was shot and killed before he could finish it. For hikers, camping at Battle Bar is on the north side of the river, at Ditch Creek.

Winkle Bar, at mile 17.5, is interesting because it was once a mining claim owned by writer Zane Gray. His cabin is still there on the private inholding.

At mile 23, you approach the community of Marial via Rogue River Ranch, which boasts, among other things, a small museum run by the BLM. The oldest known human habitation site in Oregon is an archaeological dig located near Rogue River Ranch. At the ranch's far end, the trail emerges onto Marial Road.

Options: *Rainie Falls Trail.* The Rainie Falls Trail begins on the other side of the Grave Creek Bridge, opposite the Grave Creek boat launch. It's a beautiful, easy, 2-mile walk to the falls, with much closer views of the river and falls than Rogue River Trail offers. The Rainie Falls Trail dead-ends at the falls.

Rogue River Trail west from Marial. On the Marial Road at the Rogue River Ranch, go right, uphill for 0.2 mile to Tucker Flat Campground. Or go left for Marial Lodge, the Mule Creek Guard Station, and the second half of the trail (Hike 79). It's 2 miles along the Marial Road from the Rogue River Ranch to the westbound trailhead.

Wild Rogue Wilderness

A few miles west of Grants Pass, the Rogue River enters a fantastic canyon of ancient rock walls and whitewater rapids as it knifes through the Siskiyou Mountains and Coast Ranges. A 40-mile trail follows the river from Grave Creek, where the road west from Grants Pass ends, to Agness, where the road east from the coastal town of Gold Beach ends. This is a fantastic trek, interrupted only by a dead-end road at Marial, at mile 25.

For the final 15 miles from Agness, the trail passes through the Wild Rogue Wilderness, a 15,000-acre chunk of scenic splendor that runs from the crest of the mountains north of the canyon, down to and across the river, and back up to the south-side crest. Many beautiful pathways visit the peaks as well as the canyon. Highlights are Stair Creek Falls, the tricky Blossom Bar rapid, and Hanging Rock.

Even though this is wilderness, lodges along the Rogue River Trail will serve up a hot meal and rent you a real room for the night. The jet boats from Gold Beach go as far as Paradise Bar Lodge, 12 miles into the wilderness from the western end.

79 Rogue River Trail (Marial to Agness)

Highlight:	With Hike 78, this is the best hike in the Oregon Siskiyous. The path follows a spectacular rock gorge and world-famous whitewater canyon. Marial may be Oregon's most remote community and Blossom Bar is the Rogue's most challenging rapid.
Type of hike:	Backpack, shuttle.
Total distance:	14.7 miles.
Difficulty:	Easy.
Elevation loss:	Minimal.
Best months:	Trail is snow-free all year. Marial Road is open May–November.
Map:	USGS Marial quad.

Special considerations: The trail is usually snow-free all year although Marial Road is not. In winter, the canyon is cold and rainy, side creeks are high, and campsites may be soggy. In mid-summer, the canyon can get hot and humid in the afternoon. Neither of these are deal-killers, however, and this is always a fantastic hike. Water abounds.

The description here is cursory and for trip planning only. The BLM puts out a detailed, 36-page pamphlet on the Rogue River Trail that is indispensable. Supplemental maps are also essential.

Rogue River Trail (Marial to Agness)

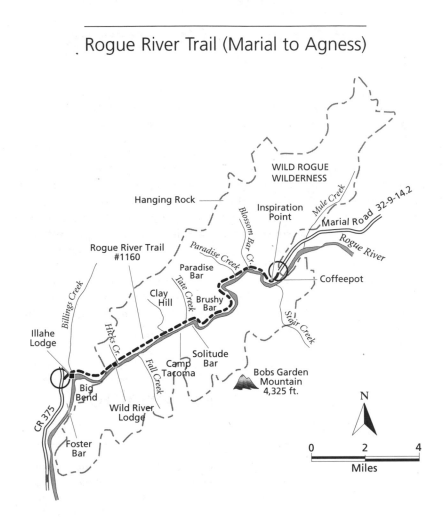

Finding the trailhead: From Grants Pass, leave Interstate 5 at Merlin and proceed 23 miles on Merlin-Galice Road past Galice to the Grave Creek Bridge and boat landing. Turn left just over the bridge and head up the mountain on 34-8-1 (gravel) for 15 miles. The road is very narrow and winding for the 3 miles between Whiskey Creek Road and Sawmill Gap. At mile 15.1, the road merges with the upper end of Whisky Creek Road and becomes 32-7-19.3. At mile 15.6, you pick up 32-8-31, a one-lane blacktop road from Glendale. Turn left, toward Powers, and go another 5 miles to the Marial Road (32-9-14.2). The gravel Marial Road is 15 miles long, very steep, very winding, and very pretty. Proceed past Tucker Flat Campground and Rogue River Ranch, through Marial, to the small trailhead parking area at the road end, 2 miles past Rogue River Ranch. The last mile is a little rough.

Parking and trailhead facilities: There is parking for six cars at the Marial Trailhead.

Key points:

0.0 Marial Trailhead.
0.5 The Coffeepot.
0.7 Inspiration Point.
2.1 Blossom Bar (camp).
2.9 Paradise Creek (camp).
3.3 Paradise Bar Lodge.
3.8 Lower Paradise Bar Camp.
6.2 Brushy Bar (camp).
6.7 Solitude Bar (camp).
7.9 Tate Creek (camp).
8.0 Camp Tacoma.
8.2 Clay Hill Lodge and Rapids.
9.5 Fall Creek.
9.8 Flora Dell Creek (camp).
10.8 Hicks Creek (camp).
11.1 Wild River Lodge.
14.0 Big Bend, Billings Creek, Illahe Lodge.
14.7 Foster Bar Trailhead.
15.0 Foster Bar (camp).

The hike: This long, level, extremely remote stretch of trail along the Rogue River is one of Oregon's ultimate hikes. The Marial-Mule Creek-Blossom Bar area is the 40-mile Rogue River Trail's most scenic segment.

People come from all over the world to run the Lower Rogue and it tends to be the domain of drift-boat and raft people. Many also hike in from Grave Creek. Few arrive at Marial by car but don't worry about that. Enjoy the scenery and cheer the rafters on as they attempt some of the Rogue's most difficult rapids.

The single-lane dirt road into Marial is steep, very sinuous, and seemingly endless. But the far wall of Mule Creek Canyon will finally appear, followed by Tucker Flat Campground and the turnoff to the Rogue River Ranch and the BLM museum there, with its neatly tended grounds.

The museum sits on the canyon's only level spot. Do visit as the area boasts much history—of pioneers, gold miners, and Indians. A nearby archaeological dig has uncovered the oldest remains of human habitation in Oregon.

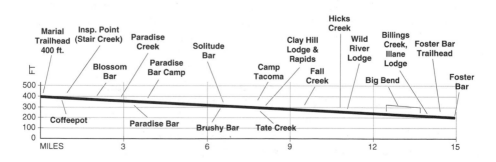

After a short walk through the woods from the trailhead, past the Wild Rogue Wilderness Area boundary, the trail (1160) comes out on a ledge above the river. For the next 2 miles, the path is gouged into sheer rock up the side of the gray-green canyon.

Soon after the path meets the river, Mule Creek Canyon is entered. The extremely narrow defile, appropriately dubbed the "Narrows," empties into a circular, whirlpool-filled hole known to river runners as the "Coffeepot" (mile 0.5). Look for boats careening from one wall to the other or spinning helplessly. The Coffeepot is fun in a raft but the tendency to crash into the wall is hard on rigid craft.

Beyond the Coffeepot, the river calms as it passes Stair Creek Falls (south bank) and, at mile 0.7, Inspiration Point (north bank, where the trail is). The aptly named falls cascades down the narrow gorge of Stair Creek. Stop at Inspiration Point for views of the double-tiered falls (with a small lake in between), the canyon, and surrounding peaks.

The canyon widens slightly at Blossom Bar (mile 2.1). A small campsite graces the mouth of Blossom Bar Creek. Just below the azalea-lined creek's trail crossing, there's a wonderful pool in which to cool your feet.

Immediately after Blossom Bar Creek, hike over to the rocks along the river for a look at the rapids. Blossom Bar is an area of immense boulders, both on the bank and in the water. Blossom Bar Rapids is the river's most difficult run. It was impassable until Glen Wooldridge, the Rogue's legendary guide, blasted a channel through in the 1920s. Wooldridge is credited as the first person to run the lower Rogue.

Blossom Bar is a favorite spectator spot, so find a good perch above the rapids and enjoy watching the rafters test their skill. Every rock, chute, and formation has a name and bystanders will be happy to explain the best routes and the technical prowess involved.

At mile 3.3, or 1.2 miles past Blossom Bar, Paradise Bar Ranch offers food and rooms. Paradise Bar Ranch makes an excellent out-and-back day hike destination. After visiting the Coffeepot, Inspiration Point, and Blossom Bar, you can have a delicious buffet lunch waiting for you if you phone ahead for reservations.

Beyond Paradise Bar Lodge, at mile 6.2, you come to the large Brushy Bar Campground, which boasts a Forest Service guard station, toilets, and real live running water. How uptown can you get?

Tate Creek, at mile 7.9, is notable for a 25-foot waterfall into a deep pool that makes a magnificent slide and is great fun. The slide is about 200 yards up the creek, to the right. Fall Creek, at mile 9.5 and Flora Dell Creek, mile 9.8, are also decorated with waterfalls but you can't slide down them. Fall Creek is across the river.

Big Bend begins at mile 13.2, where the river begins a wide, 1.5-mile arch. You can't see the beginning of Big Bend from the trail but you catch glimpses of Watson Riffle, which marks the beginning, through the trees. A yellow survey marker on a tree is a better indicator of the spot.

After a series of steep, short switchbacks and a couple of creek crossings, the trail crosses a dirt road and Billings Creek (mile 14) before emerging onto a large cow pasture near Illahe Lodge. The area is rife with history. A battle at Big Bend Pasture in 1856 proved to be the last confrontation between the U.S. Army and the local tribes and sealed their demise. The Billings family was one of the first to settle in the Rogue Canyon, in 1868. They moved to what is now Billings Creek a decade later. Marial was named for Marial Billings. You still run into the Billings family in Josephine County and the Lower Rogue Canyon.

After crossing the pasture, a gate, and two sets of stile steps, the trail ends at mile 14.6 at the Rogue River Trailhead, 0.4 mile via the road from the Foster Bar boat launch and campground. The larger Illahe Campground is located 1 mile west of Foster Bar, on the same road.

Options: *Rogue River Trail east from Marial.* The Rogue River Trail east from Marial to Grave Creek (Hike 78), begins at the Rogue River Ranch, 2 miles up the Marial Road from the westbound trailhead.

Foster Bar. For a one-way shuttle hike west from Marial (highly recommended), here's how to find the Foster Bar Trailhead, the hike's western terminus. At mile 15 on Merlin-Galice Road, just before Galice, turn left onto Forest Road 23, the road to Gold Beach. It's 37 magnificent black-topped miles, over a 5,000-foot pass, to Forest Road 33, the road along the Lower Rogue from Gold Beach, on the coast, to Agness and Powers. Turn right on FR 33 and proceed 2 miles, over the bridge, to the Foster Bar turnoff on the right. It's 3.4 more miles to the Foster Bar spur road and 3.6 miles to the Rogue River Trail spur road, both on the right. The trailhead is located 0.2 mile up the dirt spur road. There is a pit toilet and parking for eight cars at the trailhead.

Rogue River Trail, Blossum Bar Rapid.

80   Mount Bolivar

Highlight:	A short, steep hike to the highest point in the Wild Rogue Wilderness, with a tremendous view down Mule Creek to the Rogue Canyon.
Type of hike:	Day hike, out and back.
Total distance:	2.8 miles.
Difficulty:	Moderate.
Elevation gain:	1,161 feet.
Best months:	May–November.
Map:	USGS Mount Bolivar quad.

Special considerations: No water.

Finding the trailhead: From Grants Pass, leave I-5 at Merlin and proceed 23 miles on Merlin-Galice Road past Galice to the Grave Creek Bridge and boat landing. Turn left just over the bridge and head up the mountain on 34-8-1 (gravel) for 15 miles. The road is very narrow and winding for the 3 miles between Whiskey Creek Road and Sawmill Gap. At mile 15.1, the road merges with the upper end of Whiskey Creek Road and becomes 32-7-19.3. At mile 15.6, pick up 32-8-31, a one-lane blacktop road from Glendale. Turn left, toward Powers, and go 13.8 miles to the Mount Bolivar turnout, on the left. The trailhead is just off the road. Eventually 32-8-31 becomes FR 3348.

Parking and trailhead facilities: There is parking for six cars at the trailhead.

Key points:
  0.0 Mount Bolivar Trailhead.
  1.4 Summit.

The hike: The hike to the top of this highest point in the Wild Rogue Wilderness isn't particularly long but driving to the trailhead takes forever. The trail offers perhaps the best single view of the canyon. Throw in nearby Hanging Rock (Hike 81) and you have a pretty full day.

From the Mount Bolivar Trailhead, the path is quite steep with lots of switchbacks. But it's short, so take your time. It begins in a forest of Douglas-fir and white fir, with lots of rhododendron decorating the understory. The open, rocky areas are overgrown mostly with manzanita and scrub chinkapin.

The summit looks down Mule Creek to Marial and the Rogue River. Directly opposite, across the canyon, Bobs Garden Mountain can be seen with far more clarity than it can from Bear Camp Road, which runs right past it. Look for the rugged Saddle Peaks radiating southwest from Bolivar.

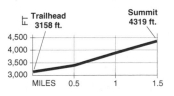

Mount Bolivar

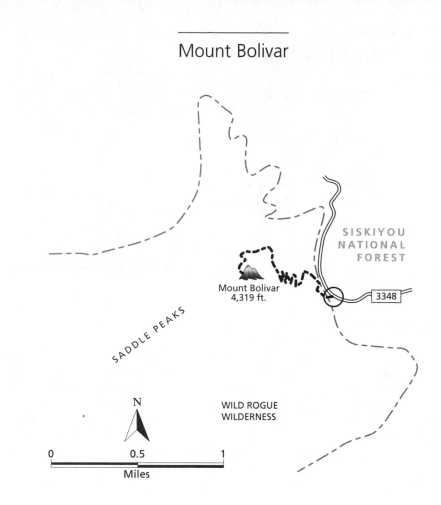

The foundation of an old fire lookout adorns the Bolivar summit. There is also a small monument with a bronze plaque. The plaque was presented to the people of Oregon from the people of Venezuela in 1984 to recognize that the peak was named for Simon Bolivar, the legendary South American general responsible for the independence of many countries, including Venezuela. It's an interesting tribute to self-determination in the middle of a vast and beautiful wilderness.

(Note: The mountain was actually named for a pioneer called Simon Bolivar Cathcart. But why quibble?)

81 Hanging Rock

Highlight: A short hike to a magnificent and terrifying rock outcrop and overlook in the peaks above the Wild Rogue Wilderness.
Type of hike: Day hike, out and back.
Total distance: About 2 miles.
Difficulty: Easy.
Elevation gain: 254 feet.
Best months: April–December.
Map: USGS Mount Bolivar quad.

Special considerations: No water. Very dangerous (overhanging drop-off with a steep slope leading up to it and no handholds or guard rails). The Buck Point Trailhead to Hanging Rock is a shorter drive by 4 miles but the trail is longer and much steeper. See "Options."

Finding the trailhead: From Grants Pass, leave Interstate 5 at Merlin and proceed west 23 miles on Merlin-Galice Road past Galice to the Grave Creek Bridge and boat landing. Turn left just over the bridge and head up the mountain on 34-8-1 (gravel) for 15 miles. The road is very narrow and winding for the 3 miles between Whiskey Creek Road and Sawmill Gap. At mile 15.1, the road merges with the upper end of Whisky Creek Road and becomes 32-7-19.3. At mile 15.6, turn left, toward Powers, on 32-8-31, a one-lane blacktop from Glendale that eventually becomes Forest Road 3348. At Barker Creek, 24.4 miles from where you picked up the blacktop, turn left onto Forest Road 5520 where a sign says, "Panther Ridge Trail— 1 mile." It's 5 miles up FR 5520 (which makes a very hard right at mile 1.5), then 1 mile (right) up Spur 140 to the Hanging Rock Trailhead.

Parking and trailhead facilities: Six cars can park at the pretty little trailhead, which is in a forested grove by a creek.

Key points:
0.0 Hanging Rock Trailhead.
0.2 Panther Ridge Trail junction (go left).
0.8 Hanging Rock Trail junction (go right).
1.0 Hanging Rock.

The hike: A segment of the 12.5-mile Panther Ridge Trail (1253), this short, fairly easy route leads to one of Southern Oregon's least-visited and most impressive landmarks. Hanging Rock is the source of Blossom Bar Creek, a principal destination among lower Rogue rafters.

The 75-mile drive to the trailhead from Grants Pass takes forever. Much of it is unpaved, one-lane, winding (and exceptionally

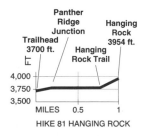

HIKE 81 HANGING ROCK

Hanging Rock

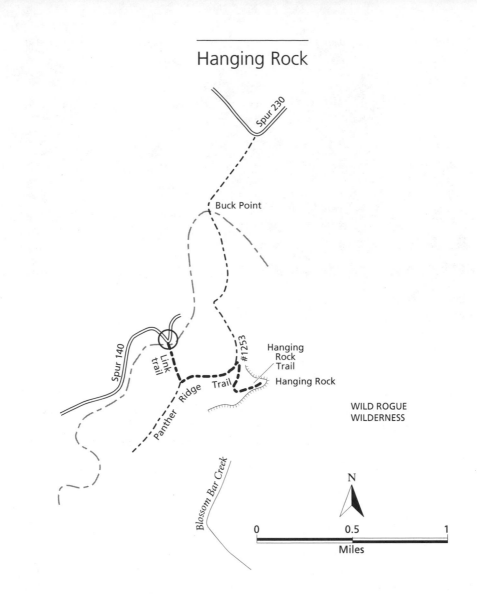

scenic). It takes three hours to reach the closest of the two trailheads that access Hanging Rock.

The two trailheads are the Hanging Rock Trailhead, described here, and the Buck Point trailhead described in Options. Both routes are gorgeous and neither is very long. They wind through verdant, old-growth stands of Douglas-fir and Western hemlock. The jungle understory's main component is rhododendron, along with salal, Sadler oak, and chinkapin. In May and June, the route is resplendent with flowers.

From the Hanging Rock Trailhead, the path winds through the woods, meeting the Panther Ridge Trail after 0.2 mile. It then traverses through more woods and crosses a meadow, a beautiful flat-rock surface, and a creek before reentering the forest and climbing slightly.

Hanging Rock.

After 0.8 mile, you arrive at the Hanging Rock Trail, on the right. If you continue straight, you end up at the Buck Point Trailhead after 1.5 miles.

The Hanging Rock Trail dead-ends at Hanging Rock after 0.2 mile. Hanging Rock is a large rock outcrop with an overhanging, 200-foot plunge. Mount Bolivar and the craggy Saddle Peaks are easily visible to the northeast while Bear Camp Summit and Bobs Garden Mountain rise to the southeast, across the canyon. A small stretch of the Rogue can be seen, probably in the vicinity of Winkle Bar. Mule Mountain blocks the view of Marial and Blossom Bar. The drainage leading from Hanging Rock to the Rogue is Blossom Bar Creek.

Reaching the top of Hanging Rock, 100 feet away from and 30 feet higher than the trail end, requires crossing a 3-foot-wide wasp-waist rock outcrop with sheer drop-offs on either side, then scaling a steep, slick-sided dome. Although reasonably doable, the worst case scenario is just a little too close-at-hand and awful. The short hike to the top of Hanging Rock is not for the faint of heart.

The rim near the trail end, adjacent to the rock, is also an overhanging, 200-foot cliff. It is safer than the summit because the edge is squared-off rather than rounded.

Hanging Rock amply lives up to its billing as a scenic wonder. Be exceedingly careful, however. Safety ropes might not be a bad idea on the summit or if you have small children along. Better yet, leave your small children at home.

Options: *Buck Point Trail.* Via the Buck Point Trailhead, the trek to Hanging Rock is 1.5 miles long with an elevation rise of 1,200 feet. That is quite steep. As it turns out, Buck Point itself is nothing more than a high spot on a densely wooded trail. The route boasts no glorious mountaintops or panoramas. So unless your agenda includes a stiff workout, use the Hanging Rock Trailhead. While the drive to the latter is 4.5 miles longer, the path from the Hanging Rock Trailhead is shorter and rises only 300 feet.

To reach the Buck Point Trailhead, go 1.5 miles up FR 5520. Where the road swings sharply right and crosses the creek, bear left on Spur 230 for 0.3 miles to the trailhead. Take the Panther Ridge Trail right, not left. The Hanging Rock Trail appears on the left after 1.3 miles.

Panther Ridge Trail. The 12.5-mile Panther Ridge Trail begins at Bald Knob, 7 miles west of Hanging Rock, and follows the ridge above the Rogue Canyon, at the north edge of the Wilderness. The 2.3-mile segment around Hanging Rock is the best part. East of the Buck Point Trailhead, the Panther Ridge Trail winds through the woods for 4 miles but doesn't really go anywhere.

Kalmiopsis Wilderness

Covering 210,000 acres between Grants Pass and the coast, the Kalmiopsis is a land of jagged orange peaks, a few magnificent lakes, mighty river canyons, and some of the rarest plants in North America. All of this is occasionally in view of the ocean. One reason for the profusion of rare species is the vast acreage of serpentinite rock and soils. Serpentinite is an ultrabasic igneous rock dredged up from the ocean subfloor by the advancing continent (so they say). The standard Pacific Northwest trees will not grow on serpentinite while many strange and stunted species seem to love the stuff. One of the rarest of the serpentinite species is the kalmiopsis flower, a dwarf, cloning member of the heath family (rhododendron, azalea, manzanita, madrone, huckleberry), which grows in a low mat on exposed mountainsides. In the entire world there are maybe 15 such mats. Finding them in bloom is unforgettable.

The canyon of the Illinois River, a Rogue tributary, is even more spectacular, if possible, than that of the Lower Rogue. The Illinois begins near the California line and skirts the edge of the immense Kalmiopsis Wilderness before joining the Rogue near Agness. A 22-mile trail follows the lower Illinois for 6 miles, climbs a mountain, then drops back down to the river for the last 10 miles. This is wild, wild country. By ascending the mountain, the trail makes a wide bypass around the notorious Green Wall Rapid, which made national news a few years ago when some rafters drowned attempting to run it during a December flood.

82 Vulcan Lake

Highlight:	A beautiful little alpine lake in the Kalmiopsis Wilderness within view of the ocean. Botanical interest.
Type of hike:	Day hike, out and back.
Total distance:	About 3 miles.
Difficulty:	Moderate.
Elevation gain:	600 feet.
Best months:	May–November.
Map:	USGS Chetco Peak quad.

Finding the trailhead: Take the Chetco River Road (County Road 784 and Forest Road 1736), out of Brookings for 15 miles. Turn right onto Forest Road 1909, which takes off up the mountain past Polliwog Butte and Red Mountain Prairie. It's 12 miles from FR 1909 to the trailhead.

Vulcan Lake

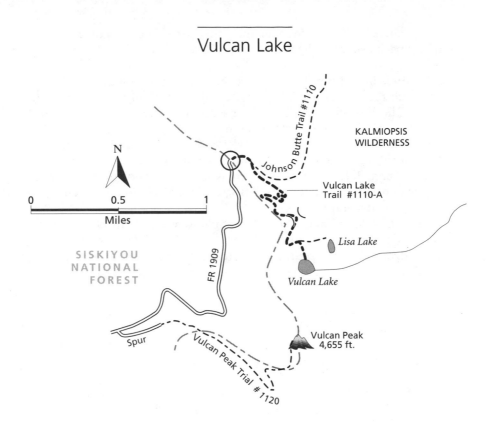

Parking and trailhead facilities: The trailhead, at the road end, has room for eight cars.

Key points:
    0.0 Vulcan Lake/Johnson Butte Trailhead.
    0.2 Valen Lake junction (go right).
    1.0 Summit.
    1.5 Vulcan Lake.

The hike: Talk about contrasts. The tan, weathered, buff-orange bedrock in which beautiful Vulcan Lake nestles, with Vulcan Peak rising abruptly overhead, contains such a high percentage of ser-pentinite rock that the area is a virtual

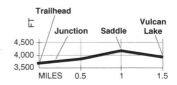

desert. The few trees and shrubs are stunted and bizarre. And yet, from the trail summit above the lake, one can see the Pacific Ocean and the lush vegetation of the coastal mountains.

Of the many alpine glacial lakes in southern Oregon and northern California, this is the only one reached from the coast. The drive up from Brookings, through vast Douglas-fir forests broken by grassy openings called "prairies," affords views of the ocean, the Chetco Valley, and surrounding peaks such as the Big Craggies. Even if you skip the trail, it's a beautiful drive.

The path is only 1.5 miles long. It begins life as the Johnson Butte Trail (1110), with the Vulcan Lake Trail (1110-A), veering off to the right after 0.2 mile. The Vulcan Lake Trail climbs up and over a rocky ridge from which you can see clear across the Kalmiopsis Wilderness to Pearsoll Peak. There are steep spots but the walk isn't difficult. The trail then descends sharply to the lake. Look for serpentinite-adapted plants such as Sadler oak, manzanita, Jeffrey pine, western white pine, and azalea. This is a great place for amateur botanists: bring a plant guide to help identify the many rare shrubs and flowers.

Fishing in Vulcan Lake's brilliant, emerald waters can be frustrating, although it's home to a few cutthroat trout. The lake sits on a rocky, orange ledge with a steep drop-off to the east and the orange summit of Vulcan Peak rising immediately overhead. One-acre Lisa Lake (unstocked) is 0.2 mile away via trail, down the hill.

Options: *Vulcan Peak Trail.* The Vulcan Peak Trail (1120) is a steep, 1-mile trek over brush and rock, to an old lookout site (elevation 4,655 feet) offering a panorama of the Kalmiopsis and the coast. The trailhead is located on a short spur off Spur 260 (go right), 1 mile before the Vulcan/Johnson Butte Trail.

The Chetco Divide Trail (1210) takes off from the same trailhead as the Vulcan Peak Trail. One and a half miles down the Chetco Divide Trail, side trails (1105 and 1105-A), lead to the Navy Monument and Cottonwood Camp. The Navy Monument Trail, actually an old cat track, drops 2,200 feet in 2.5 miles. It ends near the South Fork of the Chetco at the wreckage of a World War II Navy transport plane that crashed in 1944. The monument stands nearby.

Johnson Butte Trail. This very long route begins at the Vulcan Lake Trailhead, breaks off on its own after 0.2 mile, then winds along a forested mountain crest for 10 miles before tying in with the Tincup Trail near Mislatnah Peak (Hike 83). It's 5 miles to minuscule Valen Lake, the only landmark for the entire 10 miles.

83 Mislatnah Peak

Highlight:	An enchanted hike down to and up from the Chetco River to a wilderness mountain summit. The only entry into the beautiful Big Craggies Botanical Area.
Type of hike:	Day hike, out and back.
Total distance:	About 9 miles.
Difficulty:	Moderate.
Elevation loss and gain:	600-foot loss, then 2,524-foot gain.
Best months:	April–December.
Map:	USGS Big Craggies quad.

Special considerations: Hiking in the Big Craggies Botanical Area is permitted but there are no trails except for the short Mistlatnah Peak way-trail.

Finding the trailhead: Drive up the north bank of the Chetco from Brookings (County Road 784, becoming Forest Road 1376). Follow it 24 miles to a side road just beyond High Prairie (Spur 360). At the bottom of Spur 360 (1.5 miles), bear right at the "Tincup Trail" sign.

Parking and trailhead facilities: The trailhead is a huge logging landing with parking for 50 cars.

Key points:
    0.0 Tincup Trailhead.
    0.8 Mislatnah Creek crossing.
    1.0 Mislatnah Trail junction (go left).
    2.0 Mislatnah Prairie.
    3.8 Jack's Camp.
    4.5 Summit.

The hike: Some places do not lend themselves to trails. A path up the side of the Empire State Building, for example, would be impractical. The same is true of the 3,000-acre Big Craggies Botanical Area, on the northwest edge of the Kalmiopsis Wilderness. These formidable outcrops, resembling stoneware platters stacked on end, comprise the visual focus of the entire region. Big Craggie, 4,600 feet high, soars 4,000 feet above the Chetco River.

Several extremely rare plants grow in the scattered patches of thin soil between the cliffs of the Big Craggies. Its peridotite rock is similar to serpentinite and supports similar flora. The Big Craggies Botanical Area was created to protect those plants and the lack of trails has the same objective. The most sensitive plants include Brewer spruce, kalmiopsis, Cascade sedge, Siskiyou fritillaria, and Howell's manzanita.

The Mislatnah Trail (pronounced "mis-LAY-tna"), offers the closest views of the Big Craggies and is the only route to penetrate even a corner of the Botanical Area.

Mislatnah Peak

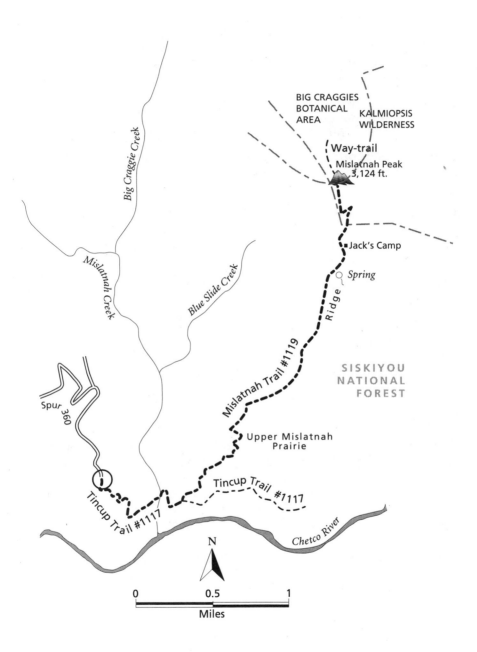

BIG CRAGGIES
BOTANICAL
AREA

KALMIOPSIS
WILDERNESS

Big Craggie Creek

Way-trail

Mislatnah Peak
3,124 ft.

Jack's Camp

Spring

Mislatnah Creek

Blue Slide Creek

Ridge

Mislatnah Trail #1119

SISKIYOU
NATIONAL
FOREST

Spur 360

Upper Mislatnah
Prairie

Tincup Trail #1117

Tincup Trail #1117

Chetco River

N

0   0.5   1
Miles

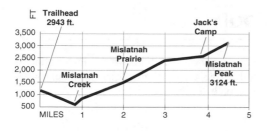

From the trailhead, the path winds sharply downhill, through a dense Douglas-fir forest, to Mislatnah Creek, where it crosses a railed, split-log bridge at mile 0.8. To follow the creek out to the Chetco (downstream 0.2 mile), it's necessary to ford it a couple times.

The Tincup Trail (1117) peels off to the right 0.2 mile from the crossing (see "Options"), while the Mislatnah Trail (1119) heads left and begins a steep climb through the woods. The next mile is the hardest, with few views except at Mislatnah Prairie (at mile 2), a grassy opening high above Mislatnah Creek.

Eventually, the path hits the ridge and levels for 2 miles. The first mile of this segment runs just west of the ridge crest while the second mile, to Jack's Camp and the wilderness boundary, follows the crest itself. Much of the route runs beneath a closed-canopy tanoak forest with occasional glimpses of the outer Craggies.

Just past Jack's Camp, a small fire ring beside an azalea-lined creek, the trail breaks out of the woods and makes its final 0.7-mile ascent up the rocky, manzanita-covered summit knob. Views finally start to get pretty good, especially the one across the Chetco to Tincup Peak.

The path ends at an old lookout site, which is as close as it's possible to get to the Big Craggies. Look for a faint, 0.2-mile way-trail (unmaintained and unofficial) downhill into the Botanical Area. The way-trail is an interesting little hike, although it doesn't pass any Kalmiopsis or Brewer spruce.

Immediately north of the summit, two unnamed peaks of the Big Craggies rise to 3,600 and 4,100 feet. To the northwest, the 3,800-foot mountain is Green Craggie while the steep, barren, 4,600-foot outcropping to the northeast is Big Craggie itself.

Options: *Big Craggies.* If you wish to explore the Big Craggies close-up, you have to do it without benefit of trail. Navigation is supposedly fairly easy because of the many prominent peaks and grassy or rocky surfaces. It's 2 miles to the top of Big Craggie, supposedly a fabulous hike for the adventurous.

Tincup Trail. The Tincup Trail winds for 6 miles along Tincup Creek. Fishing is supposedly terrific and the area is very remote.

84   Game Lake Loop

Highlight:	A loop trail with views high above the lower Illinois canyon and across to the Big Craggies and surrounding peaks, plus a pretty little lake.
Type of hike:	Day hike, loop.
Total distance:	About 7 miles.
Difficulty:	Moderate to strenuous.
Elevation loss and gain:	1,100 loss, 1,100 gain.
Best months:	April–December
Map:	USGS Horse Sign Butte quad.

Special considerations: The best route is clockwise, beginning at the Game Lake Trailhead, 0.5 mile before Game Lake. One of the trail junctions is hard to find in the other direction. Lots of water.

Finding the trailhead: Take County Road 595, the South Bank Road out of Gold Beach which becomes Forest Road 33 and follows the Rogue River to Agness. Continue for 12 miles, then turn right onto Forest Road 3313, the Quosatana Butte Road. After 7 miles, turn left on Forest Road 3680 and follow it 14 miles to the end. Where Forest Road 3318 comes in after 3 miles, you have to turn right to stay on FR 3680. Bear right at all ambiguous looking junctions. It's a long, immensely scenic drive.

Parking and trailhead facilities: There is parking for 6 cars at the Game Lake Trailhead, 0.5 mile before Game Lake. There is parking for 15 cars at the Game Lake Campground.

Key points:
0.0 Game Lake Trailhead.
2.5 Horse Sign Tie-in Trail junction (go right).
3.8 Horse Sign Creek.
4.6 End of Tie-in Trail, Horse Sign Butte (go right).
5.3 Saddle, Pupps Camp Trail (go left, then right).
7.0 Game Lake.

The hike: High in the Oregon coastal mountains, on the ridges between the Rogue and Illinois Rivers, lies some of southern Oregon's most unusual country. Two important trails originate in the heart of the region at Game Lake, and both career down to the Illinois in some of the steepest

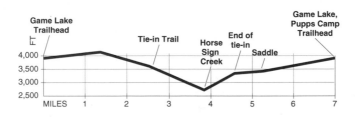

Game Lake Loop

descents in this book. Both trails involve either fording the Illinois or attempting a long and arduous hike back up.

The Forest Service has constructed a connecting link between these paths so there is now a beautiful loop through the rocky crests of the Game Lake country.

From the Illinois River looking up, all you see are looming slopes textured by dense, old-growth Douglas-fir. It's very formidable. Unseen above are rocky summits, sheer cliffs, grassy prairies, and sparsely forested serpentinite ridges. From the top looking down, the views are fantastic. The drive to Game Lake offers close-ups of not only Collier Butte and the Big Craggies but virtually every peak within 100 miles. See Hike 83 for more on the Big Craggies.

Game Lake is a pleasant, 3-acre, nonglacial pool in a wooded flat. It's quite popular so expect lots of summer traffic. The last 0.5 mile of the access road is rather rough and the shore is brushy. There are camp-grounds at the lake, Fairview Meadow, Wildhorse Prairie, and Quosatana Creek.

From the Game Lake trailhead, 0.5 miles before Game Lake, the path climbs a short distance, then plunges dramatically, following an old, rocky, washed-out roadbed. It's 2.5 miles to the Tie-in Trail, on the right, with outstanding views across the Illinois to Silver Peak and Bald Mountain.

The Tie-in Trail is far more level than the Pupps Camp or Game Lake Trails. In addition to passing much serpentinite-adapted vegetation, including azalea, Brewer spruce, Jeffrey pine, western white pine, and lots of manzanita, the Tie-in Trail crosses a number of creeks surrounded by lush Douglas-fir pockets. Look for fly-eating darlingtonia plants in the wet marshy areas.

The Tie-in Trail emerges near Horse Sign Butte after 2.1 miles (go right), at an extremely steep, closed-off road leading back up to Game Lake. Horse Sign Butte is a handsome rock projection resembling an inverted sugar cone. Head uphill on the old road to a low saddle (mile 5.3). Return to Game Lake either by staying on the old road or walking through the saddle (left) to the Pupps Camp Trail (the Pupps Camp Trail is much pret-tier than the old road). Head right, uphill, onto the Pupps Camp Trail for Game Lake.

The Pupps Camp Trail is spectacular, with close-ups of the Big Craggies and long views across the Kalmiopsis to Pearsoll and Vulcan Peaks. The little valley immediately below is particularly beautiful,

Game Lake from Game Lake Loop.

boasting emerald-green fields dotted with picturesque clusters of evergreens. Wildflowers abound, particularly azalea and rhododendron.

It's 1.8 miles back to Game Lake from the saddle, with the trail emerging on the far end of the grassy meadow next to the lake.

Options: *The rest of the Game Lake Trail.* From the trailhead, the Game Lake Trail drops 3,000 feet in 8 miles, ending up at the Illinois River at the mouth of Lawson Creek, opposite the Oak Flat Trailhead (see Hike 85). To complete the hike via the Illinois River Trail, it is necessary to ford the river, which is very wide, not always fordable, and at the very least will get you wet.

The rest of the Pupps Camp Trail. The Pupps Camp Trail drops 3,000 feet in 5 miles, ending up at the Illinois near the mouth of Collier Creek across from Collier Bar (see Hike 85). Again, you'll have to ford the river to reach the Illinois River Trail and get back to civilization.

85 Illinois River

Highlight:	A challenging path along one of America's most beautiful Wild and Scenic River canyons. Much botanical interest.
Type of hike:	Backpack, shuttle.
Total distance:	About 22 miles.
Difficulty:	Mostly easy. The 4-mile segment up Bald Mountain is strenuous.
Best months:	April–November.
Elevation gain and loss:	2,911-foot gain, then a 3,211-foot loss.
Maps:	USGS Agness, Horse Sign Butte and York Butte quads.

Special considerations: This is a long, very remote trail which is strenuous in places. Allow at least two days. The path is faint in places. The road to the eastern trailhead near Selma is low-quality in places. Both the eastern and western trailheads are at places called "Oak Flat," which can be confusing. There is lots of water but it should be purified.

Finding the trailhead: Turn right (west) at Selma off U.S. Highway 199, 20 miles southwest of Grants Pass, onto the Illinois River Road (County Road 5070, becoming Forest Road 4203). Follow the winding, unpaved, bumpy road 15 miles to its end at the Briggs Creek picnic site. The last mile can be a little muddy. The trailhead is located across the picnic site, over the footbridge.

See "Options" for directions to the western trailhead.

Parking and trailhead facilities: There are picnic tables, a pit toilet, and parking for ten cars at the trailhead.

Illinois River

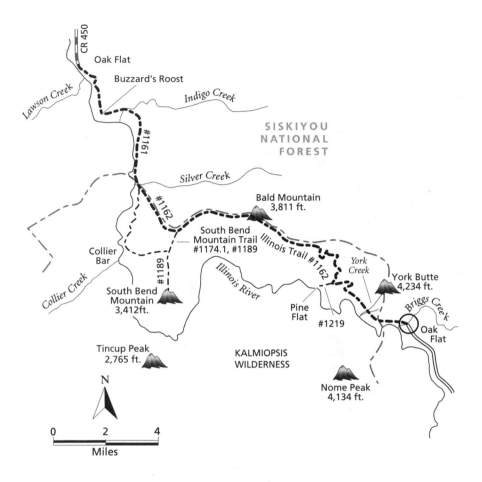

Key points:
- 0.0 Oak Flat Trailhead.
- 2.0 West Fork York Creek.
- 4.0 Pine Flat junction.
- 10.0 Bald Mountain.
- 11.5 Bald Mountain Prairie.
- 13.5 South Bend junction.
- 16.0 Silver Creek.
- 19.0 Indigo Creek.
- 20.0 Buzzard's Roost.
- 22.0 Oak Flat Trailhead.

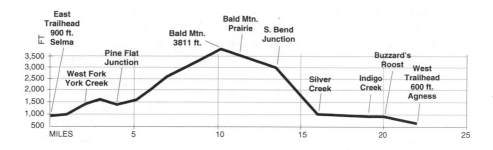

The hike: Among its many attractions, the Illinois River Trail (1219, 1162, and 1161), is the shortest path from which to view the rare kalmiopsis plant, after which the Kalmiopsis Wilderness Area is named. The purple azalealike flowers bloom from May through August. Add to that one of the country's great river canyons, remote and mysterious coastal mountain, and other botanical rarities and you have one of the Pacific Northwest's great hikes.

From the eastern trailhead at Oak Flat (the same name as the location of the western trailhead), out of Selma, the path crosses Briggs Creek via a footbridge. After 0.5 mile, you come to an old ranch with an abandoned orchard. The path then emerges high above the river. The next 1.5 miles are an area of sheer cliffs and rockfalls overlooking the rapids of the Illinois. On the other side of the river rise the orange weathered serpentinite slopes of Nome Peak and Granite Butte, with side canyons and waterfalls crashing down into the water. The trail skirts the base of York Butte, whose summit is itself an interesting day hike.

After 1.8 miles, the trail crosses the steep, rocky East Fork of York Creek. The West Fork, 0.2 mile beyond the East Fork, is similar in volume and steepness but has completely different vegetation. Instead of willow and alder, it is lined with azalea and fly-eating darlingtonia, a member of the pitcher plant family.

Be sure to pause where you come around the bend and first view the West Fork in the distance. At that spot begins a 60-foot circle of kalmiopsis plants. A dwarf rhododendron or azalea, the plant forms a prostrate mat only a few inches high with purple, bell-shaped flowers. In the entire world, there are perhaps 15 such mats, almost all within the Kalmiopsis Wilderness. The spot where you stand is also within the wilderness.

Beyond York Creek, the slope to the river becomes more gentle and the trail moves inland. For the next 2 miles, views of the river are infrequent as the path winds through forests of pine and Douglas-fir, interspersed with low-elevation oak and madrone.

Finally, the route forks at the top of a little hill. To the right lies the trail to Bald Mountain and the other Oak Flat, near Agness. To the left is the steep, 0.5-mile side trail that descends to Pine Flat. Pine Flat is perfectly named. It is quiet and out of the way, with good water, excellent campsites, and an outstanding river view. It can be spectacular in winter, if not under water.

Beyond the Pine Flat turnoff, the trail moves even farther away from the river as it rises 2,000 feet in 2.5 miles to the crest of Bald Mountain Ridge. There are several creek crossings along the ascent, and some impressive rock outcrops. At mile 10, the path crosses the forested summit of Bald Mountain, the route's highest point at 3,811 feet.

If you're wondering why the trail goes to such great lengths to avoid the river, the Illinois here lies 2,500 feet straight down in one of the most treacherous whitewater canyons anywhere. In the winter of 1997–98, the canyon made national news when several rafters, during the worst storm since 1964, drowned in the river's Green Wall Rapids. The Green Wall is a huge damlike rock formation of metamorphic greenstone that cuts across the river at right angles. The entire river pours through a tiny V worn into the formation by the relentless water. It is considered one of the most dangerous rapids in North America.

Beyond Bald Mountain, at mile 11.5, the Illinois River Trail emerges from the woods onto Bald Mountain Prairie, with excellent views into the Illinois canyon and beyond to Tincup Peak and Granite Butte. Look also for good views northward into the Silver Creek drainage. Chinaman Hat and Silver Peak are the most prominent peaks in that direction.

At mile 13.5, the trail comes to another junction; on the left is the South Bend Mountain Trail (1189), which rises 600 feet in 2.2 miles to the summit of South Bend Mountain. Viewed from the top of York Butte, above York Creek, and other vantage points above the canyon, South Bend is the canyon's most noticeable peak. Close up, however, it loses a little and the views aren't that good.

Past the South Bend Mountain junction, the Illinois River Trail loses 2,000 feet in 2.5 miles as it leaves Bald Ridge and drops back down to the river, hitting bottom just before the mouth of Silver Creek. Silver Creek, whose mouth is crossed at mile 16, runs through an extremely narrow canyon lined with vertical walls and fern grottoes. The clarity of its water is remarkable. You can stand in a pool up to your neck and your feet don't even look blue. From Silver Creek, it's 3 more miles to the mouth of Indigo Creek (mile 19).

Beyond Indigo Creek the path climbs steeply for 1 mile to a place called Buzzard's Roost, which offers a panorama of the river from a high vantage point. The spot was well known to Native Americans and is now an archaeological preserve. For more information, inquire at the Forest Service.

The rest of the trail to Oak Flat is mostly level and wooded, with muddy spots in wet weather. For 1.7 miles past Buzzard's Roost, the trail runs somewhat inland, high above the river, crossing several side creeks, one with a charming myrtlewood grove. The path's final 0.3 mile offers excellent views of the river and the canyon of Lawson Creek on the opposite bank (see Hike 84)

Option: *The (western) Oak Flat Trailhead.* The Oak Flat Trailhead at the Agness end of the Illinois River Trail is flatter, larger, and oakier than the one at the Illinois Valley end. To find it, leave Interstate 5 at the Merlin exit, just north of Grants Pass and head west on the Merlin-Galice Road, through Merlin. At mile 15, just before Galice, turn left onto Forest Road 23, the road to Gold Beach. It's 37 miles over a 5,000-foot pass at Bear Camp, to Forest Road 33, the road along the Lower Rogue from Gold Beach, on the coast, to Agness. Turn left on FR 33 and go south 2 miles to County Road 450 at the mouth of the Illinois River. Turn left on CR 450, just before the bridge, and proceed 3 miles to the Oak Flat Trailhead and picnic site.

There are many side trails off the Illinois River Trail but only the Pine Flat Trail and the South Bend Mountain Trail, both discussed in the text, are noteworthy.

---

86   Pearsoll Peak

Highlight:	Magnificent vistas from the orange-rock summit that marks the highest point in the Kalmiopisis Wilderness Area.
Type of hike:	Day hike, out and back.
Total distance:	About 5 miles from Chetco Pass, 13 miles from the river.
Difficulty:	Strenuous.
Elevation gain:	1,498 feet.
Best months:	June–October.
Map:	USGS Pearsoll quad.

Special considerations: The 4-mile road from the Illinois River to Chetco Pass is often gated and is in very poor condition. A high clearance four-by-four vehicle is required. No water.

Finding the trailhead: From Selma, on U.S. Highway 199, 20 miles southwest of Grants Pass, follow the Illinois River Road (County Road 5070, becoming Forest Road 4103), left (west). Bear left where Forest Road 4105 takes off uphill. From there to Store Gulch, the road is narrow and rocky. Ten miles from US 199, turn left on Spur 87 which drops sharply downhill beginning 2 miles past Store Gulch. Look for signs to Illinois River Falls and the McCaleb Boy Scout Ranch. Spur 87 is very steep and rutted. After driving across the Illinois River on the low-water bridge (impassable in winter), head uphill, either on foot or in a four-by-four vehicle, for 4 miles to Chetco Pass. The trail begins on the right at the pass.

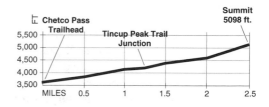

Pearsoll Peak

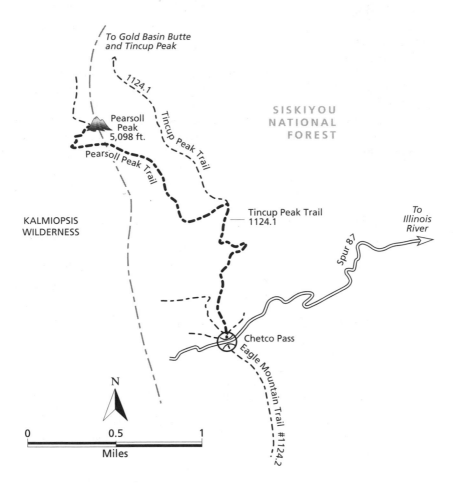

Parking and trailhead facilities: There is parking for 5 cars at Chetco Pass, 20 cars in the parking lot just over the low-water bridge.

Key points:
   0.0 Chetco Pass Trailhead.
   1.3 Tincup Peak Trail junction (go left).
   2.5 Summit.

The hike: Pearsoll Peak's beautiful orange cone, highest point in the Kalmiopsis Wilderness Area, is visible from many points in Josephine County. While not the highest peak in the county, the 5,098-foot summit ranks among its most prominent. The barrenness of the summit and its orange color result from the serpentinite rock of which it's composed. Though black, serpentinite weathers to a buff orange and supports very little vegetation, especially at higher elevations. The peak is especially beautiful when its flanks are highlighted by a light mantle of snow.

The Chetco Pass Road up from the Illinois River was originally (and still is), a jeep road. The 1976 Forest Service map showed it as a trail while the latest map shows it as a road again. The 4-mile route requires four-wheel drive and considerable driving skill. It's very steep and deeply rutted. As a hike, it's hot, dusty, tiring, and not particularly interesting.

From Chetco Pass, you can hike down to the Chetco River or hike south along the crest to Eagle Mountain and Onion Camp (see "Options" and Hike 89). The Tincup Peak Trail to Pearsoll Peak, also an old road, takes off to the right from Chetco Pass. You find a confusing network of old skid trails near the beginning. Stay on the widest uphill road, to the left. It's possible to drive this route part way but it's in even worse condition than the Chetco Pass Road. There are ruts, steep spots with loose gravel, and the entire route is dusty and out in the open. The Pearsoll summit is inside the wilderness area but most of the trail isn't.

One mile before the summit, the Vulcan Peak Trail breaks off to the left while the Tincup Peak Trail to Gold Basin Butte and Tincup Peak continues sraight ahead (see "Options"). An old lookout, where you can rest, regroup, and admire the scenery caps the summit. You can't quite see down to the Illinois but almost all the southwest Oregon wilderness, including the entire Chetco and Illinois basins, are laid out at your feet. Look for York Butte, Vulcan Peak, and the Big Craggies.

Options: *Illinois River Falls.* At some point in your life, check out the Illinois Falls Trail, taking off from a switchback just before the low-water bridge at the beginning of the Chetco Pass Road. The trail crosses an elaborate, extremely high suspension footbridge, then swings left along the river. The 0.5-mile path to the falls, while level, is annoyingly rocky and slippery, with sandy spots.

The falls are located a few hundred yards past the mouth of Fall Creek. Beyond the creek, scramble over the huge boulders for the best view. The falls aren't very high but they're thunderous and the gorge is spectacular.

Eagle Mountain. Chetco Pass marks the far end of the Eagle Mountain Trail (Hike 89, Trail 1124.2). This highly scenic, 4-mile path is better hiked in the other direction.

Tincup Peak. The Tincup Peak Trail, branching off to the right on the Pearsoll Peak Trail 1 mile from Chetco Pass, climbs over the top of Gold Basin Butte (mile 1.5), crosses Gold Basin (mile 3.0) and ascends 4,494 foot Tincup Peak (mile 4.5). These are all beautiful places with much exposed orange serpentinite.

Beyond Chetco Pass. If you keep going straight, over Chetco Pass, you end up at the Chetco river after 2.5 miles and a 1,500-foot descent into the middle of the wilderness. The road is gated after 1 mile, at Sourdough Flat, and there are 6 miles of trail along the upper Chetco. Most of these paths are closed roads leading to old mines.

87 Babyfoot Lake

Highlight:	One of the few glacial-cirque lakes in the Kalmiopsis Wilderness. An extremely popular hike.
Type of hike:	Dayhike, out and back.
Total distance:	About 3 miles.
Difficulty:	Easy to moderate.
Elevation loss:	300 feet.
Best months:	May–November.
Map:	USGS Josephine Mountain quad.

Special considerations: Lots of water in the creeks around the lake.

Finding the trailhead: Take U.S. Highway 199 23 miles south from Grants Pass. Three and a half miles beyond Selma, a sign pointing left reads, "Kalmiopsis Wilderness—17 miles." Follow this road (Forest Road 4201), across the Illinois River bridge and proceed up the steep, wide, highly scenic gravel route to the well-marked Babyfoot Lake turnoff, 17 miles up on the left. It's 1 mile up Spur 864 to the trailhead parking area.

Parking and trailhead facilities: There is parking for 15 cars at the trailhead.

Key points:
    0.0 Babyfoot Lake Trailhead.
    0.4 Junction (go right, downhill).
    1.5 Babyfoot Lake.

The hike: If you have a secret yen to stick a toe inside a federal wilderness area without working up a sweat, this is the trail for you. The only highway sign pointing to the Kalmiopsis Wilderness directs visitors to Babyfoot Lake.

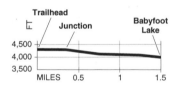

The trail (1126) follows a narrow ridge for the first 0.4 mile, towards Hungry Hill. The Hungry Hill Trail takes off to the left at mile 0.4. It's not very interesting. Stay right for Babyfoot Lake.

Beyond the junction, the path drops into a densely wooded basin of mostly Douglas-fir. It's a good place to observe light-starved understory species such as prince's pine (or princess pine—either is correct). After a while, you come to a lovely vista spot with a commanding view of the Chetco basin. From there, it's just a few more minutes to the lake.

The lake, at mile 1.5, sits in a little wooded glacial cirque with a cliff headwall on one side. The area at the base of the headwall is flat, with many campsites. Fishing and swimming in the lake are both good but not fantastic.

Babyfoot Lake

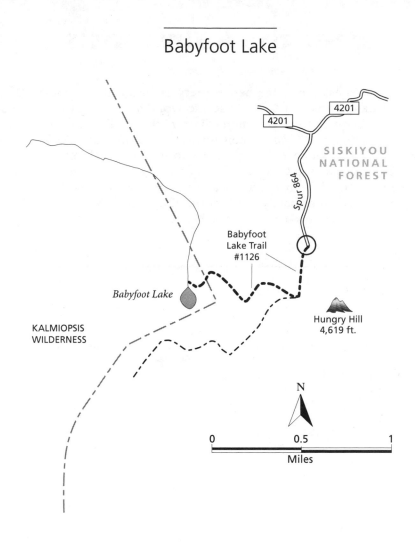

Babyfoot Lake is an officially designated Botanical Area, largely because of its Brewer spruce population. The Botanical Area was created before scientists realized how widespread Brewer spruce actually was. It is in no way endangered and reproduces prolifically within its limited range. Supposedly, the exceedingly rare Del Norte daisy also grows at Babyfoot Lake.

Near the Kalmiopsis

In most wilderness areas, the best scenery is inside the boundary. And while the Kalmiopsis boasts many scenic wonders, it is unusual in that there is just as much to be seen immediately surrounding the wilderness. Eagle Mountain, much of the Illinois River canyon, Buckskin Peak, Rough and Ready Creek, Baldface Creek, historic Josephine Creek, Windy Valley, Game Lake, and Lawson Creek are well deserving of protected status. The lack of inclusion of the magnificent and remote Silver Creek and Indigo Creek drainages, immediately north of the Kalmiopsis, has been a source of controversy for years.

88 Windy Valley

Highlight:	A beautiful hike with many vistas, leading to a secluded valley with a grassy meadow by a creek. Much botanical interest.
Type of hike:	Day hike, out and back.
Total distance:	4 miles.
Difficulty:	Mostly easy.
Elevation loss:	265 feet.
Best months:	May–November.
Map:	USGS Collier Butte quad.

Special considerations: Windy Creek, which you must cross to reach the meadow, may not be passable in winter. The log bridges get very slippery and the water can be fast and cold.

Finding the trailhead: From Brookings, follow the North Bank Chetco Road (County Road 784, becoming Forest Road 1376), for 26 miles. The route eventually crosses the Chetco River, climbs a long, steep hill and passes High Prairie. The trailhead is 3 miles past High Prairie, on the left, just past Spur 220. Look for a metal gate.

Parking and trailhead facilities: The trailhead has a pit toilet, a picnic table, and an outstanding view of the Big Craggies. There is parking for eight cars along the wide shoulder.

Key points:
   0.0 Windy Valley Trailhead.
   0.4 Cedar Camp.
   0.5 Rock outcrop/summit.
   1.6 Snow Camp Trail junction (go right).
   1.8 Creek crossing.
   2.0 Campsite at meadow.

Windy Valley

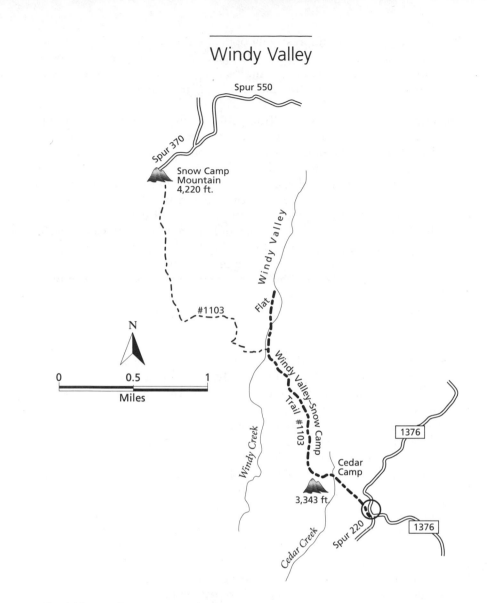

The hike: Before visiting this remote, easy trail amid some of the most bizarre country anywhere, you should first check out a few things by car. The road between High Prairie and Snow Camp Mountain is a must. Coming up from the Chetco, just past High Prairie, the dense, almost rain

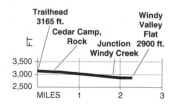

forest of Douglas-fir suddenly opens into a vast expanse of orange peridotite and serpentinite rock, sparsely covered with manzanita and stunted Jeffrey, western white, and knobcone pines.

The Big Craggies loom impressively opposite the trailhead. See Hike 83 to discover more about them. The Big Craggies are so steep and the rocks are so mineral poor that the area contains few trees except in the draws. Several rare plants grow in the Big Craggies, including the kalmiopsis flower.

The Windy Valley–Snow Camp Trail (1103) is charming and not too difficult. After passing the collapsed shelter at Cedar Camp (mile 0.4), the route winds behind the huge, unnamed rock outcrop seen from the trailhead. It's a short, steep, but rewarding climb to the top of the rock. From there, the ocean can be seen through the mouth of the Pistol River.

Just past the rock, a vista unfolds to the left in this open country stunted, scraggly serpentinite-adapted vegetation. The trail contours around a steep hillside and crosses several creeks and springs, a myrtlewood grove or two, two patches of fly-eating darlingtonia plants and endless bear grass and azaleas. Watch for views of Snow Camp Lookout.

During the second mile, the way steepens and the forest, now mostly of Douglas-fir and Port Orford cedar, grows much denser as it approaches the valley. Windy Creek soon comes into view, signaling that you're almost there.

To reach Windy Valley, go straight at mile 1.6 instead of left at the trail's turnoff to Snow Camp. Beyond, the trail is a little indistinct and muddy in spots. But it's difficult to get lost. Eventually, the large grassy prairie comprising Windy Valley proper unfolds in front of you, across the creek at mile 1.8. Several downed trees span the creek.

Across the creek, the open field is sunny (occasionally) and inviting, if a little swampy in the center. At the far end, in the trees along the creek, you find the ruins of an old homestead, a campsite, and a couple of fine swimming holes. The spot offers fair fishing and is quite popular in summer.

Option: *Snow Camp Lookout.* Be sure to drive the rest of the way up FR 1376 to Snow Camp Lookout, the actual terminus of the Windy Valley Trail. The lookout (elevation 4,220 feet) offers views of Windy Valley, every peak within 100 miles, and the ocean. To reach the lookout by car, follow FR 1376 for 4.5 miles beyond the Windy Valley Trailhead to where the road becomes narrow and takes off sharply uphill. Look for a gated road on the left (Spur 550). Park and walk 1.5 miles to the lookout.

If you hike to the lookout from Windy Valley, it's 1.5 miles from the junction at Windy Creek, with a 1,400-foot elevation gain. The short walk up the road is much easier.

89 Eagle Mountain

Highlight:	Spectacular hike along the rugged Siskiyou crest, high above the Illinois River canyon at the edge of the Kalmiopsis Wilderness.
Type of hike:	Day hike, out and back.
Total distance:	About 8 miles.
Difficulty:	Strenuous.
Elevation gain:	427 foot loss, 696 foot gain, 796 foot loss.
Best months:	May–November.
Maps:	USGS Josephine Mountain and Pearsoll Peak quads.

Special considerations: Not a drop of water. Some very steep pitches. The route ties into the Chetco Pass–Pearsoll Peak Trail (Hike 86), but it's much easier to return the way you came rather than hike 4 miles on a dusty road down to the Illinois River Trailhead.

Finding the trailhead: Take U.S. Highway 199, 23 miles south from Grants Pass. Three and a half miles beyond Selma, a sign pointing left reads, "Kalmiopsis Wilderness—17 miles." Follow this road (Forest Road 4201) for 18 miles, across the Illinois River bridge and up the steep, wide, highly scenic gravel road, past the Babyfoot Lake, Onion Camp, and Fall Creek turnoffs. A couple of hundred feet beyond the Fall Creek turnoff, look for a wide spot on the left with a sign indicating the Chetco Pass Trail. Go left (south) for Onion Camp and right (north) for Eagle Mountain.

Parking and trailhead facilities: There's parking for ten cars in the flat around the trailhead.

Key points:
0.0 Chetco Pass Trailhead.
0.8 Whetstone Butte.
1.8 Eagle Gap.
2.5 Eagle Mountain.
4.0 Chetco Pass.

The hike: This pathway following the heights of the Kalmiopsis region winds along the divide between the Chetco and Illinois Rivers. While fairly strenuous, it ranks among Josephine County's more beautiful hikes. Many of the

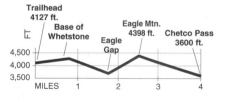

trail's highlights lie within 1 mile of the trailhead.

From the parking area, the trail (1124.2) climbs gently for 0.3 mile, through a forest of Douglas-fir, white pine, and Brewer spruce, with rhododendron and Sadler oak in the understory, before breaking out into an open, serpentinite-rock area with spectacular vistas. The sheer brown rock

Eagle Mountain

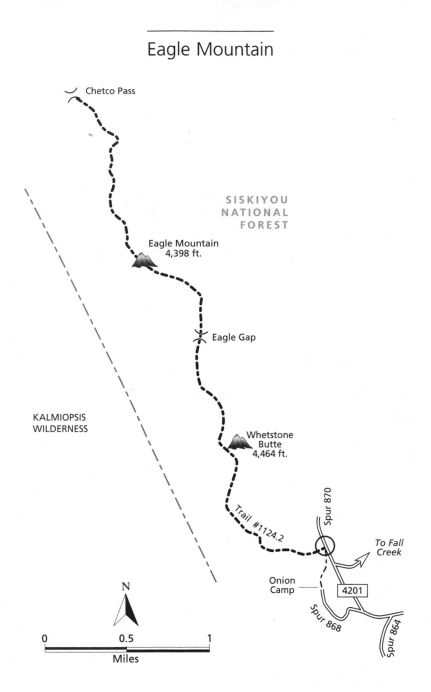

face of Whetstone Butte dominates the scene. Approaching the latter, amid stunted Jeffrey pines and craggy outcrops, you can see the Chetco headwaters (west), the Illinois Canyon (east), and towering Pearsoll Peak (north). A careful observer might also note Vulcan Peak and the Big Craggies. Far to the southeast, the often snowcapped summits of the high

Cascades, including Mount McLoughlin and the Crater Lake rim, decorate the horizon.

Whetstone Butte offers a rewarding, 0.8-mile destination. Since the trail contours around to the west of Whetstone, well below the summit, you must scramble off trail, up some steep rock faces and through a couple of dense brush patches to reach the top. The route is obvious, not too difficult, and takes about 10 minutes each way.

Approaching Whetstone Butte, the trail begins to drop as it reenters the woods. It loses 500 feet in the next mile, meeting the ridge again at Eagle Gap. The view at Eagle Gap is blocked by trees.

The segment between Eagle Gap and the top of Eagle Mountain is by far the hike's most difficult. The 700-foot elevation rise in 0.7 mile is offset by spectacular scenery. After trudging up slopes of rock and loose scree, amid stunted, windswept pines, the path emerges at the lip of a cliff which sweeps dramatically down to the Illinois.

After all that work and all that scenery, Eagle Mountain's actual summit proves anti-climactic, being flat and wooded with few vistas. Look for a grove of Brewer spruce just past the trail crest.

It's 1.5 miles on an old road from Eagle Mountain to Chetco Pass, with an 800-foot elevation drop. Beyond Eagle Mountain, there's little to be seen. Where the trail briefly breaks out into the open again, at the junction with the Bowser Mine Road, the surrounding high peaks have largely disappeared behind a serpentinite ridge radiating from Pearsoll Peak. The only reason for continuing to Chetco Pass would be to add a note of completion.

Jeffrey pine on serpentinite, Eagle Mountain Trail.

Oregon Caves National Monument

Oregon Caves National Monument, a 480-acre unit of the National Park Service, sits on the western flank of Mount Elijah. The mountain is named for Elijah Davidson, discoverer of the cave. The name "Oregon Caves" mystifies even the National Park Service since there is only one cave within the monument.

There are other caves in the Siskiyous; however, most of them are dangerous, small, and inaccessible. The Marble Mountains, immediately south in California, contain nearly 100 caves, at least one of which is much larger than the one at Oregon Caves. It was discovered in 1974.

These are all marble caverns. Marble is metamorphosed limestone. Being harder than limestone, marble dissolves into caves along vertical cracks rather than bedding planes. While limestone caves end up having miles of horizontal passages, marble caves are usually smaller, with shorter passages and more pits and domes (or "domepits" as geologists call them).

For a description of the cave tour, see the "Option" section for Hike 90.

---

90 Big Tree Loop

Highlight:	A pleasant hike featuring woods, marble outcrops, an excellent vista of the Illinois Valley, and a big tree.
Type of hike:	Day hike, loop.
Total distance:	3.8 miles.
Difficulty:	Moderate.
Elevation gain:	1,000 feet.
Best months:	May–November.
Map:	USGS Oregon Caves quad.

Special considerations: There is no water on the trail but there is plenty of water at the National Monument facilities. Parking is free but there is a charge for cave tours.

Finding the trailhead: Take U.S. Highway 199 south from Grants Pass 30 miles to Cave Junction. At Cave Junction, proceed up Caves Highway (Oregon Highway 46) 19 miles to Oregon Caves National

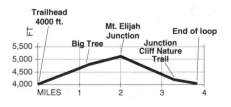

Big Tree Loop

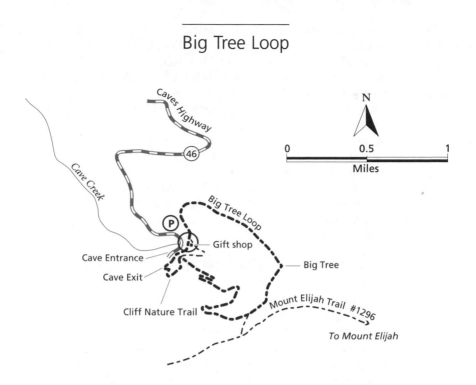

Monument. The trailhead is located through the gift shop arch, to the left of the cave entrance.

Parking and trailhead facilities: Monument facilities include restrooms, a gift shop, and parking for 200 cars. The restaurant, coffee shop, and lodge are open from mid-June to early September.

Key points:
- 0.0 Big Tree Trailhead.
- 0.3 Water tank.
- 1.3 Big Tree.
- 2.0 Mount Elijah junction.
- 3.3 Cliff Nature Trail junction (go left).
- 3.8 End of loop.

The hike: The loop trail around Oregon Caves National Monument may be the most frequently trodden path in southern Oregon. Hikers from all over the country return with glowing enthusiasm. The trail is pleasant. The experience is greatly enhanced by returning via the monument's short but spectacular Cliff Nature Trail.

The Big Tree Loop Trail begins under the arch between the ticket window and gift shop. The described hike starts in the left-hand direction, following the sign reading, "Big Tree—1.3 miles." You can also take the loop in the other direction.

The path is moderately steep as it winds through middle-elevation woods of Douglas-fir, white fir, grand fir, and Port Orford cedar. Don't get lost on two unmarked, dead-end spurs to the left.

Big Tree, at mile 1.3, is an immense Douglas-fir with an oft-broken top and an extremely thick trunk. It's what foresters call a "wolf tree," very poor in form and towering above the other trees. Most trees in the vicinity are its offspring.

On the 1.8 mile down side of the Big Tree Loop, the trail starts by crossing a wet meadow of wildflowers, Douglas maple, and the showy corn lily. Then it's back into the woods.

At mile 2, a side trail leads to Mount Elijah. Although the Mount Elijah Trail is considerably more scenic than the Big Tree Trail, its highlights are more quickly reached from the Bigelow Lake end (see Hike 73). The Mount Elijah Trail explores the Siskiyous' high peaks, none of which are visible from the cave area, the Big Tree Trail, or Caves Highway. It's 1.5 miles to the summit of Mount Elijah from the junction with the Big Tree Trail, then another 1.5 miles to Bigelow Lake.

At mile 3.3, the path merges with the Monument's Cliff Nature Trail. The latter is marked by a sign pointing to the left which says, "Chateau." This route adds 0.5 mile to the journey but is highly recommended (if you go right, you'll be back at the trailhead in 0.2 mile but will miss the marble outcrops and vistas). The trail left goes over the top of the marble formation in which the cave is located. There's a terrific vista point there, with a view down Sucker Creek of the Illinois Valley. After that, the trail winds down to the base of the marble, passes the cave exit, then returns to the entrance.

Option: *Cave Tour.* Escorted cave tours leave year-round (every few minutes in summer, once or twice a day in winter) in groups of 16. Tours take about 45 minutes. Although this isn't Carlsbad, there are lots of flowstone formations, an underground river, and a huge chamber. There are some low ceilings and very steep ladders in the 0.7-mile tour. During summer, expect a wait of 30 minutes to an hour for cave tours, if you arrive midday.

Appendix A

HIKER'S CHECKLIST

Always make and check your own checklist!

If you've ever hiked into the backcountry and discovered that you've forgotten an essential, you know that it's a good idea to make a checklist and check the items off as you pack so that you won't forget the things you want and need. Here are some ideas:

Clothing

- [ ] Dependable rain parka
- [ ] Rain pants
- [ ] Windbreaker
- [ ] Thermal underwear
- [ ] Shorts
- [ ] Long pants or sweatpants
- [ ] Wood cap or balaclava
- [ ] Hat
- [ ] Wool shirt or sweater
- [ ] Jacket or parka
- [ ] Extra socks
- [ ] Underwear
- [ ] Lightweight shirts
- [ ] T-shirts
- [ ] Bandanna(s)
- [ ] Mittens or gloves
- [ ] Belt

Footwear

- [ ] Sturdy, comfortable boots
- [ ] Lightweight camp shoes

Bedding

- [ ] Sleeping bag
- [ ] Foam pad or air mattress
- [ ] Ground sheet (plastic or nylon)
- [ ] Dependable tent

Hauling

- [ ] Backpack and/or day pack

Cooking

- [ ] 1-quart container (plastic)
- [ ] 1-gallon water container for camp use (collapsible)
- [ ] Backpack stove and extra fuel
- [ ] Funnel
- [ ] Aluminum foil
- [ ] Cooking pots
- [ ] Bowls/plates
- [ ] Utensils (spoons, forks, small spatula, knife)
- [ ] Pot scrubber
- [ ] Matches in waterproof container

Food and Drink

- [ ] Cereal
- [ ] Bread
- [ ] Crackers
- [ ] Cheese
- [ ] Trail mix
- [ ] Margarine
- [ ] Powdered soups
- [ ] Salt/pepper
- [ ] Main course meals
- [ ] Snacks
- [ ] Hot chocolate
- [ ] Tea
- [ ] Powdered milk
- [ ] Drink mixes

Photography

- [ ] Camera and film
- [ ] Filters
- [ ] Lens brush/paper

Miscellaneous

- [ ] Sunglasses
- [ ] Map and a compass
- [ ] Toilet paper
- [ ] Pocketknife
- [ ] Sunscreen
- [ ] Good insect repellent
- [ ] Lip balm
- [ ] Flashlight with good batteries and a spare bulb
- [ ] Candle(s)
- [ ] First-aid kit
- [ ] Your FalconGuide
- [ ] Survival kit
- [ ] Small garden trowel or shovel
- [ ] Water filter or purification tablets
- [ ] Plastic bags (for trash)
- [ ] Soap
- [ ] Towel
- [ ] Toothbrush
- [ ] Fishing license
- [ ] Fishing rod, reel, lures, flies, etc.
- [ ] Binoculars
- [ ] Waterproof covering for pack
- [ ] Watch
- [ ] Sewing kit

Appendix B

REFERENCES

There are any number of wildflower, bird, and tree guides in print, all of them excellent. The nature guides listed below are not necessarily the best, but they're very good. The list includes all sources from which information was drawn for this book.

Bernstein, A. *90 Best Day-Hikes, Southern Oregon and Far Northern California.* Grants Pass, OR: Cloudcap Books, 1994.

———. *Native Trees of the Northwest.* Grants Pass, OR: Cloudcap Books, 1988.

Cranson, K. *Crater Lake: Gem of the Cascades,* Lansing, MI: 1982.

Grubbs, B. *Hiking the Central Oregon Cascades,* Helena, MT: Falcon Press, 1997.

Jackman, A. and Bernstein, A. *The Hip-Pocket Naturalist: A Guide to Oregon's Rogue River Basin.* Grants Pass, OR: Cloudcap Books, 1989.

Josephine County Historical Society. *Mythical State of Jefferson.* Grants Pass, OR: Josephine County Historical Society, 1965.

Niehaus, T. *Pacific States Wildflowers.* The Peterson's Field Guides Series. Boston: Houghton Mifflin, 1976.

Randall, W. *Manual of Oregon Trees and Shrubs.* Corvallis, OR: OSU Bookstores, 1981.

Reyes, C. *The Table Rocks of Jackson County: Islands in the Sky.* Ashland, OR: Last Minute Publications, 1994.

Appendix C

FOR MORE INFORMATION

Bureau of Land Management:

BLM - Medford District
3040 Biddle Road
Medford, OR 97504
541-770-2200
www.or.blm.gov/medford

Medford Parks and Recreation:

Medford Parks and Recreation
200 S. Ivy
Medford, OR 97501
www.interrogue.com/parks/med-park.htm

National Park Service:

Crater Lake National Park
Crater Lake, OR 97604
541-594-2211
www.crater.lake.national-park.com

Oregon Caves National Monument
19000 Caves Highway
Cave Junction, OR 97523
541-592-2100 (general)
541-592-2631 (recreation)
www.nps.gov/orca

Nature Conservancy:

The Nature Conservancy
1150 Ashland Street
Ashland, OR 97520
www.tnc.org

US Army Corps of Engineers:

Rogue Basin Project/Lost Creek Lake
100 Cole N. Rivers Drive
Trail, OR 97541
541-878-2255
www.nwp.usace.army.mil/op/R/lctext.htm

USDA Forest Service:

Rogue River National Forest
333 West Eighth St.
Medford, OR 97501
541-858-2200
www.fs.fed.us/r6/rogue

Siskiyou National Forest
200 NE Greenfield Road
Grants Pass, OR 97526
541-471-6500 (general)
541-471-6724 (recreation)
www.fs.fed.us/r6/siskiyou

Umpqua National Forest
2900 NW Stewart Parkway
Roseburg, OR 97470
541-672-6601
www.fs.fed.us/r6/umpqua

Winema National Forest
2819 Dahlia
Klamath Falls, OR 97601
541-883-6714
www.fs.fed.us/r6/winema

Index

Page numbers in italics refer to photographs.

M

About the Author

Author and publisher Art Bernstein has written twelve other nature and hiking guides including the best-selling *90 Best Day-Hikes, Southern Oregon and Far Northern California*. An avid hiker and naturalist, with an M.S. in Natural Resource Management from the University of Michigan, he has lived in Grants Pass, Oregon, since 1970.